GETTING THE SEX YOU WANT

GETTING THE SEX YOU WANT

A WOMAN'S GUIDE TO BECOMING PROUD, PASSIONATE, AND PLEASED IN BED

SANDRA LEIBLUM, PH.D.,
AND JUDITH SACHS

CROWN PUBLISHERS
New York

To the women I have counseled through the last three decades, who have taught me the infinite ways in which we can embrace our sexuality

SL

For the Magical Mia, who already understands that you don't ever have to accept what you're given—with time and patience, you can edit the raw footage

JS

Copyright © 2002 by Sandra Leiblum and Judith Sachs

Published by Crown Publishers, New York, New York.
Member of the Crown Publishing Group,
a division of Random House, Inc.

www.randomhouse.com

CROWN is a trademark and the Crown colophon is a registered trademark of Random House, Inc.

Printed in the United States of America

Design by Rhea Braunstein

Library of Congress Cataloging-in-Publication Data

Leiblum, Sandra Risa.
Getting the sex you want : a woman's guide to becoming proud, passionate, and pleased in bed / Sandra Leiblum and Judith Sachs.—1st ed.
1. Sex instruction for women.   2. Women—Sexual behavior.
3. Sexual excitement.   I. Sachs, Judith, 1947– .   II. Title.
HQ46 .L39   2002
613.9'6'082—dc21   2001042469

ISBN 0-8129-3284-6

10 9 8 7 6 5 4 3 2 1

FIRST EDITION

ACKNOWLEDGMENTS

A book is created from the opinions, experiences, and points of view of its authors. But for our book, much of the credit must go to the women themselves, and those who listen to them speak about their concerns, hopes, and dreams.

We would like to thank all those who contributed their voices, knowledge, emotions, humor, and warmth to this book:

The physicians, counselors, researchers, and sex therapists:

Carol Adamsbaum, RN; Carolyn Altman, CSW; Lisa Anjou, Ph.D.; Rosemary Basson, MD, MRCP; Peggy Brick, Ed.D.; Robert Butler, MD; Marie Cascarano; David Chapin, MD; Lucius Clay, MD; Al Cooper, Ph.D.; Richard Cross, MD; Alan DeCherney, MD; Gina Delrosso, MSW; Betty Dodson; Rachel Dultz, MD; David Fergueson, MD; Jean Fourcroy, MD; Luis Garcia, Ph.D.; Mark Glasser, MD; Andrew Guay, MD; Nancy Kaplan Healey; Julia Heiman, Ph.D.; Marcia Heiman, Ph.D.; Karen Hobish, MD; Gladys Horgan, RN; Suzanne Iasenza, Ph.D.; Sarah Janosik, MSW; Jed Kaminetsky, MD; Sheryl Kingsberg, Ph.D.; Paul Lammers, MD, Ph.D.; Cap Lesegne, MD; Jeff Levine, MD; Cleo Lowinger, MSW; Konnie McCaffrey, Ed.D.; Naomi McCormick, Ph.D.; Andy McCullough, MD; Norm Mazer, MD, Ph.D.; Cindy Meston, Ph.D.; Susan Mikolon, RN; Aliyah Sabeh Morgan, MD; Ray Noonan, Ph.D.; Gina Ogden, Ph.D.; Evelyn Orozco, Ph.D.; Lisa Paisley-Cleveland; Andrea Parrot, Ph.D.; Carol Petersen, PharmD; Susan Rako, MD; Deborah Roffman, Ph.D.; Candida Royalle; Stephanie Sanders, Ph.D.; Jeffrey Scharf, MD; Kathy Segraves, Ph.D.; Evelyn Shalom, Ph.D.; Zoe Sleeth; Yasser Solimon, MD; Maryanne Styler, MD; Denise Thomas; Leonore Tiefer, Ph.D.; Sari Tudiver, Ph.D.; Sujata Warrier, MD; Sandra Welner, MD; Nina Williams, Psy.D.; Pam Wilson, MSW; Susan Wilson, M.Ed.; Craig Winkel, MD; Louise Yohalem, M.Ed.

The women and their partners:

Nancy B., Missy C. and Tiffany D., Jane and Patty; Chap and Laura; Pamela N.; Rose; Tracy Z., Maria; Ilana P.; Tara D., Amy T., Janina, Karen R., Carol L.;

Mary Pat W.; Beth F., Mary Ellen; Toni J., Anda, Pat S.; Diane M.; Libby; Sylvia B.; Bevin; Laney K.; Marian D., Marianne R.; Joan H., Lee B.; Debby W., Tammy L.; Heather W., John and Marjorie Ewbanks; Steve and Cindy S.; Tom and Linda Gayle R.; Noelle P.; Amanda P.; Rachel G., Emily F.; Tamara; Karen M.; Maria C.; Uchechi N.; Dorothy L.; Linda; Susan P., Harriet C., Donna, Deb, Reagan, Sarah J.; Julie G.; Susan M.; Joan R.; Deborah M., Kira B.; Lynn S.; Milaini B.; Janet F.; Sharon N.; Jane R.; Deena H.; Stephanie R.; Rusty B.; Denise L.; Paula P.; Phyllis G.; Lori; Judy G.; Jane Rodney; Kathleen R.; Divinna S.; Sandra S.; Beth W.; Sue F.; and many more who were interviewed but not profiled.

The various outreach and support organizations gave leads for interviews and a look at how various communities view female sexuality. These include SAGE, GLOE, Hi-Tops, and of course, the team at Planned Parenthood of Plainfield, NJ: Andre Billups, Susan Campbell, Anastasia Hardy and her baby; Janine Lytle, Charlene Minotee, Sean Dion Jones II, and Toinette Woods.

For their invaluable help scouring the literature: Amy Levin and Lissette Marrero at SIECUS, NY; Lynn Cohen at the Carrier Foundation Library; and Susan Pistolakis at the Ocean County Medical Center Library. For complete access to the University of Chicago survey and follow-up surveys: Edward O. Laumann, Ph.D.; John Gagnon, Ph.D.; and Ira Reiss, Ph.D., for his perspective on the data. And for their help with anthropological findings: Alice Schlegel, Ph.D., at the University of Arizona, and Herbert Barry III at the University of Pittsburgh. Many thanks to Dr. Gloria Bachmann at UMDNJ and Robert Wood Johnson Medical School for her critical reading of the material.

We are deeply indebted to our literary agent, Beth Vesel, for her enormous enthusiasm and clear understanding of our project, and to our editor, Betsy Rapoport, who has made it possible to get our message across.

CONTENTS

"Sex is worth dying for."

Annabel Chong (performance artist who had sex with 250 men in 10 hours), February 2000

INTRODUCTION

"My first sexual experience," said Toni, an outspoken and gutsy 32-year-old, "was with a guy in my high school theater class. He was romantic and funny—and neither of us knew at that point that he was bi. We kissed a lot, and as the months passed, we did have intercourse, although it was always quick and really disappointing. Then we'd have this long, intense discussion on how we should just be best friends, like we always had been, and we'd both cry a lot. I never had an orgasm, and I had been taught that masturbation was akin to devil worship, so of course I didn't do that. So I grew into my adult years thinking that women weren't supposed to really enjoy themselves physically.

"When I met my husband, right after college, the first things I noticed about him were his hands—he was playing a guitar and he had these huge, very expressive hands that rubbed and twanged and plucked and did everything to that instrument that I wanted him to do to me. I was so turned on, he almost didn't have to touch me. I came like nobody's business. And you know what the best part was? Right before or after sex, when we would lie there, nose to nose, one of my legs slung over his, talking softly or cuddling, breathing each other's breath. So for the first few years of our relationship, my expectations were just turned around. It was all great all the time.

"Until the kids came. Now we don't talk much. He can touch me and all I think of is, oh God, something else I have to do! It's all gone backward again. Every once in a while, I go into a chat room on the Internet, and even though I haven't talked to anyone yet, it's more exciting than getting into bed. Sex seems so hard to grab onto, and it depends on so many hundreds of things that have nothing to do with love or physical sensation. I wish it would just straighten itself out. Do you think that will ever happen?"

What do we think? After a quarter of a century of counseling men, women, and couples, we *know* that sex is a conundrum for most women. It doesn't come naturally; it's not easy. What is normal sex? What is kinky sexual behavior? What's too much and what's too little? Sex comes with a big shiny bow wrapped around it: a present that promises the ultimate physical, mental, emotional, and spiritual fulfillment, but once the box is open, everything's in pieces and there are no instructions.

A 1994 study based on the National Health and Social Life Survey indicates that more than 40 percent of American women between the ages of 18 and 59 don't enjoy sex and report a greater variety of sexual difficulties and complaints than men do. Sexual disorders in women tend to be progressive and age-related. A bad taste in the mouth for sex over the decades makes it harder to retain one's appetite.

This book is the product of years of clinical and personal experience, and it offers a view of our changing vision of female sexuality—the big picture as well as the cameos of real women who tell their own stories. Both of the authors come to the sexual arena with a great deal of professional experience. Sandra Leiblum, professor of psychiatry and director of the Center for Sexual and Marital Health at UMDNJ–Robert Wood Johnson Medical School, has been in the field of human sexuality for thirty years. She has treated thousands of women and their partners during that time. Judith Sachs, author of many books on preventive healthcare and herself a health educator, has conducted sexuality workshops in diverse settings—women's holistic centers, colleges and universities, as well as corporate campuses. Both have witnessed and also helped to create the revolution in female sexual health, a blossoming of interest, affirmation, and comfort in dealing with a subject that was previously dealt with only in therapy, in group, or in the classroom.

Sandra says: "In the 1970s, when I first went into practice, the concern was how to get young women to have orgasms; today, I'm seeing women and couples from their twenties to their eighties who want to recapture desire and enhance sexuality so that it means more than just an act of companionship. How do you get there? Not from wishing or hoping or relying on quick fixes. While the search is on for a miracle potion or fail-proof device that will transform sex and make it magical, it is my belief that ultimately, women hold the tools necessary to get the sex they want. It is their willingness to do what needs to be done—whether it means taking hormones, starting therapy, or believing that they are entitled to sexual pleasure that will ultimately make the difference between sexual apathy and sexual joy."

Judith says: "Who would ever have thought we would see *The Vagina Monologues* off-Broadway or watch *Sex and the City* on HBO? Society allows us to think differently about sex than we ever did—as long as we feel comfortable enough to tolerate the ambivalence and the tension that it produces. Seeing sex all around us, breathing it in, so to speak, makes us aware and conscious of our feelings—whether they're positive or negative. That can lead us closer to both the questions and the answers about what we want and how to get it, in bed and out of it. That's the purpose of this book."

We both see women who are reaching for that missing link between their personality and their sexuality and who are trying to keep up with the various changes that go on in their sexual lexicon. One day, they may be having a wild old time in bed; the next, they may have difficulty getting aroused. Or perhaps they have a great simpatico with their partner and then, inexplicably, they may experience a discrepancy in desire, or, even more troubling, they may lose all interest in sex. Sometimes women remember passion and mourn it—they may have had a close encounter with desire when they were younger, but then found that it vanished after they got married and had children. And after a few years of wishing and hoping, they gave up. Others say they never had it but would like to know it, either because their partner insists or because they feel that there must be ecstasy somewhere, waiting around the corner, and that they deserve to find it. And some women who are not actively sexual, perhaps after an illness or chemotherapy, find that as they grow more mature and more responsive, they can love and give love in a way that transcends physical sex.

So women are desperately searching for answers, about both sex and intimacy. Knowing the territory makes women feel safe—it's comforting to hold another warm body, to sense the presence, the smell, the familiarity of the partner you share a space with. Yet they don't always want to feel safe. Women who hit the Internet sites or have phone sex with partners they don't know or visit private sex clubs want risk and excitement. And even those who don't venture beyond their own bedroom want a thrill, not just the same old same-old.

Countless books, films, and songs would have us believe that the sexual revolution has filtered into our psyches and transformed our lives over the past thirty years. *Women love sex.* "I learned about myself from masturbating," says Tamara, 37, a divorced mother of two. "And then I took it upon myself to show my partners exactly what I wanted. Sex has never been better and it makes me a stronger person." The media would have us believe that most women are as much in touch with their desire as Tamara is, knowledgeable about how to express what pleases them to their partners and able to navigate the labyrinthine paths of sexuality as they grow up and grow older.

But another recent approach to female sexuality counsels restraint. The cheerleaders of this movement are of the opinion that the woes that beset the modern woman—sexual harassment, stalking, rape—are all responses of a society that has lost its respect for female modesty. *Women hate sex. Sex just ruins things.* "It really bothers me that there's all this emphasis on sex," says Patricia, 48, married for twenty-five years. "I mean, if that's all there is in a partnership, it burns out pretty fast. You have to work on the rest of the relationship if you have one, and if you're single, you should stay out of bed until you are absolutely certain this is the person for you." Allies of abstinence like Patricia think that women have been false to their own natures by training themselves to seek sexual gratification instead of true love. If they could only refrain from touching, they could recapture their vulnerability and romantic hopes. However, as women age, if they've kept themselves aloof from the juicy, messy fray for a long time, they may find that they can't summon the interest or the desire anymore.

Love sex? Hate sex? It's not one or the other, although women may reach both extremes at some times during their lives. In the middle of those extremes, of course, lies an array of possibilities so vast they cannot be catalogued. And probably every woman we've ever talked to—patients, friends, and acquaintances—is aware of the huge sexual split inside her—she wants it, she can leave it alone; she craves stability and family, she craves danger and freedom; she is hetero, she is gay, she isn't sure she likes men *or* women.

In writing this book, we wanted to help women understand and reclaim their sexuality. To that purpose, we've created a photo-montage of women at all stages and ages of life. We've aimed the camera at one woman after another to capture many different eclectic experiences and opinions about sex. We've talked to women from teenagers to women in their seventies and eighties; straight, gay, and bisexual; single, cohabiting, married or in committed relationships, or divorced; Caucasian, African-American, Hispanic, Muslim, East Indian; able-bodied and physically challenged. For every woman with plenty of partners, there are celibate women; for every carefree person who says she doesn't need love to have sex, there are those who swear the two can't be divided. This book attempts to look at all the problems and issues, the delights and fears, women have today, how they've changed through their lifespan, and how ubiquitous they are. Our goal is to help you discover—or rediscover—the joys of your sexuality and to understand the cycles of desire that wax and wane over many decades.

In the first half of the book, we examine a woman's life cycle to see how we arrive at our erotic destination, from the blossoming of sexual interest in childhood and adolescence through the reproductive years to the fire-and-ice changes that go on throughout midlife and on into "highlife," or older age. In the second half of the book, we explore what's new and different—the Internet, the medical and surgical innovations that may boost sexual desire and performance, and the way that, with society's evolution, the spiritual or sacred elements of sex have come to the fore. All of these permutations of the old patterns are changing the way women relate to themselves and to others.

When we started out to write this book, we were sure we were the experts, that over the years, we had seen and heard just about everything. But sex, as the stand-up comics tell us, "is bigger than both of us." There is virtually no lifestyle, from the most conservative to the most radical, that is not currently in practice somewhere. During the course of talking to researchers, therapists, and women of all ages and opinions, we realized that a huge sea-change is occurring. Ambivalence and boredom with sex, which often happens after many decades of marriage or partnership, does not necessarily doom a woman to a stagnant relationship and a body that will never feel pleasure again. Nor do one-night stands in cyberspace with partners of different genders or kinky sexual perspectives mean that all barriers have been broken down. There's always a new turn in the road, and at this point in history, there have never been so many roads with so many forks.

A woman can stay celibate or pleasure herself when there is no appropriate partner in sight; she can be sexual when there is someone around who moves her motor. She can enjoy vanilla sex or sample the many flavors of BDSM or fetishism. She can time her reproductive life so as not to disturb her career path; she can alter her hormonal output to make herself more receptive to desire and arousal, she can consider surgical repair for physical problems that make sex painful, she can explore relationships in real time and virtual time. And by taking cautious steps that will keep her safe from disease and pregnancy, she can decide on monogamy, on serial partners, or even on polyamorous groups of lovers.

But she can do those things only if she is comfortable with her changing sexuality. Ask any twenty-first-century woman about her love life and her sex life, and she'll roll her eyes and ask, "How much time do you have?" or "*What* sex life?" The stories we've heard are heartrending and clearly reveal that the anticipation and the reality of sex are at war with each other. For most women, it takes a lot more than genital friction for sex to feel fulfilling. The rest of the package includes intimacy, kindness, understanding, comfort, power. If she has an unresponsive husband, a needy child, and a hundred jobs that must be done first, it's hard to concentrate on eroticism. So we have to find a way for her to delve into her sexuality with as much intention and purpose as she gives to the rest of her life.

Where does it all start? Girls aren't taught that sex is fun or exciting, even in enlightened families. A father may get a vicarious thrill when his son gets his first girlfriend and his mom may beam with pride, but both mother and father tend to wring their hands when their daughter starts going out. How many parents stay up until the wee hours waiting for their son to return from a date, praying that nothing bad or unforeseen has happened to him? It's different with a girl, who is viewed as vulnerable and less able to take care of herself.

All of these perilous, anxious moments serve as the backdrop to women's early sexuality. *If the initiation is that dangerous, I don't know that I want in to the club.* Those experimental but clumsy erotic afternoons at the beach or late nights in the backseat were better in anticipation than in completion. There's a lot of fumbling and too many false starts. *He's* supposed to be the leader; but *she* needs to keep control. Teenage Romeos, even those who care deeply about their girlfriends, commonly lack any skill or finesse whatsoever, and for this reason, fully 75 percent of women are unprepared for their first intercourse and find their initial sexual experience distasteful. It's rushed, it's hidden, it's not all it was cracked up to be.

Of course, one bad time wouldn't cut sex off at the knees—it takes practice to quell desire. Women collect a lot of baggage over the years—bad relationships or no relationships, a fast-track career or a house full of children who each demand constant care, elderly parents or a spouse who is ill and needs attention, personal illness or disability, a poor body image, or a regular partner who never aims to please. After so much disappointment comes the rationalization *So what? It's not that important. I have better things to do. Sex just isn't worth the trouble.*

But wait a minute. Practically every woman has had an inkling of the joy and promise that her sexuality can give. Whether she finds it alone, during masturbation, or with one partner who is patient and imaginative, or deep in the recesses of her own mind as she learns what turns her on and truly pleases her, she has the potential to acquire sexual skills that will, in fact, inform her entire life. We talk about *skills* because this is not something you luck into or that someone hands you. It takes time and practice and determination to be a unified sexual adult.

In our opinion, women give up too soon. The less a woman partakes, the more she forgets what can happen when she abandons her dos and don'ts, lets go, and plunges deep. So she has to be reawakened to the possibilities of her own enjoyment. She is like Dorothy in *The Wizard of Oz,* who was unaware that all she had to do to get home was to click her heels together three times. It was so easy after the obstacles had been removed from her path. And so it can be for the majority of women.

We felt we had to write this book in order to explore exactly why it's so hard for women to have a good time in bed and to help them to turn reluctance into curiosity and then, possibly, into jubilation. We wanted to offer a respite from the misguided messages promoted by "sexperts" who encourage women to search for nonstop orgasms and perfect synchrony with a partner.

We intend to get past the overly simplistic attempts that deal only with the most obvious symptoms of love or desire and get to the meaning of the problem and how and why it evolved. We hope to uncover new pathways that will help women of all ages to reach their sexual potential. This book will demonstrate why some women adore sex, why some are dissatisfied with it, and why some have gone beyond what is conventionally thought of as sexual to experience a different type of ecstasy.

We begin by talking about how women are different from men. Simply put, what men want is the availability of sexual contact, reliable sexual performance, and release in the form of ejaculation and orgasm. Simply put, what women want is to feel attractive, to feel loved and understood, and to be valued for their minds as well as desired for their bodies. In general, men are into *doing;* women are into *being.* The common denominator, however, is bigger than any of those elements—both men and women feel the need for relationship and connection and, of course, pleasure.

Sex is good when *you* make it good, which is what so many women have discovered. It is the most personal thing we do in life, so you can't be given a road map by a kindly aunt or well-meaning friend. You need to see why it enthralls you, *specifically* you. Your sexual life is as diverse and fascinating as you are yourself—it is constructed out of the interwoven fabrics of remembrance, anticipation, concerns about body image, heightened physical sensation, guilt and anxiety, emotional ties and bindings, your relationship with yourself and another. And it projects you beyond all this. Sex is one of the only experiences you will ever have that can lift you out of your everyday life and make the rest of the world go away.

What gives women their unique sexual makeup? Is it culture that molds us—family, school, and religious influences? Is it our personal experience, starting in childhood as we attach and then detach from parental influence? Or is there something in our neurological and hormonal makeup that determines whether we turn out sexually apathetic, a tease, a scaredy-cat, or a devotee? Our sexual personality shifts and changes as we mature.

There is risk involved in female sexuality. How else can you unleash the ties of your conventional hormonal and environmental circumstances? It's not easy to preserve and promote one's own sexual development when there are so many other agendas, issues, and problems competing for a woman's attention. But it is *always* possible. The tide can turn for no particular reason, as it did for a patient we interviewed, a woman who had never had any sexual joy whatsoever and described herself as dysfunctional. She came alive to herself for the first time at 47, with no particular partner on the horizon, and had not only a first orgasm through masturbation, but a persistent sexual rush and sense of arousal that propelled her through each day.

The limits and potentials of female sexuality are just beginning to be understood. Women will be able to make new choices for their sexuality only when they are emotionally free of the responsibilities that turn them away from pleasure and make them want to hide under the bed instead of rolling around on top of it. They've got to have the guts to let go of what their mother, their partner, or their inner demons tell them, and find out what turns them on.

This book offers a portrait of women's deepest fears, desires, and possibilities. As you find yourself in these pages, rejoice and claim your birthright. Sex is the underground spring that feeds and waters the territory of your life. It's always there, bubbling up when you least expect it.

Sandra Leiblum, Ph.D.
Judith Sachs

PART I
THE SEXUAL LIFE CYCLE

CHILDHOOD AND ADOLESCENCE: THE ERUPTION OF SEX

Two girls of about five or six are standing in the rain outside a house on a warm summer day. One, with disheveled blond curls and hazel eyes, stands with her face up to the sky, her hands raised and fingers lightly grabbing at the drops that pelt her. She opens her mouth and receives the delicious drink, then giggles and runs around to the side of the house to stand directly under the rainspout. She pulls up her skirt so that the moisture can touch her legs directly; then she rubs the drops into her skin as though applying a salve. She is suddenly drenched, her hair hangs around her angelic face like wet string and her dress clings to her chubby child's body.

The other child, taller with long straight dark hair, eyes her friend with suspicion and ducks under the overhang on the side of the house to stay dry. She keeps her arms wrapped around her thin shoulders, rubbing them as though she were cold, although the rain is the temperature of a warm bath.

"C'mon, Meg!" calls the first kid, still standing under her shower. She takes the water in her two hands and splashes it in her face, then lifts her skirt so that the downpour can pelt her stomach.

"I'll get my dress wet," her friend scowls. "Katie, you come back here! My mom would be mad. I'll be all messed up and wet." She lifts one hand to wipe the mist from her face.

"It's great!" Katie dances in a circle. "Mmm. Love it."

"I don't want to stay here—too icky," says Meg. "Let's go inside and eat cupcakes. Mom got some."

Katie receives the precious christening one last time and then speeds toward the house, laughing, as Meg opens the door for her. They track up the kitchen floor and sit, one dry and one dripping, at the kitchen counter, with a box of cupcakes.

"Look at these!" Katie digs in, the first to pick a sweet treat. And in an instant, there is icing all over her mouth. She licks it off, then devours the cake. Meg giggles, jamming cake in her mouth, too. When she finishes, she scrubs her mouth with a napkin, then reaches over to clean her friend's face. Katie resists.

The girls' mothers walk in during their snack and find them arguing about who gets the chocolate one with sprinkles. Katie, wet and sticky, jumps off her stool and runs to her mother to give her a hug, which is promptly returned. Meg and her mother exchange polite pecks as the tall woman glances with undisguised disapproval at her daughter's soggy friend.

One child has so much delight in her body and the world around her. The other, even at this age, is measuring how much pleasure she can take. And that night when both girls get into bed, can you guess which one puts her hands between her legs to soothe herself to sleep?

We enter this world pushing and shoving our way through the birth canal of the woman who gave us life. A pity our tiny eyes are still squeezed shut, because this is a place we will never visit again—the opportunity to glimpse the female genitalia from the inside is gone for good. If we could only see ourselves as boys and men do, if we could reach out and touch the orchid organ cloaked and hiding inside, we might have a better sense of the normality of our sex. As it is, we struggle along, wanting to get comfortable with that clitoris, that vagina, that vulva, but for many, it's a hard fight.

Children like Katie are blessed, because they are explorers. They want to know the world—what it tastes like, smells like, feels like. They rush toward sensation and are not disappointed, even when it turns out to be different from what they expected. They can delight in the feel of the rain, the explosion of taste, the sensuality of touch. And as they grow, they will have a better chance at pursuing and experiencing the delight of physical, mental, emotional, and spiritual pleasure.

A child like Meg, though, is more the norm. She is tentative about life, not quite sure she likes being wet or dirty, always looking over her shoulder for her parents' approval. She has learned the rules of propriety and they firmly state, "When you're wearing a dress, don't get it messy." She may never even have considered touching her genitals, not because she was told it was inappropriate, but because everything else in her life conspires to hide the truth of her sensuality from her.

Where does this predilection come from? How do we turn into women who can delve into sex all the way up to our eyebrows, or barely stick our toes in it? Is it biological or hormonal, is it a personality trait, does it develop over the years as social accommodation and reinforcement?

Of course, it's all these things and more. They are harmonics around the one predominant note in our personal symphony. We can't get good sex until we find out how to tune that instrument—and it can take half a lifetime or more to do that.

Even before birth, the forces regulating female behavior and sex roles are present. Think of those greeting cards for the parents of a new baby girl. A typical message proclaims that girls are softer and weaker, but also that they are temptresses who can't help themselves. One card describes girls as charmers who are put on earth to get you to spoil them and deck them out in frilly clothes. They cast a spell on you and can't help but be enticing.

Cards about boys go on about the mudpies they'll make, the grass stains on their knees, the string and rocks in their pockets, and of course, the great games they'll play—basketball, baseball, etc. But girls are depicted as sex objects right from the start, not to mention witches who practice sorcery. Watch out—they're charmers who put you under their spells. That pink-and-white finery is all a deception, because sooner or later, the sweet mask will fall away, revealing the Lolita who will grow to be a Madonna, who will grow to be a Mata Hari.

Of course, sexuality is on the scene from the beginning, although when the curtain goes up, it plays only a walk-on part. Just a few months after birth, infant girls can and do lubricate, like their grown-up sisters. It's well known that infant boys have erections—how many parents look admiringly at that little acorn when they're changing a diaper, but when they see the moist shining around their daughter's genitalia, they hastily rub it off with a baby wipe? What's all this about girls being aroused? If we could encourage their capacity for sexual response and pleasure in their bodies from the start, they might need less reassurance about their worthiness and sexuality when they grow up.

Naming the Parts

Bringing up a girl these days is tough. A conscientious mom and dad want to make sure that she knows she is valued, that she is treated equally with her brothers, that she develops a keen sense of her mind as well as her body. But there's that sex thing. There simply isn't any precedent for encouraging girls' sexuality. As a matter of fact, most parents, even the most enlightened baby boomers who stripped and made love at Woodstock, have a heck of a time telling their tiny daughters what little girls are made of. "There's your nose, this is your chest, here's your tummy, and this is *down there.*" What *is* down there? Why doesn't anyone spell it out? If everything else has a name, why are genitals in a no-woman's land, divorced from the rest of the body?

Boys are given a choice of names for their penis—it's a wee-wee, a pee-pee, a pecker, a weiner (cock, dick, and joint come later). But for girls, it's just *down there,* a geographical area that does not discriminate between elimination and pleasure. So much stuff is included—the mons, clitoris, urethra, outer labia, the perineum, the anus—and that's only what's visible on the outside! On the inside, we have the inner labia, the vagina, the uterus, the ovaries, and the rectum. All that interior space is a mystery—whoever tells girls that the vagina is five inches long and expands to accommodate any size penis so she doesn't have to worry about being ripped apart when penetrated? What is a girl to do without a map? Where could she even request one if she had the knowledge and guts to do so?

Boys stand up and take their penis in hand about the time of toilet-training. Even if they're too tiny to get that stream up over the rim of the toilet, parents kindly provide a step-stool so they can urinate like a man. They touch themselves and see their genitals right out in the open, whether in the bath, squatting outside on a camping trip, or hanging out with Dad in the locker room after a swim. Their public bathrooms are really public—conversations take place at the urinal, or in the open shower stalls at the Y.

A girl never does get to admire her genitals. As she sits in a closed stall on the toilet, she can watch elimination take place, but she can't see where it's coming from. Ask a little girl how many openings she has *down there* and she will undoubtedly say two, one for pee and one for poop. How many mothers correct this misimpression?

As she showers behind a curtain alone in her bathroom or separated from other women at a gym, she can touch, but not see, the areas she needs to clean. And how "dirty" is that region, anyway? If she has a fastidious mother who tells her to use one washcloth for her face and another for her *private parts* (private not only from the world but from the girl herself), she is naturally going to think it is very, very dirty.

Moms and Girls

Girls cleave to their mothers. In most families, Mommy—even if she works full time—is the one who's responsible for most of the parenting and the assignment of caregiving to other individuals (family members, baby-sitters, or day-care supervisors). She's the one that girls pattern themselves after, playing dress-up in Mom's clothes and makeup, mimicking the chores that Mom does. Going to the supermarket, taking little brother to the pediatrician, getting your hair cut in a salon are life events that open a window for girls on the female-insider stuff that is passed down through the generations like a baton in a relay race.

The best kind of mother acts like a mirror to a girl—she should be able to see herself reflected in her mom's own sense of her self. If the woman she loves takes pride in her body and dresses to adorn it rather than hide it or flaunt it, her daughter will get the idea that a woman's lot is pretty good. If, however, her mother storms around the house agonizing about losing five more pounds or complaining about her skimpy breasts or saddlebag thighs, a girl will look in the mirror and begin to question what she sees. A mother who doesn't stand up for herself, who takes a lot of criticism or abuse from her husband or a boss, leaves a girl insecure, without any way to develop her own self-esteem. But a mother who feels strong and competent offers her daughter a gift.

Dads and Girls

More and more men tell us that they're thrilled to learn they're about to become the father of a girl. While women still tend to be the primary care-givers for their daughters, hundreds of thousands of men now enjoy making braids, having tea parties, playing catch, and reading aloud while a tiny head leans sleepily on their shoulder. They also relish feeling adored and idealized by their little girls, who tend to view Daddy as king of the universe.

Part of this dedication to protecting and cherishing their female children includes a tendency to overprotect them. Although anyone can tell a new dad that women typically tolerate pain better and suffer fewer major illnesses, giv-ing them a six-and-a-half-year edge over men in longevity, it is also true that girls are smaller and less physically powerful than boys. A guy gets the idea, like Billy Bigelow in Rodgers and Hammerstein's 1950s musical chestnut *Carousel,* that "you can have fun with a son/ but you gotta be a father to a girl." Men actively father their sons, too, but they seem to worry less and have more fun doing it. Girls are hard work for a man. The will-o'-the-wisp persona that may change from tomboy to prom queen to genius to moody neurotic all in the course of a day is a quandary for the most tender and well-intentioned father.

A father is vital to a girl's growing sense of herself as a competent and desirable woman. Her mother is certainly a role model of either the person she aspires to become or the person she wants least to resemble, but it is often her father who provides the reassurance and reflected gaze that assures her she is attractive. A man who appreciates his daughter—her looks, her mind, her humor, her ability to deal with others and negotiate her surroundings—tells her she's capable and gives her the internal conviction that she should wait until she finds someone who values her (just as Dad does) rather than settling for someone who happens to allow her into his world.

Unfortunately, something happens to the father/daughter relationship right around the time of puberty. As breast-buds blossom, men stop rough-housing with their daughters, fearful that they might touch them and get aroused. It is distressing for a man to see that person whose diapers he changed morph into a nubile female toward whom he may feel unwittingly attracted or aroused. The two do not compute. This sea-change very often occasions a shutdown in a father's emotional output.

The old familiar place on Dad's lap is off-limits ("Hey, get off, you're too big!" is one phrase that's guaranteed to make daughters feel totally humiliated). He may criticize her manner of dress if it's too provocative, making her responsible for his own reaction to her. And so girls find in puberty that not only have they changed, their parents have, too. Warm, snuggly, silly Dad has metamorphosed into a tough drill sergeant; kind, understanding, all-embracing Mom has become . . . to put it mildly, a bitch.

As girls grow, they may be shielded by their fathers from their mothers' boring and annoyingly insistent instructions and admonitions. Men may expect their girls to succeed academically, but other than that, they want them to stay safe and out of trouble. The first year after the onset of a girl's menses is traditionally one where both parents crack down. *You want your independence from us,* they seem to be saying, *well, put up your dukes and we'll fight you for it.*

The Blossoming—Menstruation and Puberty

A patient of Sandra's, a Greek-American woman in her late thirties, recalls the day she got her period, and the shock of the red stain, which she covered quickly with Kleenex. On that winter morning right after her twelfth birthday, she followed her mother around the house looking for a good opportunity to talk. And all it did was baffle and confuse her mother.

"What is it?" she barked. "Can't I have a minute to myself?"

"I need to tell you something—I'm bleeding," the girl said in a hushed voice.

"What? Where did you cut yourself?" her mother asked.

"I didn't."

And then, the look of comprehension and embarrassment as her mother went to the cupboard to get her daughter some pads. "Here, take care of it" was the brusque response as she thrust the box at her. No talk, no congratulations, just the practical matter of mopping up.[1]

Let's not blame her mother too much, though. It is common for a mom to think about her daughter's passage into womanhood as directly correlated with her own, and that brings a considerable amount of anxiety. Danger rears its head: drugged sex, serial partners, group sex, abortion. Small wonder, envisioning the worst, mothers are concerned.

Menses means their adorable sheltered child could get pregnant; she could get hurt by a man. And in Hispanic or religious African-American families, it means that she could lose her virginity, and then no man would want to marry her.[2] Mother anxiety often translates as mother-madness. Mothers will berate their pubescent daughters about their clothes (too tight and revealing or too sloppy and boyish), their relationships with members of both sexes ("Why do you have to go out with him?" "She's with a bad crowd—leave her alone."), and their personal hygiene ("Your hair is so greasy—why don't you wash it?").

Maybe all this ambivalence about a girl's entry into the world of women has something to do with the fact that blood isn't very nice. First, it represents injury, and second, menstrual blood smells once it hits the air. Look at the reluctance to name the actual things. In televised ads for personal hygiene products, when a substance is poured onto the pad so that viewers can see how much liquid it holds, the fluid is blue, not red. The claim of all these products is that they "protect" a woman during a sensitive time, and offer her "freedom" to continue her regular activities. Girls never really get the whole business about connecting menstruation to the positive aspects of being a woman in our society, because we are so focused on how she smells, and whether she'll leak, go on a PMS rampage, or figure out how to staunch the flow so she can jump into the pool at a moment's notice.

Historically, in female-centered cultures, menstrual bleeding was a sign of a woman's power and her association with the changing aspects of the moon and tides. She would isolate herself from men and nonmenstruating women in order to concentrate on deeply spiritual matters. But other cultures interpret this week as a time when a woman is "unclean." Orthodox Jewish women take a ritual bath (the *mikvah*) before they can lie with their husband again. Scottish women once weren't allowed to bake a certain cake during this precarious few days, for fear it would fall; in Bali, a menstruating woman couldn't even enter the temple.

So you can celebrate getting your period because now you are a woman, but you're considered unsafe, unclean, and just a little supernatural. What woman wouldn't develop ambivalent feelings about menstruation and becoming sexually mature?

Menarche comes earlier and earlier. In 1890, girls didn't get rolling until about 14.8 years old, according to a report in *The New England Journal of Medicine*. But just last year, the National Center on Health Statistics found that American girls on average begin at 12.6 years.[3] African-American and Hispanic girls may bleed as young as eight or nine. The onset depends to a great extent on body-fat ratio, and the typical inner-city diet is extremely high in fat. The Big Macs and fries that substitute for fruits, vegetables, and legumes push the hormonal envelope. And then, too, cattle are pumped full of estrogen, which means that our children's bodies are absorbing higher doses of it.

A hundred years ago, you would have been pretty close to marriage anyway when you started bleeding—it was perfectly okay to be thinking sexually. Today, you're a kid who's still cuddling up to a teddy bear at sleepovers and playing soccer after school. It's a long stretch to sexuality.

Naturally, our society has compensated for that. Little girls in bikinis mince down runways in full makeup (think JonBenét Ramsey). Their parents buy clothes for them at Ralph Lauren that are identical to their own. Eighth-graders listen to explicitly sexual hip-hop lyrics and watch R-rated movies, or occasionally flip on to a porno site on the Web. These children are precocious

and advanced beyond their years. Yet they really can't make a connection
with sexuality in their own life, so they're simply mimicking adult behavior.

Girls who grow into their adult bodies early are perceived as more mature
than their peers. You may still be playing with Barbies, but that 36D bra says
you're something other than a child. And, of course, it's at once thrilling and
terrifying to know that every boy's eyes are on your chest. Even if they taunt
you by calling names ("Look at those udders!"), you know it's kind of a back-
handed compliment. As the rest of your form fills out, and those coltlike legs
develop shape and the buttocks and hips take on curvaceous proportions, you
may panic about weight gain. It doesn't matter that your mother and the
family-life educator tell you that this is what happens to all girls—you are different, and you can't bear the idea of getting fat in a society where fat means
unappealing and undesirable. And America is prejudiced against fat (despite
the fact that so many individuals are obese)—especially fat women, who typically earn about $6,000 less per year than their slimmer counterparts and have
a 20 percent lower chance of marrying, according to a study done by the
Harvard School of Public Health.

On the other hand, would you rather be fat or out of the club? Girls who
don't start menstruating until 14 or 15 are at a real disadvantage—like Carrie
in the eponymous Stephen King novel, they look like children and are
scorned by the "big girls," who can't be bothered teaching idiots what it
means to bleed. Pelted with tampons in the shower room, flat-chested, hip-
less Carrie is a reminder of everything her sophisticated peers have left
behind. They hate it, and therefore her.

How can a girl gain any amount of self-esteem and develop a great image
of her body when she is torn between modeling herself after the anorectic
fashion ads or her own mother's body—whether that body is painfully
pumped at a gym or has begun to show signs of sagging and aging? The least
little teasing comment from Dad, a boy she likes, or another girl about her
shorts being too short or her shirt being uncool, and her universe starts crum-
bling. Teenage girls see themselves as a collection of parts—okay hands, great
hair, pretty good eyebrows, disgusting nose, and fat butt. The picture simply
doesn't come together. And as a girl dissects her own beauty and too often
finds it lacking, she loses sight of her sexual potential. Any boy who looks at
her, smiles at her, doesn't slam the door in her face, is offering her such an
extraordinary gift, because he has forgiven her for her imagined faults, that
she might just go out with him. She can't yet make a judgment about whether
this admirer is really for her or against her, so she rules on the physical evidence alone. And if she doesn't like her body, she can do all sorts of things to
it—starve it, mutilate it, burn it, neglect it—just never ignore it.

Liking Your Body

As we can see when we watch little girls get off on simple things like the rain or a cupcake, the body can be an endless source of pleasure. And as girls hit puberty, that type of sensual pleasure is heightened by the hormonal rush that starts the brain fantasizing and sets the groin a-tingle. There's something going on down there, even though it's not yet clear what it is or why it's there.

Of course, sex isn't primarily a physical act, particularly for girls, but at puberty, the brain suddenly puts a spotlight on the body. Someone touches your arm, and for fourteen years, it's been just an arm. Now it's a fur coat, an electric blanket, a new substance that's been just created to offer the greatest permeability of sensation on the face of the earth. Naturally a teenager thinks in physical terms when she thinks about sex, and if touch feels good, why not do it some more?

Because for girls, there's all that underlying concern and anxiety. Teenage girls suddenly see their male peers growing muscles, getting taller. In comparison, they are smaller and lighter and therefore more physically vulnerable. Also, teenage girls know that menstruation has put them at a distinct disadvantage when it comes to sex—they could get carried away by passion into unwanted pregnancy. Just one time cuddling in the bushes or in the backseat of a car and they could rue it for years. Then, too, their hidden, cloaked organs are more susceptible to sexually transmitted disease than a boy's. It's also more difficult to find sores and lesions on labia or the vaginal wall than it is on the penis or testicles.

But most important, there's the element of emotion. Girls want to be swept away, conveyed to a magic land where a boy lets them know how he couldn't possibly go on living without them. Every book a girl has ever read, from antique fairy tales to Judy Blume, says that sex must be coupled with love in order to be worthwhile. And because girls are socialized to please, they are torn between pleasing the boy, who's begging for it and pleasing their parents, who've cautioned against it. The only people they aren't trying to please are themselves, and here lies the crux of women's sexual conundrum: As long as their own desire and pleasure don't count, women will continue, from adolescence to old age, to make poor sexual choices.

How do we wake girls up to give them this vital message? They are deserving of delight, respect, fun, and many types of sensual and sexual experience, some of which they can't possibly savor in adolescence. It's not selfish to feel that your own interests can and must come first. Girls who settle for less become women who expect very little of themselves and of their partners, and in the end, grow to care nothing about their sexual lives. By the time they reach midlife, they say they aren't interested anymore, that the fire has gone out. The truth is more that the fire was never kindled properly in the first place.

Most girls are initiated into sex by eager partners who tell them when and how they should enjoy their sexuality—it's rare for the girl to take the lead. Too often, her sexual awakening comes as the result of an uninvited touch—a stranger or an adult she knows casually. More frequently, she starts her sexual journey with a boyfriend who is eager to score, and whose probing, prodding hands don't give her the push she needs toward finding her own pleasure. Some girls discover sex on their own, under the covers or in the shower, using their own hands to guide the way. These are the ones who may be most likely to grow into their sexuality at their own pace, experiencing new sensations at a rate they can digest and feel comfortable with, rather than being launched too quickly and suddenly by the attentions of a too-eager seducer.

How can girls develop an easy relationship with their own bodies? It's not just through touch, of course, but all manner of sensual pleasures will do it.

First, there's *food*. It tastes good, it gives energy, it offers a comfort level (satiation) for hours after you consume it. Moreover, it makes the body able to work and play hard, and that feels good, too. But adolescent girls, in their confusion about restriction and independence, often stop eating or else butcher their diet in such bizarre ways that they might as well not be eating at all. The plagues of the teen female population—anorexia, bulimia, ritualistic eating, and overeating—seem directly related to society's insistence that girls check themselves, perfect themselves, and keep pleasure at bay. According to Peggy Claude-Pierre, author of *The Secret Language of Eating Disorders,* pervasive negativity about everything—from grades to social prowess—leads to a loss of the self. A girl who can't figure out who she is or where she fits in thinks that she doesn't even belong on this planet—and if she can shrink herself down below any recognizable size, maybe no one will notice her.

Then there's the too, too solid flesh itself. Girls who have already punished themselves with bingeing and purging or not eating at all may be eager to take it farther—and this may lead to some form of self-mutilation. Taking a razor blade to yourself or burning yourself with a cigarette lighter is a method of testing the flesh. If you feel emotionally numb most of the time, slicing and ripping through your skin can provide a strange kind of solace, and give you the feeling that you've taken control over your life. The various ritualistic sexual practices of piercing and whipping are another way of achieving an orgiastic release.

Another, certainly more positive, way to explore the potential of the body is through *exercise,* although even healthy activity can be distorted and manipulated by a determined teen. Children delight in running, jumping, twirling, falling, and finding out the myriad ways in which the body can exert itself. But then exercise becomes codified as phys-ed or gym class, complete with changes of clothing that remain sweaty and smelly in the locker throughout the long months of the school year. Co-ed gym classes can kill the love of play, because once in adolescence, the boys are showing off and the girls are feeling miserable when they don't make as many baskets or hit the ball as far.

Many girls use overexercise as an extension of their eating disorder—they will rule that they must accomplish one hundred sit-ups before bed in order to "earn" a rice cracker for breakfast in the morning. The perversion of movement for the love of the vitality it can bring is complete exhaustion.

Girls' sports, on the other hand, can remedy a good deal of that. Girls who get into soccer, softball, lacrosse, basketball, track, tennis, and competitive swimming get what boys have always had—the ability to share successes and defeats in a valued arena, with or without a team. If you play a team sport, you're not out there on your own—although your performance counts—you are a group, a gang, a gaggle of great goddesses, and you can show it to the world. You wear uniforms, which help to downplay the differences in popularity, ethnicity, and socioeconomic status, and you move together toward a common goal. You find out that you can run really fast, throw or kick really far, and score to the cheers of the crowd.

And although girls can be cruel and nasty to one another, and may be enormously competitive about grades or boyfriends, they are usually able to put that aside during a game. They can be comrades on the field, and they can have compassion for those who miss a few good shots. It's more likely for girls to say "nice try" when a lesser player drops the ball than "you stupid klutz," which they would undoubtedly do in a different venue.

What's more, there are now recognizable female athletes (Mia Hamm, Joy Fawcett, and Carla Overbeck in soccer, Serena and Venus Williams in tennis, Rebecca Lobo and Ticha Penicheiro in basketball, etc.) who may not rank up there with Michael Jordan in terms of endorsement power but who pack a big punch as models for girls who want to achieve something positive with their bodies.

There is another significant way for the body to give enormous pleasure, but it's a lot more problematic for most girls than team sports. We're talking about masturbation.

Touching the Parts

If your parents wouldn't even name the parts of the body for you, it goes without saying that they would not point them out, or encourage you to see them, touch them, or own them. If you were lying on top of your covers one hot night, and your mother came in to read you a story and found your hand inside your pajama bottoms, how did she react? How did Americans react when former Surgeon General Jocelyn Elders spoke out on masturbation? This public official, who should have been able to distinguish between a healthy activity and one that could cause hairy palms, suggested that children be taught in schools that masturbation was one way to experiment sexually that did not cause pregnancy, transmit disease, or hurt anyone's feelings. And she lost her job for saying it.

Of course, boys didn't have to be told that self-stimulation feels good, because they knew that from their earliest years. Playing with the penis is a great way to learn how it works, and whether a boy is curious about urination or just wants a thrill, he may touch and fondle his genitals on a regular basis. Of course, his launchpad into puberty is the wet dream. Think how different it is to learn about being a man from ejaculation, a sexual phenomenon, rather than from bleeding, a reproductive phenomenon. Embarrassing as those stained sheets may be, a boy learns that by touching himself, he can induce the same pleasurable reaction with his hands. And the more he exerts control over masturbation, the more pleasant it becomes.

Not so with girls. Parents and teachers aren't tolerant of little girls jiggling their leg or rubbing up against the furniture. One African-American woman in Sandra's practice recalls vividly that her mother raced over to the bed and slapped her hand away from her genitals as she was drifting toward sleep, in one brief moment robbing her of years of pleasure. "Don't ever do that! Nice girls don't!" are two admonitions emblazoned on the hard drive of the libido, confused and guilty because it craves that pleasant touch.

Different cultures have different rules for early female sexual experimentation, yet in no ethnic group is masturbation smiled on for girls. (Think of a couple of boys in the backyard, jerking off to see who can spurt the farthest, feeling proud of the ability to make the penis perform so expertly.) For a girl to touch herself is for her to invade the inner space that one day may contain new life. It is seen as conduct unbecoming a lady. And so girls usually stop masturbating (if they ever started) by the age of puberty. Some have to be awakened all over again, and it's not until they are sexually active or even partnered or married that they figure out how to use a hand, a washcloth, or a vibrator to have a really good time.

Girls are forever being warned—watch out, don't hurt yourself, scream if anyone lays a finger on you. This is true even in family-life and sex-ed classes in school, where sexuality is commonly portrayed as physically risky or unhealthy, or as a set of hurdles that have to be crossed. The subject matter ranges from the changes of puberty to reproduction to contraception to STDs. And thanks to a 1996 federal entitlement program for abstinence, paying out $250,000,000 to private programs, kids can learn to sit on their hands until marriage and do nothing sexual (actually, sitting on your hands might be too much fun!). But very often, abstinence programs don't even mention masturbation. Now what kind of Pandora's box would be opened if we taught girls that self-stimulation was good?

Girls in Groups

Groups and gangs and cliques have always been there—we remember them from our own teen years, and our mothers remember them from theirs. But at no time in history has the division been so out there—you walk to junior high your first day and you can recognize the popular girls, the Goths, the Metal heads, the druggies, the jocks, the nerds, and the dozens of other groups, including the untouchables who belong to no group at all and are therefore less noticeable.

Let's start with popularity. It can be great to have it, and totally awful to have it, because it puts so much pressure on a girl. What makes you popular? In junior high and the early years of high school, it has something to do with the way you look and dress, what music you listen to, and who you hang with. Later on in high school, it's not as urgent to identify with a group, because you're searching for your own special identity, so the label "popular" is often relegated to girls who *think* they're popular, regardless of whether it's true or not. Girls who get along well with lots of different groups and make boys feel comfortable tend to be well liked. So popularity is partly attitude—a popular person is known for her charisma and self-confidence.

Popular girls tend to mature early and dress the part; they go out with boys, usually beginning in sixth or seventh grade, and they tend to stick to one boy for a few months before passing him on to someone else, often a good friend. The relationship consists of hanging out (at school, on a city stoop, by a bank, in a mall), going out for Frappuccinos (or sodas in the less trendy suburban or rural areas), getting parents to drive you to the movies, and talking, talking, talking on the phone. Sexual activity in junior high and the first years of high school follow the pattern of the "4Fs"; that is, Frenching, Feeling Up, Fingering, and, finally, Fucking. For younger kids, open-mouthed kissing (none of them ever "peck" anymore), necking, and petting with clothes on can be done anywhere—behind the library, under the bleachers, in a dark alley. It may be initiated by the boy or the girl, although even if she starts it, she may not want to go as far once she has inflamed her paramour. A popular girl may have dreams about love, commitment, marriage, and a family, but at the start of her sexual career, she is mainly after enhancing her popularity quotient.

If you're popular, popular boys pay attention to you. Some schools actually have hierarchies of ascent toward the girl of their dreams—a less popular boy must hook up with several less popular girls in a particular order before achieving the nirvana of hanging out with the "queen bee." (Incredibly dorky boys may aspire and pay attention to her, too, but if she is really out of their league, they leave her alone.)

Actually, what the girl gets out of this experience is more than attention, it's a kind of acceptance. By the time she gets to high school, a popular girl truly belongs to the same club as those she hangs with. Shared interests, socioeconomic status, religion, and race all count. According to the University of Chicago National Health and Social Life Survey, published in 1994,[4] we tend to hang out with and marry the people who are most like us. The connection between the princess and pauper, jock and nerd, black and white are tenuous. (There are increasingly more interracial couples in suburban high schools, but the numbers are still minuscule.) The specific cliques of junior high melt into one another as kids grow up and find that they relate to several different types of people.

In high school, you can play sports, be a good student, and go out occasionally, or not at all. You can socialize with groups of boys and girls without pairing off, although it becomes harder to be the odd girl out in a group where everyone else is paired. The academically inclined girls, sometimes self-designated as "unpopular," tend to steer their own course through the sexual sea. Sharon Thompson, a thoughtful educator and writer who conducted a massive study of teenage sexuality, points out that girls who have ambitions don't get caught up in the sex thing as deeply as those for whom romance is the major deal in their lives.[5] They may stay clear of boys so that they can pursue their serious interests. And boys may avoid them because they are just too scary and too much of a threat.

Every school has its outsiders, who may be painfully shy, grossly obese, depressed or in some way emotionally unstable, gay, or some combination of the above. These girls often live a hermetic existence, going to school, moving through the hallways, having lunch and study hall but rarely exchanging a word with their classmates.

Gay girls are becoming more and more common on high school campuses, although the decision to come out is just as hard as it used to be—perhaps more so for girls than boys, since there are fewer admitted lesbians than gay males. The tension and terror predictably change one's status and progress through high school, and the Department of Health and Human Resources reports that 30 percent of those teens who commit suicide are gay.

On the other hand, acceptance of gay and bi lifestyles is higher than it ever was before in urban areas. Those lucky enough to come out in New York, San Francisco, or Boston, for example, may find a totally blasé response to their daring announcement—in some sophisticated circles, the idea of picking *one* sexual identity is totally passé. You can be straight, gay, or bi, and may change again, who knows, the next time you meet someone who turns you on. This emerging tolerance should augur well for the next generation, who may find it easier to accept their peers' unconventional choices, sexual and otherwise.

Some kids say they knew almost as soon as they were out of diapers that they were lesbian; others would never call themselves gay, but may have crushes on or engage in sex play with other girls, almost as "practice" for the heterosexual relationship they hope to have later in life. They may take showers together, exchange deep kisses, go to the beach and oil each other's body while the sun warms their genitals and they fantasize about doing more.

"I knew in second grade that I loved women," said Lori, a tall, quirky-looking girl with full lips and a cleft in her chin. "I remember this one time,

I was watching a march on Washington on TV when I was 7. There were two women laughing and kissing on the screen as they held one side of a banner together. I told my parents that someday I would go to that place and live just like them. The expressions on their faces were blank, like they weren't really hearing what I was saying. But they knew, and then when I got to high school and had sleepovers with my girlfriends, it was like setting a fire in the living room. They sort of couldn't ignore it."[6]

Lori said rather proudly that she was a "bad kid"—she was in trouble constantly, she smoked, did drugs, and got drunk a lot. Although she was teased about her sexual orientation, and the administration had recently learned about her relationship with one girlfriend and attempted to break it off, she was big enough to beat up most of the boys, so she never feared for her safety as many gay women do.

Boys don't necessarily ignore gay girls, because they figure they haven't got a chance any more than they do with the ultrapopular girls. All girls, no matter their social standing or ethnicity, find that they may be the butt of sexual jokes. It's frightening to be stalked in the halls, even when it's intended to be funny—girls find out soon enough that just being a girl presents them with innumerable problems. It becomes harder and harder to volunteer in class when they begin to realize that calling attention to themselves may in the long run result in violence, infection, pregnancy, or abortion.

So what should they do about their nascent sexuality? Does it really matter if they flaunt it, hide it, or avoid it? Is it true that wearing tight tops and short skirts is an invitation to rape? Do those school rules about no spaghetti-strap fashions with bra-straps showing really have a purpose? One well-endowed eighth-grader Judith spoke to shook her head, saying, "I don't know what it is about plastic and elastic that's supposed to get these boys all fired up." Because most girls don't get it yet. They feel that sex is in the air, but they haven't got a clue as to which way the wind is blowing.

But even so, they continue to read *Seventeen* and to dream about the prom.

Everything But

Sex is everywhere. Thanks to the former President, hordes of schoolchildren in America know about oral sex and different uses for a cigar. Sex is on MTV and in the sanitized sex education classes flourishing in some states. TV and the Internet fill in where parents dare not go.

And so most kids reach adolescence both enormously savvy and also enormously ignorant about the meaning and appropriate use of sexuality. The prevalence of sex-for-power-and-popularity in high school relationships sets the tone for young women who might have idealized sex and confused it with romance. It is not largely because girls are so horny now that their hormones have kicked in that they begin to experiment with sex. They do it for a variety of reasons—to "get it over with," because they're bored or curious, because their peers will look up to them, the boys will pay a lot of attention, and they will more closely resemble their role models in the adult worlds of music, film, and television. They don't seem to be thinking about themselves or their pleasure, or how distracted they will be from their studies and extracurricular activities.

Kissing and touching in junior high give way to riskier sexual behaviors as kids are alone more often and begin to use drink and drugs to enhance feelings.[7] Where do they do it? Judith asked a group of high school seniors. It's hard to find privacy, isn't it?

The answer was, anywhere and everywhere. If they had access to a car, that was the best; otherwise, there were places behind the school, in the park, at the movies, in their parents' houses while their folks were out or even when they were in, watching TV. Very easy.

The interesting thing about sex play before intercourse enters the picture is that it is actually freer and less phallocentric than plain old routine penetration. Would that teenaged girls could remember what they got out of mutual masturbation, having their breasts and nipples sucked, their vaginas fingered and licked, and their anuses gently probed. Allowing a boy to ejaculate between one's breasts or legs can give a girl an enormous sense of accomplishment—she's made him feel wonderful but without much risk of pregnancy or disease. (Of course, these activities generally do nothing for the girl except to make her feel sticky and wet—most teenaged couples have trouble finding a place in which to get messy and then wash up.) One of the problems of "outercourse" is that kids get in the habit of not using a condom because of course they never intend to consummate the act—and that behavior leads to unprotected intercourse.

A common sexual improvisation, of course, is the blow job. According to a RAND study done in 1996 in two public Los Angeles high schools on the sexual activity of virgins, 21 percent of the students surveyed had engaged in masturbation with a partner during the previous year, and 14 percent had engaged in oral sex, often after drinking beer, wine, or liquor, or smoking grass. It has become an in thing to do in many middle schools, sometimes taking place in study hall or even on the school bus, and fellatio has become a favorite activity at unchaperoned parties for children as young as 11 or 12. In one Virginia middle school in 1999, a "rash" of oral sex broke out—or, more likely, was discovered by the administration after it had gone on for some time. The students said that they were engaging in this behavior in order to avoid pregnancy and STDs. When the teachers and principals decided to clamp down on this activity, they called only the parents of the girls involved. The implication, of course, was that the boys were passive recipients of the slutty girls' wanton attentions. Now, here's the thing—the girls aren't getting much out of it, since the pleasure part was all visited on the boys. And the girls were the ones accused of pulling down those zippers and sucking away, regardless of what the poor innocent boys wanted or didn't want.

Nothing has changed, has it? Girls are still getting the short end of the stick, or rather, no stick at all. Many girls feel they can assure themselves of a secure relationship if they suck and swallow, or suck and spit, even if the favor is not reciprocated. What do girls enjoy about fellatio? It doesn't hurt (they can control the amount of penetration into their mouths as they cannot into their vaginas), and there is no risk of pregnancy (although there is some risk of STD transmission and boys rarely wear a condom for oral sex). Girls who described their partner as caring and considerate said that they enjoyed everything they did with him—that included both giving and receiving oral sex. Those who are simply "doing sex" because of a misplaced desire to be popular or get attention from a particular boy feel subservient when they are asked to give him head. On the other hand, cunnilingus is often the only way young girls can have an orgasm. If they like their bodies—if they aren't ashamed of their genitals or concerned about their odor—this activity can be the *ne plus ultra* of sex.

Moving from outer- to intercourse is most commonly not a decision— for most girls, it just happens. Part of it is momentum. You're there, you're in the mood, and eventually, you know it's coming. For some girls, it's the pressure—the boy keeps asking, your girlfriends in the locker room are saying, Hey, what's wrong with you, I did it and it was okay. And so the next time they're halfway to the moon, and he wants to, and they kind of want to, they don't push his penis away.

The Sexual Debut

By the age of 16, virginity, for many, is a drag. And according to the 1995 National Survey of Family Growth, conducted by the Health and Human Services National Center for Health Statistics, half of all girls between the ages of 15 and 19, and a slightly higher percent of all boys, have had intercourse. The most common age for girls is 17; 16 for boys. (This is approximately two years earlier than the average age of European girls.)[8] Many girls say, "Well, everyone was doing it; why not me? I might as well get it over with. It's not that big of a deal." Of course, it's appealing to act like a grown-up, even though you haven't yet crossed that Rubicon. Girls who are most likely to jump into the sexual pool at a younger age tend to be more physically mature than their peers, more socially adult (perhaps even experimenting with cigarettes, alcohol, and drugs), and more capable of making their own decisions.[9] And although 93 percent of girls report that their first experience was voluntary, they didn't always feel it was a walk in the park.

Imagine what it would be like if someone gave you a brand-new twenty-speed racing bicycle and challenged you to enter a competition, though your only other experience was riding a one-speed touring bike. You'd have to figure out how to get on and stay on, holding your feet in those little pedal-baskets, which would occasion a few stumbles and falls. You'd have to work on coordinating the rhythm of your feet and hips so you could get enough momentum to stay on board (more falls). You'd have to negotiate traffic as you took a hand off the handlebars to signal a turn; you'd have to perfect looking behind you and in front of you to see where the other riders were. And you'd always be conscious of your goal—trying to get to the finish line. You'd feel harried, anxious, and emotionally overwrought.

That's what a first sexual experience is like. You've fumbled and groped, taken most of your clothes off, kissed and touched, and maybe indulged in mutual masturbation or oral sex. But having a couple of fingers or a tongue inside your vagina is really not comparable to a penis. Even girls who have practiced this moment in their mind over and over report that they are stunned, nearly paralyzed, when the big moment arrives.

Did you use contraception? *No, I just didn't think about it.* Why not? Researchers and sex educators agonize over this question. It's true that teen condom use has doubled from the 1980s, and nine out of ten sexually active girls use some form of contraception. But not every time, and not exactly right. This seems strange, because they're of an age when they can, and often do, make clearheaded decisions on other topics. They've been carefully taught in family-life education classes in school and reminded in church and in after-school programs.[10] Of course, one problem is that 34 percent of these classes preach abstinence only, and if you live in the Deep South, that number rises to 42 percent. Girls are told how bad sex is, how dangerous, but fewer than half the programs tell the kids where to get birth control (45 percent) and condoms (39 percent). Is it any wonder that the rate of sexually transmitted diseases is so much higher in the U.S. than in Europe?

These girls aren't having sex because they're so horny—only a small number of teenage girls talk about being so sexually aroused that they can't think straight. Girls who aren't afraid to walk into a pharmacy and buy condoms somehow manage to leave them in their locker or purse, either because it might make it seem less spontaneous and "ruin the moment," or because it forces them to acknowledge that they were thinking of having sex—a "bad girl" thing to do—or because they find themselves in a trancelike, almost hypnotized state, where they are not truly present or able to connect the importance of that little latex round with their future health and well-being.[11]

Did you use lubrication? *What's that?* (When you're anxious, say, just before you go out on a stage to make a speech before a huge audience—your mouth dries up. The same mucous-membrane situation exists in the vagina, which may feel like the Sahara as soon as that penis begins ramming its way inside.) We tend to think of vaginal dryness as something that affects women after menopause, whereas it can and does strike at any time of life if a woman is rushed or scared or unprepared.

Did you stop and talk to your boyfriend about slowing down? *How could I*? It must be said that many girls are mesmerized by the hydraulic activity of the penis—how it grows from such a little flabby piece of flesh into an engorged blue-red cylinder with a mind of its own. In addition, some of them say that they feel deep affection, even love, for the boy with whom they have decided to go all the way, and to disrupt his single-minded attention would be unthinkable. Since most high school boys are ready to shoot off like a rocket at the hint of their girlfriend's acquiescence to the "big moment," they are not exactly patient. Nor do they have a notion of how helpful it would be to stop the inexorable drive toward penetration to return to oral or manual stimulation of the clitoris so that their partner could catch up.

Some girls do report falling in love and then having sex—a novel idea for the beginning of the twenty-first century. These girls said that intercourse flowed naturally from the experience of being with the guy. They didn't plan it or discuss it ("It wasn't like, 'We'll have dinner; we'll have sex.' "), but rather, both knew that the moment was right. Those who used tampons had less pain, since the hymen had been previously stretched or broken, but most attributed their good experience to the tenderness and concern of their partner.

Other girls, without steady boyfriends, may decide not to waste the first time on some kid, wet behind the ears and at the tip of his engorged member. Girls who select older men, for the most part, are not interested in love and affection but in getting the physical part right. Many select a man who's an acquaintance of their father, or someone they met on a summer holiday— the drummer in the hotel band, the mechanic who fixes their car, the college golf pro—all of whom might be from five to ten years older. The teenage girls who offer themselves to these mature paramours can count on a guide who makes them feel more sophisticated and desirable while showing them the "grown-up" way to do sex. The girls don't necessarily expect these men to escort them to the movies or take them out for sodas. They do want the expertise that age and experience can bring.

These girls choose older partners because they've talked to their friends who had partners of the same age. The report from the front comes through with bell-like clarity: *It was over before it began; he didn't care about me; it hurts; I'm bleeding* (if the hymen was perforated); *I could be pregnant* (if no form of contraception was used); or *I could have an STD* (if no condom was used). What a sexual debut that is!

Leonore Tiefer, a feminist sexologist, points out that a young girl simply doesn't have the awareness or the technical know-how to appreciate the gift of her own sexuality, and if she misuses it in adolescence, she may turn against it for good and all.[12] In order to "keep" her boyfriend, she may agree to put out over and over, or as long as the relationship seems to have legs. Once she tires of him, or her protests make him tire of her, she once again has the chance to seal up that hymen for a while, at least mentally, and shield herself

from the potency of sexual experience. Unless, of course, her last boyfriend
has left her pregnant, or with a disease.

A Visit to the Doctor

Three million teens a year—one in four—come down with an STD.[13] And
the burden of sexually transmitted diseases rests on young women. Because
their sexual apparatus is interior rather than exterior, the infections they
acquire take hold more easily, burrowing into the mucous membranes of the
vagina and uterus. Some studies show that up to 15 percent of sexually active
teen women are living with human papillomavirus (HPV), many with a particularly vicious strain that's linked to cervical cancer. Their rates of chlamydia,
which is often asymptomatic, are shockingly high (in New York City alone
nearly a third of sexually active teenage girls are infected with it), and their
rates of gonorrhea are way above those of sexually active men and women
between 20 and 44. HIV rates are more difficult to calculate, since the disease
may have no initial symptoms, but women account for 20 percent of new
cases each year.[14]

So sex, particularly unprotected sex, could land a girl in the doctor's
office. From a medical perspective, this is a good thing, since women tend to
have regular checkups with their gynecologist throughout their lifespan if
they start young. Men, who rarely go to the doctor anyway, will see a urologist only under duress, when craterlike sores form on their penis or they're
afraid the Little Guy may be too sick to get up to bat. But they do not go back
on a regular basis for wellness reproductive care as women do.

From a pleasure perspective, of course, this is all wrong. Not only do
STDs make you feel miserable, like sex is the last thing in the world you'd like
to attempt again, but you have to go lie on a paper sheet on a hard table and
spread your legs for a white-coated adult. If you don't get pelvic inflammatory disease (PID) treated, it could cause infertility; if you don't do something
about the chlamydia, it could scar your tubes for life; if you don't get an HIV
test, you could die. So you lie back and submit to the exam. As if your parents weren't all the authority figures you needed.

The situation becomes even more difficult, however, because getting
appropriate medical care is problematic for teenage girls. There are fewer than
1,000 specialists in adolescent healthcare in the United States, which means
that there is no place to go where you really feel you belong. The exception
is Planned Parenthood, which offers not only good clinical care but also psychological and emotional support and guided groups for teens. But making an
appointment at one of these facilities requires more initiative than most girls
are capable of, and so they wind up at the office of the internist, the pediatrician, or their mother's ob/gyn. These practitioners may have little patience
for the anxiety or hesitant questions of a teen who needs time and reassurance

when undergoing what is at best an embarrassing and uncomfortable experience. Given the parameters of managed care, these physicians have only about fifteen minutes to let a girl know that her breasts and genitals look normal or that the STD she has just acquired is not the end of the world and can be successfully treated.

In addition to the exam, of course, there are the questions—the most intimate and awkward areas of a girl's life must be probed in minute detail: Do you smoke, drink, take drugs? When was your last period? What types of sexual practices do you indulge in? How many partners have you had? Are they male or female or both? Do you use condoms regularly? Have you ever shared a needle? Have you ever taken money to perform a sexual act? *Yikes!* The doctor or nurse practitioner, who may have his or her own teen at home, may be queasy about asking; the girl may be stony-faced and defensive when answering.

One high school senior described lying back on the table, her feet in the stirrups, and being faced with a picture on the ceiling of a half-naked woman (also in stirrups). A cartoon bubble emanating from her lips read, "Relax! Breathe! Calm down!" How could she? All she wanted to do was get off that table and out of that office as quickly as possible.

In retrospect, it's not so bad. You'll get an antibiotic; you won't see that rotten guy again. Everything will be all right. For now. Next time you'll use the rubber, and now of course you have the Pill or an IUD to keep you safe, at least from pregnancy. And yet you feel that in setting off the medical alarm button, you have in some way failed at sex. The romance is gone because now you know the consequences of being unprepared or overly spontaneous or just so casual and cool.

Of course, we are assuming here that the sexual experience that got you into this bind was welcome. All too commonly for adolescence girls, it is not. Imagine how much more terrible an exam like this would seem after you'd been raped.

Violence and Violation

It may happen on a dark street or in a parking lot, when someone comes up behind you brandishing a knife and tells you to pull your panties down. It may happen with the boy you've been hanging with for six months, who just happens to have had a little too much to drink and can't understand the word "no" anymore. It might be an older relative, an uncle, cousin, or stepfather, who gets more familiar than a family member should. It could be at a party, with a bunch of friends who decide to take their clothes off and go a little crazy. Rape is rape—we all know that. For a teenage girl, it is an event that can scar her sense of herself and her sexuality for years, even for life.

One in two rape victims is under the age of 18. Teens 16 to 19 are three and a half times more likely than the general population to be sexually assaulted.[15] Stranger rape is unthinkable and terrifying, but so is the more common experience of date or acquaintance rape, where reality slowly shifts and becomes a nauseating nightmare. The person who seemed so understanding and funny just a few minutes ago is suddenly out of control, humiliating and berating you for being "frigid" or "a cocktease." Grown women who've been sexually active for decades rarely know how to handle this, so how is an unexperienced girl for whom sex exists only as a romantic fantasy supposed to deal with it?

Strangely enough, although it's assumed that the woman is always going to be the victim, this is no longer always the case when we're talking about sexual violence in the very young. A recent report states that middle-school girls are often physically abusive to their new boyfriends and to boys whom they'd like to consider their boyfriends—that they will hound a young man until he gives in, and often may punch or kick him in an attempt to solidify a shaky bond. But this is a very small piece of the puzzle. Girls are much more likely to receive violence than give it, in great part because first sexual experiences often happen with older (and physically larger) boys or men. One quarter of all teens report that their first intercourse was not voluntary. Coercion, of course, comes in many colors, and sometimes it's hard to determine what exactly constitutes force. Still, at least a third of women students in one college study reported that it was impossible to stop their partner once he was overcome by sexual frenzy. Talking helps only if you say the right thing, screaming is useful only if there's someone around to hear you, running is impossible when you're pinned down, and most women simply aren't physically strong enough to fight off a determined man. Interestingly enough, acting passive and not resisting at all in a high-risk situation tends to *increase* the risk of rape, because the rapist sees the woman as weak, easy prey.

Rape is mostly about control, psychological manipulation, and humiliation. In this punishment scenario, the penis is wielded as a weapon, rammed into a vagina, mouth, or rectum. A girl's breasts may be pinched or bitten; she may be raped by an object (a soda bottle or broom handle) in addition to or instead of the male organ. The survivors of such a trauma tend to be numb, and unable to acknowledge that it took place, and/or consumed with guilt about what they did to incur this violence (*What did I say to set him off? Why couldn't I stop him?*) By the time they decide to come forward and name names, it's often too late, because the semen must be inside them and the bruises fresh for photographing to make a charge stick. Women who've survived rape often view all sexual encounters afterward as something they could have prevented.

Having to undergo a rape exam at a hospital is the ultimate in invasion. The girl is ushered into a sterile room and asked to put her clothes in a bag (so that they can be checked for physical evidence that will nail the perpetrator). The attending physician, usually a young man or woman with little prac-

tice in this touchy realm, enters with a rape kit and does a traditional biman-
ual exam, which may be extremely painful if the girl has been brutalized by
her attacker. This is followed by a combing of her pubic hair for possible hairs,
a scraping of her fingernails for morsels of his skin.

And one final misery. What do the girl's parents say? How does she face
their brave smiles and stifled tears? How do they treat her from here on, now
that they know beyond a doubt that she's had sex?

Well, it could be worse. There's only one other thing that would irrevo-
cably change her relationship with her parents forever. She could be pregnant.

Getting Pregnant: Abortion or Motherhood

Little girls grow up playing with dolls. They learn to cuddle and care for
them, bathe and diaper them, they scold them when they're bad and praise
them when they behave. Teenagers, fresh from playtime and often still in pos-
session of those nostalgic Raggedy Anns, not only tend to romanticize motherhood, they also often see it as a way out of childhood. People will take them
seriously; their families will have to acknowledge that they're involved in an
adult activity and should be treated accordingly.

A variety of schools see the siren song of motherhood as something to be
concerned about. Just as a condom might prevent an unwanted disease, so the
creation of "Baby Think It Over" is intended to stop pregnancy in its tracks.
This high-tech doll has a microchip that allows it to cry at intervals, from fifteen minutes to a mind-numbing four hours. Schools are pleased to offer this
24-hour responsibility to girls and guys as they reach the age where sexual
activity is not just possible but probable. Does the baby work? The statistics
say it's hard to convince girls after just three days and two nights with the sob-
bing robot, especially if they are certain that they can mother much better
than their own mothers. Most of them harbor the unrealistic belief that their
own child won't be nearly as difficult as this plastic annoyance. We know that
pregnancy rates are dropping in the U.S., but we are still way ahead (meaning way *behind*) of most developed countries in our teen pregnancies. Ours is
52 per 1,000 teens, while in the Netherlands the figure is 4 per 1,000, in
France it's 9 per 1,000, and in Germany it's 14 per 1,000, according to a
Reuters Health report in December 1999.

Of course, for upper-middle-class girls these days, the Pill is something to
take: first, to alleviate acne, and then, well, because you never know when it
might come in handy. If you forget to take it for a couple of days, or if you
find yourself condomless one Saturday night, what do you do? If you miss a
period, you might get jittery, but it could have been that you were working
out extra hard on the team, or too stressed or not eating enough. Maybe, if
you cross your fingers, the problem will vanish.[16]

Waiting, to be sure, is not the way to go. The longer you wait, the fewer options you have. If you act really fast, you can use Preven, the 3-day-after Pill. The advent of this potent contraceptive changed the face of abortion—it's not invasive, it's relatively inexpensive (a package costs $20, the same as a cycle of birth-control pills), and many users claim it doesn't make them feel like they're committing "murder."[17] This medication is not without major hassles, how-ever. Local drugstores often don't stock it in areas of the country where God sits at the right hand of the pharmacist. This means you'd have to special-order it, and that could take more than the allotted time. You can call the toll-free number (1–888–NOT–2–LATE) but even assuming you could find a store within fifty miles that carried it, how would you get there? No car and you're sunk. Or you'd have to ask your parents and risk alienating them forever. This is never more true than if you live in a state where Mom and Dad must have a say in your decision.[18] Most families, unless they have a moral or religious objection, clamor for abortion when their teenager reveals the awful truth. And an interesting corollary to this difficult situation is that the exposure of a teen pregnancy often brings families together. Moms become more attentive, dads get protective, and siblings get excited about the Big Secret, whatever it is. The spotlight is on the expectant mother, and what could please an adoles-cent girl more than all that attention, be it positive or negative? The fantasy of being at the center of your own universe is suddenly realized.

In upper- and middle-class families, girls are often hustled off to the doc-tor for a therapeutic abortion. In the ghetto, girls are often threatened with expulsion from the home if they don't abort, and for financial reasons, they may go to the clinic and have the deed done. You go in, you sign some papers, someone gives you a shot to make you sleepy, then the tissue is either scraped or suctioned out of you, and in a few hours, it's all over.

For the past twelve years, battles have waged at the FDA over the approval of mifepristone (RU-486), the "do-it-yourself" abortion drug. Finally, in September 2000, right before the national elections, the FDA con-veyed their blessing on the drug, and within a week, physicians were able to order the drug from Danco, the American company that is manufacturing it in this country.

Of course, doctors had already been prescribing abortifacients for patients who were leery about surgery. They used the drugs misoprostol (already FDA-approved for ulcer therapy) and methotrexate (FDA-approved for can-cer treatment) and knew the drill they would be required to go through once they had access to RU-486. Yes, it's true that almost anything is preferable to the invasive and sometimes barbarous surgical procedures that have plagued womankind for centuries. When a young woman can decide to end a preg-nancy at three weeks, as soon as she misses a period, by ingesting some pills, the political and personal choices become easier.

Or do they? The course of this new type of abortion is a tough one, and the maxim "Safe, Legal, and Rare," posited by the Clinton administration, may be supplanted by "Safe, Legal, and Just as Much of a Hassle." Doctors have little enough time as it is to spend with patients, and the RU-486 route requires three visits plus a possibly mandatory ultrasound to confirm the timing of the pregnancy (you can only use this drug up to eight weeks after your last menstrual period). In some states, physicians must report every abortion, leaving them open to protests just as potentially violent as had they been performing surgical abortions. Some local laws require that the design of offices must comply with some strange, arbitrary type of architecture, mandating that a physician's hallway be wide enough to wheel a gurney through, and in some states, fetal remains must be examined by a doctor. In North Dakota, the remains must be cremated or incinerated—and what woman is going to drive back to the doctor's office with the expelled fetal tissue just to make sure her doctor doesn't get in trouble?

How does the process actually work? The woman desiring an abortion first takes mifepristone in her doctor's office (the drugs are not available in pharmacies) to block the action of progesterone, which maintains a pregnancy. Then, thirty-six to forty-eight hours later, at home, she takes misoprostol, which makes the uterus contract, expelling the fetal tissue. So there she is, nervous and expectant, hopefully not all alone, but with no professional standing by, when she begins to experience pain, cramps, nausea, headache, diarrhea, or vomiting. Afterward, there's that vision of the bloody tissue that might have been a child in the toilet. No wonder that in France, where RU-486 has been legal for over a decade, two-thirds of women seeking abortion opt for suction.

There is, too, increasing likelihood of unregulated use of these pills—if you can get cut-rate Viagra and Ecstasy on the Internet, why not mifepristone? Without recourse to any medical assistance, with women possibly using the medication in the second or third trimester, there could be disasters that match those backroom butcher jobs of the early days of this century.

But then again, many women wouldn't ever consider abortion, no matter how it was done. Every young girl has seen the pictures of new life starting inside—in family-life ed classes, in antiabortion literature and ads—and even if she doesn't believe she'd be "killing" her baby, she can't quite get over the fact that her body has done something totally amazing. If she's from a lower-class background and isn't doing so great in school anyway, and her home life is difficult and money is tight, she may see pregnancy and childbirth as a way out of her lousy existence. She has a higher mission—raising a child to do better than she did. After the birth, she can continue her own activities, have her mother or aunt sit during the day, and begin her real "adult" life. Unfortunately, it seldom works out that way—how can she possibly give her child all the advantages when she has no model for it and she herself is so chronically disadvantaged, lacking much money, an education, a healthy sense of her worth, and most often, a partner?

Many lower-class teens want to have babies, actually *plan* to have babies. They get lots of benefits, after all—a family who rallies around them to prepare for the joyous event, a temporary promise from their boyfriend to stick around (this promise often dissolves as soon as the baby is born), and ironically, sex without any concern for pregnancy, although STDs are still an issue if the boyfriend is ambivalent and maybe has another girl on the side.

Sexual pleasure never enters into it—after the birth, many girls say they couldn't care less about hopping in the sack. True, they're tired from staying up with a crying baby, and sore from tissue tearing or an episiotomy. But even after they've healed, these girls are generally turned off to sex because of their hormones. During pregnancy, a dramatic increase in estrogen and progesterone is necessary to house and nourish new life within, and as delivery gets closer, the new chemical messengers enter the scene—vasopressin and oxytocin. These are essential to produce milk but in addition, they create a feeling of bonding and connection with the baby. After childbirth, a mother becomes biologically wedded to the baby and a whole lot less enthralled with that man who was probably a pain even before the pregnancy. Some choose to have sex just for kicks, to keep their hand in, so to speak, but it's often with a new boyfriend, someone they won't get attached to.

And others say they've had it with sex. It just wasn't that good to begin with.

Celibacy: The Big Graduation Present

Judith is sitting in a conference room upstairs at the Planned Parenthood offices in Plainfield, NJ, with seven African-American teens, ranging in age from 15 to 20. The table is laden with a picnic spread—fried chicken and rice, Chinese takeout, cheese curls, Chex mix, pineapple chunks, and Nehi grape soda. The kids dig in like they haven't eaten in a week, all except for Anastasia, who has given birth five days earlier. She hands her baby daughter around proudly, and other girls take turns holding her.

They talk about sex haltingly. One of the girls is silent throughout the discussion; one speaks so softly, it's hard to hear her. Janine, the most vocal in the group, explains to Judith about how girls are classified in the sexual ranking system.

"You're a chicken if all you do is give boys head," she says, making her neck go forward and back like a pullet pecking for seed. "Get it? And you're a sl'ore (slut-whore) if you'll do anything with lots of guys and try to cover it up."

"What about a couple who really care about each other? Is sex okay then?" Judith wants to know.

"If guys give you oral sex, that's okay, because the vagina—that's inside the body—it keeps cleaning itself, day and night. But the penis, that's dirty, it's on the outside, so if you suck it, that's disgusting."

It is curious to hear her make this distinction, since it's the opposite of what so many women feel—that their genitals smell or look ugly.

The other girls point out that if she's so down on putting something in her mouth that might be unclean, then having a penis inside her vagina would be bad, too.

"Yeah, it is! I don't do that no more."

Toinette chimes in. "I didn't do it for a year and a half."

"How was that?" Judith wants to know. "Did you feel horny a lot? Were you really eager when you went back to it?"

"I was looking forward to it, but when it happened, it wasn't so good. It was worse than it had been before. I guess I'd been expecting it to be so nice, but it wasn't."

Susan nods in agreement. "When you plan how it gonna be, it seems different than in real life."

"Did you plan for the first time?" Judith asks her.

"Yeah, I did, because I had this guy I wanted to do it with, and he looked so fine, and he was great. So I got condoms and there was this private place we could go . . . but then it turned out the first time I did it, it was with someone else. And I didn't plan for that; it just happened."

These teens are so down on sex, it's hard to figure what might ever persuade them to try it again. They are anxious about the risk of STDs, of emotional pain, abortion, and pregnancy. Anastasia had an abortion the first time she got pregnant, because her mother threatened to throw her out of the house if she didn't, but the second time, she said she was keeping this child, and no one could tell her not to. Was she more or less interested in sex now that she had a baby? She raised her eyes to the ceiling. "I won't be having sex with that guy any time soon—what he's said and done in the last week!"

Did they enjoy sex when they were in the throes of it? Well, yes and no. It was exciting, something that compelled them when they were in the mood. It was easy getting into the situation, when a guy begged them or said they were pretty, or they really had a fire "down there"—but it was over with quickly, and they didn't ever get what they wanted—whatever that was—out of the experience.

Did they have orgasms? Anastasia rolled her eyes to the ceiling. "Let me think about that a minute," she said, taking her baby from Susan to nurse. There was a long pause. "Maybe. Once. From oral sex." They went around the room—Susan had had two orgasms. Janine shook her head. Toinette said no, she didn't think so because she didn't know what they were.

"Oh, like a volcano building up," said the next girl.

"It's all tingly. Sometimes, quiet, like gentle waves," offered Susan.

Judith reminds them that it's not a sure thing; it often takes practice to make an orgasm happen. So if they had had this experience and enjoyed it, but were down on all the risks that sex entailed, why wouldn't they masturbate?

The girls just stare, silently. Finally, someone says, "A woman would never say if she did something gross like that. She'd have to be so desperate if she couldn't get a man to do that for her." Once again, the topic goes around the table. Not only was there a general negative on masturbation, the girls also conceded that they would not touch themselves in order to insert a tampon. White girls did that, but they were freaky—"they be off the hook." (This attitude is not as prevalent in middle-class African-American girls, but extremely strong in the street culture of urban blacks.)

Sex, for these kids, was problematic. You had to try it, because everyone you knew did it, and you got a lot of pressure from friends (even those who were not sexually active) to go with whatever boy looked good and was supposed to "do things" well. But after you tried it, there were all these headaches. You could get a reputation as a "hood rat" (a little scurrying rodent, running around the 'hood doing it with everyone) and who wanted that?

Maybe this is a good thing, because we don't want our children to take so much responsibility when they aren't ready for it. Although the girls oohed and aahed over Anastasia's baby, there was a wariness—this could happen to me and what would that do to my life? And a lot of the black brothers they knew were picking white girls to go out with, because they were easier to control and didn't talk back as much as their black sisters. So they were going to sit back and wait and see.

"Would any of you miss sex if you succeeded in staying away from it?" There was a moment's pause. Not one of them was jumping out of her seat.

Toinette smoothed her hair and speared a chunk of pineapple. "Nothing replaces it," she said, and nodded sagely. "Someday I'll find somebody else."

They all still believe, despite their rocky introductions to the relationship game, and their awareness that they've given all and received nothing, that someday, it will be different. For these hardened, street-wise but sexually naïve young women, hope is the thing they cling to. And how can we dare to persuade them otherwise? No matter how old and savvy we get, we yearn for the same thing ourselves.

2

THE YOUNG SINGLE WOMAN:
SEARCHING FOR LOVE

Once you've passed the hurdle of the self-conscious agonies of adolescence and the shame and guilt that you should or shouldn't be sexual, it usually gets a little easier. This is not to say sex is a cinch—it's the rare woman who feels that way!—but by the start of the third decade of life, most women are ready to accept the challenge and delight of being sexual. Women in their twenties are still wrestling with their sexual identity and trying to make sense of it, but most are eager to pursue desire much as they do their college degree or a good job.

They are no longer content to wait for an invitation to the dance. It's tempting (as long as you've got a condom handy and you can persuade your partner to use it) to go ahead and enjoy the whole smorgasbord of sexual play without much thought to marriage or family. Many singles are content to fool around (with affection) and keep the notion of "the relationship" in the background. Once the chore of losing one's virginity is accomplished, many women find that they can give themselves permission to experiment with sexuality and really enjoy it.

There is probably nothing akin to the rush of delight that zings through the body when a partner touches your genitals for the first time. "I always loved masturbating and coming," one 22-year-old told. "I've been doing it since I was 11. But when this guy went down on me, I thought my head would blow off. My initial reaction was, Wow, I read about this but I couldn't believe anyone would actually do it to me. My whole body tensed up—but just for a second—worrying about whether I smelled or tasted okay down there. Then his tongue started working and I totally forgot my self-consciousness. I couldn't believe the difference in sensation from my fingers to his mouth. Even better than his fingers inside me. It was so soft, so warm— I thought the orgasm would never end." At last there is a witness to the total lack of control and complete sense of joy that we feel when we celebrate the spirit and the body in that unique event called orgasm.

Just like guys, many single women search out excitement, variety, and stimulation. At this time of life, they may try oral or anal sex for the first time, use a vibrator or watch a porn flick, or get tied up with scarves. Trust is evidently the most important element in choosing someone to have fun with—women are concerned about the number and *quality* of the partners they choose to experiment with. Too few and they might feel hopeless or unwanted; too many and they could be slapped with the label "slut," which is exceptionally hard to live down.

Young women want physical pleasure, but they want a lot more, too, because a woman's sexual identity is bound up in her own need to protect what's hers. A romp in bed is great, but in order for it to feel fulfilling to many women, it has to be part of the all-encompassing emotional and spiritual umbrella that includes a sense of femininity, her self-confidence, love, romance, companionship, and other elements that tend to be difficult to achieve. It is still a conundrum—can a woman separate love and sex? Yes, kind of, for a while. As long as there appears to be some way for her to delve into her sexuality with as much intention and purpose as she gives to the rest of her life.

Trying to Write New Rules

For the last half-century, women have been leaving home to get an education, to make a living, and to meet a life mate. This foray out into the world gives us a certain amount of freedom of will, desire, and choice. We can select a variety of paths—go to work full-time or part-time, go to school, date casually and have sex with the ones who seem suitable, or cohabit with a partner (male or female). For most, the looming prospect of a reproductive life where sex becomes a conduit to a child and a family is still a distant goal. Most women don't want to bed every attractive man they run into—as a matter of fact, they are increasingly cautious of sex when they suspect that their partner has no emotional involvement in the event.[1]

Young single women may have sex for any number of reasons, positive and negative: *I wanted to have fun; we were fooling around and it just happened; I wanted him to like me; I wanted a better grade from my professor; I loved him and he loved me back; I was drunk and lonely; I was horny; I was looking for a good time when I didn't have to think about anything.* As much as women may love sex, they often have trouble with the aftermath. Even a fling, a casual one-night stand, an easy falling into bed with an old friend takes on significance far beyond the physical act. Because every time a woman chooses to express her passions, she encounters all that extra stuff that goes along with sex—her need for kindness, thoughtfulness, and intimacy. She wants some sort of investment—of a partner's time, interest, or affection. Even if her initial intention is just a delirious roll in the hay, it's the rare woman who can look at fooling around as simply a physical expression of freedom and desire.

Still, how do you know what you want if you only look at the first one who comes along? Dating is increasingly becoming an outdated concept—women and men (or women and women) just don't do that anymore. You either hang out with someone until you end up going with them, and therefore, sleeping with them exclusively; or you "hook up" with several partners for mutually agreed upon casual sex. However you meet and greet, the process becomes a complex phenomenon with many goals, one of which is finding someone with whom you are sexually compatible. This requires at least a little shopping around before making a final purchase.

Sex for singles these days is easy, because there are so many places and opportunities to meet people, and it's also complicated, because nobody knows what the rules are once you do meet. Romances begin in singles bars or coffee bars, in the laundromat, at the mall, in class, at the library, at work, on teams, through the Personals, or on the Internet. These meetings are usually fraught with ambivalence as you both juggle the niceties of social intercourse. Your eyes meet, you feel attracted, you speak of common interests, you decide (in a moment) whether to exchange phone numbers or email addresses, and you plunge into what may or may not become a Relationship.

But on the other hand, sex for singles has pitfalls. In opening the door to desire and arousal, women usher in a host of difficult choices. And here's the funny thing: Decades after feminism, most women don't like to call the shots in bed. They still admit to wanting a man to sweep them off their feet, and even as they claim responsibility for their own orgasms, they want a guy to make them feel delicious and desirable.

"I want to be seduced" is the comment Sandra hears over and over again from the young women who come to her for therapy. "I want to be bowled over—not brutalized. I like somebody who says 'I'll call you,' after we've had a first date, and then he does and admits he's been thinking about me or he missed me. I'm on his mind. It's not that I don't make my feelings known to him—I certainly do—but it doesn't feel right if I have to do all the initiating and all the work. It's not exciting if the guy doesn't pursue me a little." Women are looking for a man who can script a sexual scenario. Then, when the two of them start the rewriting process together, it can become a true collaboration.

What a burden this places on guys! Every college has come out with a list of precautions for couples who are hanging out together. Permission must be given for each and every step across the minefield of sex play.

"May I kiss you?"

"Yes, you may."

"May I take off your bra and play with your breasts?"

"Yes, you may."

"May I insert my penis inside your vagina?"

"Oh, well, I don't know about that."

How can anyone have a fabulous time when they are always keeping score, playing sex like a game of chess where the pieces can block or even destroy each other's equilibrium? Women are desperate to experience pleasure in some way, but at this age, most seem confused as to where to look for it, how to approach it, and how to do the necessary negotiation in order to achieve it.

A scan of the past few years' *Cosmopolitan* and *Glamour* magazine articles gives a clear idea of the things that preoccupy women at this stage of their life. *What should you do after a one-night stand?* Don't be ashamed—be self-confident afterward, the magazines advise. Don't hang around waiting for him to call, but don't beat yourself up if he doesn't and you think it's not going to go any farther. *How can you get closer to a man?* Tell him personal, private things, including not just what you like in bed, but also secrets you recall from your childhood. *Should you tell a guy you love him?* Before you do, ask yourself the following questions: Does he treat me with respect? Does he call me when he says he will? Does he want to see me regularly? Is he kind and compassionate? *Should you always wait for a guy to make the first move?* No, you can initiate—call him up and ask him out. Don't be submissive and helpless. The message here, clearly, is don't let a man call all the shots.

The magazines allow us to measure ourselves and our behavior against other individuals who are, in demographic terms, just like us. So when *Cosmo* says that on average, most women have ten partners before they settle down with one (some count only those with whom they've had an orgasm), the reader can feel confident that she's not "easy" if she's had nine or even eleven.

Stop Before It's Too Late

Intercourse is the Maginot line of sex. A 30-year-old "technical virgin" echoed the adamant feelings of many young women—"I think sex is terrific—I've done everything in bed except that. I grew up believing my mother, that intercourse was just for marriage. And even if it seems a little weak as a dowry, that's what I want to bring. Guys just don't seem to get it. Why I would do oral and anal sex and play with toys and blindfolds and all kinds of stuff, but never let him put his penis inside. It's not my hymen—that's probably gone from tampons and vibrators—but it's the principle of the thing. There has to be something I don't give away."

Fear of STDs is a big deterrent to intercourse, but the real concern of young women is retaining a sense of balance among romance, lust, and practicality. They learn to strike a bargain every time they strike a pose, hoping to avoid getting hurt emotionally, physically, or mentally. As adolescents, women were taught that they had a right to say no—sex-ed classes emphasized respect for one another's bodies and private space. So teens figured out how to barter their sexuality for popularity. This isn't true for mature 20-somethings who bargain for a lot more—their independence. They award points to the guy who always wears a condom, more points for flowers on a birthday. A woman who always pays for her meal on a date tells me, "That way, I'm in charge. If I want to seduce him, I can. If I want to say no to sex, that's my prerogative."

In 1995, a little book called *The Rules* became a controversial sensation. It reversed the *Cosmo/Glamour* formula for being honest and straight-forward—in a sense telling a woman that it was a mistake to uncover the deepest recesses of her personality in a search for love. She was to pay atten-tion to only one thing: *What's in it for me besides sex, since that's not all I'm after? When do I get the ring?* The woman who dates right always insists on a call by Tuesday for a Saturday night date. No excuses. Each woman is advised never to call a man except to return his call, to look wonderful, to act as though she is on top of her life and doesn't need a man *ever,* and not to take casual flirt-ing seriously. She is to ignore all but the most formal methods of pursuit—it's a grave error to accept a spur-of-the-moment invitation for lunch or coffee, because that would mean she didn't care enough to demand the very best. If she's nuts about the guy, she should keep that under wraps.

Play hard to get and you will get what you want. The attitude, expressed not only in *The Rules* but in several other books of the same ilk, is that you should devote as much time to finding a mate as you do to learning to play the piano. Practice every day and even though you may not get to Carnegie Hall, at least you'll get more familiar with the difference between good practice and bad.

The Rules dicta on sex are similarly strict. Physical expression of connect-edness has nothing to do with desire or personal fulfillment. Instead, it's just another way to keep your man. If you make time for sex in your relationship (once you've nabbed him securely, that is), he'll be less grouchy, he'll think about you when he's not with you, and it will ultimately strengthen your bond.

So cold! So mercenary! The message is play hard, play fast, and play like a man, using strategy and cunning. How could this attitude contribute to what we assume the woman wants all along—a loving, committed relationship that will take her from her twenties to her nineties? The authors of this book take a very Scarlett O'Hara view of life—that women are smarter than men and can therefore con them by twisting them around their little finger. Also, that the goal is more important than the game. And finally, that the only way we are ever going to feel a sense of self-worth is to stay out of the emotional fray. *The Rules* imply that our own sexual gratification isn't a worthwhile priority.

People who need rules like these don't trust their intuition that what they believe or see is valid. Women tend to worry about not one but two jobs in a burgeoning relationship—first, they feel they must monitor their own response sexually (the ultimate *Cosmo* question is whether you do it the first, second, or third time you go out with someone), and second, they must maintain a precise temperature for the relationship itself. It should be warm, but not too warm.

Be Modest. Be Abstinent. Be Holy.

On the heels of *The Rules* came another set of regulations, one that harked back to an earlier generation. Don't have sex at all. Save it for marriage. Recently, several authors, most notably Wendy Shalit in her polemic *A Return to Modesty,* have denied the rewards of the sexual revolution and instead would have us believe that female power lies in sexual restraint. The theory here is that the woes that beset the modern woman—sexual harassment, stalking, rape—are all responses of a society that has lost its respect for female modesty. In training themselves to seek sexual gratification instead of true love, women have been false to their own natures. They can increase self-esteem by deciding that they are worth waiting for. If they could only refrain from touching, they could recapture their vulnerability and romantic hopes.

As if you could erase your sexuality by wishing it away! This is not to say that there is anything pathological about periods of celibacy—if there's no partner that attracts you, or if you need a period of time alone after coming out of a relationship, or you prefer to hold on to your virginity until marriage, not having sex makes sense.

But for most young women today, it's difficult to stay celibate and have a social life unless you belong to a community, perhaps a religious youth group, where everyone—males as well as females—are on the same wavelength. If you go without sex or masturbation for a significant period of time, fantasizing generally drops away and the sexual life force goes dormant. Women who made it through high school without being part of a couple (even for a few weeks at a time, which is common these days) or who are under the wing of a church youth group have little trouble adjusting to their sex-free status in college or on the job. They couldn't care less about flirting; they aren't turned on by adorable gestures of the guy in the next dorm. Many women who have not yet come out as lesbians also choose to be celibate, because they are still confused about their desires for sexual expression, and same-gender contact may be completely at odds with what their faith teaches. So it's easier to stay away from it entirely. Abstinence is also a logical option if you are shy, socially awkward, or a workaholic.

But somehow we think that the "modesty" approach may be just another ploy, similar to *The Rules*. In not having sex, not thinking about sex, using all your time for work or study or "wholesome" activities like choir practice or chess games, women can announce to the world that they are serious. They have values, morals, and a sense that love *must* precede sex. The questions are: Can't a sexual being be taken seriously? Can love be cultivated in such a vacuum, without any form of physical contact? (Masturbation, by the way, is also a no-no, since it is prohibited in the Bible. No mention is made of what it might offer a twenty-first-century woman in terms of self-esteem and fulfillment.) Most women don't buy the notion of sex without love, so why would they consider love without sex? The fantasy of what it'll be like after the wedding may get in the way of the real-life development of a relationship.

There is another reason to remain celibate, and that is that abstinence before marriage is the socially sanctioned way to behave, as it is for millions of Muslim and East Indian women whose families keep the old ways even though they may have lived in America for several generations.

Traditional Muslim women spend their public life under wraps. The clothing that covers them literally from head to foot is a reminder that sexuality is a visual time bomb—any man who sees their flesh will be inflamed, and their own reticence won't protect them. According to Dr. Aliyah Morgan-Sabah, coordinator for Community Medicine at Brooklyn Hospital in New York in the Department of Family Practice, the religious life is paramount for a Muslim woman. There is no intermingling of the sexes, even with chaperones, and although some practitioners of the faith go to regular colleges, it is far easier to be educated and to work with your own kind. "When women and men are together, the Devil is the third party," reads a line from the Koran.

It's freely acknowledged that women in this culture have wants and needs—under their long shapeless dresses they may wear lacy T-shirts or Victoria's Secret underwear; they may hope and dream like any American girl of finding the Right Guy. But he has to be Muslim, and he has to be observant. A girl who takes off her head scarf outside the mosque after Friday prayers is asking for trouble, not only from Muslim men but from non-believers on the street.

It's acknowledged that women might just have desire before they're married (although most families arrange early marriages—some as young as 14—in order to legitimize temptation). If you feel horny, the prescription is fasting and prayer; above all, avoid stimulants like cigarettes, alcohol, even spicy foods. Cold showers are essential, along with more prayer. If you can't make it, masturbation is a possible solution, although it is frowned on and the faith counsels you to take a shower afterward. Anything is better than *fornication,* which is defined as "sexual intercourse between two unmarried people."

But the restrictions are mutual—neither women nor men have license to fool around. That is not true in the East Indian culture, particularly for women whose families come from Northern India, where more conservative cultural attitudes prevail than in the south. Dr. Sujata Warrier, director of the New York City program of the state Office for Prevention of Domestic Violence, says that young women in the Indian community are focused on marriage. Despite a good job or a college background, a young woman hopes for a union that will build social, political, and economic ties between families. The passion of male and female conjoining doesn't count for much—love and sex are sacrificed to the greater good. Even in America, Indian marriages are usually arranged, to be certain that one caste doesn't intermingle with another.

People do sometimes choose their own spouses, but they tend to feel more comfortable with partners from the same economic caste and stratum.

An Indian girl learns very early in life that when she marries, her body belongs to her husband and she is to submit completely to him—this doesn't make for a lot of enthusiasm about what life will be like after marriage. Many young women are fortunate to have both a love match and a financial one, and others fall in love slowly over the years they spend with their husband. There are, certainly, young Indian women who experiment before choosing a life partner or having one chosen for them, but it is not talked about or encouraged, except in the world of Bombay films imported into the U.S. in record numbers to feed the fantasies of young girls. The torrid love scenes portrayed in these films are a brief respite from reality. But a girl can still dream—so she does. Girls who never hear from their mothers or aunts what sex will be like watch the screen and wonder whether it could be better in America. It usually isn't. But it's hard to get rid of those idealized images.

Fantasizing About Life and Sex

So what do we make of these contrary sets of guidelines for young women? That the anticipation and the reality of sex are at war with each other. Because whether a woman offers fake or real messages to a man, she may still not get what she wants. At this time of her life, a woman is not necessarily hoping for a ring, but rather for keeping her sense of self-esteem and capacity for different types of intimacy intact. She may meet one man who loves hiking and the great outdoors and another who enjoys snuggling in front of the TV with a bowl of popcorn. She may have a ho-hum, no-fireworks relationship with a man she sleeps with occasionally after they have dinner or see a movie, but be totally overwhelmed with her fantastic sexual response to a guy she met in a bar and doesn't intend to see again. Having serial partners is one way to reaffirm that life has great variety—a big sea of messy emotion and possibility.

But it's hard for many women to make sense of these contradictory feelings so that they can develop good sexual self-esteem. It's virtually impossible to take those baby steps toward the bedroom with a new man—or even a familiar, comfortable man—without going over the legacy of self-hatred that many girls grew up with. Hark back to those early days when they were cautioned for touching themselves, dressing provocatively, or sitting with their legs apart and you will begin to understand why very few women can look in the mirror without an extremely critical eye. *Am I okay?* (That's the first, most basic question, which of course extends beyond the realm of sexuality.)

But then there are those specific questions that women torture themselves with: *Why does my body look like this? Do I like it or hate it? Why don't I have bigger breasts and smaller hips? Why does my nose get really broad when I smile and are my teeth crooked, so maybe I shouldn't smile, but then how will he ever know I really like him?*

In a study by Luis Garcia, Ph.D.,[2] women revealed a big gap between their feelings of attractiveness and how they felt about their sexuality. The men in the study felt okay about the way they looked, and about their likelihood of attracting a woman. Females, on the other hand, had trouble seeing themselves as really desirable. It wasn't just that they needed the "male gaze" approving of them; rather, it was that they didn't approve of themselves and couldn't fathom anyone else doing so either.

It's not enough that we pick ourselves apart all the time. We also have to use that incriminating ideal to twist and distort what we perceive as a man's interest. *He can't really like me, can he, looking the way I do?* that little internal voice whimpers. *Why is he paying so much attention to me? Is it only for sex? It's not really possible that he could like me for me, is it?*

When they stray into this gray area, lost in between the cynicism of youth and the self-knowledge that comes with practical experience, young women can get themselves into trouble. Because the longer they hold out hope that there is something good to be found in a relationship, the less likely they are to pick up on the clues that something is wrong, and unless they fix it, it's not going to get better.

Campus Craziness

It is increasingly important for women today to have a seventh or eighth sense about their own participation in the sexual dance, because the world isn't such a safe place, as many girls just sprung from the shelter of high school and family quickly discern.

Most young women who opt for college don't go to meet a husband as they did decades ago. Rather, they go to find a range of interesting people who will accompany them through the four years they spend in the growing-up process of learning, doing, and feeling. (Of course, for those who cleave to academia like moss to a rock, or wish to become a doctor or lawyer, this is a much longer process!) The boyfriend/girlfriend paradigm happens as much as it used to, and an exclusive sexual relationship tends to develop out of a close friendship. You spend hours on the phone, you go to movies and grab a bite to eat, you hang out, and everyone knows you're a couple. Over the course of several weeks or months, you decide to do something about the physical attraction. On the other hand, if you are simply "hooking up," the reverse occurs. The attraction and flirtation are the *primary* draw—one party (most commonly, the man) will suggest a "hook up," which usually means a casual sexual contact. Everyone's eyes are open; the cards are on the table. Hooking up doesn't have to be sexual—it can be a platonic relationship built on mutual interests, minus romance or commitment. But nobody gets hurt because everyone's playing by the same rules.

The social world of a college campus may feel like a warm sea with plenty of good fish in it. And yet, there are sharks in those waters. Andrea Parrot, Ph.D., who sets up date- and acquaintance-rape programs at colleges and universities all over the country, says that young women and men simply don't grow up with the tools they need for this precarious time of life. There you are, away from home, no curfews, nothing at all to stop you from doing whatever you want. You can drink, and drugs have never been hard to find. You're 18 years old, your future just one step ahead of you. And sex, well, it's anywhere and everywhere you look, but most often in places where you aren't looking and aren't paying attention.

You've just traveled a thousand miles from your home state to attend college, and an upperclassman meets you as you're moving into your dorm and helps you carry your bags in. He says he'll show you around, tells you which courses are guts and which are killers, looks through the high school yearbook lying on your bed and makes funny comments about a variety of your "dorky" classmates. He seems confident, sexy, and he's interested in you.

You go out with him that night. You're tired from your trip, but eager to get into the swing of things, to meet and greet. You go to a local hangout and have a burger and soda, and as you're leaving, he runs into some of his buddies. He doesn't bother to introduce you—they just exchange a few words—and anyway, you're rushing to a movie. Afterward, he takes you to a local pub and orders a beer for you, although you protest that you're exhausted and just want to go to bed. He insists it will help you sleep, it's just a beer, after all, what are you, a wimp?

You drink alcohol every once in a while, when your family has wine with a meal, but you're not really used to it. You sip it delicately until he starts teasing—making fun of you, actually—for being too "ladylike." You barely finish half your drink by 1 AM, which is way past your bedtime; in the meantime, he's consumed three.

You get in his car, and he starts back toward campus, but then turns off somewhere—you're not familiar with the area, but you know he's not going in the direction of school. When you ask him about it, he says nothing, but keeps driving. You're getting uneasy, and ask him more urgently to take you home. He turns to you with a glazed look on his face and says, "Oh, baby, I'll take you home."

You can piece together the rest of this scenario, can't you? He parks the car, makes a pass, which you fend off. He gets more insistent, you try to talk him out of it. You are saying no, you remind him—that's the universal signal to stop—but he ignores it. You can feel his erection through his pants as he pins you down on the seat and puts his mouth on yours, to stop your noise rather than to kiss you.

And then he rapes you.

Why, after all the sex-ed classes and all the training so that young women will watch out for themselves, does this disaster continue in drastic numbers, both in college and in the workplace? One in four women will be raped in their lifetime, and as we saw in chapter 1, younger women, particularly when they live alone or in an unprotected environment, are ripe for assault. In several studies, students accounted for 25 to 27 percent of all rape victims.

Rape can leave devastating effects—Susan Brownmiller, in her landmark book, *Against Our Will,* quotes the testimony of one woman who was raped at the age of 14 and didn't menstruate again until she was 21. Another reported that after her rape, none of the girls she knew were allowed to have her in their homes, and all the boys stared at her as she walked down the street. Women report, years later, feeling that they must wash obsessively to get "the smell of come" off them or that they live with a fear that dormant HIV or syphilis from the attack will suddenly blossom inside them.[3]

According to Dr. Parrot, there's an insidious pattern that offers clues to the incipient rape. It can be broken, but this must happen early in the relationship, even if that relationship lasts only an hour. Look at the clues the rapist in the example above left in his wake—first, he made fun of photos in your yearbook, belittling an experience that was, at the very least, a nostalgic trip for you. When you ran into his pals, he didn't bother to introduce you. He forced alcohol on you (hoping to loosen you up) when you said you didn't want any, and called you names when you didn't drink it. Everything in this scenario screams "get away from this guy," yet you went along with it. Only at the very end, when he was cloaked in a testosterone haze, did you say no. By then, it was much too late.[4]

Women are socialized to be understanding, not assertive. They typically make things nice when conflict starts. These are the wrong attributes to possess when confronted with a confused, drunk young man who has one thing in mind. Actually, it may not be in his mind at all—his rational, sensible side is asleep while the old brain, the limbic system that sought only domination and pleasure, comes to the fore. He may even have dosed his partner's beer with Rohypnol, better known as "Roofies," a hypnotic sleeping aid that, in liquid form, can easily be slipped into a drink to render the victim incapacitated.

Whenever Dr. Parrot comes to a campus to set up a date-rape program, she asks the administration to provide her with ten students from every conceivable ethnic and social group. She gets some kids from the track team, some from theater, some from the Christian fellowship, some from the gay and lesbian group. She asks them to pretend that they are directing a movie about two kids who start seeing each other—the movie is to take them from their first meeting to right after their first sexual encounter, whether that takes an hour or a year.

Invariably, she said, the script is exactly the same. The two kids selected are a male and a female, the boy always coerces the girl (even if she is clearly interested and flirtatious, she never initiates the sexual encounter), and at the end, the boy always has an orgasm; the girl never does.

Both the women and the men are interested in expanding their social horizons, in having a good time with their peers, and in experiencing that risky, frisky feeling you get when you're pushing the physical envelope with another individual. But where men and women part company is how far and when they want to push it. The process of sexualization in a relationship—how much sexual stuff goes on and when—unfailingly causes major breakdowns between the genders. The same things don't offer that jolt of delight to both sexes, and they don't go about getting what they want in the same way. It's hard enough to get both people to speak the words "we've got to use a condom" to each other, let alone "not tonight, babe."

Rape would be horrific if it were just a physical assault, just a painful reminder of how women, no matter how assured and self-confident, may not be strong enough to protect themselves from harm. Of course, the nature of the attack goes to the heart of the matter, where it hurts more: A man who rapes a woman is defiling the private, intimate place that has previously given a woman enormous pleasure. In addition, he may leave a residue that is hard to combat—pregnancy or an STD.

Taking Responsibility—Condomania

We know what to do about sexually transmitted diseases, and yet they have proliferated to epidemic proportions in this century. Whether a woman is raped or has consensual sex, she runs the risk of picking up one of those dastardly organisms. It would be great to know that you could jump in the sack without a care in the world, but that just isn't going to happen in the near future. Until some extraordinary vaccine appears, a woman who is not in a mutually monogamous relationship has to rely on condoms.

Although 70 percent of women in long-term relationships reportedly use some type of contraceptive, it's a lot harder to get guys to use condoms when you're just hooking up or hanging out together. Guess why it's always been hard to get men to cooperate? When their excitement is stirred and they're with a woman they don't know well, they're in fantasy land. They are not thinking about being responsible or careful. And when they're with a woman they know and supposedly care about, they want the full experience of tactile sensation. They want to be close—and if they feel strongly about this person, they have undoubtedly rubbed out of consciousness all former partners that either of them ever had. A man who's thinking only with his little head has trouble understanding why he should bother to put one of those nasty things on—unless there's something at stake.

The advent of rampant HIV in the early 1980s institutionalized the condom, and in the 1990s, it was even introduced into the public school system. It was also now essential to master the techniques of partner interview—you had to know a person's whole sexual history because if you went to bed with him or her, you were also going to bed with every other partner he or she had ever had. The fun part is always mitigated by the midnight monitor in your head that reminds you of the high price of spontaneity. So you become the latex sentinel. Surely you have a lot of other things on your mind, like whether you really want to have sex, and whether you like the guy enough to be this vulnerable with him. But you have a duty to perform if you want to protect yourself.

Sex can leave a woman scarred—pelvic inflammatory disease can curtail her reproductive life; HIV can turn to AIDS. Sexually transmitted diseases have a more deleterious effect on women than on men, since the delicate mucous membranes and rugal folds of the vagina are prime breeding grounds for bacteria and viruses, and cervical cells divide quickly, facilitating the multiplication of any virus that invades the area.

There are so many of these infections. Vaginitis, particularly trichomoniasis, is just unpleasant, but it certainly can put a damper on sexual pleasure. Beyond those minor ailments legion among the female population, we move on to lesser known but truly contagious ones. There are pubic lice, those malevolent pediculosis ("crabs") and scabies. There is gonorrhea and the recently revitalized syphilis. Chlamydia and herpes simplex virus (types 1 and 2) are rampant in the population, as are shigellosis, genital warts (HPV), and finally, HIV. PID, pelvic inflammatory disease, can affect the cervix, uterus, fallopian tubes, abdominal cavity, and ovaries, and may result from a variety of other untreated infections.

Talking about condoms makes many couples queasy, and physically going to the store to buy them is harder on the psyche than on the pocketbook. Clinics abound in urban areas where condoms—and a quick sex-ed lecture on why to use one every time from start to finish—are free for the asking, but what does it take to get young people to walk into one of these places? Men generally go kicking and screaming when their girlfriends drag them—once again, the woman is the one who has to turn somersaults for sex.

Even if you got everyone to wear a condom, you can't guarantee the quality of the rubber. Condoms break. Then, too, not every STD goes away because you use one. Think about HPV (human papilloma virus), which nabs 40 million Americans each year, causing genital warts. The warts themselves are relatively painless, but the infection that causes them has been linked to both cervical and penile cancers. One-third of all college women are believed to be infected with this virus, and the likelihood rises with the number of partners. With four different partners, you have an 80 percent chance of ending up with warts. Even with a condom on, a couple who enjoy oral sex or frottage (rubbing the penis between a partner's legs or external genitalia) can catch it, since the warts often congregate at the bottom of the penis's shaft, which is untouched by a condom.

The strange and mysterious thing about women is that their insistence on using condoms every time tends to weaken with the longevity of the relationship. The first talks, awkward as they are, are incentive to the man because at the end of this harangue, he's going to get what he's after. The woman has a game plan, and she sticks to it so that everything goes smoothly. But once the couple is bedding down on a regular basis, it gets harder to stop and talk first. The next few dates, and the next few occasions for sex, may be more spontaneous, less planned. There's no pattern, no ability to sit and think when the sex is fast and furious.

Then, as weeks and months go by, the intensity may lessen, but the inclination to consider all the ramifications of the act is gone. No longer is intimate touch a novelty; now it's one of the activities that makes them a couple. So the woman who continues to put her foot down about condoms before she will acquiesce is suspicious, domineering, and probably doesn't like sex. Or that's what the guy says. And what does she do? She stops thinking about the possibilities that could make her sick, make her pregnant, or get her thrown out of her house or dorm, and she opens her legs along with her heart. No condom? Well, maybe next time. If luck is against her, she can always see a doctor who can make things right again.

The Medicalization of Sex

In decades past, you went to your mother or an older relative for advice about cycles and reproduction and painful periods. But young women today go to a gynecologist years before their mothers and grandmothers did, who typically made that first doctor's appointment when they were married and became pregnant. Twenty-first-century sexuality is highly medicalized—if you're a smart and savvy sexual consumer, you don't wait for trouble to strike. You make an appointment at your college infirmary or your best friend's ob/gyn, you hop up on the table, put your feet in the stirrups, and ask for the Pill.

Oral contraceptives, a mix of estrogen and progesterone, fool the body into thinking that a pregnancy has already occurred, so there is no egg waiting to ovulate and possibly get fertilized. There are currently OCs with graduated amounts of estrogen that mimic the body's natural cycle, and also 28-day packs with seven dummy pills so that women won't forget to take a pill a day. Some dial-paks suggest that you begin at the middle of the pack rather than the beginning, to avoid breakthrough bleeding. And although most packs have all seven dummy pills, several formulations now have only two hormone-free days. And you don't even need to remember to take a pill a day, if you don't want to. A newly FDA-approved intramuscular injection, Lunelle, from Pharmacia Corporation, is a monthly dose of medroxyprogesterone and estradiol that takes care of thirty days of birth control (and at about the same price as a dial-pak of pills) with one trip to the doctor's office per month. Many women get a partner to learn to give them the intramuscular shot, which saves them the cost of the injection service. A contraceptive patch is also in the works.

A new oral contraceptive, Seasonale, due to hit the market in 2003, requires a woman to bleed only four times a year.[5] She will take a pill every day for twelve weeks, followed by placebo pills for one week. This appears to be a safe way to administer OCs, since the pill contains less estrogen than conventional birth-control pills, which should lower the risk of the uterine lining overgrowing. The endometrium will still fluctuate under the influence of the estrogen and progesterone in the pill—simply not enough to cause breakthrough bleeding.[6]

The early medications of the 1960s contained a great deal of estrogen—undoubtedly too much—and there was some risk of heart attack, stroke, and thrombolytic events for long-term users. But dosages have come down to below 50 micrograms (today, there are pills with as little as 20 mcg of estrogen) and minipills are also available—"lite" contraceptives containing long-acting progestin that can be used by women who cannot take estrogen because of cancer risk or because they are breast-feeding. Most side effects have been eliminated because of the lower and more sensitive dosages. It is also apparent that there are noncontraceptive benefits to taking birth control pills—a decreased risk of ovarian and endometrial cancers, prevention of benign breast disease and pelvic inflammatory disease, menstrual regulation, and even clearer skin. In addition, they can increase bone mineral density.

But the newest kid on the block is the FDA-approved Nuva-Ring, a flexible plastic ring that slowly emits low-dose estrogen and progesterone over a period of three weeks. You insert it after your period stops, leave it in for three weeks, then discard for the last week when you bleed again. You insert a new ring the following week. The nice thing about this device, which, studies say, is very safe, very effective, and very easy to use, is that you get your hormones exactly where you need them—right in the vagina—and they don't need to be metabolized by the liver as a pill does.

Of course, what we'd like is to get men into the act of being responsible for birth control. Women have been the gatekeepers of contraception since the beginning of time, but at last men will be able to take steps to prevent pregnancy. This pill, projected to appear in pharmacies within the next decade—should women be able to convince men to take it!—will use androgens and GnRH-agonists to render sperm unable to pierce an egg. Also in the works is a vaccine that will do something similar.

But in the meantime, our arsenal of protection is securely in the hands of women. And this can be embarrassing for many women, who are concerned about what guys will say.

"If I'm on the Pill," one college junior said to me, "it means I'm ready, I'm out looking for it."

Isn't that also true if you have a condom or a diaphragm in your purse? Judith wanted to know.

"No, not a condom—you can just go to the corner drugstore and get one when you need it. And diaphragms are yucky and messy, so I wouldn't consider one. But a pill in that little dial-up container means you think about sex all the time, all month long! That's a pretty strong statement to a man."

So women who think about sex aren't just thinking about passion, fun, eroticism, or excitement. They're thinking about pregnancy. That's the thing that really separates us from men, and perhaps colors every sensual and sexual encounter we have until we pass through menopause. Each time we reach out for pleasure, we are slapped down by that suspicious little hand waving in the air over our heads—*Is it safe? Can I proceed without triggering a reproductive time bomb?*

Doctors find potential Pill-takers primarily in women who've already had a pregnancy scare or an abortion. More upper-income women are likely to take Ortho Tri-Cyclen or Mircette or Alesse because their mothers dragged them to the doctor's office in high school when they first became sexually active, or as an excuse to regulate their periods or control their acne.

Other birth control options aren't appealing to most young women. The IUD has a reputation of causing heavy, painful periods, and for most singles, it seems too permanent a solution. So many "bad" IUDs have gone by the wayside that now only Progestasert, which emits a low dose of progesterone, and ParaGard, the copper T, which is good for up to ten years, still remain in use. According to Dr. Jeffrey Levine, who teaches at Robert Wood Johnson Medical School and runs a women's health and counseling center in New Brunswick, New Jersey, IUDs are underutilized in America although they are still popular in third-world countries. Dr. Levine emphasizes that IUDs today are very safe, extremely effective, and a great choice for women who are interested in getting a career going and waiting a significant amount of time before considering pregnancy. That doesn't mean women want them, however. It's this business of a foreign object protruding from the cervix that gives pause.

Norplant, five hormone-emitting sticks that are implanted under the skin of the upper arm, which was pioneered in low-income ghetto populations, seems coercive to many women, a way for the medical establishment to control who has babies when. The Depo-Provera shot involves a trip to the doctor every three months, and has considerable side-effects, including a danger of blood clots. That leaves the old diaphragm of our mother's day, which requires a woman to put her fingers not just inside her vagina but all the way up to her cervix. Many Hispanic and African-American women have been taught since childhood that you don't touch that area or put anything inside the vagina. If it's that difficult to persuade them to try inserting a diaphragm in the doctor's office, you know it's going to end up sitting unused in its little clamshell, tucked away in a drawer in the bedside table.

What else have we got? There's the contraceptive sponge, whose track record isn't as good as other methods. The Reality "female condom," a solution only a celibate researcher could love, is a nonlatex device that serves as both diaphragm *and* condom. It gives a woman a lot of control, since it can be in place before she ever meets up with her date, and a man can ejaculate into it more than once. It's placed inside the vagina, but has a rim that extends outside the labia, which may protect much more efficiently against genital warts that sit on the bottom of the male shaft. Aesthetically, however, it's not at all pleasing. It moves around a lot and makes a burping sound during intercourse, which would be funny if it weren't so gross. And at $2 a pop, it's not exactly the first item on a single woman's shopping list.

Yet with all these available options, the majority of women just don't use them. They get carried away, or they can't speak the words necessary to use protection. And so we end up with that old American tradition—fixing it after it's broken. Another chemical boon to women's sexuality is Plan B, the emergency contraceptive pill. When the race to stop a pregnancy is paramount, a woman now has seventy-two hours from the time of unprotected intercourse to take her first dose of levonorgestrel, and then a second dose twelve hours later. This pill stops the implantation of a fertilized egg. The 3-day-after birth control pill, Preven, manufactured by Gynetics Inc., can also take care of those glitches of sexual indulgence. The "morning after pill," which actually can be taken for up to seventy-two hours or three days after unprotected sex, uses special doses of regular birth control pills to prevent or delay ovulation. Because the pills work prior to implantation of a fertilized egg, they do not serve as an abortifacient such as RU-486. But try to tell that to the religious right. Many pharmacies in areas of the Bible Belt don't carry the stuff. Wal-Mart refers customers to Planned Parenthood health centers and other approved providers, but they do not currently stock any emergency contraception.

The success of the real thing, RU-486, in a Catholic stronghold, France, will probably never be matched in the U.S., where the Right to Life movement often trumps a woman's right to deal with her own fickle body.

Do doctors explore the issues of women's sexuality as well as their reproductive health? They should, but most are so embarrassed by the topic that only a tiny minority even ask if a woman is sexually active, let alone whether she has any problem with desire, sexual abuse, sexual orientation, arousal, or orgasm. There is a picture hanging in Robert Wood Johnson Medical School that should be a cautionary tale to women today. It shows a Victorian gynecologist engaged in an examination of his female patient. She is standing, fully clothed; he is kneeling, with his hands up underneath her voluminous skirt. He looks away; she looks away. They are both pretending that this is a perfectly normal, socially acceptable event. If he were to stumble on a diagnosis, it would be nothing less than a miracle.

Now, it's true that we have inched forward in sexuality training for physicians. Some medical schools around the country, including Robert Wood Johnson, actually have a required sexuality course, but unfortunately, there aren't many like this one. More often, a human sexuality curriculum, if offered at all, is likely to be optional or brief. In any event, it's one thing to take a sexual history in a classroom setting and quite another to fit it into the ten minutes you're mandated by the HMO for an exam.

So it's up to the patient to ask—but how realistic is that? We want young women to have good guidance and get their questions answered, but at the same time, we cringe at the collaboration of medicine and sex. What if, for example, you have bruises around your labia from rough play with sex toys? What if you come out to your doctor and he or she acts shocked or upset?

Women get spotty healthcare in general, and it's worse if they're lesbian. Unless their physician is also from the gay community or has gone to medical school very recently, women are probably not going to get the treatment they deserve. Traditional thought was that lesbians didn't have sex with men, so they couldn't get pregnant or contract an STD. Consequently, doctors never even mentioned protection to these women. Some never even did Pap smears, feeling that it was unlikely that such a patient would get cervical cancer. But this is patently untrue. Since women can transmit herpes, chlamydia, bacterial vaginosis, and HPV, it's essential to counsel them to use some form of latex protection like a dental dam and to wash carefully all sex toys that might enter the vagina or anus. Lesbians have to demand appropriate care, and often, change health plans several times, to be sure they stay well or get well. But the physical end of this is only part of the picture. A woman who is confused about her sexual orientation needs reassurance and guidance, and a woman who is thrilled but anxious about her new sexual partner and wants to ask questions about her difficulty with orgasm requires a doctor who can put down his speculum and just listen and talk.

Gynecologists are trained to perform wellness exams and take care of diseases, yet in recent years, they have been asked to probe into areas that give them *angina*. Fortunately, there are some lesbian gynecologists and nonhomophobic physicians around. While it may take some ingenuity to find them, it's certainly worth the effort to search them out. But of course, doctors aren't the only ones who have trouble dealing with lesbians, as any lesbian will tell you.

Gender Bending

Most lesbians are fairly confident that their primary attraction is to women by the time they reach their twenties, but there are some women who remain uncertain. Maybe they're gay, maybe not. "Straight," however, doesn't cut it, especially if they're attracted to a man one month and a woman the next. "Bi" means more, yet there is still a great deal of prejudice from the gay and straight communities for those who have not chosen one or the other. A recent movie showed a female character climbing into bed with another young woman, who had been jealous of her attentions to a man she liked. When the woman expressed surprise, the ambivalent star replied, "I didn't know I'd have to declare a major." The line between gay and straight and bisexual has blurred. Many women talk about "pan-sexuality."

It's now a common occurrence to pledge allegiance to the lesbian community rather than declare one's homosexuality. Women who belong to the club may be political or totally uninterested in radical feminism; they may wear leather and short hair or dress like suburban housewives. The point of having an intimate same-sex relationship is the consolidation of affection and interest—actually, it's not much different from having a best friend, except that you sleep together. The old-fashioned dichotomy of gay women dividing up as either butch or femme hardly exists for young women of today who have broken out of the mold of patterning themselves on a heterosexual relationship. Several sexual theoreticians have postulated that it's curious why more women aren't lesbian, because women love the kind of emotional, analytical, in-depth communication that is characteristic of such unions.[7] This is not to say that men can't be perceptive and sensitive—but those essential qualities are more apparent and more valued in a relationship with a woman.

So is sex the only sticking point? Not exactly. Some women identify themselves as lesbians, but never make love to a woman. Others call themselves heterosexual, but cohabit with a woman. Probably every woman who's honest with herself can admit to being attracted at some time to another woman (this is not true of most men). And those women who are willing to admit that they enjoy sexual relationships with both sexes are probably just recognizing the tendency that most of us have—we fall in love with a person, not a gender. If that makes us bi, well, so be it.

If lesbian or bi identity is to have a meaning, it probably exists along a sliding scale, similar to the one Kinsey proposed, in which a few individuals were either exclusively homosexual or heterosexual, and the rest of us had a little of everything—depending on the situation in which we happened to find ourselves and the erotic possibilities we discovered in many different people.

Being Young and Out and Still Looking for Love

Although she's in love with a woman, Tory wishes she wanted a man. Being young, single, and gay isn't easy. "If I were just in it for fucking," she says, pronouncing the word loudly and distinctly, "I would pick a man every time. No dates, no commitment. Hey, men're so simple! No man has ever rejected that offer once it's made. Women, on the other hand . . . " She let the sentence trail off.

Tory is 27, wiry and fast-moving, her straight blond hair cut close to her head, her sweet, open face bare of makeup.

"What's the difference between sex with a man and sex with a woman?" I ask.

"Oh, everything. Well, with a man, of course, there's a hard body and a penis. So I only have vaginal orgasms with a man."

"Only?" I was thinking of the long-standing debate over clitoral and vaginal orgasms—how the latter were considered superior since Freud made women cringe before the mighty penis. Yet Tory described them as though they were somewhat lacking.

"Yeah, well with a woman, you can have these amazing blow-your-head-off clitoral orgasms, and at the same time it's more like your whole body is coming. You don't have to stop and wait for your partner to get ready to go again. You can just spend the whole night making love, talking about, 'Hey, that was a mild one . . . maybe this time we should use a vibrator or the velcro restraints, or just our mouths instead of hands.' You know, there's a lot of variation."

Tory had always lived alone, although she'd been in long-term relationships. "You know that joke?" She grinned. "What does a lesbian bring to her second date? A U-Haul. It's a woman-thing, I guess. Well, first, maybe because there aren't that many gay women, so when you meet one that you'd like to date, you figure you should stick around to see how it pans out. I've gone to gay bars just looking for a one-night stand, and gotten hooked because the other woman decides that we're an instant couple. Like your girlfriends don't understand it. *What? You've had four dates and you're not getting a joint checking account?"*

She said that she had to have a lot of sexual chemistry with a partner, although she was with one woman, Billie, where they had sex—and not very passionate sex—only once or twice a week, which she considered a piddling amount. Billie was an incest survivor and was terrified of being touched, which Tory respected. She said her own considerable sex drive took a beating in this relationship. "I stopped being as interested, you know. I didn't even masturbate that much—it just wasn't so much a part of what we did. But I think the relationship eroded because there wasn't any sexual tension. I really need that—my best relationships have that edge to them."

She has been involved with a woman about fifteen years her senior for the last two years. And if you wanted to pick a problematic union, this would be it. "I had just broken up with Billie, and I was feeling like it was time to do something on my own, something good for me. So I joined a local women's softball team, and my first week up at bat, I see this person staring at me, flirting with me, for God's sake. She was about my size, dark, long hair in a braid, with these piercing green eyes and this round body you just wanted to hug. All I could think about was touching her. And she had a fabulous laugh, you know, she used to make us all crack up.

"Well, then I find out Anna's married and has two kids—two girls, 12 and 15. So the fantasies were like, okay, it's nice to think about it, but it's not gonna happen."

"You wouldn't have asked her?" I was curious as to how assertive she was when it came to taking what she wanted.

"No. Hey, there's plenty of women who had girlfriends in high school or college and swear they're straight, like even my own two first girlfriends are married with kids. That was just playing around, practicing for 'the real thing.' But to expect Anna, who for all I knew was a classic suburban housewife, to go to bed with me, I think that would be asking a lot."

"But you would have accepted her as a friend, without the sex?"

"Yeah, that's how it was. We'd all go out for beers after practice, and she'd sit right next to me and she was outrageous. Flirting like crazy. I thought, What is with this lady? She just doesn't know that she's turning me on. (But she did know, I found out later.) And a couple of times she drove me home when my car was in the shop. We started doing things together—going to movies and museums on Saturdays when her kids were at their friends' houses. Her husband, Pete, he was really great. We'd watch sports on TV together. I became like a member of the family.

"So one night, Anna drives me home and we're sitting in the car and she's coming on to me—I swear I never did anything!—and I said, 'You better watch it or you'll get more than you bargained for.' And she said, 'Like what?' So I kissed her. And that was it."

Although Anna had never had a relationship with a woman before, Tory said, she was a wild woman in bed—they had terrific sex that was open and experimental. They would go to Tory's apartment after practice, and Anna would leave at four in the morning so that she could be home when her daughters got up. Over time, the connection they'd made—the good friendship and the fabulous sex—grew into a deep and close love affair.

"What about Pete?"

"Anna and Pete hadn't had sex in two years, so she was starving for it. Frankly, I don't know what he did to get satisfaction, but she said he'd always had a real low drive. We started by keeping it a secret, but she felt rotten about that. So we told him. He was hurt, of course, but I think not that surprised.

"I think for him, it would have been harder to lose her to another man— you know how men think that lesbians don't have 'real' sex, so it's not a comment on their manhood if their wife walks off with one. Also, I think he was relieved that I was taking Anna off his hands, because she was a handful."

"And now what?"

"Well, lately, I've been thinking about my future. Like I want to be with her, set up house, spend the rest of my life with her. But not like this. Not sneaking in and out of bed so the kids don't find out. I'm not stopping my life for her."

When we last spoke, Tory had put an offer on a house in another town. She told me firmly that it was about time she had something of her own. She gave Anna a date—her Y2K, as she called it—that she wanted an answer. "I'm not sitting around and waiting for her," Tory said. "Sex is one thing, love is another, but my life is more important."

She has come to that realization that women generally have to make over time—matters of the heart can't take precedence over one's personal development. Yes, it's important to have a lover, but it is more important to love yourself.

Orgasms—Where to Find Them and Do They Really Matter?

Whether a woman is gay or straight or hasn't yet decided, finding that illusive gold nugget buried in the sexual experience is often extremely difficult. Where are all those multiple orgasms women read about in magazines, and do they feel compelled to achieve them?

Women as a group tend not to be big pleasure-seekers—it is virtually impossible to get a group of women together and ask what they do for fun. The answers range from cooking to gardening to painting murals on the bathroom wall—some household chore that they've restructured to become a hobby. They are generally proud of taking so much time away from work to enjoy these pursuits. But ask about pure pleasure with no end-product, like masturbation, for example, and they will clam up. The topic creates instant discomfort. A great deal of this anxiety about masturbation has to do with society's phallocentric model of sex—i.e., if there's no penis present, it can't be good. Women just aren't educated to find female models of erotic stimulation. In addition, the poor self-image so many women have isn't conducive to super-hot fantasies where they are being massaged and licked and serviced by a battalion of horny admirers bent on giving them dozens of orgasms. Ask the average woman in the street if she touches herself "down there" or inserts anything inside her vagina in order to get off, or stimulates her clitoris, and her mouth will drop open.

Also, a sexually inexperienced woman is not reliably orgasmic. There seems to be a sequence of stages that lead to knowing and claiming pleasure, and they generally begin with masturbation, which is, of course, having a good time when no one else is watching, and no one else expects anything of you. The woman who's been conditioned throughout childhood to take care of someone else's needs (a doll's, a younger sibling's, a parent's) before her own is going to have a hell of a time thinking about her own orgasm if her partner is lying right there next to her and hasn't come yet.

Masturbation itself requires practice. How do you know whether you like touching the clitoris directly or you prefer the sensation of rotating circles right around it? How do you know if you want both clitoral and anal stimulation while you fill up your vagina with a dildo or vibrator? You have to experiment and try again and again. Suppose you are interested in those sequential, if not multiple, orgasms? You have to get good at letting the feelings subside slightly after one peak and then starting in again rubbing or tapping or stirring the area so that you can come back to the plateau you left.

In addition, there are those shadowy areas you've heard about but aren't quite sure what to do with. Anal stimulation, for one, makes some women uneasy—do you really want to touch that opening that has always been connected with elimination? Do you want a partner to do that? But many women really get turned on by having the anus touched, even licked (if both parties have scrupulously showered first), or having something—finger, dildo, or penis—inserted inside. Next, we have the G-spot, the cushion of tissue wrapped around the urethral sponge, which was discussed by a Berlin gynecologist, Dr. Ernest Gräfenberg, in the 1950s and later popularized by John Perry and Beverly Whipple in the 1980s. This little joy button, described as a lima-bean-shaped protrusion on the anterior wall of the vagina, can create mind-blowing orgasms in those women who can locate it—and even help trigger female ejaculation. It is more likely that a partner or a specially designed, crooked dildo or vibrator will be necessary to find this spot, since it's way high up and most women's fingers just aren't that long. It's also easier to stimulate in various positions (doggy-style is good), which means that a woman has to be experimental enough to get up off her back and do something to achieve this reputedly incredible orgasm. It may be that not all women have this distinct area or that it is really difficult to locate—which would suggest that there is no universal female sexual response that we need to strive for!

Another rarely plumbed area to stimulate is the tip of the urethral sponge at the base of the clitoral shaft. The urethra is a highly sensitive area, just like the anus, and can be used to good effect for sexual pleasure. Then, too, some women need a great variety of simultaneous stimulations to achieve orgasm—their partner's hand on their clitoris and U-spot, his penis in their vagina, a butt plug in their anus, and their own two hands manipulating their own nipples. (If they are daring enough to touch themselves, that is.)

And what about female ejaculation? What exactly is going on? This is still a matter for debate in many circles. The clear, odorless liquid that exudes from the paraurethral glands, which may be produced from many different types of stimulation, is distinctly different from urine in chemical composition. Some women who ejaculate just feel that they're getting extra-wet, and others can shoot a spray across the bed—in any event, once again, the woman has to feel comfortable enough to let go and not worry that she's about to pee when she gets excited. The expectation, the anxiety, the confusion about what's going on may stop an orgasm in its tracks—or else, the wild abandon and new sensations may allow it to overflow. The key, of course, is practice, practice, and more practice.[8]

Women who are longing for one of these dramatic physical events, unfortunately, may be missing out on a lot of the real fun of having an orgasm. An orgasm may be delicate as a sigh or overwhelming as a tidal wave—depending on the time, place, and circumstances. This lovely release isn't always a physical event—it can occur anywhere and everywhere in the body at once, regardless of the area actually touched—or *not* touched. There are women who can have "no-hands" orgasms, simply by fantasizing. There are some disabled men and women who report fantastic sexual feelings by meditating or daydreaming. We really don't have a clue as to all the various permutations of this experience, but it can only improve with a lot of experimentation and permission.

What images turn you on? One day it might be the thought of getting stuck in an elevator with no underpants on and a masked man beside you. Another day it might be lying spread-eagle in the sand as two women suck your nipples and two men put their hugely engorged penises into your two openings. But you'll never know this until you try the fantasy over and over again.

Because practice is so essential for mastery, cohabiting and married women have a much better chance at reaching orgasm, whether through partner manipulation, oral techniques, or intercourse—the last being the hardest to achieve. A single woman, even one with a few partners under her belt, will have to have a regular sex life to become reliably responsive. This is not to say that you can't be single and get aroused easily, but it's taking it to that next step that requires faith.

Once you get good sex, you want it again. You look forward to it because you remember that you had a wonderful time the last time. And then you're ready, primed, already lubricating when that first kiss or touch on the hand signals the start of a sexual experience. And after it's all over, you reminisce about the best parts and concoct a videotape that you can play over and over in your head until the next time, when once again, you're at the brink because of the last time. If, of course, the last time was four months ago, you need a whole lot of help—mental, emotional, and physical—to get to the same place. (This works in reverse as well. Women who have been abused, either as children or teens, have to overcome their past memories in order to feel comfortable enough to try sex again.)

If only we had older mentors to reassure us about the progress of our sexual abilities. Our mothers and aunts help us decorate our new apartment and tell us how to live on a budget, but they never provide guidance as to how to get the most out of sex! It really is like riding a bike—you need someone to hold on to the back when the training wheels come off, just in case you fall the first few times. That's what we could use in mastering sex—an older mentor who offers encouragement that we're doing just fine, and will undoubtedly get better, if we're patient and do it as many times as it takes to get it the way we want. We also need to be told that falling off (in this case, *not* having an orgasm) is also perfectly all right.

There are cultures where older women serve as guides to female sexual contact—in Polynesia, for example, menopausal women were traditionally recruited as sex educators. But our civilization has turned sex on its head—we've got to have it, and yet, the doors to the library with all the information are locked and barred. There's no way to find out how except by taking the plunge.

How do you do that? It takes some women half a lifetime to find out.

Alone but Not Lonely at 35

Advertisers have been targeting baby boomers for the last decade or so because they're the people with money. They'd buy houses and cars, they'd buy stuff for their houses and cars, they'd buy stuff for their kids, they'd go on vacation, they'd divorce and remarry and do it all over again.

The new group that advertisers are targeting is never-married and never-to-be-married-again women. The number of women living alone in this country has increased by more than a third in the last fifteen years to 30 million, according to the Census Bureau. Single women are no longer under the age of 30, but rather, straddle all generations. And as women have been earning more and spending confidently, they have become major players in the economy.

According to the National Marriage Project 2000, a large survey from Rutgers University of 20- to 29-year-old non-college-educated individuals, a great majority of singles are looking for "sex without strings, relationships without rings." Casual sex, careening around the twelve-lane highway of dating, is perfectly fine if you're not ready for a relationship, which will bump you onto the one-lane road of mutual fidelity. Most women of this age like the idea of love, but they can't handle all the emotional baggage that goes with looking for it. Many of them, especially African-American women who may have seen their mothers, aunts, and cousins abandoned by men who couldn't make a commitment to come to dinner let alone to get hooked up, feel that they have to get ahead on their own. They want good jobs, nice homes, and sex whenever it's available. They'll even supply the condoms.

You may know—or you may be—a woman who has been searching for a viable relationship for a very long time:

A Definite Keeper: I am a smart, funny, adventurous woman, comfortable "in town" or in the woods. I've spent my time until now creating a professional life. Now I want to find my life partner. Are you honorable and self-aware? Can you laugh and cry? Do you need more play and tenderness in your life? I am the treasure . . . come find me.

Being single is no longer a stigma. You can place an ad like the one above in a Personals column at any age—all you have to do is describe everything you are and everything you've longed for in fifty words or less. The term "old maid" has almost left the lexicon. The reason for this, of course, is that society has given us permission to grow up more slowly than we ever did. With a huge number of individuals living at home after college for financial reasons, or starting a new career path every ten years, it's now considered okay to lag behind in the romantic arena. Even childbearing doesn't have to conform to the old timetable.

It is preferable, many women say, to be a whole person before you start looking for a relationship. Becoming someone's wife isn't the issue these days—it's making a partnership that feels comfortable and right, no matter what age. And so single women can enjoy the company of men and not be man-hungry. Think of the proliferation of co-ed volleyball teams and swing-dance classes, or the new trend of female participation in classes at Home Depot to learn to put up drywall or tile a bathroom floor. Yes, they might meet someone cute there, but the real purpose of the visit is to learn a skill. A skill to practice when a man is not around.

Patricia: The Self Before Relationship

Patricia has a big circle of close friends, men and women. Everyone loves spending time with her. She's a great cook and interesting groups of people are often found at her kitchen table on weeknights and weekends. But at 35, she has never had a serious, committed relationship. She says a guy has to hit her over the head, otherwise she doesn't notice that he's interested in her. "I think some of it goes back to my parents—they were much older, Hungarian-Jewish immigrants who rarely spoke English at home. I was their little *'ketze-lah,'* their kitten, and they treated me like I was a lot more fragile than my brother, who was two years younger than me. Things might happen to me, I could get myself in trouble—that was the attitude. I think that's why up till a few years ago, when I was alone with a guy, I started feeling anxious and tensed up. I felt like I was doing something I wished I hadn't and then, bingo, I'd go mute. We'd get cozy and I wouldn't be able to say a word. *Yes, I want to; no I don't.* I couldn't say what was on the tip of my tongue. I felt paralyzed."

Patricia's verbal paralysis carried over to her physical state of being—she was rigid when she tried to have sex, and it was extremely difficult or impossible for her partner to penetrate her.[9] She was desperate to change this part of herself, to become the wild and crazy woman she really felt she was, but opportunities never seemed to present themselves. She was in her mid-thirties when she ran into a man she had known fifteen years earlier and they started a relationship.

"He was helpful, very sensitive. He understood how hard it was for me and he just said, 'Well, we're going to make this happen.' I felt a huge load lift off my shoulders, because he was going to do it for me. He called me 'sexy'! I can't tell you how relieved that made me feel. He took his time, touched me all over, and he was so complimentary about my body—not in a fake way but like he was really seeing it and appreciating every part of it. He'd hold me, kiss me, then eventually, he'd say, 'I'd love to go a little further.' He was so tender and nice, and he kept repeating that we were going to be fine." She smiled. "I guess I believed him. My muscles finally relaxed and there was no problem. Except . . ."

"Except what?" Judith asked.

In a steady voice, she confessed that she had never, in all her thirty-five years, had an orgasm. At a friend's suggestion, she bought a vibrator. "I bought it and put it in the closet. I just wouldn't touch it. My friend kept teasing me about it—Well, do you still have it? Is it getting dusty? So one rainy afternoon, I took it out and tried it. Then I got obsessed with it. I wanted an orgasm so badly I was pushing it and not allowing my body to react."

Patricia says she's not sure if she's come. Maybe sometimes she feels these little waves that could be orgasmic. But in the meantime, she is doing something else that would have been impossible for her a couple of years ago. She is maturing sexually and experimenting with her sexuality. She's been with her current lover for a year and a half, and has become comfortable just playing with sex.

"We have such a good time," she said. "He lives far away, so sometimes we meet in hotels, which is kind of forbidden and luxurious, and we've done things like use whipped cream and sex toys, and done a little bondage with silk scarves. Once I came to his house wearing high heels and a coat—that's all—because he dared me to and never thought I would. I've actually used the vibrator in front of him, but I'm trying to get away from that because I don't want to rely on it. Also, I've finally discovered the wonders of oral sex. I'm really close to having an orgasm with him when he goes down on me. I pass this imaginary line that's been holding me back, and it makes me realize that there is potential there, and all I have to do is tap in to it."

I asked her if this man was a keeper, and she sighed. "No, there are too many complications—it's not a forever thing. But I'm emotionally open to meeting people now, as I never have been. And I've had more experience in the last five years than ever. It's like Pandora's box was opened—I've been wanting to have this part of my life feel good. And I'm eating it all up, loving it. Between my last two lovers I have a great chance to experiment and play out things that people usually do in their twenties. I guess my growth was stunted a little, sexually. But I have hopes."

There is something *stuck, tight,* about Patricia's description of sex. Here is a competent, self-aware woman who goes mute at the thought of speaking up for herself in an intimate setting, who couldn't open her legs to a man because everything inside her screamed, "You'll be hurt! Don't do it." Yet she wants to get over this. She has taken on sex as a creative project, something to delve into like renovating an old house. It's possible, with enough time and a lot of effort.

Who needs marriage? Many of the single women Sandra counsels don't care whether they ever march down the aisle. At the same time, however, they are aware that their single status makes sex a large responsibility rather than a delicious game. There's so much work involved in enjoying intimacy that many find it hard to reach their sexual potential.

Marriage, however, isn't the answer. This enormous institution that society has codified and ritualized for hundreds of years means less to many women than it ever did. Jewelry stores now advertise "wedding and commitment bands" to take advantage of the new trend for gay unions and partnerships that are not sanctioned by law but imply togetherness in a different way. The looming reproductive clock that used to press women into marriage has stretched as though manipulated by Salvador Dalí, and it's not quite as potent a factor these days as it used to be. You can have a baby in your forties by using the new technology; even in your fifties if you're willing to adopt or take an egg from a younger donor. So you can postpone marriage as long as you feel it's appropriate.

Some women, however, are terrified of the prospect of being alone at 50, so they feel they have to hustle at 25. Maybe watching their mother suffer through a bad marriage and divorce, maybe reading too many of those *Cosmo* columns about spending New Year's Eve alone. It just gets to them after a while. They have it burned into their hard drive that women menstruate, gestate, and lactate; men impregnate; and that's how it's been and will always be.

For this reason, there will always be women who are desperate to have that legal document, even if the nature of the relationship they are about to celebrate is significantly different from the one their mother or grandmother expected. The wedding ring is a symbol of the wholeness they crave, in bed and in life. It shows they've grown up, established roots, and are in the running to produce a new generation. Their families think more highly of them; they may even get a better seat in a restaurant. Sex is legit, and so is spending a long Sunday afternoon with your sweetie without feeling that you have to wear makeup or act smart or be anyone that you don't want to be.

There's a kind of relaxation that sets in as soon as the wedding band is slipped on. As the old song says, "A man chases a girl/ Until she catches him." After years of pursuit, of longing, of wondering how whole you can be with just sex or just romance, there it is—the grand slam home run. *Marriage.*

3

COUPLING:
AVAILABLE SEX

There's a cartoon that's been circulating in dorms and women's groups for several years. The illustration is of two pie charts that show how we think—one's for men; one's for women. The man's pie is roughly divided into three major sections: sports, sex, and career. The sex quadrant has a tiny subdivision known as "the relationship" and there are also a few extraneous categories that get small slices of the pie, including "going bald," "aging," and "strange ear- and nose-hair growth."

The women's chart is much simpler. Fully three-quarters of the pie is devoted to The Relationship, and within this category, there is a small sliver labeled "sex." The other tiny pieces that make up the rest of the pie include "food" (with a subdivision labeled "things we shouldn't have eaten"), "pets," "aging," "having to pee," and "men trashing." We laugh, but we grudgingly agree: There is arguably no woman who does not factor her relationships into everything she does in life.

We bond with women we happen to stand next to in a movie-theater line, or with whom we exchange comments about the tomatoes in the supermarket. It's never just the movies or the tomatoes—it's how we *feel* about seeing a film or squeezing a ripe fruit. That's why women tend to be so discontented with men even as they desperately desire to hook up with them—for most men, a movie is a movie and a tomato is definitely a tomato. For a woman, it is commonly something more—sometimes it can express the whole range of human emotion. Why don't men understand that?

It's not so much that men and women don't communicate effectively, it's rather that they are working with different tools on the same material and coming up with different outcomes. And this, of course, leads to the problems that men and women have about dicing, peeling, mixing, and matching their sexuality.

Women are experts at finding ways to use The Relationship in every conceivable manner. They can think and talk about The Relationship they don't currently have and obsess about having, The Relationship that is ongoing and has its good points although it also has a lot of problems, The Relationship they just got out of and good riddance to it, the extra Relationship they are considering or in the midst of because their primary Relationship is slightly unsatisfying but not enough to end it, The Relationship they've never had but are now ready for, one that they can imagine in all of its various hues and permutations.

The easy way out would be to say that women have a serious need to expand sex and combine it with the more problematic themes of coupling. Because they are always grasping for those love straws, they can't simply enjoy the physical and emotional pleasure that comes when they're touched, kissed, and fondled. They can't let go with the greatest orgasm of their lives because they just can't be that vulnerable with someone who may not be there tomorrow.

But this is not a childlike concern that women have to get past. For the majority of women, it is a clearly established fact—most are adamant that some type of relationship must develop before sex and continue after sex or it just doesn't work for them. The great majority of women want affection, cuddling, and a guy who remembers their six-month anniversary, more than they want a great stud.

What Is a Relationship and Why Do Women Need One So Much?

Let's define "relationship" so we can all get on the same page with it. It's a connection between two individuals that encompasses dozens of interlocking roles and expectations—from friendship to attraction to curiosity to power-balancing to silliness to comfort to the sharing of many different interests.

Women can, of course, manage a life alone—many do, particularly as they age, as long as they can put down roots in an area where they have access to work, sustenance, and entertainment. But they tend to send out shoots wherever they are to family, friends, and acquaintances in ways that men don't. They make relationships wherever they are.

Most women with interesting lives are okay with being single, no matter what their age, but they are generally hungry to have a partner hovering for times when they choose to share themselves and their world with another who is sympathetic as well as sexy.

Erik Erikson said that for women, intimacy precedes identity. And being intimate means being with someone else. Love is something that the majority of women feel they're entitled to, and they'll make a lot of concessions in order to get that jolt of feeling. It is possibly for this reason that so many staunch loners begin to think that staying single may not be all it's cracked up to be.

Is It Less Sexy to Be Single?

Being single is no guarantee of sexual fulfillment, even in these egalitarian times when women are free to ask men up to see their etchings and premarital sex is almost de rigueur. Singles are mythologized as carefree souls who have sex here, there, and everywhere. But *are* they, really?

Despite the moaning and groaning over the sad state of marital sex, the institution isn't doing badly. Fully 65 percent of couples have sex more than once a week even after ten years of marriage.[1] How many singles could run that kind of tally? If you're hooked up with someone, maybe not the perfect one but *someone,* you have a better chance of doing the mating dance than if you live alone with your cat.

During the course of any couple's lifespan, sex will wax and wane depending on many other factors—how much privacy they have, whether they feel secure in the relationship, whether they're rapturously in love or bored to tears or just barely tolerating each other. It also greatly depends on where sex falls in the lineup of all the other things that they share and must do. Even when partnerships are not ecstatic, they may be quite workable. People have more sex when they live with their partner, because availability is, in most cases, more important than passion.[2] Sure, it's fun to feel that surge of delight when you attract one mate after another, but what adult woman wants to sustain that type of frenetic lifestyle forever?

If you look at what popular culture says about singles today, it's clear that the unattached have more angst than orgasm. The four chic urban women in *Sex and the City* don't really get laid as much as they talk and fantasize about it, and at least two of them—Carrie, the heroine who writes a newspaper sex column, and Charlotte, the demure WASP—desperately want to get connected to a man. But despite Charlotte's marriage and Carrie's committed relationship, the four women are bonded to one another, not to a male partner. The disaster that is Ally McBeal's love life is a mournful commentary on the young professional woman—she was forced to work side by side with her childhood sweetheart who married another woman (and then he died of a brain tumor), and the dancing baby is more present in her fantasy life than any man she dates. She pines, she yearns, she itches to walk into the sunset with a man.

Most women side with Carrie and Ally. Even those who value their personal and sexual freedom over everything else want to be part of a couple someday. Eve did it because she was encouraged to do so by a higher authority (also because Adam's first mate, Lilith, did not work out); but nearly everyone else since that first pair have decided to cleave together because it feels . . . right. A woman doesn't just settle in to being part of a twosome because of loneliness or peer pressure (although those elements do come into play for some), but rather because if she's spent any amount of time getting to know herself, she realizes when she is ready to share all that bounty with someone else. Creating a household, making joint decisions, being one of two has an appeal all its own. Even women who've coupled and uncoupled once, twice, three times, never lose hope that the next emotional bond they make will be the perfect one.

The practice of living together in a formal or informal union has stretched and grown over the last decade—women have demanded balance in relationships and they are getting it. Men have become better partners as women have insisted on more equality at home. Of course, women who are comfortable with a "traditional" male-dominated marriage pair up with men who will conform to that standard. And women who desire a peer relationship often find men who are willing to supply that type of giving. There are also couples who aren't quite sure what they want when they get together, but work it out along the way.

These days, there are dozens of variations on the theme of committed relationships, some sanctioned by law and some not. We see three major overlapping types of partnerships and marriages: those that are primarily family-based, existing in order to provide security for a group of individuals rather than just two; those that are primarily friendly and companionate; and those that are primarily romantic and sexual. Most every bond has elements of all three, although one of these generally sounds a dominant note.

Nearly half of all marriages end in divorce, but a whopping 40 percent last throughout the partners' lifespan. The leftovers are people who never marry and those who divorce and remarry each other, because it turned out their bond was stronger than any they could form with two other partners. There are commuting marriages, where couples see each other only sporadically because the other travels for work or even lives in another state. There is serial marriage, a phenomenon that becomes increasingly popular as people grow up and grow out of initial bonded relationships. There is lesbian commitment—tantamount to marriage, since gays rarely get to pass "Go" and work their way up to the Nirvana of legal matrimony. There is also cohabitation for straights, a trial run for the married state that has fewer rules and regs and that some couples extend into infinity. There are also partnerships that have opened up traditional boundaries to accommodate children or different lifestyles. For example, there are individuals who may be married to one person but living with another, or separated and alternating nights in different houses. There are communal arrangements such as lesbians living with gay men in order to provide their children with a male role model, where each partner is allowed to bring his or her respective lovers into the mix. And there are also coupled individuals who love their privacy and maintain two households.

Sex for coupled individuals is a reflection of what George Bernard Shaw said about marriage a hundred years ago: "Marriage is popular because it combines the maximum of temptation with the maximum of opportunity." Your partner is there all the time, so if you want it, you can have it.

Looking for a Partner

How do women find that special one? Most of us are looking for a man or woman who has a variety of traits that we admire, because they help us feel valued, loved, and supported, and balance the deficiencies we think we have. You might be a traditional-marriage seeker who wants a man, first and foremost, to be a good provider and a stable individual who will protect and comfort you and help you to raise and nurture children. Or you might be more inclined to settle down with a comrade in arms, a person to whom you can tell everything, a buddy who will help you to share the challenges of daily life. Then again, you might be a thrill-seeker who requires a heightened sense of emotion, a person who craves a Vesuvius of a marriage where the fights and the loving are equally hot. A good deal of what we require in this mix has to do with the attitudes and ideals we developed as little girls and teens and the role models of our own fathers and mothers. It also harks back to the life experiences we've had so far.

There are probably several people in the world with whom we could fall in love and become happily paired. And yet, according to the 1994 sex survey on American patterns of sexuality,[3] most of us choose life partners who are from approximately the same class and same intellectual bent as ourselves. Factory workers marry factory or shop workers; Ph.D.s tend to marry Ph.D.s or MDs or JDs. The social rules bend a little, but they're not totally flexible. This may be slightly more liberty than we got when our families arranged the match (of course, even today, many cultures in America continue to do this) but we can delude ourselves into thinking we have freedom when we get to do it ourselves.

The overlay on top of all these criteria, for most women, is love—however we each define it. This set of complex feelings is vital to the majority of long-term relationships. Most women want affection and caring in order to go to bed with a man, and if the relationship continues, they need to feel attached in order to establish a "coupled" commitment. Even if that attachment should eventually break, many women still remain loving toward the man they once shared a life with.

Getting Attached

"After the first few months of marriage," said Sue, "sex wasn't as frequent or spontaneous or daring, but it had a different quality. It was deeper, richer, filled with something that didn't belong to anyone but us." Sue, and so many other women interviewed for this book, talked about a special kind of intimacy in coupled sex that might have something to do with possessiveness or, to look at it from a more evolutionary point of view, attachment.

Helen Fisher, noted sexual anthropologist and author of *The First Sex* and

The Anatomy of Love, explains that humans have conveniently separated sex drive, or lust, from what she labels either attraction or attachment.[4] These three distinct emotional systems may be married to different brain functions. Sad to say, the great romances of life may be welded by a power surge of neurochemicals that tell us whether to get hot in the pants, sigh and dream, or plan a wedding.

Lust, the first, most basic of the trio, is instinctive. Animals feel lust and so do people. It doesn't much matter who the object of this craving is, as long as you can have him or her. This type of feeling, out of control as it may be, is determined by the androgens, which in turn are triggered by production of brain hormones FSH and LH.

Next, let's think about attraction. It can be fatal, yes, because when you're attracted, there's a specific target of your interest. Not just any person will do. You may dream and fantasize about that partner to the point that intrusive thoughts overwhelm your consciousness. The attraction component of our emotions seems to be dependent on catecholamines, neurotransmitters such as dopamine (which produces euphoria, loss of appetite, and a decreased need for sleep) and norepinephrine, which not only excites us, but also causes us to imprint, just like baby geese, on the object of our affection. We're stuck; we waddle around in a daze.

High levels of serotonin, interestingly enough, can make us lose sexual interest because it fills us with such a great amount of well-being, we don't need anything or anyone else—that's why Prozac is such a downer for many lovers. But low levels of this neurotransmitter may help us rewind the videotape playing in our brain—that sense of fixating on the time, the place, what he was wearing, and how he smelled may all revolve around that chemical.

Then, there's attachment. Attachment means home, family, nesting, seeing your babies filtered through your partner's eyes. It means feeling like a piece of you has been ripped away when you're not with the one you've bonded with. This is the monogamy cocktail: two peptide chemicals called oxytocin (which is also released by nursing mothers) and vasopressin (which, in animals, is associated with male parental care). As we know from studies on individuals in arranged marriages, they may feel no lust, no attraction, but they are committed to the one who has been selected for them as their life-long mate. Women literally gush the hormones of bonding, which are released both in orgasm and in nursing. (Males, of course, can ejaculate into a variety of partners without getting stuck on one. Talk about compartmentalizing.)

It would be nice to think that attachment was wedded to the earlier two stages, and in many cases, it is. The person we choose for a mate is usually someone who turns us on. And for sophisticated women who have tried on a few partners for size prior to marrying, sexual compatibility is one of the top prerequisites.

Not Quite Married: Cohabitation

According to the U.S. Census Bureau, the number of unmarried couples living together rose 454 percent between 1970 and 1990, to a whopping 2.9 million couples.[5] Sixty percent of all married couples have cohabited before the wedding, even if it's just for a month. (Only 10 percent did so in the neat-and-proper 1950s.)

One of the most common motivations for deciding to share living quarters is to ensure that sex will be available and accessible. Cohabitors have sex more than anyone else in America—19 percent of men and 17 percent of women are intimate with each other four or more times a week.[6]

The problem with cohabiting is that it has no real character of its own. There's no name that we give to the "significant other," and there's no insurance that cohabiting will lead to a future together. And sometimes, a relationship that was built on lots of sex doesn't stand up. Once the initial flush of all that hot passion is past, the two people may look at each other and wonder what the fuss was all about. If you find that you aren't compatible, you split up your stuff and hire a moving van. No formal covenant must be broken. There is emotional turmoil, of course, but it's a lot easier in terms of paperwork than a formal divorce.

For many women, the idea of living together is very appealing for practical reasons. "I hated getting up in the morning to go to work knowing that my favorite sweater was at my apartment. The sex was so fabulous, but everything else was such a hassle, it took the glow out of my orgasms. But when we finally decided to get an apartment together, everything suddenly got much simpler. I had a place for my stuff, and my aromatherapy pillow lived under his pillow. And making love was a lot more equal—it wasn't coated with the idea of my place or his place."

Are cohabitors faithful to their mates? In Blumstein and Schwartz's 1983 study on the American couple, 17 percent of male cohabitors strayed during their first two years with their partner, and 16 percent of women did (the numbers increased for both the longer they were together). This is a significantly higher number than the authors' tabulation of marrieds (only 9 percent of husbands and 7 percent of wives were unfaithful during their first two years of marriage.)[7]

Cohabitors don't develop the same deep roots as married individuals whether they live together for a year or for ten years. They are always creating and re-creating what they do and are together, which is wonderfully liberating but, at the same time, unnerving for many.

Abigail, married after two years of cohabiting, told me, "When we lived together, I was never sure it would really work out, although we had talked about getting married from the first week we met. Before the wedding, I used to have these dreams twice a week where he had just walked out, and I couldn't find him—and there was nothing wrong between us. But after we got married, those stopped."

Of course, her dream is founded in a rather practical concern. Approximately 38 percent of people who live together before marrying break up within a ten-year span as opposed to 27 percent of those who live apart before the wedding. Being loosely joined is no preparation for marriage, nor is it insurance against divorce.

Cohabitation is an exploratory experience that serves as a convenient method of learning about your partner's habits, likes, and dislikes. The big question usually comes after the two have spent about a year together: *Do we split up? Or do we pledge our troth?*

The Marriage Option

The numbers are overwhelming: Over 90 percent of American women will dive into the marriage pool before they turn 49, like salmon swimming against the current, uncertain of their goal at the top of the stream. Women are marrying later now than they used to—the average age for first marriage is 26.7 years[8]—which means that they generally have a good deal of sexual experience by the time of the wedding. This is in sharp contrast to women in our mothers' generation, who were more likely to have had intercourse for the first time on their wedding night or just shortly before it.

How much does sex matter in the big picture of a marriage? If it's wonderful, most women agree, it accounts for 10 percent of the whole; if it's awful, it's 90 percent. About 35 percent of couples have sex at least two times a week, if not more; and 35 percent have an average of one to four times a month. The remaining 30 percent are abstemious or celibate—they have partnered sex a few times a year or not at all.[9] Anger and hostility are the biggest factors in the erosion of a marriage's sex life. Next is fatigue, then boredom, and finally comes infidelity—often an offspring of anger and boredom. We'll talk about extramarital affairs in chapter 5, but suffice it to say that when most partners stray, they are looking for a diversion outside of their commitment or searching for a loophole that will get them out of an untenable situation. Since 85 percent of married couples say that monogamy is a necessity, those who tread over the line are in some way dissatisfied or looking for change.

Men seem to benefit in more obvious ways from marriage than women. Studies show us that men tend to live two years longer when they marry, but women a year less than if they'd stayed single. Men gain greater opportunities for professional advancement when they wear a wedding ring; women lose out as they bang their head against the glass ceiling. Men's mental health improves dramatically; women suffer depression and symptoms of stress more frequently when married than single.[10] Maybe this isn't because of the men they partner with, but rather, because of the way women change subtly as soon as they consider themselves responsible for a household, particularly if there are children in it. Since most of us are raised to take care of others first and ourselves last, it's common for married women to knock themselves out making a "nice home," leaving little time or energy to be sexual.

Latina women are more likely than either Caucasian or African-American women to opt for a wedding—their culture upholds the idea that a woman is more herself as she becomes part of a couple. It's okay for a Hispanic woman to concede that her man is on top—whereas many African-American women are too independent to want to submit to any man, and many Caucasian women may suffer from that perennial anxiety that the one they chose might not be the right one in the long run.[11]

Family-Based Marriage

Marriage is a formidable institution, molded over the centuries and slowly, oh so slowly, becoming more malleable and flexible. It provides a way for families to link up for advantageous economic benefits and a way to pass along inheritance from one generation to the next. If the couple like each other, so much the better. If they love each other or grow to love each other over time, it's a grand success. Sex becomes legitimized by marriage. Your prospects are all locked up in the formal contract you have signed. Sometimes this realization can make women antsy—*Is this really all there is?* they ask when they come down from the honeymoon high. But on the other hand, if there are many more pieces to the marriage equation than attraction, they may find themselves quite content. "More belongs to a marriage than four legs in a bed," wrote Dr. Thomas Fuller in 1732. And in the family-based marriage, this is evident.

In this traditional form of wedlock, the rules are carved in wet cement pretty early on. Typically, the man tends to take the lead in most everything the couple does, including sex. His spouse defines herself as "a wife" rather than "a partner" and is responsible for the majority of the housework and childcare even if she works full-time and earns more money than her husband. The structure of the relationship is based on her dependency. This type of marriage can be found on all socioeconomic levels in America today, although the more money and education a couple have, the more likely they are to reject this conventional arrangement and want to equalize their partnership.

The pull of family can be as strong or stronger than sex drive. We all truly value our independence and autonomy, but if we grew up in a close-knit group and adhere to their beliefs and mores, we will find ourselves increasingly impelled to repeat the pattern that gave us so much support and sustenance when we were young. If we hated our family, we may feel, as we bond with a partner, that we can do better—and should, for the benefit of the next generation as well as for ourselves.

Stick to your own kind sounds very chauvinistic, and yet we do, most of us, even those of us who think it's okay to buck society's strictures.

"I had to stop dating Gentiles," one young Jewish woman told me. "In college I never decided who I'd go out with or who I'd sleep with based on his last name, but now that I'm ready to find someone, I have different criteria. Like I could never marry a man who didn't roar at Marx Brothers movies, or sprinkle Yiddish into his conversations, or know the Four Questions from the Passover Seder. I was never a religious Jew, but I need to make my life with a Jewish man."

Although most Americans choose their mates from their immediate culture, some still allow the community to choose for them. Arranged marriages aren't common in America, but they do exist in ethnic groups that have not become completely acculturated, and they offer women a unique type of security. It's not that they've abdicated their decision-making ability; they've simply ceded it to those they trust.

"I'm extremely modern and liberated," said Asha, a first-generation East Indian woman. "But when I married I expected my parents to pick my husband. We were chaperoned the whole time we were dating, and when we had a gorgeous Indian ceremony, I felt so much like a link with my past. My husband spent three nights cuddling and talking to me before he even suggested sex. Because I was a virgin—and so was he—and we both had to get used to the idea. I found it incredibly romantic. And our relationship has always been like that—courteous and respectful."

Muslim women pick their own husbands, but the culture dictates that family comes first, so falling in love or being physically attracted is not as much an issue as is feeling a sense of comfort. A Muslim couple are supposed to establish harmony together and create a home where children can flourish. Religion and prayer are paramount—a woman would never confront her husband about being rough or insensitive in bed; rather, she would pray over it and ask a family member to intervene for her if she couldn't indicate indirectly to her spouse that she wasn't pleased with him.[12]

Catholic, WASP, and Jewish traditional households offer all members comfort and connection. Even if you ran around a little when you were single, it's more likely than not that you'll return to the bosom of your family when it comes time to find a suitable mate. In the family-based marriage, sex is both for reproduction and for bonding. The couple are more often than not devoted to each other, and since they may come from observant religious backgrounds, they are also usually monogamous. If the woman finds, over time, that passionless sex is boring, she may simply incorporate that activity into the vast number of other household chores that have to be dealt with during the course of her busy week or month.

Friendly or Companionate Marriages

There are others for whom the quality of friendship is more urgent than a person's family background. It's common to hear that a woman married "her best friend." Any woman who ever cherished a womb-to-tomb pal in high school remembers the relief of knowing that no matter what was going on, there was someone who loved her unconditionally but gave her good feedback. She could share secrets, act like a fool, eat a whole quart of Häagen-Dazs crying over the misery of a rotten boss or an extra five pounds with someone who thought and felt as she did.

That urgency for a best friend who is also a lover is the criterion of many women today when they go looking to link their lives with someone else. For lesbians, this is a natural outcome of the friendship—it's easy to find that you are sexually attracted to the woman with whom you've spent hours drinking coffee, seeing movies, and walking in the park. For straight women, the quest is usually more difficult. First, there aren't that many men who behave like a female best friend—and most heterosexual women wouldn't want them to. Then, too, do you want to share everything with the partner you live and love with? If you don't leave just a little mystery, will the two of you lose your boundaries and start to merge together?

At the beginning of any pair-bonded relationship, typically, there's a lot of sex. Both parties are thrilled with getting to know the other, and delight in finding out all the various things that they can do together. "We had sex literally three times a day right after we met," said Daria, who now, after eighteen years with her husband, typically has sex once a week. "I was in therapy at the time and I remember laughing about the fact that I'd never wanted to screw so much before and I was really sore but loving it. I said, 'Well, this can't continue,' and the doctor asked why not, and I said, 'Because you can't live your life this way.' Life isn't about sex. But what I didn't know then was that the start of any relationship—at least for me—*had* to be about sex. If I hadn't been that overwhelmed by the look of his hands on me and his smell and his deep rumbly voice in my ear, I wouldn't be here so many years later."

There are friendly marriages that are completely sexless, but most women value some type of physical intimacy. One woman who nervously told me that she and her husband of two years hadn't had intercourse for the last six months hastily assured me, "But we do lots of other things—we snuggle and spoon in bed a lot." Holding hands and kissing is, for many friends, just as good as any other type of sex play. It may be tamer, but it says the same thing: I love you.

To be friends over the course of a long-term marriage is so valuable that sex can't stand in the way. It's at this point that we should point out the other type of marriage of pals, which happens between two women.

Lesbian Commitments

As the restrictions of traditional marriage dissolve, we look to lesbian women for hints on how to make this institution even more equal and equitable. As a culture, we are still a little queasy about same-sex marriage—the state of Vermont is the only one in the country that guarantees the same protections (for matters of adoption, inheritance, health and pension benefits, and tax breaks) to gay and lesbian couples as it does to straight married ones.

The idea of gay marriage is frightening to a good portion of the heterosexual population. Visions of wild orgies, complete with strap-ons and vibrators, dance in the heads of those who decry the union of two men or two women. As it happens, experts are concerned about the dearth of sex in lesbian relationships, not the excess of it.

Two women who bond together usually start off as best friends, and the issues of power and control, although they may exist, are less apparent than they are when a man and a woman get together. If you think about the way that most of us are indoctrinated at an early age into the texture and fabric of a relationship, you come down to the fact that it's desirable to be a little less "you" when you come together to be part of a couple. Women may tend to lose themselves more in a relationship with another woman than they might with a man. The *vive la différence* maxim of heterosexuality does not apply here.

If you look back to chapter 1, you'll recall that little girls are rewarded for being compliant and cooperative—they usually raise their hands before calling out the answer in class and they often defer to male classmates to see what they think first. This sometimes (although not always) translates to their behavior as part of a couple. Many experts feel that for lesbian women, it's more politically correct (and more emotionally comfortable) not to initiate activities or ideas. Symbiosis is prized more than it might be when a man and woman set up house together.

So what does this do to your sex life? If you're always waiting around for your partner to suggest a little fun and games, or you really want to be seduced but your partner does, too, will sex happen? The Blumstein/Schwartz data indicate that lesbians have sex less frequently than any other type of couple. This has been the prevailing theory for many years, but current feminist thinkers find it a destructive myth. According to Suzanne Iasenza, clinical psychologist and sex therapist, "lesbian bed death" is a concept that exists in the heterosexual consciousness in order to downplay the warm, close bonds that women can form when they make a commitment to each other. Iasenza contends that there is a natural falloff of intimacy in *all* coupled relationships, but it sticks out more when you look at lesbian partnerships, because intercourse is not in the lesbian lexicon.

For two women, "having sex" can include a huge repertoire of different activities. This means that when lesbians do interact sexually, they typically spend a lot more time at it than straight people do. Iasenza also points out that in these relationships, "passion is a slow burn instead of a bonfire."[13]

One common phenomenon in lesbian partnerships is that one woman may have identified with her sexuality very early on and had only lesbian relationships, while the other has just recently come out to herself and has previously dated only men. It can be unsettling to hear from your partner that she is still attracted to the opposite sex, even if she does nothing to upset the balance of the current relationship. "I never really trusted the fact that Leslie was completely mine," said Faye, whose commitment of four years had recently ended, "not that you can ever say that about anybody. But I guess there's still some suspicion in the lesbian community about bi women. Like they just need that penis inside them to feel feminine. Which made me feel less appreciated in bed."

A lot of gay women who come into a partnership have experienced years of shame living in the closet, where they may have slept with men or indulged in promiscuous (but covert) behavior with women. When they do fall in love and decide to commit to being a couple, it may take a while to discover exactly what it is that feels great to them and affords them the most pleasure. They can let go of the obligation to play a set role in the relationship and instead be a friend, a lover, and an equal partner. What a good model this could be for heterosexual women searching for that even–Steven equitable relationship with a man.

The more trust evolves, the more each woman will feel empowered to be sexual when she wants to be. As in any couple, discrepancy in desire (see below) can make a big difference in how well or poorly the two women adjust to each other's needs—sexual and otherwise.

Romantic and Sexual Marriages

Yes, Virginia, there are still those couples who can keep it hot and heavy over the course of a long marriage, be they gay or straight. And what is their secret? These individuals have prioritized sex. It's a vital piece of who and what they are. To look at, they're not much different from other couples—they aren't necessarily more attractive or more hip. There is a hint of the magic in their eyes, though—you can tell the instant you see them together that they adore each other and crave that physical bond. Somehow, they have discovered a way to block out distractions, worries, and duties, in the service of their mutual pleasure. They may have had loveless or sexless first marriages and feel that they have finally found their true mate, someone whose high sex drive matches their own. A good many of them have no children (or they share children with their exes and therefore have a lot of free time), and they have great imaginations that allow them always to see their lover as fresh and new. In addition, some of them don't live together all the time, which makes the heart grow even fonder.

"I remember being so sad when I got this government job where I had to travel to Pakistan three months out of every nine," said Eleanor. "I was just married and all I wanted to do was stay home in bed with Steve. But it turned out great for us. We couldn't wait to see each other and tear each other's clothes off. I could sit in my hotel room any night and get wet just staring at his picture. It was as if he had his hands all over me anytime I closed my eyes. Then, when we finally did get together, it was ecstatic. I had one orgasm after another, and he'd barely touched me."

This type of marriage is possible when the couple share living quarters, too. Francine talked about a look her husband would give her whenever they went to a party together. "He said the rest of the room went away and only I was there. I guess his being turned on made me want him more, too. We're very verbal about our plans for what we are going to do together. Of course, sometimes, like at that party, we just end up kissing in a back room. It's like we're dating, but since we're married, we feel this complete bond. Even when we get mad, it doesn't last long. It's just not worth it to us to hold on to lousy feelings."

Of course, good sex spills onto the rest of the relationship and lubricates its inner workings. In order for a twenty-first-century partnership to be ful-filling, it seems clear that the institution of marriage needs to be adjusted and custom-fitted for the wearers. Hopefully, it will evolve into a more fluid and more creative institution as women play a more active role in the coupling process, and feel entitled to an equal voice in their domestic and sexual lives.

Coupling Means Never Having to Make a Date

If you're dating someone, you tend to dream about the time you get to spend together. You begin to plan events around things that you both enjoy doing, both in public and in private. If you're an outdoorsy duo, you'll go for hikes and canoe trips; if you love nightlife, you'll try fine wines and take a tango course. But the way you connect—with glances, words, and touches—when other people are around will certainly have an impact on what you do when you are alone together. For most couples, the effect of that synchronicity is the desire for privacy and intimacy.

Regardless of why you made the date, you anticipate that, at some time, you're also going to fool around. This may happen before or after other scheduled events, or right in the middle (remember those meals you started to cook together where you simply had to turn off the oven?).

But look what happens after you start living together: The opportunity is there all the time. You're in the same space, doing homey things like raiding the refrigerator, taking a shower, walking around in a partial state of undress (which can be either alluring or sloppy). Men see their wives wearing facial masks; women see their husbands picking their teeth. Coupling takes the mystery out of sex—when you date, you can leave afterward and dream about what you just did and what you'll do next time. When you're joined at the hip, all you do is turn over and go to sleep.

This works differently depending on the balance of power in the relationship. As a society, we have assumed for centuries that men want more sexual frequency and that women are content to mirror their partner's excitement. The man pursues; the woman acquiesces or declines. (There are many couples where the woman initiates and the man responds, but the data indicate that they're not as happy, because the man feels like a failure when he doesn't jump first, and the woman tends to see him as wimpy if he's always waiting for her to call the shots.)[14]

This traditional call-and-response pattern in the bedroom balances the power between the couple—one gets to put the agenda on the table, the other gets to accept or reject it. If the sexual harmony in a marriage is fueled by this formula, there's a lot of tension and suspense. Does he want to or doesn't he? Will she say yes or won't she? The sexual blend usually reflects the balance of power in other realms, such as work and money. If one partner earns more and has a more prestigious job, it is common for the couple to assume he's the "leader" in the bedroom as well. And it's much harder for the two individuals to keep on an even footing if one is incredibly successful and the other is just getting by. (This is also usually true when one works and the other parents.)

The millions of couples whose sex lives follow this traditional pattern have an advantage—their erotic interest may be quite high. As sophisticated as we may think we are, most women tell us they like the chase. We want to put out feelers, and then we want the person we crave to come to pursue us. It can be a real turn-on to fantasize about situations that take us to the edge, but not quite over it. An open-minded woman who likes sex a lot may dream about having a particular man strip for her just as she dreams about him demanding that she go down on him. But in both imaginary situations, someone is taking the sexual initiative. The ancient dance of male and female tends to increase in intensity as those roles are better defined.

But in a "peer marriage,"[15] there is no leader or follower. If we are exactly like the one we love, then who goes first? Who seduces and who succumbs? In a perfect world, we would each play the dominant role half the time, but most of us haven't yet evolved to that point. The type of civilized behavior that goes along with sharing everything equally down-regulates hot and erotic sex.

"I want to be wanted," Toby told me, "and so does he. That means that it's darn near impossible for one of us to ravish the other. We respect each other, we like each other, we're absorbed by the kind of communication we have together, but we don't set off fireworks anymore."

Toby and Len were both working in the same design company when they met ten years ago, but when the company merged with a larger firm, they went out on their own and established a freelance business. They worked and lived together for three years, building their client list slowly before deciding they were ready for marriage.

"We even had our wedding in the apartment we were living and working in. It was like, Hey, can't we get out of the house? The problem with our sex life started with our environment—we could never figure out if we were at work or at home. We never fooled around in the offices—those two rooms were off-limits—but even moving over to the bedroom in the middle of the day felt weird because we were still at work. Geez, we were *always* at work! Of course, when you run your own business, you want to be on top of everything. So there we'd be, naked in bed after lunch, and the phone would ring and maybe Len would be going down on me and I'd be moaning and thrashing and have to stifle it so I could talk to a client. Len, who's even more nervous than I am about making enough money, encourages me to do that. He'll talk shop to me in bed when I'm trying to tickle his balls. So it's always tough getting any momentum going. And I'm usually too exhausted after the long workday to have sex before going to sleep. Mornings are our best bet, when we're both kind of dreamy and relaxed. Except that the dog has to go out," she added, sighing.

Toby longs to be a great sexual partner, but how can she be when she's wearing her business hat? She wants to be playful and seductive with Len, but their work comes first. The type of equality in many coupled relationships—cohabiting or married, straight or lesbian—requires a new kind of juggling of sex roles. Women who have grown up in a marriage and discovered their own potential are often the catalyst for this brand of partnership. If they really don't want to play the coy submissive, they need to show their partner that they want to be accepted as an equal in the bedroom.

What can people like Toby and Len do to make those sparks fire again? Evidently, they both have to agree to lead and to follow. They have to make dates for sex at times when they mutually decide to put the office on hold; they may have to leave the house for a bed-and-breakfast or a no-tell motel on the highway. The intensity of peer relationships offers a real challenge—to allow respect and admiration for the person you have chosen as a life partner to metamorphose into a delight and anticipation that maybe you don't know everything about that individual after all. You have to be willing to take a risk and create something new in your sexual repertoire that will replenish the depleted stores of sexual interest and tip the teeter-totter excitingly off balance.

Discrepancy in Desire

More than no sex or bad sex, the problem most couples encounter is finding a time when both want to have sex. Our libidinous urges arrive and depart precipitously. When one's up, the other's down; when A is donning some sexy underwear, B wants to sleep or watch TV. And the more they don't click on their sexual timetable, the more they doubt that they're really meant for each other, the soul mates destined to be together for all eternity.

Why can't he read my mind? ask hundreds of women. *If he loved me, he would know when I was eager and just what I wanted in bed.*

Well, it doesn't work that way. Simultaneous orgasms and mind reading are great, but they are usually due to luck or a great deal of practice or knowledge or communication, not to extrasensory perception.

In a classic scene from *Annie Hall,* we see a split screen, with a man and a woman talking to their respective shrinks. Woody Allen, desperate for more sex, moans to his therapist, "She only wants it three times a week," while Diane Keaton complains to hers, "He wants it all the time!—like three times a week!" One of them has the hots; the other has the colds.

"I don't get him," one of Sandra's patients said to her in disbelief. "I walk into the bathroom to brush my teeth wearing my underwear, and he jumps me. He's waving his penis around like a big flag. But all I want to do is brush my teeth—sex is the last thing on my mind." Another woman told of being totally turned off when her partner put her hand on his crotch in the middle of an action film at the movies, and still another was dumbfounded to find her husband with an erection in the middle of a serious discussion about money. "Why does he want sex when we're clearly doing something else? It's like he's not even thinking about me—it's just that I'm conveniently there to accommodate his other little head."

But it can work the other way, too. Men who had huge sexual appetites prior to taking vows now delight in being settled. They hardly need to reach out for that breast or thigh, because it's right there, staring them in the face day and night. Many women describe how their husbands turned quiescent, almost *shy,* after their wedding night. The rakish bachelor who had whispered hot suggestions in the backseat of the car or on a deserted beach suddenly clammed up in his new bed. Now he was content to have sex once or twice a week in the missionary position with the lights out, under the sheets.

Whereas many women, after marriage, want to bust out and do things they might not have considered before. Now that they wear that ring, they feel comfortable enough with their partner to experiment with oral or anal sex, to watch an erotic video or do it in the bathtub under the bubbles. But when they come on to their husband, all they get is a fish-eyed stare. "Why do we need all that extra stuff now?" asks the puzzled husband. "We're married, we can just *do* it."

It takes two, of course, to alter the sexual chemistry. A woman who is ready for a romp, greeted by a man who's content to doze by the fire, may start questioning her own sexual appetite. "I used to check my watch as it was getting time to leave the office because I couldn't wait to get home to him," one woman told me. "For the first few months, he was just as ready as me, but after a while, he'd have something else to do. Now, two years later,

I sometimes stay late at work. Sex is still okay, but I don't think about it all the time."

Well, all right, you do anything a thousand times, it's not the same as the fifth time. The seduction factor declines, the romance is dulled—courtship is over and done with. And it's harder to say no even when you don't particularly feel like it. Part of the adjustment over the first years of a marriage is a grieving process—both partners mourn the loss of the passion that brought them together like a thunderclap. But that's what being a grown-up is all about. It's as if both partners are looking at each other much the way Adam and Eve might have in the Garden, minus their leaves. *Wait a second,* they are saying. *This isn't slap and tickle anymore. This is serious.*

For hardworking married women holding down a job (or even two) in addition to managing a home, sex may be a brief interlude at the end of a busy week, or it may be the solder that binds them to the life they didn't necessarily choose but got anyway. Sex may become the commodity with which a woman maintains economic parity. There are certainly women who "put out" in order to feed their family. This is true whether or not they love the man they wedded, or he abuses them, or he wants their kids, or is furious that he is stuck with kids. "What's love got to do with it?" asked Tina Turner, and for lots of women, that question is significant.

The Wifely State

Dalma Heyn, an insightful reporter on the love-and-marriage scene, talks about the process by which women turn into wives.[16] This subtle alteration doesn't happen to every female who dons a wedding band, but it does to a significant number. It all has to do with identity. Women tend to grow and mature best in a symbiosis with others—so it feels good to be part of a twosome. On the other hand, women also crave autonomy. They desperately fear a loss of personality within the entity of the couple they have helped to form.

Consequently, a kind of numbness often settles in around the married state when a woman tries to have both—to be herself and to be half of the partnership—which may effectively cut the sexual pipeline to her husband. It's hard to have the abandon and erotic mystery surrounding great sex when you are also attempting a joint venture that has to be settled and organized.

"I think my husband was really ready to get married when he met me," Marilee, a wife of a year's duration told Sandra. She was a fabric designer from Oregon who had met her true love in New York on a visit to friends. "From the first week we met, he was interested in commitment, and no one I ever dated talked about the future, so it was really flattering. But you know, I was 30, I was tired of the dating scene, and I was looking for someone serious about life, about me. Gene was 36, and he'd spent most of the last ten years establishing his computer business. Now, in one week, he meets me and says, 'This is it! She's the one!' "

Sandra asked whether she was sexually attracted to him. "Oh yes, I mean, he was handsome and had a great smile. I found myself looking at him a lot when I didn't think he noticed. We had so much fun together. We went to the beach and stayed with my friend, we had a cookout, we lay under the stars— it was really romantic. I think it was the third day we were together that we just took off our clothes when we got back to the house to take showers and stayed that way. I have to say that I didn't have an orgasm with him, and I still don't unless we have oral sex, which he doesn't enjoy very much. So we lived together for a year, and then we got married." Her voice sank and she shook her head as she realized how depressing she'd made that word sound.

"You know, I love him a lot, but he's the kind of man who has to go to the bedroom, take off his clothes and fold them, turn out the light, and get into bed. Then he can think about sex. It's not spontaneous, not . . . creative." She sighed. "I had this lover once when I was on vacation in Jamaica. Just some-one I met. And that's the only person I ever had an orgasm with during inter-course. I had nothing in common with this man—it was total chemical attraction—and he took his time and seduced me and said all kinds of sexy things to me as he undressed me and I undressed him. I wasn't myself, you know—I was so excited. When he got on top of me, his balls slapped against that strip of skin that's very tender and sensitive [the perineum], and I couldn't believe what was happening when I started to come. And it didn't stop there— we had sex several times that night—I just didn't get tired. It's nothing like that with my husband," she said finally. "But I love Gene. And it's really going to get better, because I'm going to work on it. I'm going to talk about it."

The determination is so poignant, and it is echoed in the voices of many married women. We have both talked with women who adore their husbands but describe their sex lives as "in a rut," or "pretty uninteresting—you wouldn't want to hear about it." One woman confessed that she was just about to broach the subject of getting a sex manual or going to a sex shop to buy toys. Many of these women—the determined ones—still masturbate (although if they didn't as girls and young women, they typically don't start after the honeymoon). It's a sad dichotomy—to achieve the married state and find it difficult or impossible to match reality with the fantasy that was so hot and seductive. Familiarity is not a good bedfellow for passion.

Supply and Demand in the Bedroom

Why should the sex life of a couple be so unstable? Think of a coupled rela-tionship as an economic system that works by the law of supply and demand. The commodities are sex, romance, and affection. For singles, there's a lot of demand, but supplies are ephemeral—some days you may find what you want, but then you might have to go through a long period of depletion (celibacy) before the shelves are stocked again.

Cohabitation and marriage eliminate that problem. The supply is endless, particularly when the relationship starts up. Sex is available and demand is high. Both parties are flush with the heady rightness of how their bodies fit and how great it is to spend so much time together doing all the things they can to give each other pleasure.

But as time passes, although supply is still bountiful, demand lessens. Other demands force their way in—it becomes more important to decorate the house or go to a class or prepare for the holidays or catch up on sleep. The important time that has been set aside for sex is relegated to new pursuits. The consequence is that when demand for sex becomes very low, supply also starts to diminish. Whereas one partner might have insisted that this was a priority, he or she will stop trying after too many rejections or lackluster responses. When no one tries, and no one cares that much about physical intimacy, it becomes a chore. It's almost embarrassing to recall those times when sex was at the top of the list. With both demand and supply dwindling, the couple reorganize their relationship around something else—the work they do, the money they have, the children, whose needs are placed first.

There is a way to get the system online again, and that is for demand to reappear. Ideally, both partners have to rethink their attitudes toward sharing this very important part of the relationship. If they don't, the bedroom will take on the qualities of Miss Havisham's dining room—a ghostly arena of memories and old dreams.

It's true that these days, we don't need to be coupled. We can be economically independent and have our sex, too. But the lure of union is often just too much—maybe cohabiting or marriage isn't a panacea, but most women feel that it's better than the alternative. And we should expect sexual activity to fluctuate as supply and demand go up and down.

"Seldom, or perhaps never, does a marriage develop into an individual relationship smoothly and without crises; there is no coming to consciousness without pain," wrote Carl Jung. Coupling is not easy, but it can get better over time. So many little things entice us to become one of two and to remain that way with one or another partner. Think about the calm comfort of sleeping with that person whose scent is unlike any other. Think about finding the one person in the world who understands you. And if you are really lucky, you may discover that your best friend, soul mate, and sexual turn-on is the same person to whom you said "I do."

If not, well, he may be great with the kids.

4

MOTHERING:
WHAT'S SEX GOT TO DO WITH IT?

You don't need a husband to be a mother, nor a partner, nor a uterus, nor an ovary. Not anymore. What you need more than anything else is the motivation, the money, and the management skills. Our new reproductive technologies have finally split procreation from sex.[1]

Any bonded couple eventually faces the question—Do we have kids or don't we? For most married couples, children are a priority, sometimes at the beginning, but certainly more so as years begin to pass and the possibilities for conception narrow. It used to be that you got married so that you could start a family. Now, with advanced reproductive techniques, procreation no longer goes hand in hand with physical intimacy. And once the children arrive, where does sex go? For a lot of new mothers, the answer is *who cares?*

In 1960, only 24 percent of married women between the ages of 20 and 24 hadn't yet had a child. But as the baby boomers grew up and decided to finish college, or began earning more than subsistence wages, it was more important to remember to use that diaphragm or take that pill. By 1981, with so many women postponing conception until they had a college degree, over 80 percent of first births in the population were to women over 25, and 20 percent of first births were to women age 30 and older.[2] In the 1990s, women waited even longer, establishing their marriage, their career, and themselves before even dreaming about a baby. You could be 47 and having your first child and no one would look askance. You could have your second one at 54 with an egg borrowed from a younger donor.

It is not true that all women who want to get married also want to get pregnant. Nancy Chodorow, one of the most convincing voices to speak out against the idea that all women possess a natural mothering instinct,[3] makes the case that *both* men and women in the presence of a newborn will start to bill and coo and perform "mothering" duties. She suggests, as do many feminists, that women have had more role training to be mothers than men have, and that girls who've had the necessary background (playing with dolls, watching their younger siblings) just fall into the role when the opportunity to be a mother presents itself.

Until very recently, it was assumed women would bear children and stay home for a while to rear them. Today, that's not necessarily the case. Many young couples decide even before they marry that they will never have children. Voluntary childlessness grows more popular as society nods its approval.

But for many more couples, having at least one baby is somewhere on the "to do" list. There comes a day when, either because the woman's biological clock is running fast or because the couple is finally in a place where finances and career seem on an even keel, they figure it's time. This is not always a comfortable choice, especially for women who are competitive and ambitious.

When women reach a certain point in their job or career where it seems appropriate to make this drastic life change, they start rationalizing: *It won't be that different; I can do both; my husband is a great guy and he'll share all the childcare chores.* Others are resigned. They feel if they don't do it now they never will, and that instinctive pull drags them inexorably toward pregnancy. Others determine that they won't be a slave to motherhood and will get help from relatives, friends, and/or professional baby-sitters or opt for day care. The type of domestic equality that exists in many marriages liberates the woman to do all the things her husband does in the workplace *and have children as well.* And this subtly changes the sexual dynamic between the couple. As on a computer screen, the parenting window drops in front of the romantic/erotic page on the marriage website.

So they start trying. And hopes are high.

The Scourge of Infertility

The number of couples who desperately want a baby but can't conceive has grown exponentially in the last two decades. Fully 10 to 15 percent of American couples, or one in six, are classified as "infertile." The diagnosis is given when six months of unprotected sex (one year if you're over 35) has not yielded the whiff of a pregnancy, once the doctor has ascertained that the problem isn't lack of information about how to have intercourse or an underlying sexual dysfunction.

Those infertile couples for whom the infertility problem is emotional or psychological are in the minority. It's much more common to be dealing with a physical or hormonal problem—either male factor, female factor, or combined male-and-female-factor infertility.

If this were just a private problem for the couple, it would be hard enough. But society expects couples to try on the parenting hat for size eventually. Everyone asks, "Well, so what are you waiting for?"

And if you're actively trying to get pregnant, and it just doesn't work, the sense of failure is monumental. You think back to all those near misses in college when you were so relieved to see that monthly stain coming right on time. It was such a burden to remember not to get pregnant, and now, when you want just the opposite, you have the feeling that the gods are looking down and laughing. No baby? Have some more sex—maybe it'll work next time. Except now, there's not much incentive to get back into bed.

If you think about that trio of sirens that draws us to sex—procreation, desire, and intimacy—and you take one away, how does that affect the whole mix? Most of the time, we're happy to remove the first one, and there are certainly plenty of individuals who make do without the third, but when the goal is the creation of new life that comes from a loving home, it's hard to play the game without all the pieces. Where the pregnant couple get to have good associations between their sexual play and what blossoms from it, the infertile couple see sex as barren, going nowhere. So sex may become something that happens infrequently, and the fewer chances at bat, the fewer possibilities for a home run.

Once a couple decides to put this problem in the hands of professionals, they begin a set of routines that make going to the bedroom about as appealing as swimming the English Channel. It's cold, it's exhausting, and there's no guarantee that you'll make it across. There may be tubal surgery to correct anatomical problems or adhesions caused by pelvic inflammatory disease; there may be drug therapy, to encourage many eggs to ripen in the ovaries; and of course, there is "calendar sex," to be certain that the sperm have their best shot on those days when ovulation is most possible.

The ritual coupling that comes right around the time of ovulation may be fraught with such pressure and anxiety that the rest of the relationship starts suffering, too. The tension is subtle at first, then increasingly, frustration and criticism may hang in the air like a bad smell. Sex may be an ugly reminder of how terrible they are at fulfilling their biological destiny. The infertile woman tends to think about sex only a few days before and during ovulation, and she's not concentrating on pleasure—she just wants to conceive. But she can't.

Or maybe it's him. Maybe she married a guy who wasn't all he seemed on the surface. It's not enough that he can get it up—he should be able to produce. The word "sterile" keeps floating back into her mind.

Sex becomes a chore, one that is divorced from eroticism, playfulness, or even female orgasm. Imagine how it used to be, lying in bed, your partner beside you, wanting to snuggle or tell a dirty joke, or tell him how aroused you get when you feel his erection growing in your hand. Now imagine how it is when sex suddenly becomes goal-oriented. All you really care about is getting that geyser of semen spurting up toward the interior Valhalla between your legs. Having sex to have kids is hard work, especially when it's not working. Ejaculation is required in order to get those sperm moving in the right direction, but some experts feel that it makes no difference at all if the woman climaxes, since the uterus may be just as receptive to sperm in its quiescent state. Those little swimmers can get up toward the fallopian tube without any help from female orgasmic contractions. In addition to the anxiety about not producing, you don't even get a pat on the back for letting go and enjoying yourself while trying.

The other ongoing anxiety, of course, is money. The medical menu of baby-making is extremely expensive. Couples have run up bills over the years of $50,000 and more—they have taken second mortgages on their house, forgone vacations, and delved into retirement accounts. This in itself can create a lot of friction in the bedroom. Putting your faith in a reproductive endocrinologist means that you are always conscious of a third party who gives you instructions on what to do, when to do it, and how to do it. Only certain positions are approved (man on top is best for gravity); only certain times for sex are auspicious. Although couples are counseled to have two types of sex—one with a goal and one without, the stress can be overwhelming as the months pass without result.

"We used to have 'fun' sex on the futon in the TV room," one aspiring mother told Judith, "and 'baby' sex in bed. But we could never keep them straight. It got so he could only get it up for the TV room, but when I was fertile, he simply couldn't maintain an erection. Needless to say, the subject of my own enjoyment didn't come up much. I could see my husband felt the kind of sex that was just for us was less important, but it was the only kind he liked, or should I say, the only kind his penis liked. Then I started questioning whether he really wanted to have a baby. We'd have terrible fights about it. Eventually, he'd grab the clicker and see what was on the tube. It would have been amazing, during this time, if we'd been able to get pregnant."

As the process of having a child drifts farther and farther away from sex, interestingly enough, sex can get better! In many surveys at infertility clinics, about a third of couples who couldn't make a baby the old-fashioned way and opted for in-vitro fertilization managed to let go of their guilt and blame and went to bed just to have a good time. They abdicated their responsibility for doing sex "right," and left that to the doctors who were mixing and matching their eggs and sperm in laboratory test tubes. In the meantime, they found each other again. Although the feelings of grief, loss, and injury over infertility rarely ever vanish, one healing factor is that a couple who are truly in love figure out that they have a lifetime ahead of them. If the high-tech procedures don't work or they run out of money, they can make other choices together—they can adopt or they can live together without children.[4]

Babies and Sex—Are They Compatible?

When sex leads to pregnancy, whether it was planned or not, the landscape changes once again. The first flush of making that decision is enormously exciting. Some women report that desire for their husband is overwhelming, that they never initiated as much in the bedroom as when they were trying to make a baby. Others say that the attempt to create new life added an almost mystical specialness to the act.

"I felt such a rush of love for him every time we touched," one young woman said, "even if we were just holding hands. It was different from feeling horny, although I certainly wanted sex more than I ever had. I couldn't wait for work to be over so that we could be together and maybe conceive. The bedroom felt charged with energy."

When conception actually takes place, another shift usually occurs between partners. There's a sense of terrific joy but, on the other hand, a sense that things are not really settled yet. Many fathers-to-be see their newly pregnant wives as more vulnerable, fragile, like a soap bubble that might burst if touched too much or too roughly. Many women also talk about the fantasy of being "invaded" by something they can't quite describe.

Female sexuality is an *internal* art—we are conscious, when we feel sexual, of inner waves of uncontrollable intensity coursing from clitoris to vulva and spreading throughout the pelvic area, and from there, throughout the whole body. It feels excellent to have sexual touch on the outside, as men do—the breasts and labia respond—but it's quite different to feel something going inside you and opening you up. As the baby grows, we are once again overwhelmed when nothing inside is the way it used to be. We can feel the fetus kick or turn over or rest on our bladder. These inner monologues of the child we have helped to produce offer us another glimpse at our sexuality.

During the first trimester, the two-in-one phenomenon doesn't seem quite real, because it's not usually visible. No one need really know except the couple, and for superstitious reasons, most elect not to tell any but the most immediate family. For the first hazy weeks, the new mother usually feels out to sea—nauseated, tired, and about as far from sexually interested as she's ever been. Her body begins to betray her in little ways—she gets suddenly clumsy; has indigestion; or doesn't see as well at night. Her body balloons with new life, and as the months pass, she can no longer sleep on her stomach or tie her shoelaces.

The hormonal picture is vastly different than it was prior to conception. Estrogen and progesterone levels are simultaneously high in order to get the breasts ready to receive their milk, to thicken the uterine lining for implantation and then to prevent miscarriage. Having so much of both gonadal hormones does a number on sexual interest—the mother-to-be may be horny from estrogen and at the same time too sleepy and moody from progesterone to have the energy to do anything about it. Blood volume of a pregnant woman increases 40 percent from her pre-pregnant state, which makes for leg cramps, bloating, and bleeding gums. Her ligaments start to soften in preparation for labor and childbirth, which can make her feel like her bones are melting around her internal organs. Even her eyes change shape due to fluid

retention, and pressure on the bladder from the increasing size of the fledg-
ling fetus is nearly constant.

So sex becomes a challenge, and this is not such a bad thing. The old
boring routines simply have to be changed—as the missionary position
becomes impossible, and the woman-superior position becomes uncomfortable or unwieldy, a couple has to start exploring new options. Being nauseated or exhausted at certain times of day means that sex play has to be
apportioned differently—if you always did it first thing in the morning, you
may want to experiment with lunch breaks or making love before dinner as
the sun goes down.

The pregnant woman feels sexy at times when the pregnancy seems safe
and not too obtrusive—that is, primarily in the second trimester. When all's
well inside and estrogen makes a woman lubricate like a fountain, fantasy
returns. In the third trimester, even with a bulky, awkward body, most
women are interested, as long as their husband continues to find them beautiful and they can explore some new positions to accommodate the swell of
the belly and the growing baby inside. Toward the end of the time, it often
becomes too much of a chore to make love. Husbands report being exceptionally nervous when they see their wife's belly bulge as a random foot kicks
out or they actually feel the baby press on their penis during intercourse. It's
too much like a voyeur peeking out from inside, judging Mom and Dad for
their lascivious acts. Many doctors suggest that right before the birth, husbands stimulate their partners to orgasm by sucking their nipples or manipulating their clitoris in order to get labor moving along. And giving birth, that
painful but brilliant process whereby what was inside comes out, teaches many
women how to let go for the very first time. Physiologically and psychologically, they may be better prepared in the future to become orgasmic.[5]

There are pregnant women who adore everything about their pregnancies, including sex, and then there are those who are cautious. Being pregnant
and married is a sign to the world that you did have sex (we all know our parents did it once), and are now usually washed clean of all erotic traces. Even
women who considered themselves quite experienced sexually tend to haze
out a bit when confronted with questions about other lovers or even other
times with their partner that were in any way wild or freaky—they forget the
sexy lingerie or quickie in the backseat or getting it on in his mother's pantry
during those long hours of preparation for Thanksgiving dinner. That's all
ancient history—the ripe belly makes it so.

But for some women, being pregnant helps to associate those three basic
elements that drive us to sex in the first place—desire, reproduction, and a
longing for intimacy. If we didn't have the attraction and instinctive push to
couple, we'd never come together to make new life, nor would we search until
we found that special individual who could help us achieve that goal. But

when all three systems work together, sex can take on new meaning. Some pregnant women feel they've come into their own sexually for the first time.

Ellen, a special-education teacher who grew up in a conservative Presbyterian family, started to feel really sexy late in her first trimester, and those good feelings spilled over into her marriage. "The really big change for me was that I wasn't as distracted as I typically am. You know, the tape playing in the back of your head about all the things you have to do and why are you wasting time in bed? Well, as soon as I hit the fourth month, sex was distracting me from everything else, including my work!

"I had these great sex dreams. I used to wake up on the verge of coming and sometimes I'd masturbate. I was really aroused, and felt so loose and good in my body. I know a lot of women hate the way they look pregnant, and are nervous about fitting back into that size 8 the minute the birth is over, but I didn't have that reaction. I enjoyed eating; I enjoyed looking at myself in the mirror, especially because my tiny breasts finally had some shape. My husband loved that—he wanted to play with them all the time. Unfortunately, they were terribly sore during my first trimester, so they were off-limits, but we did so many other things.

"I initiated sex for the first time in our marriage and he thought that was terrific—he would love it to be that way forever—and I found that I was taking responsibility for saying exactly what I liked and didn't like in bed. Where I used to get impatient and turn off if he didn't guess exactly what I wanted without my saying, now I was more relaxed about it. I wondered sometimes how that related to preparing me to be a better parent. My husband would be too rough on my clitoris and I'd tell him to slow down and ease up. And I kind of giggled to myself thinking how I'd say the same kind of thing to my child who was playing with another kid: 'Be nicer to Susie, be gentle with her.'

"And this was weird—there were times when I didn't need to have an orgasm, although I'm usually pretty orgasmic. But the goal wasn't just pleasure, it was bigger than that. It had to do with this process that had brought me together with my husband and what we'd created together. I mean, it was really intimate."

There is a font of power that Ellen has discovered, and it's one that mothers have possessed from the days when we swung in the trees and camped in caves. Recent research suggests a strong Darwinian component to successful mothering—that instead of our old notion that women have to retreat to home and hearth and give up their autonomy when they procreate, they begin to dominate the social order. Dr. Sarah Hrdy, a noted primatologist at the University of California at Davis, compares human moms to chimpanzees and finds that the high-status primates are those who reproduce successfully and, in fact, become the progenitors of their own dynasty.[6] So ambitious, striving women actually use their skills in the bedroom to continue the human race.

There is a big transition between being a married couple and being a married couple about to become parents, and this requires a shift in expectations and priorities. Sex, while vital to a man and woman who share a life, is part of a bigger picture to those who choose to create a family. The feeling of merging with another, or having no boundaries (as many people in love attest to), is subsumed by the framework of parenting, which has its own limits as well as its hugely expanding borders. If you're adult enough to decide you can give away some of your own pleasure in order to nurture young, you may also be adult enough to ask for what you want in bed and not settle for less. The nausea, weariness, and physical displacement of a pregnancy can be put aside for something truly essential—sex as a codicil to love of not just one other, but of several.

Moms Without Men

You don't think much about the difficulties of being a lesbian parent until you go to the local library looking for a classic kids' book called *Heather Has Two Mommies*. It is not in the children's section, but rather, in the adult nonfiction, shelved with women's studies and sociology texts on alternative lifestyles, sexuality, and teen suicide.

"Why?" we asked the librarian. "Well," she said, somewhat defensively, "you wouldn't want just any child accidentally taking it out. Not that it would hurt the child," she added quickly, "but the parents might be upset." It should come as no surprise to anyone to learn that lesbian moms may be living right in the middle of communities where this book is looked on with such ferocious suspicion. They might even work at the library.

The old goddess religions portray a hermaphroditic deity who can pull strong women from her womb without any male assistance. And though we're not quite up to that, we can certainly forgo everything but the sperm in the baby-making equation. Lesbian women are having children together in growing numbers, with the assistance of sperm banks or guy friends who donate a sample once a month during those fertile days.

How many lesbian mothers are there these days? It's not possible to say, because so many lesbians are still in the closet. Even those who are out and partnered are not legally wed, so there's no way to tabulate their "marriages" or their offspring, but numbers have surged as more women acknowledge their choice. Charlotte Patterson, a researcher who covers the lesbian and gay parenting scene, has published estimates that range from several thousand[7] to one to five million,[8] reflecting the confused tabulations in the field of women who are hiding their orientation and those who've come out. Suffice it to say that the last ten years have seen a huge growth of new lesbian families via donor insemination and/or egg donation and adoption or foster care.

Motherhood with a man in the picture is difficult because the man can never feel what it's like to carry a child to term, to labor and deliver her, and nurse her. After the birth, many men stand around waiting for instructions— *You're the woman, you know these things instinctively*—even when we haven't a clue. New fathers often talk about feeling more protective toward the woman in their life (instead of just to the new child they have borne), which can make sex less buoyant and carefree.

But with another woman, the question becomes *Who's the real mommy?* For this reason, many lesbians who have the resources go the high-tech route. They have a reproductive endocrinologist harvest eggs from one partner, fertilize them with sperm from a known or unknown donor, and then implant them in the uterus of the second partner. That way, although only the DNA of one of them is represented in the child, the other has all that intrawomb interaction going on. And they can always have another child, if they're both fertile, and reverse roles. Another choice is adoption or foster care, where neither woman is related to their offspring and there's no competition for who's more related.

The gender question fades before the role delineations. There are so many roles! Do both women work? Are they both taking time off? Will one play the traditional stay-at-home housewife for a few years and then switch with her partner when she returns to the workplace? Does a perfectly equal partnership start to shift subtly when one does more disciplining and the other more comforting?

How does this affect the sex life of the parents? Sheryl-Anne and A. J. both work at a record company in New York and feel grateful that they have such a tolerant work environment. "I can't remember when I didn't want to have a child," Sheryl-Anne, an African-American/Cuban woman who grew up in Harlem, told me. "I was thinking about being a single parent, but then A. J. came to town and all I could think of was her."

A. J. said, "I grew up in Nebraska with a father who said he'd much rather have whores in the house than lesbians. Of course, I didn't know I was a lesbian until I got to New York, so I didn't know to be ashamed. I just dated guys and hated it. But after I got to New York, this whole world opened up to me. I started hanging out with a group of women and then I got this job and met Sheryl-Anne. After we started going together, she started pressing me about the baby. I said let's wait a year and see if we're still together. I really like the guy who's our donor—we plan to have a second, which I'll carry— and he's promised to do the job again so the kids can be biologically related. Our doctor gave us some syringes, and sterilized cups with lids. We started trying in February and got pregnant in July.

"The only thing that's not so good," A. J. said, "is that as soon as we got pregnant, we could feel our sex life slipping. There was just so much else to think about. Like how we deal with homophobia when kids tease our kid about not having a daddy, and how to make sure she isn't all confused about her own sexuality the way I was. I've been scouring the stores looking for nonsexist toys—also, I want her to have the message right from the get-go that people can fall in love with men, women, or both. There used to be one set of 'the facts of life,' but now there are lots more facts. Sex seems much more fraught with meaning, you know? I can't just jump into it the way I used to."

"We don't do it much," Sheryl-Anne agreed. "We each masturbate—it's not like we've lost the urge—but we can't seem to get in sync on when we want to be together."

A. J. added, "We both decided that we would never have sex just to please our partner. That we would only share intimacy because we each wanted to. There are some times, though, when I'm lying in bed and I want her and, like, she knows. She just comes into bed and holds me. That feels terrific."

Sheryl-Anne and A. J. are clearly projecting their feelings about being intimate together to what it will be like when there's a third party in the mix. It's also possible that they're anxious about the changes that are sure to result in their relationship after their baby is born, and this makes them less eager to be sexual with each other.

There seems to be more equity and equality when lesbian mothers have a child who is not biologically related to them, but the road to adoption is paved with conservatives, which makes the process incredibly tough. A lesbian couple cannot adopt—it must be a single-parent adoption—and how do the two women work this out? Private adoption via advertisements or foreign adoption are other possibilities, but these require "home study" on the part of the courts or social services agencies, as does getting permission to be a foster parent. Just when you thought it was fine to own your sexuality, here you are being judged all over again.

The excitement of making a life with a partner is not necessarily compromised when you decide to have a child, but it certainly presents new challenges to the relationship. With two women together, there's the opportunity for different personalities, different parenting styles, and a shared perspective. If sex goes by the wayside for a while, well, it can come back. But suppose you have no one at all? Suppose you've made the decision to parent all by yourself?

Single and Divorced Moms

The ranks of single women with children are growing steadily. The Bureau of the Census tells us that 10 to 15 percent of Caucasian families have single heads of household; for African-Americans, the number rises to 40 to 50 percent. Most of these are women. In 1960, only 5 percent of the population had children out of wedlock; today (counting teen births), that number is 30 percent. And many of that number are having babies alone by choice. Other single-family households are headed by divorced women, who might wish they had a partner—just not the one they came in with.

How do you date or develop a sex life when you need to work to pay the bills and your income doesn't cover the high cost of baby-sitters? If you have supportive parents, siblings, or friends, you are extremely lucky.

"It was hard enough to find men before I had a kid!" one woman with a six-year-old son by choice said. "And now I come with baggage, so it's unlikely I'll develop a lasting romance. But that's sort of why I figured, why wait for someone else to help me do something I'm going to do anyway? It's not that I dislike men—I have great men friends as well as women friends—but I'm not wild about making a life with a man. I like the idea of Alex having a few male role models who will be around when I want them around."

So it's nice to have a guy over for a trip to the zoo or Christmas-tree trimming, but what about filling that space in the bedroom? Many single mothers are celibate, not by choice, but by situation. Attracting a man while you have a child in tow can be difficult, but figuring out when and how to be intimate can thwart the hottest passion. There's his house—but who will stay with your child if you want to stay overnight? Many single women don't want to introduce their dates to their kids because it's hurtful to inspire a fantasy that maybe this man will stick around and become "Daddy." In addition, women who are determined to be good role models themselves don't want to give the message that sex is a casual activity, even though they will admit that it's a relief from the difficult job of raising a child solo.

But what if your child happened to find your bedroom door locked when it never was before? Or what if she ran into your boyfriend in the bathroom in the middle of the night, or saw the two of you naked? None of these events would likely provoke lasting trauma, but they certainly can take the delight and spontaneity out of sex. And what if the person they encounter is another woman? As children of single women get older, they are bound to wonder about their parent's sexuality. It is far easier to talk honestly with children in an age-appropriate fashion than to simply wait for an accidental meeting and then own up to the truth.

"It's too hard to get their hopes up and your hopes up when the likelihood is that it'll end after the first three dates or maybe a few months," one single parent told me. "I love being in charge—and you have to be with a kid on your own—but that turns off a lot of guys. They want to wear the pants in bed, and I'm so used to doing that. I like initiating sex, I like being on top; I even like talking about exactly how to touch my clitoris. And one guy said to me, 'You don't have to be so pushy.' I thought all I was doing was expressing myself, for God's sake! But I think to him I had stopped being all soft and feminine. So to hell with him."

Masturbation is a life-saver for a lot of single women, and some claim to love their vibrator more than any man they've ever met. Although this is the

sexual activity that most people are embarrassed to own up to, a lot of single
women look on it as a delightful experience that they can indulge in at least
once a week.[9] They may rent a sexy video once in a while, or go out to male-
stripper clubs like Chattertons with a group of female friends who can laugh
about their dearth of sexual outlets. The idea of building a relationship takes
on new meaning when you think about the many parts you have to fit into
the whole, and lack of sex seems like a small price to pay for security. "I have
to know he's the one," a woman who had dated for six months without doing
anything more than kissing said. "I know myself—I get totally wrapped up in
a guy when the sex is good, and I can't take that kind of attention away from
my two kids."

A woman with a man and a child is seen by the world as a person who
plays a few roles—she is simultaneously viewed as mother, wife, lover, partner, etc. But a woman alone with a child is seen by the world as a mom—the
dedicated caregiver whose image is more matron than Madonna. The fact is
that a single parent is not a "single"—she is coupled with the children she has
brought into the world. She and they comprise a family, although sex had little or nothing to do with cementing the bonds that tie them together. The
woman who is emotionally on top of her own needs is more concerned with
preserving time alone for herself (to meditate, go to an exercise class, or take
a piano lesson) than with scrambling to find a mate who will fit in to her
ready-made family.

Mothering All the Time

A young Syrian-Jewish woman of 26 from Brooklyn waxed poetic about her
three children. "I dreamed of the day when I would give birth," she said,
"when I could name a daughter after my mother (who had her ninth child
when she was 39). It's a blessing; it's the most beautiful thing in the world.
When I sit with them in the park, I can't believe how lucky I am to wake up
every day and realize that I can help to shape their lives, their futures, their
happiness. Of course, there are the everyday chores, and those are . . . all
right, just chores. But what draws me is the closeness and love I have from
them and that I can give to them. I can't imagine doing anything else in life
but raising children."

The Bible extols a virtuous wife and mother as worthy (Proverbs 31, "her
price is far above rubies"), and in a Muslim household, too, motherhood is
about as terrific a role a woman can play. Muslim men are allowed to have up
to four wives, and must treat them all equally. When one has a baby, her influence rises. One Muslim woman from New York told Judith that it takes four
women to keep a man in check—to keep him on his prayers and duties.

"It's hard to share the man you love, but for some families, it works out
well. When you get those kids, you start having a lot of responsibilities, so it's

good to have someone to split the work with. You've got a house to take care of, a mother, a mother-in-law—you have your plate full. He must provide for all of you and give you security—food, housing, clothing. And if you're busy with a new baby, it's not bad to have another woman to provide sex for him until you're ready to feel that way again. The Koran talks about the four angels that surround the marriage bed—one to the right, one to the left, one front, and one back. But at the time of intimacy between a man and woman, the angels leave so you can have your privacy. It's very romantic."

The Muslim woman is able to split her priorities. She can be completely alone with the man she loves (no angels, no kids, no other wives) when she is feeling sexy; and then devote herself to the home and family when another woman is filling the conjugal bed. This makes it possible for women to play one role at a time instead of simultaneously having to be a seductress and a mother and a best friend and a housekeeper, and all the myriad other selves that spurt out of that main quartet.

But if you don't come from such a culture, if you grow up feeling that you have to succeed in the "real" world of career and intellect, and then manage to have children before it's too late, your priorities are quite different. Most mothers who hold down a job and take a few months off for each birth tend to have twelve ears, a hundred hands, and a fragmented sex drive. "I close the door and it's 10 PM and I know they're asleep," one young African-American woman told me, "and Bill is nibbling my ear, and all I can think of is, 'Did I empty the diaper pail in the baby's room and put my first-grader's favorite shirt in the wash?' I split myself in half and now I can't mend the rip!"

Most women agree that the split-screen phenomenon starts in pregnancy and divides even further after the children are born. Men have a wonderful ability to turn everything off except the sex channel. Women, on the other hand, are juggling all the time. If you're distracted and exhausted by dozens of chores and responsibilities, it's hard to drop it all and suddenly feel desirous and erotic. It's hard to feel sexy when covered with spit-up; it's also difficult hormonally to recapture desire while lactating.

There's another blockage, and that is the relationship of the woman to her child or children. Thanks to the magic of the hormones oxytocin and vaso-pressin, most of us take one look, one smell, one touch of the infant who came out of us and we are hooked for life. This is a vital evolutionary event—if we didn't care so much, we wouldn't bother with the nuisance of feeding, diapering, washing, and protecting our young from harm. What we feel is the intuitive pull—how many women who are miles from their baby feel let down at the exact moment their child wakes up and starts crying? This can't just be timing—it has to be magic.

The Breast, from Sex to Nourishment

When a woman finds that she is more in love, more attracted, more delighted with her new companion (her baby) than with her old one (her husband), she very often is turned off when approached for sex. It's as if the brain had emptied its cache right into the baby file, and the husband file is depleted. Nursing one's baby clinches the deal—those hormones are flowing, not to mention the hours spent in feeding, which curtails a lot of other activities, including sex. These days, thanks to the persistent lobbying of pediatric nutritionists, most women breast-feed for at least a month so that their child can reap the health benefits. Many go on for a year or more. And this means, during that time, that their breasts belong almost exclusively to the child.

Hundreds of years ago, female breasts were looked on as productive organs—the human race would never have survived as long if there were not women to give suck. Upper-class women always opted out of this activity, leaving the job to wet nurses, and their clothing became increasingly structured to prohibit access. (Think of trying to get your breasts out of one of those Victorian corsets!) So breasts were hidden and, like anything that's tucked away, became more alluring. Over time, female breasts took on a sexual rather than a nutritive significance.

And then styles changed and necklines were lowered to reveal a glimpse of mammary magic. That clinched it—breasts had to be sex objects. Maybe it's because vaginas never peek out of clothing, giving a tantalizing promise of what they're for. But breasts spill almost but not quite into public view, offering anyone a free fantasy. When a woman becomes a mother, her breasts become even more beautiful and expressive—but wait a minute, they're not sex toys anymore, they're milk machines! And most women feel a radical change as their body shifts in purpose and function. Most men see this—but don't quite get it. To the husband, those are still his breasts, which happen to have taken on a new, secondary function.

How do you retain your delight in having someone fondle your breasts, lick them, and suck them when you have relegated them to your child? All that stimulation is bound to bring on a let-down response, and then you start thinking about your kid and suddenly you're not aroused anymore.

Some women are able to juggle—when their husbands want to try a little breast play, they switch gears internally and allow this sucking to feel tingly and erotic as opposed to the exact same sucking from their baby, which is not supposed to feel sexual. But many think of their breasts as off-limits to their husbands as long as they belong to the kids.

In America, sex is encouraged, or at least permitted, after the first six weeks postpartum, and contraception does what abstinence and those hormones of lactation might otherwise accomplish. But there are plenty of women who can't concentrate on desire and arousal when their kids are their first—and sometimes only—priority.

When the Last Thing on Your Mind Is Sex

When milk starts to flow, estrogen supplies decrease, and this can make the postpartum period seem bleak and sad, since this vital hormone is the one that interacts with brain chemicals to give us a sense of well-being.

New mothers are hormonally challenged, and this really knocks the stuffing out of most women. Fatigue is as constant a companion as the new baby, and it rarely lets up. At first, you must get used to having a tiny insomniac in the house who is up when you want to be down. Then, just as you get the baby on a schedule, you realize that you can no longer sleep the way you used to, because you have a hundred new chores to do and you have to rehearse them all in your head before the next day dawns. Women talk about falling asleep at the wheel, at their mother-in-law's dinner table, or while standing up in the kitchen while waiting for a bottle to heat. They are so bone-weary that the idea of doing anything else in bed other than sleeping— like sex, for example—seems like a bad joke. This fatigue is often compounded by going back to work too quickly, or having another child on the heels of the first.

Of course, you may be more than tired—you may be tired *and* depressed. After all, you've been waiting nine months for the blessed event, it happens, and then you can't sleep, your episiotomy hurts, and your body is in hormonal chaos. Both new mothers and new fathers experience postpartum depression (the father because he often feels like the odd-man out, helpless and pushed away). This can have an enormous impact on libido.

Women are struck by depression twice as often as men, and it generally happens at times of stress. The anomie of the teen years may trigger it; lack of a partner can do it several years later; preparing a wedding can make women weep; and midlife is a common time for "the blues" that turn black. But for some women, the postpartum period is the one in which they're most vulnerable—they may become so distressed and disoriented that they feel they will harm their child or themselves. Sex is the last thing on their minds.

The couple's relationship is key to restoring a kind of equilibrium, as is a great support system. "If my mom and my sister hadn't been there to spell me, I think I would have jumped out a window," one woman said, reflecting on the birth of her first child. "My husband hadn't a clue what to do with me, and I didn't either. I didn't like him, or my baby, or myself. But when I had time alone and knew that my daughter was in great hands, things looked better. I went out and started running so I could get my body back in shape; I went to my room with earplugs and had marathon sleeping sessions. In about a month, I was okay. At least I could talk to my husband again, if not have sex with him. That took about four months more."

The question is, when sex returns, what will it be like? Is it possible to recapture the old joy and spontaneity with kids around? Or is it possible to create something else that feels equally meaningful, even if it lacks the passion of the pre-pregnancy days? Even when a woman's body is back to its old self again, desire often lags behind. And that may be true, not just for the post-partum months, but for years afterward.

"It's not that I don't like sex anymore," a mother of three school-age kids told Sandra. "It's just that so much else gets in the way and feels more urgent. Then, too, we don't have the privacy we used to, and I'm always concerned about them hearing us. I used to be really loud in bed—I think orgasms feel better when you can yell about them—but I can't do that when they might wake up or walk in. So sometimes I feel like I'd rather not do it at all."

Those mating calls that inform your partner that you're attracted and involved and in the moment are terrible losses for some women. And just as they may have lost the ability to communicate verbally with their partner, so they also lose the knack of revealing to him—and themselves—what it *sounds like* to feel enormous pleasure. Sex isn't only about touch and taste and smell—sound is a big part of the sensual play that draws us to our partner. This downward spiral of silence makes it harder and harder to keep sex at the forefront of the marriage.

There are also women who get so bound up in mothering that they become numb to their sexuality. And this can last and last. "Ten years . . . it's been ten years since my son was born," Sally, 32, told Sandra. "And I've felt my need and desire for sex dwindle more and more each year. They say that a woman reaches her sexual peak in her mid-to-late thirties. Is my body just gearing up for that point? Will I ever get there? What happened that caused my libido to go bye-bye?"

See how she plaintively mourns this long fast of her desire! She even expresses the loss in words she would use with a very small child. It's not a Madonna/whore teeter-totter, with the balance shoved to the left side; rather, it appears to be a changing loyalty. The affiliation is so passionate in some women, it leaves little room for any other true love. It's also incomprehensible to a lot of mothers how fathers can be involved in their children's lives and yet find no trouble having an erection when the baby is crying, the toddler is screaming, or the third- and fifth-grader are having a water fight in the backyard.

As the years of mothering separate a woman from her sexuality, she may have trouble remembering what it felt like to feel sexual desire. And her relationship may devolve into a purely practical partnership where the function of mother and father replace the joy of being lovers. Mothers, who are so good at multitasking, need to find a way to turn off the switch and do only one thing at one time when they are alone with their partner. But how?

When we consider Claire, a mother of a one-year-old with a troubled marriage who came to Sandra for help, it becomes clear how deep this split between the mother and the lover inside us can run. When she started to talk about her marriage, she kept interrupting herself, resettling uncomfortably in her seat, then apologizing.

"Let me tell you about Pete," she said proudly about her baby as she sat down in Sandra's office. "He's a handful, but I'm nuts about him. I want my marriage to be better for his sake."

She started in immediately on a description of her relationship with her husband, Jim. She had married a young man she had fallen in love with in college. After a whirlwind courtship, they were treated to a lavish wedding and all-expenses-paid honeymoon, courtesy of her father, who also bought them a new house and gave Jim a job in his business. Claire had initially been filled with adolescent fantasies about fixing up her dream cottage, picking out the perfect curtains, paint, and decorations. Instead, she soon found herself in a disappointing marriage to an emotionally immature man who would spend evenings with his pals in the garage fixing cars. He came in only for meals— accompanied by his best friend.

"I thought sex would feel better after we got married and we had more privacy, but instead it's gotten worse. You know, before, we'd stay out really late and have midnight picnics and drive each other wild going almost all the way. I remember being excited when I'd hear his voice on the phone. And then we got married and I got busy with the house and he kind of went back to hanging out with his friends. After a while, he treated me just like . . . another pal. One of the guys. He never seemed to really appreciate having me around. I was sort of like the TV—you keep it on for company even if you're not watching."

She sighed. "And sex. It used to be better. I mean, I would occasionally look forward to it. But now, since the baby, not ever." She paused and rubbed her nose. "It's probably because I'm always tired. There's always something to do that gets in the way of our being alone—feeding, diapers, laundry. Some days I don't get to take a shower until noon! Anyhow, wanting sex kind of has bad associations for me."

"How so?" Sandra prompted.

"I don't really want to let go."

"Why not?"

She looked away. "Well, when I was in college I got pregnant and had to have an abortion," she said softly. "Swore I'd never have sex again! Of course, I did. But I never really liked it after that. God, I was convinced I'd never get pregnant after getting rid of one baby. I was sure I'd be punished."

"But you weren't."

"Oh, no. We got pregnant so quick! Almost too quick." She gave that little laugh again. "But we were lucky. We got Pete. My little man is so sweet, so terrific. Sometimes, when I'm sitting in the rocker nursing him, I feel so much pleasure, I think this has to be Heaven." She looked embarrassed. "It's not a sexual thing—I didn't mean that."

"I know."

"I just want to hug him to pieces." Her face got a faraway look when she thought about her son. The love affair was clearly defined.

"Did you and your husband intend to get pregnant?"

"Sure, of course," Claire said enthusiastically. "We really wanted kids. And all my friends were getting pregnant. I guess I could have waited a little longer, but Jim never liked using protection, and it just happened. I was so happy. I was kind of hoping it would make him fall in love with me all over again. You know, bragging, *'the mother of my child.'* "

"So how have things been with your husband since Pete was born?" Sandra probed, but she already knew the answer.

Claire pursed her lips. "Well, it's good for him. He has such an easy time of it, and I guess I kind of resent it. And I always feel so rushed, because Pete might wake up. So I can't come at all."

"Did you use to have orgasms? Before your son was born."

"Sometimes. Now I don't even remember what it feels like. So the idea of sex just doesn't really interest me— I'd rather play with the baby or watch a video. But don't tell Jim that! He thinks he's God's gift to women!"

"You haven't told him how you feel?"

"Oh, it wouldn't make any difference. I guess he knows I'm totally exhausted from being with Pete all day, so it only happens every couple of weeks, if that."

She crossed her hands over her chest, hugging herself the way she might have wanted to be hugged by someone else. "I don't desire sex. I don't desire him," she said in a small voice. "I just want to go to sleep at the end of the day and not get woken up for some stupid reason, because he needs some attention." She sighed. "But the funny thing is, I do want to feel differently. I want to want sex, and I want to want Jim. What should I do?"

The Middle of the Road

Claire, Sally, and the millions of women who have exchanged good sex for mothering are not doomed to a cold, unattached marriage. But they are going to have to work harder to recapture their pleasure, and what this means is that they have to be motivated.

There are technical strategies to employ: make dates, use the grandparents, hire sitters, plan bed-and-breakfast weekends away from the home front in order to recapture romance and physically tear yourself away from those octopus arms of your kids and all that caring for them entails. But the difficult part goes way beyond using sex toys or massage oils. The crucial factor is whether you can balance two types of love affairs—one with the partner you came in with and the other with the new partner who is completely dependent and offers unconditional love. If you sincerely believe that sexuality is your birthright, you'll make it a priority, put it on the calendar, talk about it, plan for it, claim it as your own. But you must separate out your life with children from your life as woman. (We offer many strategies in Part II of this book.)

For some, this chore is too difficult. And like Sally, they hang in limbo, waiting. Waiting for the kids to be grown and out of house, out of car, and out of mind. Waiting for a time when life doesn't revolve around soccer games and play practice. Finding it in you to feel warm and responsive even when your husband doesn't get a Christmas bonus or, worse still, loses his job. Waiting until midlife, when the rage of hormones crests and then, finally, ebbs. It is often only at this point that the sexual woman can reemerge, older and wiser, maybe not quite as juicy as she was before, but ready for all kinds of action.

THE WOMAN IN MIDLIFE:
STUCK IN NEUTRAL OR
SURGING AHEAD

As a generation, we baby boomers are awfully lucky. We came along late enough to have the Pill, but early enough to avoid much of the scourge of HIV/AIDS. Some of us came of age and married young, before the sexual revolution, and had little more freedom than our mothers. But those of us who trembled with possibility at the brink of the 1960s knew that sex, drugs, and rock 'n' roll were ours for the taking. We didn't have to worry a lot about the consequences of our sometimes hasty and thoughtless actions. We were concerned about pregnancy, but most of us could find an abortion if we wanted one, at least after 1973 *(Roe v. Wade)*. Those of us who dared to defy our early memories of our parents and teachers as "sex police" took matters into our own hands—if we had no partner available, we masturbated or went to bed with our trusty vibrator.

We knew about sexually transmitted diseases, although the ones that were most pervasive when we were growing up—gonorrhea, crabs, and pubic lice—were a cinch to treat in comparison with HPV and HIV. A good many women who are now passing the menopause border might have had twenty or thirty partners and never thought of themselves as promiscuous. Casual sex wasn't considered unusual in the 1960s and 1970s, and for some, it was a social nicety to get out of the way so that the relationship could proceed. Even those of us who were not experimenting widely at the time grew up in an atmosphere where sexual freedom was a permissible option. Consequently, we are a group of women who are not easily shocked, particularly about sexuality. And that gives us the opportunity to face midlife with a large palette of choices.

When you turn 50, it's hard to see your hand in front of you without your bifocals; when you go for a long hike or play touch football with your kids, your body is not so forgiving the next day. You just don't feel like yourself anymore. Which means that sex also feels different. An intimate relationship that has nothing to do with attracting a mate or making a child can be intimidating to women who have never considered a broader perspective on their sex life.

By the time a woman has reached her sexual prime—whether it's 45 or 65—she has probably had her children, been in numerous relationships both good and bad, and knows the type of pleasure she wants to pursue or avoid. She is tired of letting sex float over the relationship as a gentle reminder of those big romantic dreams that she put aside years ago. And she wonders, *Is this all there is or am I missing some essential elements? Am I happy, and what does that really mean? Is there some other way of doing what I've been doing? What do I risk if I change the pieces on the board?*

All her options are tough ones because they involve a personal quest that will change the status quo. Some women decide, after many years of putting up with sex, to avoid it entirely, whereas others decide to jump into it with abandon. Still others feel they must change course to explore some areas that previously might have appeared only in their fantasies. Midlife sexuality, depending on your attitude and life experience, can become a challenge, a scourge, or a delight—and sometimes, all three.

About 30 percent of women in long-term marriages, according to a University of Chicago survey, have sex once or twice a week,[1] simply because this is part of what most couples do, whether they're thrilled with each other or not. Most of the time, it's all right—often fun—even if it's not at the top of the "to do" list. Very often, these women describe their marriages as fine, or at least, as workable. They have a great deal in common with the life mate whom they know as well as they know themselves, and they don't want their partners searching elsewhere for comfort and excitement. As one woman said when Judith asked how often she fantasized or masturbated, "Well, that's not really what I'm about anymore." Over the years, she had come to think of herself as a collection of roles: wife, mother, career woman, house decorator and maintainer, chauffeur, exerciser, dieter, etc. It had become harder to feel like an object of desire—hers or anyone else's. So sex turned into a rote drill, accomplished when she was too tired to care much whether she did or didn't get aroused, and did or didn't have an orgasm.

Other women talk as if they got to the party just as it was breaking up. "It used to be nice, but my lover and I don't connect that way so much," a 50-year-old lesbian from Chicago said. "A lot of our friends are going through the same thing, although we don't think of it as a bad thing. We just don't need sex that much if we have the rest of the relationship. I never had a very strong sex drive."

Still other voices are adamant about the lesser importance of sex to an older woman. Sex was okay before the kids, but it became useless or annoying while listening to the patter of all those little feet in her head, so why bother? "I don't think much about sex," a 52-year-old office manager from

Queens stated bluntly. "I like my husband, my kids, and I just had a first grandchild—that's what really interests me. There's too much talk about sex anyway, and it gives people the wrong idea about what holds a marriage together."

There are women who never married, or who are divorced or widowed and still mourning the lover they can't imagine replacing. Women without partners grow more numerous as the decades pass. Although it's possible to meet that special someone after menopause, and there are many late-in-life partnerships and marriages, single midlife men are often looking for younger women. Being without a regular partner for a long time can lead to both sexual apathy and diminished arousal. When you're sexually active, your genitals stay primed for sex—your body is in the habit of "turning on." But periods of abstinence in a 50-something can gum up the works, which means that any midlife woman who wants to stay sexual has to work a little harder. Kegel exercises, masturbation, hormone replacement, and water-based lubricants have been the salvation of many a woman who anticipates a return to sex at some point.

There is, of course, the midlife woman whose sex life has ground to a dead halt and who has no interest whatsoever in starting it up again. She never really enjoyed sex during her reproductive years, and since she's been inactive for so long, it's become the norm not to feel any excitement. She is shaped differently—her body has softened; her attitudes have hardened. She knows the kind of relationship she has, and can't imagine changing it. She can continue this way, not quite celibate but not quite sexual, until she and her husband are old enough for twin beds or even separate bedrooms. She no longer feels tolerant of his snoring, and values her privacy more than their intimacy.

The midlife women who are stuck in neutral are not necessarily depressed or angry. They have simply dropped sex as a major activity in their lives. As a matter of fact, the majority of midlife women report some loss of appetite for bedroom fun. But let us not forget that there is another group of midlife women, who are eager and hungry for intimacy. Midlife marks the first time that many women actually think about their sexual identity and come to discover how they really feel. Those who loved sex in their younger years are more likely to want to continue being sexual at this time. They have the experience and self-awareness to complete their circle, the one that started at their first menses or their first kiss, when that indescribable rush of delight coursed through them.

A lot of their inhibitions are gone—they can walk naked in front of a mirror, they can yell and laugh when they orgasm, and they don't need to worry that their lovemaking will result in a pregnancy. They are ready to shake up their marriages, to go for counseling, or, failing that, to consider taking a lover (male or sometimes female). They want to break out of the matrimonial box they've been in for years. Maybe they feel attracted to or desired by a younger lover, or perhaps they're content with someone of their own age with lots of experience and a huge appreciation of women. They may finally learn to masturbate, they may become interested in erotic literature and film, they may experiment with extramarital and Internet affairs. Somehow, in the years when they sat home watching *Sesame Street* and vacuuming up the Cheerios, they began to diverge from the "straight" path. Now at midlife, these women feel entitled to will their newly found sexual energies into existence.

Sometimes a shift in marriage—separation, divorce, or the death of a spouse—can catapult a woman out of her cocoon and back into the real world. No longer sheltered by the demands of the house and home, many women in midlife go exploring. As they watch their parents grow old and die and they develop a healthy sense of their own mortality, they realize that this may be the last moment they've got to make a break for it.

These intrepid souls are learning by doing. Even if they never initiated sex before, they are itching to start something. "I woke up on my forty-eighth birthday," Layla, an administrator for a national teen coalition, told Judith, "and I thought, What is going on? I have sex maybe once a week for twenty-six years; my husband hardly understands what oral sex means except if I'm giving it to him, and I recently bought a vibrator online because I figured, what the hell, I'm not getting any younger. I used to fiddle around with masturbation like it was something to be ashamed of, but I've recently discovered exactly how and where I like to be touched. My body feels alive, more responsive than ever. I'm thinking about buying my husband an erotic video for Christmas because I'd really like to show him what's going on with me, but if he's too uptight, well, I'll just watch it myself."

Midlife sexuality is a turning point. You can just stand there, waiting endlessly for something better, or you can take your chances and surge ahead, although you don't know exactly what you'll encounter. And a large group of midlife women, those who are feeling strong, secure, and confident in their own sexuality, are taking that heady risk.

Why do some embrace sex and others shun it? It's hard to tease out the many overlapping reasons—from previous rewarding sexual experiences to an effortless passage through menopause to the availability and interest in a partner, to the new lack of inhibition that may come with the development of a stronger, healthier self-image.[2]

Finding Meaning in Menopause

You stop bleeding once a month. You get a few gray hairs and crinkly lines around your eyes, and you put on a few pounds. What do these physical changes really stand for? Nobody paid much attention to menopause until the baby boomers made it something special.

This is not a bad thing. After all, the more discussion there is, the more education we get, the more attention our healthcare providers pay, the more prepared we are. We need to be aware that eating soy can help us to protect our bones and heart; we have to know that exercise is vital at this time of life. It's equally important to know that the onset of vaginal dryness doesn't have to mean the end of sex—going to the doctor may not only provide a prescription for hormone replacement therapy, but also support and understanding. When we get together with groups of women just like us, we don't feel like we're alone in the desert.

Menopause can be interpreted in many ways, depending on your worldview, and although some women are pressured and depressed by it, others find it enormously liberating. What exactly is going on? The process is physical, mental, emotional, social, and certainly spiritual.

Just Before the Change of Life, a Change in Expectations

The premenopause and perimenopause[3] mark the beginning of a hormonal cavalcade of events in most women, which may engender either increased fantasy and interest in sex or total turnoff.

The physiological reasons are apparent when you look at the changes in the endocrine system that occur during the forties. During the perimenopause, estrogen levels rise as the brain hormones FSH and LH (follicle stimulating hormone and luteinizing hormone) are produced in greater quantities and they, in turn, stimulate the output of testosterone, the hormone of desire.

For the majority of women, there's not a lot of change from perimenopause to menopause. Physical and emotional alterations are so gradual, the aging process barely seems an intrusion. Many women are liberated by menopause because at last all the booby-traps are sprung—with no more worries about bleeding or pregnancy, they can start to consider sex for its own sake.

When Sex Doesn't Feel Good—Problems with Desire, Arousal, and Dyspareunia

But for some women, things don't run smoothly. Within eight or ten years of their rediscovery of sexual pleasure, the body may take a unpredictable turn. They may suddenly find that they lack all desire for sex, or they can't get aroused, or have an orgasm, or they have dyspareunia, where sex is excruciatingly painful.

Some of the above-mentioned problems have to do with another hormonal riptide raging through the body. During the late forties or early fifties, the endocrine system goes into overdrive, trying to keep up the pace it has maintained throughout the perimenopause. But over the next few years, the higher FSH output can't stimulate the ovaries to make much estrogen at all.

After menopause, estrogen levels typically decrease to a fifth of those we had in our reproductive years. As a result, many women feel fatigued and exhausted a great deal of the time, which makes the idea of sex less appealing. The vaginal barrel narrows, no longer stimulated with an estrogen bath, and its lining becomes thinner and less elastic. This can make penetration difficult or painful, and the possibility of repeated uncomfortable sexual encounters reduces the frequency of pleasurable fantasies. If a woman anticipates pain every time she climbs into bed, it's not surprising that it becomes harder and harder to become aroused.

The Bartholin's glands, which kept the rugal folds of the vagina bathed in lubrication, simply don't produce as they used to, making sex an awfully dry run for some. Even when aroused, a woman's genital tissues—labia, clitoris, vagina, and uterus—don't have as much blood coursing through them, which can mean diminished sensation in the clitoris and labia, the breasts and nipples, and other areas that used to be highly erogenous. Consequently, sex may not feel as good as it used to. Although menopausal women are constantly worried about encroaching pounds of fat, they actually *lose* subcutaneous adipose tissue in the vulva, which also slows a woman's ability to lubricate and may also make the thrusting action of sex into an unpleasant battle rather than a harmonious dance.[4] And one more insult—the pubic hair starts to fall out. It's one thing to listen to your husband complain about his comb-over, but what can you do to replace your fluffy "bush"? The sparse look of the vulva is reminiscent of childhood—or extreme old age—a time when the genitals were open, exposed, and lacked the allure of a fur-covered mons.

The hot flashes and flushes of menopause, caused by a falling off in the temperature regulation managed by the hypothalamus, can make sex a draining affair, literally too hot to handle. Leaking urine during orgasm because of improper closing of the urethral sphincter, can make sex too embarrassing to attempt. Less elastic tissue around the clitoris and labia may become irritated or infected during sexual manipulation or penile thrusting. While relatively few women will have all these complaints, many experience at least one or two. With so many possibilities for these internal mechanisms to go haywire, about 40 to 60 percent of menopausal women[5] get sidetracked from sex, at least for a while.

There are many options these days to alter the female hormonal landscape, and they can make a positive difference (see chapter 8). The gold standard treatment for midlife women is hormone replacement therapy (HRT), a combination of natural or synthetic estrogen and progesterone (for those women with an intact uterus), which will protect the heart and bones as well as make arousal easier and sex feel more comfortable by adding back lubrication and elasticity to the tissues. Estrogen is an extraordinary multitasking hormone, which affects over three hundred tissues in the body. But progesterone, the counterbalancing hormone, which protects the lining of the uterus from overgrowing and becoming cancerous under the influence of estrogen, is a pharmaceutical double-edged sword.[6] The role of progesterone in breast cancer has been debated vehemently over the years. One recent study (1999), by the National Cancer Institute, of over 46,000 women suggests that progesterone may increase the risk of breast cancer after menopause. But then we have to ask, what's going to help and hurt the most? Of course, if you're thinking about sex, it's the estrogen component that is generally thought of as a benefit.

But here's the ironic twist. Good sex requires not just lack of pain and easy arousal, but also true desire. The combination product (Prempro) of estrogen and progesterone commonly prescribed for women with an intact uterus robs the body of testosterone. We need to *want* sex in order to have sex, and it is testosterone, the "hormone of desire" produced mostly in the adrenal glands, that helps to accomplish this goal. Most of the testosterone in our system travels through the blood attached to a protein known as sex hormone binding globulin (SHBG), leaving just a small percentage free in the blood. But estrogen stimulates the production of this protein, which effectively binds up most of the testosterone we've got. So an HRT regimen may make sex feel better physically but, at the same time, dull the libido.[7]

And testosterone bears another, even more crucial, role of retaining our zest to get out there and participate in life. The draining fatigue and exhaustion that so many complain of at menopause may have to do with a decline in this hormone, which starts slipping away in our mid-thirties, and for most, only becomes evident when we reach our fifties. If you're too tired even to think about sex, desire will plummet. As desire wanes, so does intimacy.

Testosterone output has an even more rapid descent, of course, if the ovaries are tampered with or removed. For those women who've undergone an oophorectomy (removal of the ovaries) or chemotherapy (which effectively knocks out ovarian function), the libido decreases from the day after surgery.[8] Even for women who've had a hysterectomy (removal of the uterus) with their ovaries left intact, hormone levels start to sink about three to six months post-surgery and never regain their former output. Since there are testosterone receptors in the breast, clitoris, and vagina, it's not surprising that less of this hormone would discourage sexual sensitivity in those areas. As we get older, we don't have as many receptors, nor do we produce the same number of enzymes that allow us to use testosterone on a cellular level.

A great deal of current research is devoted to this fascinating hormone, and many clinicians have gingerly started treating women with replacement testosterone. It won't regrow pubic hair, but it will restore vitality and oomph, which is a lot more important in bed. It is becoming increasingly clear that a great deal of what has been labeled "menopausal depression" may actually be a testosterone deficiency. Instead of plying women with anti-depressants (which may further diminish their libido), it might be advisable to try Estratest, a combination of estrogen and testosterone, or a replacement testosterone gel or cream. (See chapter 8 for a complete discussion of hormones and other medications that affect sexual response.)

The loss of desire makes some women enormously sad, while others claim it's "supposed to happen" this way. One interesting corollary of the feminist movement was that women finally woke up to the fact that they didn't need to be appreciated by men in order to appreciate themselves. "I waited forty years to think a good thought about myself," said one midlife woman, who had recently let her hair grow out to its natural silver and had taken up yoga. "I had such a perverse introduction to sex—by my step-father—and then I married at 19 to a man who totally loathed women and let me know it. After my divorce, I was celibate for so many years—nothing turned me on. It was only after a lot of therapy that I found out what I deserved, and what only I could provide. Suddenly, I was interested in mas-turbating, and my fantasy life revved up. Like Sleeping Beauty, I woke up when I discovered that I was the prince, as well as the princess."

Not wanting sex, of course, is more significant than not wanting a part-ner. Lonnie Barbach, a sex therapist and noted sex researcher, points out that turning off to sex may have little to do with sex and more to do with our rela-tionships or our changing feelings about ourselves as we age.[9] Desire is a very complicated matter, much more so than arousal. A woman who has plenty of testosterone in her system may be completely turned off to sex because she's angry with her partner, or because her mother just died. She may feel horny, but if she's been brought up to believe that it's not nice for older women to be sexy, she may well squelch all passion. But it can work the other way—she may be hormonally deficient and yet feel such intimacy and closeness with her partner that she may feel impelled to nibble his ear or buy herself some fancy new lingerie. A low sex drive, like a low car battery, can be charged. It's nor-mal, too, to feel abuzz with juices one day and to feel nothing the next.

Feeling nothing *all* the time, however, is depressing. That nunlike calm with nothing bubbling under the surface that may descend during the late for-ties or early fifties tends to make women feel less feminine and attractive, and can mar their sense of self-worth.

The Changing Body—Our Sexual Image at Midlife

Despite our best efforts to preserve that youthful glow, the body goes through its own metamorphosis over time, and this can be a thorny matter for a lot of people who never considered themselves vain. Many women in midlife view their own less-than-elastic skin, breasts, and belly as embarrassing, or at least unsexy. "I always liked my body, even though my hips were a little on the wide side," one 53-year-old woman told Judith. "But I turned around after putting on my underwear the other day, and I saw my mother—you know, the folds of skin lapping over the band of my bra. I eat right, I exercise daily, and I still have two little bellies, which just bugs me. Parts of me still look toned and muscular; parts of me are falling from grace. I guess when the whole thing looks one way it won't be so incongruous, but right now, I feel like that picture of Dorian Gray in the closet, ever so slightly changing—and not for the better."

If you can't stand in front of a mirror and accept your heavier or more wrinkled self, how can you show yourself to a partner? Can you still have a bedroom romp in the early morning or at lunchtime, or have you relegated sex to a darkened room at night? Are you self-conscious about love handles or cellulite, or the way the skin of your stomach, which seems more or less flat when you stand up straight, hangs in folds when you're straddling your partner? Suppose you've had a mastectomy, and can't bear the thought of showing off your altered chest? (See chapter 9 for a full discussion of the way that breast cancer can affect sexual response.)

Most of us have issues about our weight and looks, enlightened as we may think we are. We know, of course, that it's going to be harder to take off the three pounds we gained over the holidays, and what if we don't, and next year, we put on another three? What does this mean in terms of the way we view ourselves as sexual beings? We live in a society that makes a fetish of wasp waists and willowy limbs. Small is perfect; a little larger is suspect. And the truth of the matter is that the body allocates more of its fat stores abdominally as we age, which means that no matter what you do, you probably don't look the same even if you weigh the same after menopause. It's a good thing to weigh a little more in midlife, since the body is able to replace some of the estrogen it's losing by converting androstenedione, a substance produced by the ovaries and adrenals, into a weaker form of estrogen in the adipose tissue. This is easier when the body has a little more fat on it.

Some midlife women and their partners are finally acknowledging that fuller figures are fine—maybe more than fine. How refreshing it is to report that a group of philanthropic fund-raisers in a small village in England recently printed a midlife "cheesecake" calendar to raise money for leukemia research. These matrons, from 45 to 66, posed naked, wearing only hats and pearls, hoping to come up with $2,000 for their cause. Instead, their calendar sales topped $550,000.

Men were delighted to "see real women instead of stick insects with pouty lips and pipe cleaners for legs."[10]

The stereotype of the menopausal woman from our mother's day was the Edith Bunker character, a slave to her hormones, red-faced and moody, the last person in the world that anyone would think of as sexy. But these days, she is portrayed more accurately as a woman who knows what she wants and is finally old enough to go out and get it. The new crop of gray-haired models and actresses is testimony to the aging of the population—the older the very old get, the younger we seem in midlife.

The body in midlife doesn't change only on the outside. Sometimes there are also internal alterations. The most common of these is hysterectomy, the most performed surgery in the United States, which most typically takes place in midlife.

Hysterectomy: The Upside and Downside

Far too many hysterectomies are performed in this country every year (650,000, according to most sources). Women who complain a lot about their gynecological health to physicians, who are pressed for time, particularly poor women and women of color who may not have access to the best healthcare, are routinely encouraged to have this operation once they've passed menopause. It's just easier to cut out the offending organ than work with a patient on time-consuming and more expensive treatments that may or may not resolve her physical and medical problems.

But does that make this procedure wrong? Certainly not, if it's done out of medical necessity. For someone who has been in enormous pain or has been bleeding profusely and continually, or has had to contend with huge painful fibroids, removing the uterus makes good sense. It may also help to restore a woman's comfort level and interest in sex.

How does a hysterectomy affect a woman's feelings about herself? What impact does it have on her sexuality? Before answering these questions, let's take a step back and first consider the more drastic procedure—an oophorectomy—and what that does to the hormonal equilibrium. Excising both ovaries in one swipe removes the major testosterone-producing organs and quickly puts a woman into menopause, with all of its attendant signs and symptoms. In the past, nervous physicians who lived in dread of leaving in anything that might subsequently become cancerous recommended removal of the ovaries every time they performed a hysterectomy. In recent years, however, women have been making a stand to retain at least a piece of one ovary, which can keep the hormonal production going, albeit at a slower rate, and may ease the transition into menopause. And most miraculously, preserving even some ovarian tissue may mean that a woman who has not yet had children may be able to preserve her fertility. If you are a candidate for this surgery, you should make every effort to convince your physician to save any healthy tissue you may have.

The value of keeping the uterus, however, is not as apparent. It can become filled with fibroid tumors that may put too much pressure on the bladder, rectum, or vagina; it can become cancerous; it can bleed so profusely as to rob you of all strength; or it can collapse into the pelvic cavity. So is there any good reason to hold on to it if it's not functioning properly?

Once again, the question of hormones comes up. There is some evidence that hysterectomized women go through menopause about four years earlier than their sisters with intact uteri because removal of the uterus affects the blood supply to the ovaries, resulting in a decrease in hormones. This can potentially bring on premature bone loss and heart trouble.[11] If you've been having a difficult time with the classic symptoms of menopause—hot flashes and vaginal dryness, irritability, sudden bouts of depression—you may find that sex doesn't always seem as appealing.

But for many women, the change after hysterectomy is a positive one. Alan DeCherney, professor and chair of the Department of Obstetrics and Gynecology at UCLA Medical School, says, "I find that once women have recovered from the operation, they feel great and their sexuality improves, not because of libido changes, but because whatever problem they had is gone—fibroids or endometriosis or bleeding or pelvic pain." A woman's reaction also depends on how much she liked sex in the first place, before she started having uncontrollable symptoms. Needless to say, a big part of the equation is her relationship with her partner. The loss of an internal organ can't take the rap for a marriage gone sour.

Probably the most distressing part of gynecological surgery is not knowing what kind of reaction your body will have. According to Diane Hartmann, MD, assistant professor of obstetrics and gynecology at the University of Rochester, patients say that postoperative sexual concerns are a contributing factor to preoperative anxiety. The night before, you think about that organ inside, the one that maybe carried several babies to term, the one that bled monthly, letting you know that your reproductive system was chugging along, that everything was okay. It has always been a hidden participant in your sex life, and now they're taking it out and throwing it away.

To compound the problem, women don't get support from those who could give them the lowdown, if they cared enough or were less embarrassed about sex. More than 55 percent of respondents in a 1999 survey of 258 peri- and postmenopausal women said that their doctors *never* brought up the subject of sexual health, although 70 percent of those women wanted them to. And if physicians don't discuss this issue when the body is completely healthy, imagine how they clam up when there is disease present.

Hysterectomy can involve more than just the uterus. Does it matter if the cervix is removed as well? There is some evidence that retaining the cervix reduces the incidence of both leaking urine during sex and painful intercourse.[12] (Unless the cervix is diseased, it is no longer routinely removed, although once again, you have to be proactive and talk with your doctor about it—never leave it to his or her professional discretion.) Since the tenting of the uterus during sexual climax is less pronounced after menopause anyway, it may not affect women who weren't conscious of it before.

For those who have suffered for years from profuse, sometimes continual bleeding, a hysterectomy can restore and improve sexual relations. Over a thousand women who were followed for two years after their hysterectomies felt that sex was better—less pain, more frequency, more desire, more orgasms—after surgery than before it.[13] With a boost in general good health and less pain and bleeding, less concern about urinary incontinence, less anxiety about stained clothing and sheets, sex greatly improved for many women.

"I was really depressed when my doctor said he had to take the cervix and at least one ovary," said Pauline, a 53-year-old lawyer from New York. "I'd had years of awful sex, or no sex, because I was bleeding almost all the time, and I got anemic. After my divorce, I didn't date much—just buried myself in work. When push came to shove, the doctor said, 'Look, you can't wait any longer—let's do it now.' Anyhow, just around this time, I met this wonderful man, a guy in the music business. He was so much fun, and so different from my ex-husband, and did I ever desire him! I told the doctor he had to leave my vagina exactly the way it was, because I was going to be using it a lot. And as soon as I could make love, about six weeks after surgery, I did. We went at it slowly—lots of touching and teasing and oral sex. When we finally had intercourse, I felt a real difference—it was fabulous! All that worry about what sex would feel like without a uterus and a cervix . . . well, it was totally unnecessary. My body felt more whole than it ever had."

But for some women, none of this helps—not even an attentive and responsive partner. For many physical, emotional, even spiritual reasons, there are women who become more fatigued and anxious and have more limited physical function and less pleasure after the surgery. Granted, not every hysterectomy has the same good outcome as Pauline's—there may be scar tissue around the vaginal cuff, which means that this foreshortened organ may not accommodate the same sized penis as it did before, and penetration may be painful. Nerves have been severed that run through the uterovaginal plexus, which may negatively affect orgasms, especially if the cervix is removed. Then, too, the loss of estrogen after surgery may hasten menopause if it hasn't started already and cause vaginal dryness as well as a host of other symptoms, including fatigue, depression, and arthritis and other types of joint pain. The women with the most postoperative complaints seem to be those with the most preexisting health and sexual problems.

But women who like sex tend to keep liking it, even after surgery—they actually get more experimental and more communicative. And those who were never partial to it or had difficulties with their spouses say that it's not worth trying anymore, or that they do it only to keep their partner satisfied. There are women who never had orgasms prior to hysterectomy but had multiple orgasms afterward; and vice versa.

Of course, sex is not just a connection between nerves and flesh. For some women, in some cultures, the uterus is an icon of their femininity, and to lose it is to forfeit some essential part of what makes them female. This is particularly true of those who never had children and now won't be able to. You may know, rationally, that the uterus is simply a sack that holds a growing child—the ovaries are the organs responsible for fertility—but feelings about femininity are complex, and many grieve over the excision of this symbolic organ.

Mark Glasser, chief of obstetrics and gynecology at Kaiser Permanente in San Francisco, points out that the decision to have a hysterectomy may have deep roots in a woman's ethnic and cultural background. "In the South, there are four times the number of hysterectomies than in Marin County," he says. "Southern culture is steeped in family history—if a woman's mother or grandmother had a hysterectomy, and she's a possible candidate for the surgery, it's a lot more likely that she'll have one, too. But in this part of the country, women and their partners are very eager to keep their organs—in certain ethnic groups, a woman is less valued without a uterus." African-American women, who make up the backbone of a strongly matriarchal system, will usually protest that they don't want the surgery because they can't lose their "nature." Muslim and East Indian women, who are valued for their reproductive potential, will nearly always opt for myomectomy (an operation that removes fibroid tumors but leaves the uterus) or endometrial ablation (a procedure where the lining of the uterus is removed with a laser) rather than lose their precious childbearing organ.

Women who get an early diagnosis for cervical cancer do have an option, although the treatment, known as a radical trachelectomy, is still not performed by the majority of American surgeons. Pioneered a decade ago in France, the organ-sparing operation involves retracting the cervix by pulling it down through the vagina, cutting out the cancerous lesion, taking a sample from the surrounding tissue to confirm that it is disease-free, and stitching a pursestring suture around the cervix to tie off its opening to the uterus. Pregnancies that occur post-trachelectomy are high-risk because the cervix has been weakened by the trauma of surgery. However, 55 babies have been born to women who have been through this procedure. Since there have only been 300 trachelectomies performed worldwide as of this writing, and none of the women have passed their fifth-year anniversary of being cancer-free, the verdict is still out on the efficacy of the procedure.[14]

Of course, our sexuality is not dependent on our physical organs. We certainly don't need a uterus to be sexual. Getting along without it may be better or worse for you—it will certainly be different—and may give you the opportunity to redefine what it means to you to be a sexual woman.

Our image of ourselves is vital to feeling desire because it's like a boomerang—what you give out comes back to you.

The Harmony of Good Sex

"I never quite understood why my mother used to sing every Sunday morning but never any other time," said Olivia, who at 57 had been married for twenty-nine years. "She sure didn't have a great voice. Finally, when I graduated from high school, she and I went away for a weekend alone at the beach together and I asked her. She grinned and said it was because she and my father made love every Saturday night, and that never failed to make everything rosy for the next week. And I have to admit," she added with a grin, "that it's exactly the same with me. I know my husband's going to be in a better mood after sex, so I will be, too. Sometimes he buys me little things—silly presents that would mean something only to the two of us. And frankly, I think that's really a big reason that I still have sex with him. We enjoy each other more when we've been intimate, like two people sharing a secret no one else can guess at."

Many women are simply not as driven by their sexual appetite as men are, and particularly in midlife, when the body itself isn't as receptive, and when years of marriage have dulled the thrill, it's important for women to have another source of stimulation to make the physical act desirable. We used to think it took desire to trigger arousal, and if you weren't feeling overwhelmed with passion for your mate, your sex life was doomed. But Rosemary Basson, a professor in the faculty of medicine at the University of British Columbia, Canada, talks about the cycle that keeps women interested over the long run.[15] Intimacy is the key factor that spins the cycle of responsiveness.

To get the cycle started, first, they must to be willing to become aroused, and then they will seek out sexual cues that they might otherwise ignore. Once aroused, they will begin to feel desire, and desire, in turn, will lead to more emotional intimacy. There's real incentive to say yes to a sexual invitation or initiate sex themselves in order to keep intimacy going.

The cycle can break down at any point—if the couple has an argument, for example, those potentially rosy thoughts will turn black. Instead of fantasizing positive things about the man she wants to get close to, she'll spin off a series of antifantasies—*he's getting fat, he doesn't make as much money as I do, he repeats the same stupid stories twenty times*—that will stop sex in its tracks. The cycle may break because the woman is feeling depressed, she's overwhelmed with nonsexual distractions, or she allowed the "moment," when something warm and spontaneous might have occurred, to pass.

But if she expects that sex will increase communication and bring some reward, whether it's an occasional bouquet of flowers, an enthusiastic compliment, or more help around the house, she'll see to it that the cycle keeps going, in Basson's view. Because women are fixers. Just as they kept their finger on the emotional pulse of the relationship in their teens and early years of dating and marriage, so now they find it necessary to nurture—sometimes coddle—the relationship as it gets older and less frisky.

Of course, it's not all up to the woman. A lot of the ease or difficulty of tending the emotional and physical flames depends on the person who shares her sex life.

Partner Problems

The Beatles wanted to know if we would still need them—and feed them—when they were 64. Many midlife women find that they are doing more feeding than needing. It's hard to sustain passion over eight or ten years; even harder over twenty or thirty years. Can we really be everything to one partner for that long? You change, he or she changes, and suppose you're not going in the same direction?

In addition, midlife men are starting to discover the difference between fear and panic in the bedroom. Fear is the first time you can't get it up twice; panic is the second time you can't get it up once. If your husband is having erectile dysfunction, do you sigh and bear it? Do you rush him to the urologist for a Viagra prescription (see chapter 8), or do you stop having sex because it's too embarrassing and too much trouble?

Of course, even if you have a completely functional partner, it doesn't mean you're passionate about him or her. And for a great number of women in midlife, sex simply doesn't have the priority it used to. It is common for women who were not sexual self-starters, but who became aroused because their husband had an erection and desired them, to find that they no longer respond to the same triggers. One woman recalled that her husband's cue to have sex was to put his foot over hers in bed. Just the thought of what that meant—the remembrance of other times when he'd done the same thing and the expectation of what it would lead to this time, would make her wet and excited. But suddenly at midlife, his foot no longer started those colored lights going. And she was too anxious about hurting his feelings to tell him that she needed some other kind of foreplay.

Then, too, midlife is a time when a variety of health problems rear their heads, and doctors prescribe medication. Since most women marry men who are several years older, it is likely that their partners will begin to experience physical problems before they do themselves. A husband who is on antidepressants or heart or diabetes medication or going through cancer treatments may find that the drugs as well as his less-than-optimal physical state depress both his desire and performance. And if his wife is healthy and able, as most women in midlife are, she may find it extremely frustrating to want physical affection but have no outlet for it.

One of Sandra's patients, Melissa, at 49, a small dynamo of a woman with a smooth cap of gray-blond hair, expressed her dismay at her husband's diminished interest in sex. They'd be lying in bed together, and she would cuddle up close to him and start to kiss him, but he'd put her off with a comment about how tired he was and how early he had to get up the next morning. It was an excuse, but not an excuse. After all, lovemaking doesn't *have* to keep you up all night. Sandra asked what she thought was going on.

Melissa sighed. "It used to be the reverse. He used to want hot and heavy sex, and I used to want to talk and touch. Now I'm the passionate one, and I think this embarrasses him. He always had to be the leader."

"How long has this been happening?"

"Probably since my youngest child started going to school full days. I remember I was standing in the kitchen one morning feeling so . . . unencumbered. No play groups, no finger painting. I could do whatever I wanted. So I made tomato sauce from scratch. You know how you throw the tomatoes in boiling water, and in a few seconds, the skins shrivel up, and you can peel them right off? Well, I was just like that. I was ready. I was popping out of my old skin. Like I'd reached a stage in my life when everything had come together. The kids were on their own and so was I. It all clicked. Except Jack just didn't get it. We'd go to bed and I'd get all hot and bothered and he'd be talking about the water bill. I would want to do things that I'd read about in the magazines, like having him postpone his orgasm or maybe get in some new position, but I got so self-conscious, because he'd wonder where I learned that stuff. He's not cold or nasty or anything—he's always sweet, always so kind when he explains why he's too tired, or he's feeling under the weather."

"Does he have any medical problems?"

"He takes blood pressure pills, and he sees the chiropractor every week."

"And in bed . . . ?" The question hung in the air.

"Maybe once in a long while he has trouble. It's just that it's *always* a long while in between. He turns me down nearly every other time. And I mean, how many times can you get turned down by your own husband?"

She was clearly hurt—women assume that men are always ready for sex, so when the woman has to ask, it's humiliating. And when she's rejected a few times, she begins to think it's her fault, that she's not attractive, or not "good" in bed.

"So what would you like to do about it?"

Melissa sighed but didn't answer. Then she sank back in her chair, looking dreamily into space. "I want Jack to pay attention to me, to touch the back of my neck or my ankles and set me on fire. But how do I suggest that?" Sighing, she murmured, "You know, I really love my husband. . . ."

Then her face changed. "I have to get to Jack some way. I didn't used to, but now I need more. It's more than just being a woman with an itch—sex makes me think differently, be differently with other people I meet. Sometimes," her voice dropped to a whisper, "when I get in bed with Jack, I imagine there's another man there, too. That's really a great fantasy. I want Jack to come to therapy with me, because if I gave myself permission to change, then he can, too. Otherwise," she shook her head sadly, "I don't know about us. This is a trip I don't really want to take all by myself, you know?"

Melissa has just discovered what she's worth. She's old enough and sophisticated enough to stop agonizing over what sex is "supposed" to be like and to start imagining what place it could take in her life. She doesn't look to her childhood or the church or her husband or the sound bites on the news about better orgasms. She wants to rewrite the notes of the old standards and sing them whenever she wants to. She is also aware that her frustration in the bedroom is probably connected to problems that have nothing to do with sex. Over many years together, couples build up patterns of miscommunication or resentment or unresolved power struggles (including who initiates sex or what's appropriate to do in bed).[16]

Finding ways to be sexy together that aren't specifically physical—like learning massage or reading erotic stories or sharing fantasies or watching erotic videos—may all enhance the *idea* of sex (which for some, can be better than the actual thing!). Short-term therapy is clearly helpful to Melissa, and hopefully will be to her husband and to both of them as a couple, as well.

Women who don't have a clear notion of what to do about their love lives often close their eyes to moral dos and don'ts and allow the fantasy to become real. Another path that many midlife women have taken—some with guilt and some with self-justification—is an extramarital affair.

Extramarital Affairs . . . and Their Aftermath

If you've been in a marriage for several years, you know exactly what you have and what to expect. You and the person you wedded so long ago feel like one unit—you may even have come to look or sound a little like each other. There are the ties of family and finances. If you never had kids, there may be an even more focused bond between the two of you. It's the comfort of having that one person beside you in bed and at the table, the ease of uttering only part of a sentence and having it completely understood.

So why risk all that? Why have an affair? Clearly, some women are tempted by more than physical pleasure. They want an affirmation of the person who has been hiding inside for so many years, the one who saw a glimpse of delirious passion and put it aside, only to have it raise its head again and demand attention.

Can women today deal with sex without love? The anonymity of a one-night stand—someone you pick up at a bar or at a convention—is degrading to most women, yet an Internet or phone-sex relationship (see chapter 7) can be intriguing. And there are those few select women who say that they can have "just sex," the way men can when they find a regular partner who gives them total release without any other strings attached. But most women, when they stray, are usually looking for a relationship that's *more* emotionally fulfilling than the one they have at home.

Flirting is fun and it certainly makes us feel desirable and interesting. The question is, are we aware of when we cross the line from flirting to invitation? And once we've crossed it, can we turn back? Psychiatrist Stephen Levine points out that affairs put us at the brink of abandonment.[17] By taking this step, we could in fact lose everything we've worked so hard to accumulate over the years—the trust and closeness of husband, children, parents, and friends, not to mention the lover in question. The decision isn't always a logical, conscious choice to test the waters. It often feels like aliens have invaded the psyche, causing a perfectly normal, rational individual to cheat on her mate, even though she never would have considered it before. If things are getting stale or stagnant, maybe they need shaking up—the new lover may be a convenient repository for all those longings to make life new and exciting again.

"I love my husband and I like him, too, but that's not enough sometimes," Anitra said to Sandra in one of their therapy sessions. At 50, she had a 27-year marriage behind her, and four children, one of whom was just about to go to college and the rest in high school and junior high. "He's a wonderful person," she acknowledged, "but I never felt lust for him. Never looked at him and thought, Oh, I'd like to have sex tonight.

"Well, the big change in me happened six years ago. I met someone else, someone I was on a town committee with. I'd seen him around town for years, but that first night we sat together, I was on fire. I felt myself blushing—and, you know on me, it really sticks out with my Swedish complexion! I had butterflies and a rapid heart—all the classic infatuation stuff. I don't know where it came from. I was so overwhelmed that when he poured me a glass of water and I took it and our hands touched, I dropped it. Got water all over the two of us and the floor. What an idiot!"

"Did you think about having an affair that first night?" Sandra asked, seeing that even in telling the story, Anitra's color was high.

She shook her head. "He knew before I did. He teased me, and said something about now he knew what it would be like to take a bath together. Later in the week, fantasizing about him, I kept imagining the two of us in the tub. I had this need—I can't describe it any other way—to see him naked. I mean, for God's sake, he was married and I was married. I kept thinking there was someone else in my body doing this—it couldn't have been me. You know, as I got to know my lover . . . I'll call him Ed . . . I didn't really have the same respect for him as for my husband—I mean, clearly, his moral values aren't as strong as my husband's. James has extremely high ethical standards—maybe that's why he doesn't turn me on. He's very upright, and uptight."

Sandra asked about sex with Ed and how it was different from the physical experience she had with her husband.

"Like two different activities." Anitra laughed. "Making love with Ed was like dancing with Fred Astaire. I was good at it! I was creative and flexible and completely spontaneous. For the first time in my life I didn't feel inept in bed. Of course, James was the first and only man I'd ever slept with, and after a couple of afternoons in a motel with Ed, I understood that my husband wasn't a very good sex partner. You know, I'd never been attracted to my husband's genitals. I rarely looked at them. But I can't tell you how beautiful Ed's penis is. I loved touching it, and his balls. I loved putting them in my mouth. His mouth and his hands were so expert—I rarely have an orgasm with my husband, but I did all the time with Ed. The two of us could talk about sex. We could talk about everything and anything!"

"Like what?" Sandra asked.

"Oh, like how things feel and saying dirty words. I don't think I ever said anything like 'I want your cock inside me.' It sounds silly saying it here," she added, blushing again. "Because after all, it's not real."

"What do you mean?" Sandra decided to put her on the spot. There was a long silence. "It was a fantasy that I could have both. My husband and my lover, forever, whenever I wanted them. Sounds pretty immature. It's not right." She coughed and looked away. "But I wouldn't say it's wrong either." She sighed again. "Well, it ended. Both of us were just too nervous about someone finding out. We were sorry and not sorry, if you know what I mean."

Shortly after the breakup, Anitra's mother died and she went back to Sweden for the funeral. "I really felt like a stranger in a strange land. It was as though I'd been abandoned in the middle of nowhere without a map," she said. "All the lights had gone out."

In order not to fall apart, she worked on her marriage, spent more time with her children, and took up crewing. Rowing that shell every morning with eleven other strong women made her feel competent and successful—it also changed her body.

She was in wonderful shape physically, emotionally, and spiritually when she ran into Ed. "We saw each other and it was like it had never ended. All the longing, the curiosity, and the passion were still there." But when he asked her to start up the affair again, she turned him down.

"I wanted to, more than anything. I could taste him all over again, remember the feeling of his hands on me, and how I loved that feeling. It went completely against my instincts to say no. But one big thing had changed—I now have a 14-year-old daughter. I had never felt guilty about sex outside my marriage, and I still didn't. But now I had to be a sexual role model for my adolescent girl. I was exactly the same age my mom had been when she divorced my dad. So my history was pulling on me to make a choice. For me, in the present, I wanted that delirious, wild excitement I'd had with Ed all over again. For the young girl I had been, and for my child, I had to correct the past. So instead of indulging myself with an old fantasy, I masturbated a lot, and

I got my husband to make love with me in the car. He was dubious at first, but I think he actually enjoyed it, although I shocked him."

She paused a moment, then said. "I don't think I've hurt my marriage, and I think I may have helped it. Look at this top I'm wearing," she said, pointing to the neckline of a black sweater that crisscrossed her breasts, exposing a bit of cleavage. "I never would have shown off like this before—everything I owned had a high neckline. But loving to be touched gave me a whole other sense of what kind of fabric I wanted on my body, and how I wanted to look—it brought out a whole sensual side of me. I kept up the crewing, went to the gym and started working out; I stopped smoking. Really, a lot of amazing things happened because of my affair.

"You know what?" she exclaimed. "I like myself. When I was young, there were times when I thought I was too masculine, I didn't really feel like a woman. But now I do. I'm a different person now—I feel sad that for so many years I wasn't really myself when I was doing all those things in my marriage just to please James, not because I enjoyed them. I'm so much more assertive because I had that affair and I learned to speak up for what I wanted. That's the side of me that was there all along and I was afraid to let out."

There is a stage beyond the discovery of erotic potential, and that is the one where the woman assumes responsibility for her own pleasure and takes it past mere gratification. Anitra knew what the affair meant to her, and how it might affect the rest of her life, and she was able to reconstruct the puzzle out of her new self-awareness and self-worth.

Anitra's new determination to stand up for herself—to live where she wants, to dress as she likes, and to be the daring new person who has recently emerged—may yet improve her married life. And her husband appears to be titillated by her self-confidence, if not yet quite comfortable with it. "He better come around," she told me. "I've decided to give my marriage four more years and see how things go. I want to start working again, and have a financial base of my own, just in case things don't work out between us. But I really hope they will."

Because of the slow burn in women's sexual trajectory, it takes a long time for some to wake up in bed and figure out what sex means to them. The closeted maenad with Bacchanalian tendencies can tear off her cloak of responsibility and guilt and learn exactly what she needs to do to howl at the moon. Women take longer to mature sexually because they are so aware of the risks—and it takes time to appreciate the costs as well as well as the prizes.

Taking Different Paths: Lesbians at Midlife

The older lesbian population has been growing steadily over the last two decades as society slowly but surely makes it easier to be gay, at least in urban America. Celebrities like k.d. lang, Melissa Etheridge, and Ellen DeGeneres made coming out into a daring and wonderful act. Much popular culture celebrates the look, the sound, and the edgy attitude of lesbian women. In the real world, however, lesbians are still ostracized, persecuted (think of the two women killed on the Appalachian Trail not long ago), and reviled.

There are currently lots of midlife women who have lived together for decades as "roommates" who are finally out. Two women going through menopause together typically have fewer problems, because they each relate to the hot flashes, palpitations, or whatever symptoms they may share, and have undoubtedly always used vaginal moisturizers and lubricants as part of love play. Ellen Cole's study of midlife lesbians indicates that because the nature of power in the relationship is more equal than in most heterosexual pairs, both women commonly experience a stronger identification and integration of their personalities.[18]

Being intimate with other women (or one other woman, which is more to the point) is a small piece of what it means to be a lesbian. "My identity is gay," one woman said to Sandra. "Sometimes that means I want sex; sometimes not. When I met my partner, I was so relieved to feel I could trust her. With women, trust has been a focal point of being with whom I chose to be. Really, a decision to spend my life with women had to do with communication—less to do with sex than with trusting."

Some women identify themselves as lesbians, but never make love to a woman. Others call themselves heterosexual or bisexual, but cohabit with a woman. In midlife, this may be even more pertinent because the older generation of women who make love to women have lived with such a long legacy of homophobia that it may be hard to admit, once and for all, that they carry the banner for other women who have made hard choices. Many say they know, within an instant of meeting a heterosexual, whether it's safe to be out—they're not going to take chances of being rejected or abused.

For many lesbian women, midlife is simply the crest at the top of the hill. They had a vague idea of who they were in early childhood; they came out in college or just afterward, and they've spent a good deal of time consolidating their feelings about themselves and their current partners. They are not at a stage where their identity can coalesce and regroup.

The interesting thing about midlife—whether we are gay or straight—is that we all start growing toward the middle—the most feminine among us become a little more masculine; the more masculine allow their feminine side to emerge. This type of healthy androgyny gives midlife women the edge—having fulfilled their nurturing roles as wife, mother, and caregiver to an elderly parent, they are now ready to develop more assertive and self-promoting qualities that may entice them to explore pleasure and the deeper elements of their sexuality as they never have before.

What Lies Ahead?

Women now live one-third of their lives past menopause, which means that the road ahead is long and filled with possibility. The divergent tracks of midlife sexuality—dropping the ball or learning new ways to carry it—may not be quite as far apart as they might seem. It's okay to love sex one day and be cool to it the next. When we can accept that, we have acknowledged that sex isn't an act; it's *what we are,* which means that it's changing all the time. Wouldn't it be grand if we could tolerate days of abstinence and shrug off less than exciting orgasms because we still possessed the expectation that captivating passion was just around the corner?

Sex is not simple, as must be quite apparent by now, and it tends to become more volatile the older we get. We may go through periods where fantasy crumbles into dust and the most devastating invitation leaves us cold. And yet, one spring morning, we may wake from a dream feeling wet and desirous and reach between our own legs or across the bed to our partner to recharge the cycle of intimacy.

It can change again, dying down and flaring up with the turn of the seasons or the particular mood we're in. The older we get, the more vital it is that we never close our eyes to the potential that our sexuality offers us when we allow it to inform our entire lives, not just those hours spent in the bedroom.

6

THE WOMAN IN HIGHLIFE:
STILL SEXY AFTER ALL THESE YEARS

In the cult movie *Harold and Maude,* a young boy falls in love with an ancient woman. Their ages don't matter at all—the discrepancy in years becomes inconsequential as the story proceeds. But this woman, played by a 70-something Ruth Gordon with all the verve of a young sex goddess, is a spur to the rather dull kid to start looking at life so that he can wake up to himself. Maude receives Harold's "engagement ring," which she then promptly tosses into a lake, "so I'll always know where it is." She's dotty and canny, and his love for her touches her but doesn't affect her plans to commit suicide on her eightieth birthday. When you're that old, you have priorities that come before sex. (We don't actually see them coupling; we see only a love-struck Harold, blowing bubbles toward his sleeping beauty in the morning light.)

Maude is Harold's tour guide through life. Her position as mentor and guide wouldn't be considered unusual in many cultures, where an older woman always indoctrinated a boy in the ways of the world. The idea of a love tutor, of course, is to prepare a man properly so that when he takes a bride, he'll know just what to do to please his wife. Maude has a huge appetite for the sensual—she is wild about sunflowers and delights in the taste and look and smell of food. She loves driving fast and feeling the wind in her hair. She, like many women of her age, is more interested in the relationship than in physical satisfaction. And like many women currently in their seventies and eighties, she is her own person, unmoved by what others want of her, undaunted in her zeal to attain her goals.

Her sexuality, however, is never much of an issue. Why don't we get to see the main characters making love? Because the viewing public couldn't take it. In real life, society sees wacky old ladies as sexless, and the idea of matching 20- and 80-year-old genitals on-screen would be considered by most to be bizarre, even repellent. Elderly people acting sexual have broken a sacred commandment—*Thou shalt not do it, or even think about it anymore.*

As recently as the 1960s, even Masters and Johnson, the doyens of healthy sex, didn't condone "eldersex." (Remember that Virginia Johnson was a good deal younger than her mentor and colleague, with whom she had a sexual relationship.) In their landmark work, *The Human Sexual Response,* they write about how difficult it is for a healthy older woman to get her physically unfit mate to participate in bed, and add, "It is also *obvious* that extramarital sexual partners essentially are unavailable to the women in this age group."[1] (Italics ours.) That type of youthful enthusiasm and derring-do in highlife (our word for the stage that follows midlife) is still suspect in an older woman, although we condescendingly applaud it. Isn't Maude fabulous to be in such great physical, mental, and emotional condition? Wouldn't we all like to be just like her when we're her age? But she decides to end her life at its zenith instead of waiting, as most of us do, for a slow, steady decline.

Truth be told, the body at 70 or 80 isn't what it used to be. The aging process often robs us of our vitality and physical well-being. Incontinence, which may develop for any number of reasons, makes sex embarrassing and uncomfortable. General fatigue and depression may add additional burdens to the increasing load. It's harder to do any physical activity, including sex, when you feel ill or disabled.

Thankfully, more and more of us are aging really well, and don't see signs of debilitation until our eighties or nineties. Obviously, there are a lot of benefits to healthy aging. The hormonal changes of menopause typically come to an end by the early sixties, which means that the body begins to find its own equilibrium. The hot flashes and palpitations die down, and though the short-term memory loss may not magically desist, long-term memory usually improves. Vaginal atrophy has usually stabilized, and those women who have been on hormone replacement therapy for a decade may not have much more trouble with arousal now than they did ten years ago. Masters and Johnson found that women from 50 to 70 masturbated more than they used to[2]— could this be because they found that it was easier to come to orgasm the longer they persevered or because in the absence of a partner, they were determined to continue being sexual?

Arousal and orgasm become a journey— even the woman who has little difficulty in lubricating will take a good deal longer to get where she's going. As one clinician explains it, sex when you're younger is like downhill skiing— you get towed up to the top of this mountain and then, whoosh, you come straight down. But sex when you're older is like cross-country skiing. You get to take your time, see the scenery. It takes time to enjoy yourself, but in highlife, you've got a lot of time. You may be retired, or at least not tied to any schedule, and you can make love whenever you choose. A male partner of this age will take an hour to respond to Viagra, but while waiting for him to have an erection, anything goes. It takes a lot longer when you're 60, 70, or 80 to become aroused and lubricated, and it may take an hour or more to come. And orgasm is no longer as crucial to many at it used to be—the sensations, smells, tastes, and warmth of sex may be valued more than the physical release of climaxing. Because the tissues are far more delicate, a gentle touch is paramount, particularly if lovemaking is going to continue for a while. Yet another good reason for sex to become more than just physical—a couple can achieve new levels of intimacy.

Then there's the matter of desire, which can be problematic at any age. Women over 65 are three times as likely as men to be widowed, and if there's nobody around to get your juice flowing, desire may ebb. An interested and interesting partner is harder to find. For every one hundred women over 65, there are only seventy-seven men, so competition is keen.[3] Women in America typically live alone for eleven years after the death of a spouse, but that may span the remainder of their lives. Some of these women remain in their own homes, some choose independent living facilities, some move in with family or a close female friend, and some move into assisted living or long-term care facilities.[4] The stories in retirement communities are legend about the older women who "rush" a recent widower, plying him with casseroles and cakes, eager to nab a likely candidate who might offer companionship, chauffeuring services, and maybe a warm and warming bed.

Women in their seventies and eighties have lower testosterone and DHEA levels than their younger sisters,[5] which means that "desire" may stand for something other than the instinctive urge to couple. When asked about fantasy, sexual dreams, and masturbation, older women are usually reticent to confess to what they may very well feel. But libido can be quite active, even in extreme old age.

"My mother hadn't been herself in so many years," Jessica, 69, told me, "so she wasn't really aware when we had to make the choice for a nursing home when she was 93. She was a frail, delicate woman from another country who was 40 when, by mistake, she had me—she'd grown up in England in the Victorian era. She was always so proper—never talked about sex to me or my sisters. Anyway, when we moved her to the home, it was all I could do to visit. I couldn't stand the place—it was so cold, so functional. So I paid to have a massage therapist come in and give her a treatment once a week. It made the most amazing change in her.

"One day, when I was sitting with her, she started singing. 'I'm tired of living alone; I want a young man of my own/ A man to undress me/ A man to caress me/ I'm tired of living alone.' I don't know where this ditty came from—it was probably some old 1890s popular tune. But getting touched regularly had awakened something in my mother, something that literally made her want to sing."

Desire is evidently generated in more ways than simple androgen output, and a woman who feels deeply, either because she is in a committed relationship or because she has found a kernel of excitement in her own soul, is going to feel like a sexual being, no matter her age.

What Do We Know About Highlife Sexuality?

There are few statistics and very little hard evidence about highlife sex—few sexologists have been bold enough to ask this population about sex, other than Starr and Weiner,[6] two researchers who studied individuals (age 69 to 91) in 1981 and Bretschneider and McCoy,[7] who looked at 80- to 102-year-olds in nursing homes in 1986. So the most current information comes from surveys by the AARP and the National Council on Aging. The AARP asked one thousand of their members—all over 50, but who knows how much older than that—to answer a simple survey in 1999.[8] The results were heartening: About 60 percent of this primarily healthy and active group were satisfied with their sex lives; 18 percent said they felt that they would challenge the statistics for their age group. A full 61 percent said that sex was as good or better than when they were younger—and 70 percent had sex at least once a week. Even if they had been without a partner for years, they could instantaneously spark new desire and feel psychologically and emotionally ready to be sexual when an appropriate lover came on the scene. Thirty-four percent said that their sex life was bland to nonexistent, mostly due to illness, loss of a partner, side effects of medications, or treatments such as dialysis or chemotherapy that robbed the respondents of energy and enthusiasm. Many of the latter group also had no private place to be sexual, since they had moved in with relatives or were institutionalized (a smaller portion). Bottom line: There might have been a slowing of sexual frequency and behavior, but not of appetite.

Of course there are also older women who want nothing more to do with sex and can't see what the fuss is about. (They never could when they were younger, but felt obliged to pretend.) If sex before highlife gained them little self-esteem, if it was embarrassing or painful or stressful, either physically or emotionally, they might be quite comfortable with abstinence, whether they had a partner or not. The authors of this book are obviously biased toward encouraging women to remain sexual throughout every stage of life, but not wanting a sex life is not necessarily an unhealthy choice. Affection need not be physical to be meaningful, and many women prefer to use their final years to grow and change in ways that have nothing to do with sexuality.

Sex in highlife depends to a great extent on the earlier foundations you've built. A woman who has always adored her body and her partner and felt that intimacy is her birthright isn't going to retire her sexuality. This sexual freedom and blossoming on either end of the lifespan is a symbol of the new wave of acceptance of types of intimacy that used to be forbidden or avoided. The ancient religions—Tantric and Taoist traditions of India and China, the South Pacific islanders, and the Native Americans—teach that sexuality promotes longevity and the longer you continue being sexual, the longer you'll live. What seems to be more to the point for women in our society is that once they allow themselves the freedom to be sexual all the time, they have more reason to take good care of themselves so that they can enjoy every facet of life.

You know when you encounter an 90-year-old who is vital and alive that the flapper she used to be in the Roaring Twenties is in there somewhere, waiting to get loose. "I have a lot of wrinkles," one woman said, "and he has a lot of wrinkles, but we can't see them so well, because our eyesight isn't so good. But we can sure feel our way around."

A New Perspective on "Old"

If you ask a group of 50-year-old women if they can see themselves having sex at 80, most will make a joke about it. "I'd sleep with my husband when I'm 80, but then he'll be 82, oh God. You couldn't give him enough Viagra!" Another said, "There aren't any men to have sex with when you're 80. If they're still alive, all they want is for you to take care of them. Even if they still had the urge, you'd be afraid they'd have a heart attack and die. Unless you can find a younger man, what do you do?"

But if you ask 65- to 75-year-olds, those who will talk about sex are quite comfortable with the idea of continuing the practice until death. This is because women in highlife are annoyed that others see them as sexless just because of their age. "I am constantly infuriated by the assumption people make that there is a kind of watershed after which you are old. I don't feel old unless I am sick, or hungover a little, like I am today,"[9] said a woman who had lived long enough to have strong opinions and not be afraid to express them.

We make it hard for the elderly to see themselves as sexy. The body of an 80-year-old is constantly desexualized in our society—and indeed, how often do we get to see one? A turn-of-the-millennium gallery exhibit in New York City of photographs of extremely old nude women by Manabu Yamanaka was more shocking than the supposedly blasphemous elephant-dung Madonna on display at the Brooklyn Museum. The skin of the subjects in these pictures is mottled, a map of wrinkles that makes it hard to decipher exactly what part of the body you're looking at. The women are bent over, their bones prominent, their breasts hanging to the pelvis. They smile at the camera, gap-mouthed, toothless, perfectly happy to be seen just as they are, in all their imperfection and simplicity. Yet a *New York Times* reviewer described these women as "aggressively naked," and said that some viewers found the photos too disturbing to look at.[10]

Judith once took a vacation in a seaside town in Mexico that was frequented by elderly German tourists. The women in their sixties and seventies were topless, as they were at home, although the Midwestern couples in the next cabana nearly choked on their margaritas when they saw that ample, unrestrained flesh. Their wide-eyed stares seemed to scream, *Those lewd old bags! Where do they get off exposing themselves?* Let's cover up the wrinkles and age spots, lest they should remind us that we, too, are growing old and approaching, ever so slowly, the time when flesh matters not at all.

But it does matter until we breathe our last, and as a matter of fact, paying attention to the sight and smell and touch of the body can normalize sexuality and lessen our fears about what old age presages. It is also important to remember that even if intercourse is no longer desired or possible, there are dozens of other methods of being intimate, and women may start exploring them only when other avenues are cut off.

Thinking Back, Living Forward

The group of women in highlife encompass a wide span of history. Those in their late sixties came to sexual maturity and motherhood in the 1950s, when falsies and girdles to restrain the body mimicked the coyness and fake orgasms that would "trap" a man and make him roll over and propose. It is difficult to imagine a more repressive atmosphere for learning about the delights of the flesh and spirit and the importance of women's autonomy in bed and elsewhere.

"Sex was dangerous," Eileen, a recent widow of 66, told Judith. "My mother let it be known that one could not ever touch—if you did, you'd be a runaway train out of control. Never spend time alone with boys, she said, although I did and she caught me and I was grounded for days. Several of the popular girls at school had to drop out because they got pregnant, and I was determined that wouldn't happen to me. So my husband was my first and only lover, and we consummated our relationship only after we were married. It was a relief to know that nothing awful would happen, but I didn't have orgasms, and he had no idea how to please me. Also, he refused to use condoms and I knew nothing about birth control, so I always associated sex with baby-making. It was okay, but we were Catholic and we did have eight children—which is really excessive!" she laughed.

"Sex wasn't much good until the kids were mostly grown. I was really bored, and he sort of liked the idea of having an adventure, so we decided to try a few new things—that summer, when the kids stayed with his sister in New Hampshire, we ran around the house after each other; we got some videos; we put up a mirror in the bedroom. That period lasted quite a few years, until my menopause, when I kind of lost interest. Then he had his heart attack, and for a while, I was a caregiver, and the sex got put on a back burner. It's hard to think of a man as a stud when he's winded or napping all the time. But he got well after rehab, and slowly, sex started getting good again, although we didn't have intercourse that often. My husband couldn't perform like he used to, he needed time in between to recharge. But then he'd get on a kick where we'd make love at night and the next morning when we got up. Then it was a long time in between, but that was okay. The frequency was less but the enjoyment was the same. You know," she said, a flush coming over her face, "I really miss him.

"I talk to other women who are without a man, like me, and find a lot of them don't think they need sex at all. I know one whose husband died long ago; she enjoyed it but they slept in twin beds, which I think is weird. It's difficult for me not to have sex—I miss the closeness, giving pleasure to someone, it's like you're whole, in a way. Everything came together when you were so close to one another."

Eileen is aware that her chances of meeting a man her age are not good, but occasional masturbation and fantasy fill the gap for her right now. A woman with traditional values and a foursquare view of sex, she cannot imagine herself with a younger man. This might not be as difficult if she had been born a decade earlier. Some of the women who grew up during World War II had more extensive sexual experience and are more frank and open than their younger sisters, possibly because many of them came into their own when the men were overseas and they had a brief period of freedom from their traditional roles. Women in their seventies who enjoyed sex and are still sexual tend to be less fearful of what's rightfully theirs.

Beni, born in New York to German-Jewish parents, is 72. Like Eileen, she was brought up to believe that sex was dirty. "I saw my mother's rubber thing in the bathroom one day, and she nearly blew a gasket. My sister and I would talk about what it was for, but I don't think we really figured it out other than it had something to do with sex. I did masturbate, although I don't think I ever had an orgasm, but I was a senior in high school before I actually made out with a boy. Naturally, my parents had let me know in no uncertain terms that I would marry a Jew, so I guess I thought that sex would be okay if the person I was involved with was Jewish and it might lead to marriage. So one night at this country club, this guy asked me to dance. We ended up necking and then he took me outside and started fingering me. It was wonderful! I really didn't want him touching my breasts, though—I was one of those kids who thought if I didn't look like Mae West, I should jump out a window.

"I went to NYU and lived at home. One day, my freshman year, my mom and my aunt took me shopping, and this Hollywood star was in the aisle with us. Well, my aunt got his autograph, and we started talking and he invited us to see his show at the Copacabana that night. During intermission, he invited me backstage and he asked me out to lunch the next day. So I'll cut to the chase—the lunch was in his suite at the Waldorf, and within two minutes of my stepping through the door, we were in bed. He had an enormous penis—it probably hurt a lot, I don't remember—and after he penetrated me, there was all this blood. Of course he was horrified to realize I'd been a virgin, and he looked really scared that maybe I wasn't as old as I'd said I was.

"But then he started making love to me again, and as sex goes, he really knew what he was doing—I couldn't fully appreciate it at the time. He said I was beautiful, how much he loved my ass . . . he said things I'd never heard, and frankly, never did from either of my husbands, because most men are completely tongue-tied in bed. He said it was great to touch me, and he'd name all my body parts and show me what to do to him. He had me suck his penis and he'd kind of coach: 'longer, gentler, rub it, lick it, use your hand like this.' It was so erotic. Then the phone rang, and it was his wife, calling from Hollywood. I lay there, frozen, but he had no trouble touching me and talking to her at the same time. Afterward, when I asked how he did that, he laughed and said they were two separate things.

"My life got totally skewed wrong because I was so sex-crazy, and men liked that about me. So my first husband—he was a sex machine—we had intercourse on the third date, which was really soon in those days. He was seventeen years older than me, very nasty, very controlling, but he was terrific in bed, and that's why I said yes, but I can't tell you why I stayed with him for sixteen years, except that in those days, you felt it wouldn't be fair to the kids to divorce. I had several affairs, one with a neighbor who was so kind and sweet that I thought, I don't have to stay here—there are other ways to live my life. And finally, I got out. It was scary to be on my own, but I did that for a while—I was so lonely, I did nutsy things, like have sex with a workman who came to the house.

"Then I started seeing a therapist, and really got my head straight, so that when I met my second husband, I was ready for a grown-up relationship. He's a sweet, caring, sensitive man, and we worked at marriage, and have been for the past seventeen years. He's not as sexual as I am, and we used to fight about that, also because we had so much time, with no kids at home and no particular job to go to. It would have been nice to just get in bed after lunch and stay for a while. I'm the kind of person who can separate sex and love . . . I like *lust,* like to play—to my husband it's a big deal serious thing. Anyway, age has slowed me down—in the last ten years, I find it's not so terrible to do without. If it's a choice, say, between going out for a bike ride or staying in bed and making love, well, biking might be just as fun.

"I have to say that I don't like not feeling as much like a sexual person—it ties into my appearance. I mean, I can still hold my own with makeup on, and I'm not out of shape. But the closer I get to being elevator music, the less significant it is in my life. I have fantasies; I go to this ballroom-dancing class and flirt. I even have a guy who likes to have phone sex with me every once in a while. Mostly he's just a friend. I admire his drive—he's older than me but he thinks I'm the greatest. I have a feeling that he'd be too nervous about performance to actually suggest we do it, but it's safe for both of us on the phone. And it's good for my ego, too. The best thing about sex is the aliveness of it, with every nerve-ending tingling and experiencing sensations of being present with what you're doing, it's all working at one time."

Beni's sadness over the changes of aging echoes the sentiment of many women her age, although in her case, it didn't become so uncomfortable that it turned her against sex. As long as you have your health, as our Jewish grandmothers would have said, you have everything. In highlife, it just takes you longer to get it.

The Healthy Elderly

Beni and Eileen are robust, healthy, involved women, and they're not unique, by any means. The more we know about aging, the more infirmities and disabilities we can probably prevent or at least reduce. But a great deal of the aging process is apparently luck. Will you want sex if you have no partner? Will you go out and join volunteer organizations and go on Elder Hostels and take up tai chi just for the purpose of meeting a new guy? What will it feel like to date at 70 or 80?

For one thing, many older women tell me it's nice to lose your self-consciousness about your body. At last, you have to say, what you see is what you get. So you have a big rear end and a mastectomy. So you take out your bridge at night and put it in a glass. The body becomes less a temple than a factory—as long as all systems are pumping out product, you don't need to renovate.

Dr. Robert Butler, a gerontologist who is an internationally acclaimed expert on aging and sexuality, is optimistic about the possibilities for intimacy and closeness as we age. "We need a broader definition of sexuality," he told Judith. "There are many reasons for wanting to be sexual, including friendship, security, and safety. It's comforting to have another person to look after you. But if a woman marries an older man, she might wind up as a caregiver, not a sexy job."[11] This means, for many women in highlife, that it may be better not to commit yourself quite as thoroughly as you might have done some years earlier.

Cohabitation or two separate dwellings makes a lot of sense, because marriage over the age of 65 comes with lots of problems—joint tax returns cost more; your pension and Social Security don't necessarily benefit your partner if you die, and the kids from former marriages get jittery about their inheritance. Also, how do you heal from the grief of losing the person you spent a third or even half your life with? It may not be as much grief as it is familiarity—that was the person you knew better than the back of your hand, and he's not around anymore, so nothing feels right.

Then all you have to do is get over the guilt. For women born in the 1920s or 1930s, who may have had limited or no sexual experience before marriage, the idea of feeling excited again may be quite upsetting. If you grew up believing that there was no justification for sex without first, true love, and then, a desire for children, you may be stumped as to what these new feelings are and how to go about mediating them. You like this guy, or maybe you even like two and spend some time with each. Is this playing the field? Are you fast and loose? Suppose you are more sexually attracted to these new suitors than you ever were to your lifelong partner, the father of your children? For a generation who let the man make all the moves, the heady liberation of initiating or overtly enjoying sex can be a shocker. How do you get over the feeling that you're cheating, even if your spouse is dead?

Maybe you won't, and your new delight in being assertive, even doing what you consider *bad,* will add an edge to the new relationship. It can be a wonderful boon to your ego to find that not one but several people are very interested in spending time with you, and it doesn't matter whether the interest is sexual or personal or social. Many women in highlife find that they like themselves, their bodies, and their minds, better than they ever did.

Butler sees a new tolerance for alternate lifestyles among the elderly—it's no longer shocking for a woman to have more than one partner (though she may live alone in her own home), or have no partner, and instead, rely on groups of friends for social contact, and use masturbation, flirtation, massage, and physical exercise for physical and sexual release.

This is, he says, a sign of wisdom on the part of women, not to get stuck with a guy who statistically is more apt to become a burden.

"I like living with myself," Amy told me over a cup of coffee one afternoon. She is 73, living in the house she and her late husband, Ed, bought thirty-five years ago. "I never want to marry again or even live with a man. Wash his socks and cook his meals just to have a warm body beside me! It doesn't make sense." She served as caregiver until her husband had to be moved to a long-term care facility, and now, she wants to meet some new men, but on her own terms. Nor is she interested in hanging around the house waiting for her daughter to ask her to baby-sit—she doesn't want to work full time, but she enjoys her part-time receptionist position at a local museum, which leaves her free to take long weekends if she wants to go away, or sleep late in the mornings if her arthritis is bothering her.

"My kids want me to sell the house and move to one of those leisure villages, the kind where you have your own independent-living unit to start with, but if you need it, you can step up to an assisted-living facility, and then, for those who really want to stick around even when they're decrepit, the nursing home. So depressing to see those tired 90-year-old babies being pushed around in wheelchairs and fed like they were infants. That is not for me. I'll find a way to get out before that happens."

As to her sexual prospects, she is rational and lucid. "Sex with most men my age doesn't appeal to me because they're all so performance-oriented and I'd probably have to spend most of my time making *him* feel good. Also, there's a big new incidence of HIV in old men, because with the Viagra and all, they've been feeling their oats and visiting prostitutes. I can't imagine having a discussion about using condoms at my age! So I've been making do by masturbating, although I can't climax that way. The only time I can come now is when I have a massage, if a person I don't know is touching my lower back and legs. It's so pleasant and relaxing. I'm not aware of any particular fantasy— I just go with the moment and then, very quietly, I come. I don't think the massage therapists, all female, ever notice.

"I do go to singles nights at the senior center and concerts and card night, and there are dances sometimes. Ed and I used to go dancing a lot and I adore that—it's really sexy, especially if you get a partner who knows how to lead. Dancing is almost as good as sex."

We tend to think that our options narrow the older we get—we can't move as fast, see as far, or make love long into the night. On the other hand, the healthy elderly may have imaginative solutions to old problems and find that they enjoy themselves enormously, although they may not be setting any records for erotic Olympics. What they want—the release, the relaxation, the companionship—is theirs for the taking.

Sexual with Courage

Betty Dodson is now 70 years old. She came to the forefront of the field of human sexuality at least three decades ago, when she spoke up passionately about the importance of self-pleasuring. After years of a conventional marriage with once-a-month sex, she broke out at 35 and experimented wildly with men and women, but mostly, with herself. By her fifties, she was famous for being an iconoclastic masturbation coach, and for spending time helping women to move, to breathe, to make sounds as they discovered their genitals and the power they could give themselves. She found penetrative intercourse uncomfortable after menopause, and spent ten happy years without having anything other than a finger, a tongue, or a small dildo inside her vagina and an electric vibrator on her clitoris. By 65, she needed two hip replacements, but now at 70, she has turned another corner and boasts a 25-year-old male lover. They like to have sex every other day. "He'd like it every day, but I have to leave some energy for my creative work," she laughs. "So he fills in with masturbation."

Will the real Harold and Maude please stand up? What does a 70-year-old woman see in this young lover? "It's wonderful, refreshing, and I get to wield all my power," Dodson says. "He's an assistant, an apprentice, a passionate lover, and he says he sees my soul and my beauty when he looks at me, rather than my wrinkles. After all, I'm giving him years of invaluable sexual knowledge from all the work I've done. Think of all the older women who could share their experience with a gorgeous young man. But most women," she sighs, "don't know shit from sex at 70."

Dodson's therapeutic practice involves helping women to take charge of their own sexuality, and she sees women of all ages, including those in their sixties and seventies whose husbands are worried that they're not having enough fun in bed and want them to enjoy themselves. Her sessions are conducted with a vibrator and her own design for a vaginal barbell that's used for penetration. She watches the women stimulate themselves and then coaches them to loosen up, let go, laugh, and breathe. "Most women come to see me because they're tired of not having orgasms and pleasure during sex. They are ready to take charge of their own sexuality."

There is a lot of prejudice against masturbation—we are supposed to put away childish things when we become adults, and self-pleasuring is, for most of us, the first sexual experience. Those who continue doing it when partnered often won't confess it, and it is the rare couple who will share masturbation as part of their lovemaking. And yet, for all the bad press the activity has received, we know that it's safe, it releases tension, it can fill our days and nights with a sense of well-being, and for elderly women, it affords a great many physical benefits, keeping the genitals lubricated and elastic and encouraging hormone production. It also enhances proprioception, the ability to feel our body—we get a better idea when we touch ourselves how to touch others.

In a similar fashion, self- and partnered massage can take the place of sex or make it more enjoyable. Getting to rub and stroke and slap and knead the muscles, tendons, and joints may seem a small thing, but when those body parts are sore or painful, the more we touch, the better. Massage is one of the oldest therapeutic techniques around—Jesus Christ was a firm believer in the laying on of hands to encourage physical as well as spiritual balancing. By working on the body in this way, you can relax muscles, reduce tension, release toxins from the lymphatic system, promote better sleep, and make the recipient (and incidentally, the giver) feel cared for and nurtured. The sexual organs, of course, become more friable with age, and a delicate hand moisturized by oil or lotion is necessary.

One of the interesting things about massage is that you can't assist the person who's giving it to you. If you try, the techniques fail. The more you remain passive, the more you yield to the comfort of those healing hands, the more you gain. Now, of course, sex isn't usually like this—think of all the performance anxiety you can feel with a partner, or the frustration when you're not receiving what you think you want. But with massage, it's all there for you. When you allow yourself to lie back, put yourself in someone else's charge, and let go, you can receive the true spirit of sexuality. The hands and fingers, even the elbows, knees, feet, and toes, can become instruments of enormous pleasure.

Lesbians in Highlife

By the time you're an "old dyke," in the parlance of the lesbian community, you'd better have accepted yourself. Having been accustomed to betrayals, to failures, to ostracism in one way or another throughout the lifespan, it may be easier to deal with the losses that naturally come with aging. Two women who have shared a good part of their lives together know the drill—they are attuned to each other's changes, and possibly more flexible than straights about the roles that they may have to play. "When Jill got cancer at 55, I couldn't imagine how we'd get through it," said Evelyn, now 70. "She was the major breadwinner, first of all, and she was the big organizer around the house. She was terrified of dying and leaving me penniless, because of course I wouldn't get her pension the way I would have if we had that man-woman-marriage thing going. I was just terrified of her dying. Somehow she got through chemo and radiation and we got matching buzz-cuts, which was kind of fun. Sex went out the window, and we'd been really wild in our younger years. I missed it at first, and then I was too busy to miss it. As long as I could hold her, that was the important thing. Who needs more than one breast, anyway? She's beautiful, just the way she is."

Having a partner in our old age is something that most of us aspire to. But many lesbians and bisexuals are alone by the time they reach highlife. Although plenty of young lesbians are now having kids, that's not true of the last generation, who may not be fortunate enough to have anyone to take care of them or even help them make decisions in the last years of their lives. They may have no pension and no insurance (making it difficult or impossible to secure adequate health care with understanding practitioners).

The loneliness of the older woman who may not have any resources at her disposal can be somewhat mitigated by new types of "families" that are springing up in lesbian communities. Just as gay men bonded together through the AIDS crisis (when many of their birth family disowned them), so women have also created extended communities where they can socialize and network. From the days of the Stonewall uprising in New York's Greenwich Village in 1969, it became apparent that there was strength in numbers. And like their male counterparts, lesbian feminists banded together in the 1970s and 1980s, creating formal and informal structures and resources that the group could rely on.

If you are a heterosexual and you arrive in any urban center in the United States, you'll get the official Chamber of Commerce publicity, with flyers directing you to sights, events, restaurants, and hotels. But if you have "gay-dar," you'll go out on your own, seeking the bookstores, theaters, clubs, and community centers that have become the foundation of that city's LGBT (lesbian-gay-bi-transgendered) underground. This is still harder for older lesbians and bisexuals, who may suffer from their own form of ostracism, based on their age. Narrow-casting even further, you need to find an older gay population to hang with, not just a gay population.

There are very few organizations dedicated to social support and services for elderly gays and lesbians—places to direct them to appropriate healthcare, food stamps, and legal services, as well as a comfortable environment where they can be surrounded by their peers and be assisted by counselors who know what their needs are. In New York City, there is SAGE (Senior Action in a Gay Environment); in San Francisco, there is GLOE (Gay and Lesbian Outreach to Elders); and you can also find social services if you live in Fort Lauderdale, Palm Beach, Minneapolis, Buffalo, Ottawa, and a few cities in Rhode Island and Massachusetts—otherwise the pickings are slim, especially if you live in the suburbs or in rural locations. For the most part, elderly lesbians are on their own. Some of them may never come out of the closet.

Women of this age group commonly passed as straight most of their lives, living in the shadows of their true orientation, and didn't care to come out until they were past retirement because knowledge of their secret might have endangered their job and/or pension. But many older lesbians tell us that after a divorce or the death of a spouse, it feels like the right time—time to let your own children know who you are, and to affirm your identity to your own self. Time to lead an open life as a lesbian, even if you're 60, 70, or 80, claiming your sexuality fully at last.

Where Do Women Go When They Get Old?

If we could only track the moment when it happens. One day, we are caring for young children and our own parents, and then, in a blink, the world is topsy-turvy. The kids are grown, back in the house (sometimes with children of their own), then thankfully, out of the house. We retire from the job; we lose a spouse. And suddenly, no one can see us anymore. Those who belong to the invisible brigade of women may play a mean game of tennis, volunteer at the hospital, cook up a storm, but they are not the first, or even the fifth, invited to an exclusive dinner party (unless they're very wealthy, of course). When does the changeover occur?

Ruth, a widow of 68, lives by herself in the house she and her husband bought in the 1950s. She is in good health, actively involved in her community, a great reader, and she takes a weekly yoga class with a couple of good friends. She has a boyfriend, Sam, who spends about half the week at her house—and she spends one or two nights a week at his. Her kids are slightly ashamed of this—Ruth once overheard her daughter explaining to her grandchildren that Sam's car was in Grandma's driveway a lot because it was hard to find parking in his condo complex.

One day, while trying to chop her car out of the ice, Ruth slips and falls, breaking a hip. Since her bones are not as dense as they once were, it takes a long time for her to heal sufficiently to be on her own. She can't climb the stairs in her house, so she moves into the spare bedroom in the home of her daughter and son-in-law. Because it's harder for her to be active, she puts on weight. Her children persuade her to sell her house, and although this depresses her greatly, she feels she has no choice. Although Sam tries to persuade her that she'll be good as new in just a few months, she has a hard time seeing beyond the next doctor's appointment. Bereft of privacy, arguing about independence, she and Sam drift apart. She is no longer as concerned about her clothes and makeup, and stops thinking of herself as an attractive, sexy woman. After all, no one tickles her feet anymore, or licks her eyelids, the way Sam did.

How many women go through this transformation? To switch places with your children, who now are the decision-makers, despite your best efforts. To sense their uneasiness when you and your boyfriend hold hands or kiss. To be dropped off at a day-care center once your eyes are too bad for driving, just as you did with your kids when they were 2 or 3. Although you are more mature, self-actualized, and wiser than ever, you are whisked back to childhood, so that you can be safe and "taken care of." To be robbed of your possessions, your environment, your health, and your dignity all at once is numbing. It's not hard to see that sexuality would vanish at a very fast clip under these circumstances.

A life of one's own becomes more difficult to salvage if you have any debilitating condition. Illness and disability are the enemies of sex, as are the medications that accompany them. Many drugs that are the staples of highlife can dampen the libido and wreak havoc with performance. A woman who is on antidepressants, antipsychotics, antihypertensives, chemotherapeutic drugs, or even antihistamines may feel she is swimming upstream when trying to feel aroused or have an orgasm. In addition, many older women abuse alcohol to assuage loneliness—a sure prescription for a damaged libido.

When you're ill, it's hard enough to feel pleasure in general—pleasure from a sunset, a good meal, or a windfall check in the mail—let alone feel sexual pleasure. If you have cancer, a good many of your waking moments may circle around how long you will live, and what your family will do without you. The treatments are time-consuming and exhausting, and if you've lost an organ—a breast or bladder or vulva—how can you begin to feel whole when you're clearly not? Heart disease leaves you breathless and, perhaps, terrified that too much exertion in bed will bring on a heart attack. Although your doctor may have told you that you can safely make love as soon as you can climb two flights of stairs, you may not want to try. And what about arthritis, which cripples and deforms the body in painful ways? And then there's incontinence, where you blush to admit that you need a rubber pad on your mattress, just in case. Your embarrassment about mixing excretory function with lovemaking is compounded if you have an ostomy; you have to worry about cleaning the stoma and doing all the unhitching and reattaching after the act.

Sex takes more work, it's true, although it's really the independence factor that's more crucial. A hospital bed or a wheelchair won't squelch sexual

interest, if you can shut and lock your door. But for women who are completely dependent on a caregiver, the road is rougher.

Disabled and Still Sexual

Older women sit in wheelchairs for a variety of reasons. Of the 40 million
women over 50 in the United States, 15 million have some disability, and it
has an impact on their sexuality—just how much depends on the attitude of
the woman, but also on her particular problem. These individuals tend to
have increased joint pain, spasticity, incontinence, weakness, or immobility. If
you can't even open your legs wide enough for a pelvic exam, you can't relate
to a *Joy of Sex* vision of what it means to make love.[12]

Being a free sexual woman entails a certain amount of personal freedom,
and if you're disabled, you have less and less of that. You may travel the world
in the wheelchair or need two canes to get up one step. Anatomical mis-
alignment may put a great deal of pressure on the bladder and rectum, and
you develop more perineal infections than other women. Many disabilities are
tied to problems with the connective tissue of the body, which means that
lubrication is lacking at any age, and becomes even less abundant at
menopause. Women who are tied to a chair typically have the cardiac problems of any very sedentary individual—they may be obese, short of breath,
suffering from a rapid heartbeat or great temperature irregularity.

Disability, of course, is not an illness, and if a woman has been able to get
appropriate medical and occupational attention, she is one up on the game. "I
find it really interesting to make love now," one former athlete who'd been
injured in a car crash and had been in a chair for thirty years told me. "You
have to do things you never did before—you do it in the chair, you do it
doggy-style, you do it side to side. We got some great big body pillows and
use them as support anywhere and everywhere. I love it when my partner and
I take a bath together, or exchange massages—it's so much more intimate than
it used to be. People see me and I know they think I don't do it anymore, but
actually, sexual exchange is more frequent now than it was, even though we
don't have intercourse very often."

Some disabled women say that it may take longer, and they may have to
take analgesics or select a time of day when they're in the least amount of pain,
and that they may not feel as much in certain areas but feel more in others.
Arousal causes muscles to relax, which means that sex can reduce the spasticity so common in disabling conditions. Certain studies of patients with crip-
pling arthritis report that orgasm offers up to six hours without pain after the
erotic event is over—it may be a placebo effect, caused by the sense of well-
being that sex confers, but who's quarreling, when it means feeling more at
ease and more comfortable?

Mastery and Sexuality

Where will we be if we live to extreme old age? (The number of centenarians grows apace—a recent estimate is that a third of those infants born in 2000 will live to their hundredth birthdays.) More and more of us will be on our own, although there will be those who end up in long-term-care facilities or nursing homes. And these days, even the institutions are changing their policies as more of their clients are demanding conjugal rights. There are enlightened nursing homes that allow conjugal visits and cohabitation, even when the parties are not married, although many residences separate couples either because the medical or psychological condition of one partner is upsetting to the other or because the children (who pay the bills) feel it's inappropriate for Mom to sleep with her new boyfriend.

Of course, the problem of whether you're allowed to be sexual never comes up if you can stay independent. Being old and healthy means that you live an autonomous life—you don't need other people to tell you what to do and you trust yourself more, both physically and mentally.

Erik Erikson created a model of the stages of man as a sequence of challenges, the last one being ego integrity versus despair.[13] Those adults who have really matured can look beyond themselves—they don't see their petty accomplishments or lack thereof as the beginning and end of the world; rather, they can integrate all the things they've been with what they've become and resolve to make the most of the results. They have a sense of the dignity of their own life; they can renounce the various dreams that they cannot fulfill, and this ultimately provides them with a type of wisdom that only the very old who've been around for many decades can achieve. Erikson saw the most evolved elderly as accepting of their lives, able to deal with death, and having a uniquely spiritual view of the universe.

Erikson's worldview offers a wider perspective on sexuality. If there is no partner to share ecstasy with, or the body is in too much pain to experience it solo, what do you do? The act of sex—the purposeful grasping at desire or arousal or orgasm, may fade into a kind of pleasant oblivion. But the meaning and feeling of sex may shine brighter as new options present themselves. True mastery of sexuality may take us beyond the body. A master, after all, doesn't need the extras—the candlelight and massage oils, the sweet whispers in the ear—because she already has the motivation and wisdom to create her own pleasure.

There is a woman named Anna Wilmot who, at the age of 102, lives alone by the edge of a pond in western Massachusetts. When interviewed on National Public Radio, she described her life as quiet, perfectly delightful. In winter, she would watch the birds flying over the frozen water; in summer, she would go skinny-dipping.

"Really!" the young reporter fairly chirped.

"Sure," Ms. Wilmot told her, laughing. "I wait for nightfall and watch out to make sure none of those fishermen are around, and then I take everything off and go splashing in. It's my way of reminding myself who I am. It's the best."

Here is a woman who ventures out under cover of darkness, not caring about her fragile bones or her wrinkled flesh or what anyone else might think of her if they knew her secret. She loves the sound of the crickets, the earthy smell of the mud beneath her toes. She loves the feel of the water moving over her legs, gentle as any lover who had ever touched her. She has learned how to give herself pleasure and isn't afraid to take it all in. She is closer to ecstasy, after ten decades of life, than most of us can hope to be.

Maybe, when we're masters, we won't need to hope for sex. It will be there, part of us, without our even trying.

PART II

GIVING YOURSELF PERMISSION FOR MORE AND BETTER SEX

"My grandma was never naked," laughed Evangeline, a 68-year-old retired schoolteacher. "She raised me on the homestead that's been in my family since the Civil War, and she was a proper Southern lady. My sister and I slept in the loft over her bedroom. When it was time to go to sleep, she'd throw her flannel nightgown over her head like a tent, and I'd watch her busy under there, taking things off, until she had a pile of clothes and underthings on the floor. In the morning, she'd reverse the process. She bathed in the kitchen bathtub in her underwear. She told me that Grandpa and her had never seen each other undressed—that it wasn't proper. Can you imagine! That woman had six babies, and lived with her husband for fifty-three years, and she was never naked!"

Evangeline had a knowing look on her face as she went on. "There was no way I could escape that kind of indoctrination. In my first marriage, I was so ashamed of my body and sex. I remember being thankful for the steam fogging up the bathroom mirror so I didn't have to look when I got out of the shower and could just throw a towel around myself. I'd jump into bed before my husband every night and turn the lights off. We always made love in the dark. And I was very, very quiet. I didn't make a peep, even when I climaxed. It was 'nice' sex, you know, familiar, like a worn pair of pajamas.

"So after my husband died, it really didn't occur to me that I would ever be intimate with another man. Then, after I'd been alone for about eight years, a friend introduced me to Joe, and over our courtship, I felt like I woke up. Joe was the most physical person, never aggressive, never pushy, but he touched my hand or my shoulder, and it would send me reeling! I started seeing myself through his eyes. He thinks I'm just the greatest thing, and he loves to look at me. And so I took off my clothes and made love when it was light out. I'd been brought up to believe that only 'bad girls' showed off, or made a spectacle of themselves, but I didn't feel 'bad' at all. I felt entitled to open up something that had been walled off inside me for so long. I guess what I felt about sex had been right for me at one time, but now it was different. It wasn't that sex was bad or good, or that I was good or bad. It was like thinking I would fall off the edge of the world and finding out that it was round."

Being naked is being vulnerable, exposed. It means revealing yourself, leaving yourself open for judgment, open to experience. You have to like yourself to bare your breasts and your soul, and this process can take years.

The truth is, most of us grew up with Evangeline's dichotomy: Sex was either clean or dirty, right or wrong, sacred or profane, too much or too little. This dualism has kept us from feeling comfortable with the fact that we are not one thing or another, but in fact, a broad range of sexual possibility. We may start out our sexual life in a kind of figurative missionary position *(I may be boring, but at least I'm probably normal)* and end up as a sexual pioneer, daring to be dominant, in charge of our feelings and behavior, and realize that that's normal, too. The old convention, that sex is split between the two poles of romance and lust, may be relevant at one stage of development, but as we boomerang back and forth from one to the other, we get glimpses of the huge range of choices in between. And they begin to look more and more appealing as we give ourselves permission to think differently about sex.

Just as women experience menstrual and reproductive cycles, so we also experience cycles of new romance and breakup, birth and motherhood, grief and loss. Running though all of these is a sexual cycle where interest and desire appear and disappear wearing different disguises. The sex life we've got right now isn't necessarily the only one available, nor is it likely to be the one we'll accept indefinitely. Thanks to birth control, increased economic and social freedom for women, better access to improved medical care and greater longevity, every woman has the potential to be anything at all—to assume one role, put it down, and take up another—over and over throughout her life-span without committing to just one. We may be ravenous for sex, constantly fantasizing and seeking out a partner, and then, with a change of circumstances, such as having a baby or losing a spouse, we may drop the sexual spark completely. Then, as we grow a little, perhaps caught up in an Internet affair or enthralled with a cosmetic change in our face or body, the urge may return again, with greater or lesser force than before. We may lie dormant for years, ignoring hormones and fantasies, or simmer at a slow boil, or bubble over. The more fluid, the more aware we can be of this continuum, the more we will be able to take advantage of new opportunities or think differently about our current options, and the result will be a different—and often improved—sex life.

Our society provides few ways to think about sex—it is treated either as a health concern or a recreational diversion. There is little discussion or celebration of marital or long-term partnered sex. Most times, once we're ensconced in stable relationships, we don't prioritize this activity—work, school, children, eating, and sleeping come first. We don't have any celebration that respects our interest in sexuality, as the ancient and tribal communities did when they devised puberty rites and initiations. But if you value sex, if you make it a potent force in your life, and if you realize that you always have the option to change your mind, draw back, turn around, and start again, you will, like Evangeline, find that the world is round, and that naked is perfectly okay.

Making Sex a Priority: Reclaim Your Desire

If you don't like what's going on in your sex life right now—or if you have no sex life—it's time to take a deep breath and do something about it. Of course, you have to *want* to change, and that's the goal of this part of the book. It's time to think about sex differently, and about your own pleasure, so that you can get the sex you want. It's time to invite sex to take center stage and give it permission to perform brilliantly. In order to tempt you to do this, we will give you concrete ideas and specific suggestions to pique an interest that you thought wasn't even there or couldn't be resurrected. If you're the type of woman who passively waits for things to happen to her, we suggest adopting a more proactive approach. If you think you have run out of ways for making that quick half an hour between the sheets once a week personally satisfying, take heart. Make sex a priority, and it *will* get better. When you're thinking about it, and you sincerely believe in your ability to become a more sexual woman, you'll become stimulated enough to take steps to improve what's going on both inside you and with your partner.

Decide right now that you're going to reclaim desire, or create it anew, if you never owned it before. Understand that you *can* make your sex life better, more interesting, more engaging, and part of the fabric of your life.

How do you do this? In the pages that follow, we offer a gamut of ideas, skills, and cutting-edge technology, as well as some good old common sense. Some of the ideas you'll find here are easily accessible; others may require considerable time and effort. If you are truly motivated to be a sexual woman, you won't stop with the playful suggestions offered in most sex manuals. While they're fun to contemplate, and you may enjoy them once or twice, they won't make a lasting difference in your life if that's all you do. You need to go further, to try out a variety of new options until you hit on ones that work for you—that challenge, extend, and expand your view of yourself and your sexuality.

We want, first, to give you *permission* to think about options you've never considered before. Then, we want to give you *information*. You may be surprised to find that some old myths or fears you had are based in error, and once you have the true story, you can proceed differently. Next, we'll give you *specific suggestions* that we'd like you to try out, first alone, and then with a partner. Some will seem relatively easy and comfortable; others will require a leap of faith. If it doesn't feel good, all you do is stop and go on to something else. Finally, we'll talk about *therapy*. Therapy helps women reclaim—or claim for the first time—their own right to be sexual and to realize that they are entitled to pleasure. If none of the ideas we've offered is working, it's possible that you are dealing with some old, unresolved issues. A professional can be a guide to lead you through the dark forest and into the light.

We're about to offer you a varied menu of options in the hope that you'll try them all and then settle on the ones that fit you best. Will you try out a sex toy, or an escapade on the Internet? Will you experiment with a drug that might make you feel more intensely or get you aroused more quickly, or will you actually consider changing your body with hormones or surgery? Will you experiment with reading sexy stories or more explicit erotica, or will you play with fantasy and take on different roles in the bedroom?

Society is in a lot of flux and turmoil about what's "right" or "appropriate." We see women in power, but we also see them used as sexual fodder for the advertising industry. We see women holding hands and kissing on the street, but we also fear that our Supreme Court judges might revoke our right to freedom of choice. As more social barricades are toppled, we have more plasticity in terms of the roads we take—but it's up to us to put on our walking shoes and start exploring them. We don't have to find one magic bullet to affect our sexuality—we can and should mix and match ideas and therapies. We don't have to be exclusively homosexual or heterosexual or monogamous or polygamous or sex-loving or sex-avoiding—there are dozens of shades in between. The 50-year-old who danced at Woodstock and the 20-year-old with multiple piercings grow closer in their sexual metamorphoses.

Look at the options we're offering in this half of the book. You can turn on to the world of cyberspace, which allows for any and every permutation of sexual expression; you can delve into a treasure trove of pharmaceuticals. You can have your body altered with surgery; you can alter your mind with meditation or mindfulness. You can also expand your sexual being into a sacred practice with skills and beliefs that have been around for centuries.

Thousands of years ago, women worshipped goddesses who were the idealized icons of their own power. Today, that power is within each of us. All women, if they choose to do so, can select from a sexual smorgasbord of partners, objects, activities, and feelings. When we are confident enough to turn sex from work into play, the sacred and the profane aspects of it can come together as one. Take a look at the choices we offer you and **try something—*anything*—you haven't considered before.** The challenge to get the sex you want is ongoing, and that's a great thing.

CYBERSEX:
VIRTUALLY TURNED ON

When you log on to the Internet from the office or the privacy of your bedroom, you are in good company. Fully 70 percent of Americans have used the Net at some time during their lives, over half are online regularly at work, and 43 percent have Internet access at home. Some intrepid explorers are connected 24/7 with DSL (digital subscriber line) service, which serves as a permanent tether to the information highway. If you're looking for a date, if you're looking for others with the same sexual interests, or if you simply want a question answered about a sensitive subject, this is the place to go.

A recent study at Stanford University posits that the more time we spend on the Net, the less time we spend with *real* human beings[1] (italics ours). Of course, our definition of "real" is very fuzzy in cyberspace. If what we want from sexuality is a sense of instant communication that spans space and time and offers us pleasure that is immediate and ever-present, it's readily available online.

If you have lived a sheltered life, possibly marrying your high school or college sweetheart, with little or no opportunity to investigate the wide world of sexual options, the Internet may be the place to go to expand your horizons. Even if you consider yourself comfortable with what you know about yourself sexually, the Internet provides both a safe and provocative way to go a little farther—to see what else turns you on, gets your juices flowing, or triggers some new and exciting fantasies.

The Web can be an important medium for exploring your sexuality safely and securely. If you can't stand the way you look, or feel too awkward and reluctant to hunt for a partner in RL (in real life, in cyberspeak), you may succeed brilliantly in VL (virtual life) on the Net, where you'll be valued for your facility with words and your mental agility. Instead of being judged instantly by your appearance, occupation, or age, you will be valued online for your sense of humor, your perceptiveness, and most important perhaps, your ability to abandon yourself to the moment and share hidden aspects of your personality.

One of Sandra's patients, Laura, was terribly shy. She'd had a congenital endocrine condition, dwarfism, that never allowed her to grow and, at three feet tall, very well endowed, she said that physically, she "felt like a freak." Laura had been abused by a piano teacher when she was a child, so sex had never really appealed to her as an adult, and she was phobic about traditional social situations, like parties or community meetings. "I worked in an office and went home," she said, "and my sex life was, well, let's say on a scale of one to ten, it was a zero. When I started moving around the Net to find people, it was with the thought that I was interested in women, but I didn't want anyone to see me, looking the way I did.

"My passion is books, and I found a couple of lesbian chat rooms devoted to literature. It was like a new world exploded in front of me, and it was all mine. Women really talked to each other—they were passionate about what they read and what they said. I didn't say anything at first, but when one woman who called herself Buddachild posted on a bulletin board, I answered her post and told her some of my ideas. So we got friendly that way, and finally, I felt brave enough to talk to her when she was online. Eventually, we put each other on our buddy lists and arranged a private chat. That was the beginning of our online affair—and it was incredibly wonderful."

The Internet can serve as an equalizer for women—by going into chat rooms, answering a post on a bulletin board, or responding to a sexy email, you get to initiate or direct an online relationship. If you are house- or wheelchair-bound, you can travel easily in cyberspace to locations and sites otherwise closed to you. You have control without risk—at least as long as you keep the relationship on the screen. There is no danger of pregnancy, rape, or STDs with an online acquaintance—if you protect your anonymity. Online, you can find others like yourself, people you can talk to and listen to, allowing you to feel that you're not alone on earth. The Internet offers you potential—and that in itself is a positive thing.

SURFING

Navigating the Net—Learning the Basics

Whether you are a total newbie or are completely familiar with many aspects of the Internet, it's important to know what you're doing when you explore sexually online so that you don't feel frustrated or embarrassed or get yourself into difficult or compromising situations. What we'll do in this chapter is take you through the four major avenues of sexual exploration—*surfing, shopping, chatting,* and *dating*—and lead you, step by step, through each one so that you can navigate swiftly and surely in this brave new cyber-world.

If you come across sites in your netsex investigations that turn you off or depress you or make you cringe, if you find yourself "flamed" (yelled at, belittled, or insulted) by someone in a chat room who disagrees with your ideas or behaves toward you in a hostile manner, you don't have to take it. Remember, a computer is a machine. You can always turn it off.

But can it allow others to track your movements? Everyone is paranoid about getting discovered when they're looking for sex online. Suppose your sister sits down at your computer and accidentally sees that you've been surfing in a bondage and discipline room, or your husband discovers your latest message to an online sexual friend. It's essential that you learn how to take precautions so that this won't happen.

When you start out to explore the Internet for sexual resources and stimulation, you have to decide which area you want to explore first. It might be best to start by accessing information on topics that interest you, where you feel that there are gaps in your education. To find information on sexuality, start with a search engine (e.g., www.google.com or www.excite.com) and be as specific as possible in your search words. Instead of just asking for "sex," you might want to look at "female orgasm," or "anal intercourse." Be sure you put quotations around your key words so that you don't get a million sites for each word you've written. The search sites usually provide some information on what can be found on the sites they list, which means you can figure out pretty quickly whether pornography is a highlight of this site.

Remember, though, that the Internet is a vast, unregulated arena with no rules. If you want to be very sure you won't run into any triple-X links, stick with the tamer women's sites, such as www.ivillage.com, www.thriveonline.com, or www.oxygen.com. (See Resources page 270, for more like this.)

If you get more adventuresome and start surfing away from the tried-and-true women's health and sexuality sections of the Web, you may run into pornography sites. If you do happen to log on to something you find seamy and off-putting, close all Internet windows you have opened by clicking the X in the upper right-hand corner of your screen. Then simply reopen your Web browser and continue.

If you're surfing around some particularly exotic areas, you'll want to think about the cookies that get deposited on your machine. A "cookie," an adorable name for a not-so-adorable phenomenon, is a little piece of code that the sender uses to determine when you've signed on to a site. He then can figure your service provider, operating system, browser type, and the server you were on last. Cookies can be used to store information about where you go online, so companies can put up specialized ads that they think will appeal to you. If you're wandering around sex sites a lot, you can imagine what type of ads you'll get!

If you want to see the current cookies you've accepted, simply type "JavaScript:alert" (document.cookie) into the address bar when you are logged on to a site. You can also choose to find out whether you're getting cookies in advance. In IE (Internet Explorer), go to the View Menu, then click "Options," then go to Advanced and click on "Warn Before Accepting Cookies." This is slightly cumbersome, since you'll constantly get warning messages, but you can also go back and disable this function if you don't like it.

You can also allow the cookies to come thick and fast, and then cleanse your system of them on a regular basis. In IE, on the C drive, go to Windows, Temporary Internet Files, click on the main folders, go to Edit and click on "Select All," go to File and click on "Delete." In Netscape, you will find a file—or do a search for it if it's not apparent—called cookies.txt (or magic-cookie on the Mac). You can delete the entire contents of this file—pay no attention to the warning you get. After the file is empty, save it and set its attributes to Read-only, Hidden, and System. When you exit Netscape, all the cookies will clear out.

Don't want anyone else to see where you've been exploring? You may also wish to clean out your history as well as your cookies, particularly important if you have cyber-savvy children or a parent or partner who might not approve of your exploration. Before you sign off for the day, either press Ctrl H or go to the History window on your browser and select all, then delete (on most systems, using your right mouse). Clear out as many weeks as you have been fooling around online.

Finally, use common sense. Don't access porn sites if you're not prepared for the crotch-shots and often degrading pictures of women in gory and explicit detail. Don't accept email from anyone you don't know. Just click on it, hold it down, and drag it to the trash. Don't respond to any junk mail you get, and don't respond to opportunities to "unsubscribe" from the site sending you the junk mail—that just opens the door for them to send you more junk. Once again, click, hold, drag, and trash it.

Dealing with Guilt or Discomfort About Online Sexual Exploration

While surfing the Internet provides lots of opportunities for losing your inhibitions and for experimenting in ways you might not in real life, it can also cause discomfort and anxiety. Sandra has many women in her practice who have been startled and upset by becoming aroused by images, descriptions, and stories that they find intellectually or psychologically objectionable. They become threatened and anxious by discovering that they are turned on by pictures of women with huge breasts or women spread-eagled on beds or hung from hooks, or stories of women being ravaged by groups of men.

Jennifer, who had been overpowered and raped when she was 19, had repeated fantasies long after her abuse about being turned on by forceful, even degrading, sex. She checked out some of the sites that pictured women being forcibly restrained, and it threw her into a tailspin. She became aroused looking at these images, and her reaction was to shut down sexually. "I always assumed that what I needed to get turned on was candles and romance, loving words and gentle caresses," she said. "I couldn't believe that I actually got wet by looking at aggressive, explicit, and violent pictures. I found it upsetting and frightening." It took her a year of therapy to help her accept that the fantasies were a way of coping with her rape, rather than a genuine wish to be violated.

Sandra had another patient, Mary, who was always told by her mother to "cover up." She had always undressed in the dark and was shocked by the thought of showing off her genitals, even to her husband. And yet, when she started roaming the Net, she found women who had posted their amateur porn shots. At first, she was horrified, but found that she kept coming back to look at these pictures. One day, she explored some sites that sell sex toys and costumes and started imagining herself in a leather G-string and collar. Sandra asked her, if she actually ordered them, would she wear them? She told her she wasn't sure, and yet, within a month, with a click of a mouse, she had herself an outfit that would have worked nicely in a *Penthouse* or *Hustler* spread. She hasn't yet worn the clothing for an encounter with her husband, but she's thinking about it. Whether this will enhance or diminish her feelings of attractiveness and desirability is entirely dependent on her own self-confidence and sense of autonomy.

Another rather conservative heterosexual patient found herself turned on by a photo of two Asian women kissing. She wondered if, deep down, *she* might be gay. It took some convincing to reassure her that it was normal to respond sexually to beautiful bodies doing sexual things.

Cyberspace affords you the chance to explore and realize your most private fantasies, but it does not supply a barometer for how to interpret them. You may find that you feel ashamed of becoming aroused by something you've always considered wrong or repugnant. Then again, you may look at these forbidden acts and decide *This is something I'd never do in real life, but it does reflect some aspect of myself—I don't have to be afraid of my fantasies, and I can decide how I want to use them.* By accepting the inherent contradictions in your own sexuality, you may be able to open the door to greater understanding of yourself and others.

Cybersex Education

In first exploring the Net for sexual stimulation, we advise you to start with sites offering female erotica, where you can get your feet (and another part of your anatomy) wet just by reading. Try sites that offer literate porn that's directed at women, such as www.nerve.com, www.libida.com, www.askisadora.com, and www.blowfish.com to begin the process. We offer more sites to select from in Resources p. 270.

You can also find information about more general sexual topics by going to sites that are educational in nature, such as the Sex Information and Education Council of the U.S. (www.siecus.org), Kinsey Institute for Sex, Gender, and Reproduction (www.indiana.edu/~kinsey), or the Institute for the Advanced Study of Human Sexuality (www.iashs.edu).[2] Whatever you intend to pursue online—go to the source with your mind wide open.

Sandra usually suggests that female patients initially go online with the goal of learning something new. There are no "dumb" questions about sex. Most of us are still battling the legacy of repressive messages and half-truths from our childhood; the Net offers information you might be embarrassed to ask about elsewhere. *Is it okay for me to have cunnilingus when I'm eight months pregnant? Where can I get an abortion for under $200? Is it safe to have intercourse while I'm being treated for a yeast infection? Can I take my husband's Viagra if I take medication for hypertension? How do I know when I'm too old and it's time to stop trying to have a baby with my own eggs?* Recent post-op transsexuals can find others who can advise them about negotiating new relationships; women who have been intellectually cloistered from a complete sex education—Hindu, Muslim, Orthodox Jewish, or Southern Baptist—can pick up the basics or more explicit areas of sex. The Net will both educate and titillate.

But be prepared. There is no telling what you'll get as you jump from site to site or whose opinion a particular webpage espouses. Prowling around the virtual corridors of cyberspace, you will encounter any number of answers to your questions, but not every answer is accurate. Sandra always tells her patients to look for the same information on several different sites, first using the national organizations for sexuality education mentioned above so that they can weed out the wildly erroneous from the mild exaggeration. If you get too much information too graphically, it can be a real turn-off.

Sandra counseled a young Hindu woman who was about to enter into her arranged marriage. She'd been told that she would need two saris for the long event—one magnificent dress for the ceremony and one rather dark, plain one for afterward—but no one would explain why. She had no way of knowing that the two-sari custom evolved to save virgins from bleeding all over their good dresses. In an attempt to educate herself (she knew, at least, that the extra clothing had something to do with sex), she logged on to a women's website and followed one link after another until she arrived at a sexually explicit site that frightened her with its raw footage of bizarre behaviors. She was so put off by these vivid images that she was unable to consider sex for at least a month after the wedding and finally sought short-term therapy.

There are those women, however, who find this type of exploration to be liberating. A 40-year-old nun who just left the convent said it was better to know something than nothing. "I was paralyzed with fear about going out on a date," said Elaine (formerly Sister Agnes). "I had sexual fantasies, but I had been told that they were evil, so I couldn't even begin to think about realizing them. The Internet helped. I logged on to a discussion group about virginity, and found that there were other women like me! Some had sexual aversions, others were too scared to go on dates. But we held each other's hands online, and that made it easier."

The Net, of course, is not just words, it's also pictures. And with sex, a graphic image is sometimes illuminating. You can find archives of pictures showing people doing the most outrageous things (which you might find enticing or repellent) and private sites that charge a fee to see rare photographs, very often classic or ancient representations of sexual positions and behaviors. Even real-time sex shows are available online, if you have a yen to see what others do when they couple.

The Net's visual displays can satisfy our voyeuristic tendencies—or perhaps demystify sex. But it can also flatten the experience and make us blasé about the more shocking aspects of sexuality. Research suggests, however, that visual images make fleeting impressions on the brain. For the first few hours after seeing something distressing, we can recall it exactly as it was. After twelve hours, we can recapture most of the image, but it's blurry. And after twenty-four hours, it's unlikely that we remember much detail at all, although the idea may still have impact.

The type of mental and emotional liberation that women can achieve online often motivates them to want to try out some different behaviors; for example, buying a sex toy or wearing a costume to bed. Here, too, the Net offers a brave new world of plastic, rubber, leather, lace, and feathers.

ROAD RULES FOR THE SEX EXPLORATION ON THE INFORMATION SUPER HIGHWAY

1. When using a search engine, be specific in what you're looking for. Use quotation marks around the words in your phrase to limit the search.
2. Don't access any porn sites unless you want to be bombarded with ads and junk mail and don't respond to junk mail—not even to "unsubscribe."
3. Clean your system of cookies on a regular basis, or set your browser to alert you before accepting cookies.
4. If you're concerned about others finding out where you've been (especially your kids), go to the History window in your browser, select all, and delete. Make sure you go back in time as far as you've been looking at sex sites.
5. Start with reputable, more mainstream sites that deal with women's health or sexual education, and follow their links. To be sure that the information you're getting is accurate, check out the same question on several sites.

6. If you accidentally get onto a porn site, simply X out all the boxes or turn off your Web browser.

Technology, like anything else, can be used for good or evil. Practice common-sense computer usage and you'll be fine.

SHOPPING

Buy and Try

For women who feel that they've lost touch with their sexuality, Sandra often recommends that they go online to purchase something sexy. Wearing sexy undergarments is a way of reminding yourself—or discovering for the first time—that you are a sexual person, even if you don't currently have a partner or feel you will never again get any pleasure out of sex. Almost all women can enjoy the feeling of having something soft and sensual against their skin, whether it be a silk teddy or a lace camisole or a velvet bustier. Wearing something slightly illicit or kinky under your regular clothing, like a pair of split-crotch panty hose or a vibrating leather butterfly, not only provides private thrills throughout the day, but serves as a reminder that you are a sexual person.

We'd like to give you permission to spend a little mad money for a shopping excursion on the Net. Don't leave it up to your partner to buy sexy clothing or sex toys! By making choices and selecting something that really appeals to you, you are taking a positive step toward reclaiming your sexual self. Go to sites online that offer clothing and toys specifically designed with women's fantasies in mind. Try www.goodvibes.com, www.evesgarden.com, www.bettydodson.com, and www.websexshop.com and the others in Resources, p. 270. (See chapter 11 for a discussion of what to do once your goodies arrive.)

One married woman of 45 complained that she and her husband had tried for years to help her have an orgasm, and she had just about given up hope. She'd had one a few times when she masturbated, but even that was difficult. Sandra suggested that she might consider using a vibrator, and she laughed. "I would love one of those, but I have no idea where to get one!" Once directed to a website that specialized in sex toys, she was eager to finish the interview so that she could get online. "I knew there had to be something better than those back massagers with attachments," she giggled.

Books are always a safe bet when you go shopping, and the various sexuality sites offer how-to informational guides as well as coffee-table picture books about sex. There's also audio erotica, so that you can listen to hot tales of passion while you masturbate or have sex with a partner. You can even buy tapes that you listen to with headphones so it sounds like you're in the midst of an orgy, with all the moans, heavy breathing, and even a few slaps or spanks highlighted in vivid stereophonic sound. Erotic films, like those of the feminist eroticist Candida Royalle, allow you to see others engaged in acts that you might want to fantasize about, even if you're not ready to act them out in real life. (See Resources, page 270, for a list of great sexy films for women.)

The biggest hurdle, of course, is ridding yourself of old attitudes that might prevent you from getting the most from your new toys. Consider a vibrator as an investment that delivers dividends. Many women aren't initially thrilled with the idea of making love with a piece of plastic or rubber; still, they feel they have to do something—*anything*—to change their feelings about the importance of sex in their lives. One single woman told Sandra, "I gave it a name—Sam—and I'd take it to bed with me. After delaying for days, I finally put it between my legs, listened to some jazz, and fantasized. I began to feel aroused for the first time in years! I had always had problems touching myself with my hand, but Sam was easy. He was a really good partner—he kept on giving long after my hands would have become tired. I bought him online, anonymously, and he came in a brown mailing bag, and absolutely no one in the world knew. Thank God for the Internet!"

It's important to give yourself permission to do something that isn't your usual behavior, to move from *I never* to *I might*. Doing something different from your usual patterns can break the sexual doldrums. If you don't like your new purchase, you can at least say you tried it. But you may be surprised—a vibrator or a dildo can be a way of getting back in touch with your own sexual arousal. No one can see or hear you or complain that you're taking too long. And you can have as many orgasms as you like without having to worry about a partner.

It's safe to use your credit card for sex shopping since these are secured sites. Unless you check the box giving away your personal information (or uncheck it if that's the default setting), the vendor is not allowed to sell your name to any other site. (If by any chance, you click without thinking, just follow the earlier instructions on page 155 about not responding to junk email.) Your purchases will arrive in plain packaging, so that even the FedEx man will think you're getting some new clothes or books rather than a leather G-string or a set of ben-wa balls.

The Net, of course, is the *Ur*-university of sex. And there are plenty of other people in it who would love to take classes with you. It's the ultimate playground for ideas, and of course, for relationships.

CHATTING

Chat Rooms—Learning the Basics

Looking around a sex site, whether it's for information or for shopping, doesn't involve you emotionally. But meeting and greeting on a site to talk about intimate matters is a different story. Finding like-minded companions in cyberspace is a little like going to college for the first time—you are thrown together with many individuals who come from different backgrounds and have different expectations. You don't just make small talk as you would when you first meet someone in an office, real-time, or at a neighborhood block party. You may share your deepest feelings; you may talk about philosophy, erotica, fantasies—and you do it almost immediately. The Web is always running in present time, which means you have no past and no future. Self-disclosure is not only accepted, it's expected, and you may find that chatting at this intense level can be a real challenge. But if you learn the rules of the road first, you'll feel a lot more comfortable.

No matter which chat rooms you want to visit, your first priority is selecting an onscreen name or set of names that can't be traced back to you. If you're on AOL, you're allowed from five to seven screen names on one account, depending on the version you're using. Only your original sign-up name is traceable, because you have to give your real name and address and credit card to get started—the other onscreen identities and the instant messaging services you establish with them are hidden from the general public. If you don't have AOL, you can set up a separate account on any of the servers that offer free email, such as MSN, Yahoo, or Excite. In order to enter any chat room or post on any message board, you must log in. You'll be asked for your email address and a password as well as a nickname to which all future postings will be sent (if you forget to pick a nickname, they'll send everything to your real email address, *which you don't want*).

Be aware that when you select your different identities, you are telling the cyber community how you would like them to imagine you. The names you select are self-advertisements. So if you call yourself hotstuff@msn.com or virgingirl@yahoo.com, you will receive attention worthy of your name.

Mary Anne, a patient who was very nervous about talking in chat rooms, created one name for her family (that was the one that was traceable to her original account), one for casual acquaintances, one for her explorations of sexual self-discovery, and one that she used when she was interested in no-strings-attached, hot-and-heavy cybersex. "I'm a different person when I write under the 'cumgetme' name," she confessed with a laugh. "I feel like I'm flying when I'm talking to my online lovers, and I'm easily aroused by descriptions of how I'm being touched on my nipples or licked on my clitoris. It's funny—I can't talk dirty in real life, but it comes easily online."

The Net can provide a safe haven for those who have been so badly hurt, they can't ask for help. "I had a patient who came to me after venturing into a healing-after-rape chat room," said a colleague who subsequently treated the woman. "She spent a month just listening, and finally got up the nerve to reveal this secret that she thought would mark her for life. It was only because the other women in the room had told their stories first—some more horrendous than hers—that she was able to seek professional help."

If you're dealing with a particularly difficult issue, like rape or sexual dysfunction, you might want to try a support group. These online forums are held for women who are experiencing similar issues and want to share with one another and talk about their pain and recovery. It must be said, however, that support groups aren't always supportive, and some members may be downright unpleasant. The phenomenon of flaming exists all over the Net. Sometimes you may also encounter women who are bitter and angry, eager to recruit others to their cause or conduct marathon bitching sessions that can be antitherapeutic in nature. If you do run into someone who gives you grief, don't start arguments, don't talk back, just get out. You're not held hostage—you don't owe it to anyone to appear in the room if you're being treated badly.

Stay out of chat rooms where there is no moderator to put a stop to bad behavior. Online moderators (sort of like bouncers in a bar) are online nearly all the time, and their purpose is to keep "flaming" to a minimum and bar personalities who are disruptive or abusive.

If you find that you are pursued against your will by someone online, abandon the name under which they know you. Simply don't collect messages in that mailbox and don't respond to any messages sent to you under that name. You can also ban certain pests from your personal cyber-world. The "locate" feature on AOL allows others to find you online. But if you find someone annoying or scary, you can get rid of them by typing their email address in the box that asks if you will accept messages from this party or if you want to block them from accessing your mailbox.

Where to Chat

We suggest that you experiment with a few chat rooms—not necessarily the romance and love variety where people are alternately gross and coy, but rather a room devoted to one of your major interests. If you're into politics, art, film, or even gardening, that's a good place to get started. One of Sandra's patients joined the Jewish singles chat room on AOL and found a group of like-minded people in New York City who met every Sunday evening at a bar or coffee shop. "I loved those guys," she said. "They practically had the same background, the same parents, the same education as me. By the time we all met, we called each other 'roomies.' We dated online and off." This was a perfect melding of virtual and real life.

One common way to find companionship or love online is by looking through "profiles" and by designing one of your own. Profiles are shorthand résumés, descriptions you create that will attract people who have interests and ideas similar to yours. (Of course, if you have five identities, you'll need five profiles.) This is the crux of the matter—how do you define yourself? It's hard to be insightful *and* truthful; and in fact many shy away from honesty online. If you're just window-shopping for fun, you can say whatever you please. But if you really want to use the Web effectively for dating, whether in your virtual life (VL) or real life (RL), you need to figure out what it is about yourself that *you* would find sexy.

People describe themselves as they wish to be perceived, of course, and the range of disguises is endless—your new buddy can pretend that he or she is a different sex, or race, or age, or religion. This is self-protective in many instances. Think about a woman in a wheelchair who decides to regale her contacts with stories about the time she ran the marathon. Or a shy, reticent type who would never dream of being on top, but who plays a dominatrix online and tells men to "lick" her goddamn shoe, or else.

Cyberchatting and Cyberdating

There are endless opportunities to meet partners online, whether you're looking for a buddy, a soul mate, a lifetime companion, or as Erica Jong described it in *Fear of Flying,* a "zipless fuck." Your message and your name are the medium—you become the image you chose to project. There's a whole language of abbreviations and icons for cyberchatting—you can find these on www.netlingo.com. You can be witty or irreverent, poetic or sardonic, or silly or sad. You can think about what you want to say and then revise it—you've got all the time in the world after you create your missive to press "Send," so you don't have to feel rushed or pressured. Chatting, for most women, is enormously gratifying. Sandra's patients uniformly tell her that the sexiest thing they know is to have a person who listens to them and responds to their words.

So let's say you've met someone in a chat room, and you two are getting cozy. You've read each other's profiles and you're really simpatico. You post a message on a bulletin board in the morning, he answers by the time you're home from work. He's already in the chat room in the evening when you log on. The two of you flirt a little—maybe other people in the room notice. The next step is a "private chat," which gives you a space away from the crowd to talk one-on-one. These one-on-one encounters can be done in a variety of ways. On AOL, you are members of a closed system and can put each other on your "buddy lists." By using instant messenger (IM) software, which you download from the AOL homepage, you can talk to each other, in real time, in a box that appears on your screen. If you don't choose to download AOL, you can still have privacy online with two other types of software—ICQ (webspeak for "I seek you") and IRC (Internet Relay Chat). These two systems give you access to information about who's online at any particular time on any particular site and can be downloaded, free with plenty of instructions on how to use them, from their homepages. This can be the start of a good friendship, or a romance. Or it can fizzle after the first time, in which case, you simply don't respond again when summoned out of the room by this person. And if they're persistent, see above for ways to block communication entirely.

The Lover Who's Never Seen but Always There

"It was one of those sleepless nights," Rachel, a patient of Sandra's, told her in a therapy session. "My husband was asleep upstairs, and I was surfing, because that's how I deal with my insomnia. I logged on to AOL to see who was there, and saw this name that threw me back decades. It was 'Lysander,' which was not only a character from Shakespeare, but also a neighbor from when i was growing up outside Seattle. So I joined the chat and posted an IM to this guy, asking if he knew that family. No response for about five minutes, and then he said, 'Sure, that's my aunt.'

"We talked for about an hour, and one thing I really liked was that he never asked, 'ASL,' which is the mark of a total asshole online. They want to get your age, sex, and location right away to decide if it's worth their while to spend all that time with you. So we got to reminisce a little, and even though I figured I had to be about twenty years older than him, it was okay. We never asked if the other had posted a photo in our profiles. I had, but I really didn't want to tell him to go look at it, because he'd see that I was 55, and it might spoil the fantasy. I was having too much fun.

"Over the next two weeks, I looked for him online, and eventually, we made dates so we didn't have to guess about when to log on. I found out that he's never been married."

"Was he telling the truth, do you think?" Sandra asked.

"Well, I'm married and I always tell the truth. But you have to have a gut feeling about the other person. What are they hiding? Are they making something a little better, a little shinier about themselves? I thought he was for real, and anyway, I was very attracted. I started flirting, asking what kind of woman he liked, asking whether he liked kissing—things like that. He seemed a little shy, I don't know.

"But the next time we talked, he asked what I was wearing. I told him— it was a hot night—I was in my underwear, which was true. He asked me to describe it, and this was really sexy. I told him all about my tap pants and the lace on the underwire bra. Then I asked if he wanted me to take my bra off. There was a big pause."

Sandra asked how she'd felt. Had she been excited, physically aroused?

"I can't tell you how much. I'd never had sex online with anyone, but I thought, Now it's going to happen. I was very wet, completely ready. I wanted to touch myself, but I wanted him to tell me exactly how I should do it. I didn't think about my husband, my marriage, nothing but this. I think I would have done anything—although in real life, well, I'm not particularly abandoned. I wait for the man to get excited, and then I can catch fire."

Rachel and her lover, interestingly enough, didn't go any farther that night. They were on the brink and then he told her he had to think about this some more. Rachel was disappointed, but she said she was taking it light-heartedly. After all, she'd probably never meet him, and it would be fun just to flirt. Anyhow, in the clear light of day, she might end up really guilty about "going all the way in the privacy of my own study," as she called it. She knew that to endow the relationship with a lot of unrealistic expectations would be a way to get sucked in, and she didn't want that. She wanted to stay loose.

When Sandra saw Rachel three months later, she said she had finally "cybered."

"You know what that is? We typed to each other exactly what we were doing and how it felt. *I'm typing with one hand now; ooh, that feels great; my nipples are so hard—can you feel them? I want you to touch my clit. Oh, yeah! My hand just slipped off the keyboard.*"

Sandra asked Rachel how she would characterize this relationship. "Is it an affair? Have you met this man in real life?"

Rachel shook her head wistfully. "No. I had the chance. I was flying across the country on business and I changed my airline ticket so I could stop off. He seemed happy about that. But when I thought about it some more, I decided I didn't want to see him. Ever. I had a vision of him that was all mine, and reality would have killed that. It was enough that he'd helped me to recognize a piece of my sexuality that I'd never acknowledged. And something else. It would have been really bad for my marriage. And devastating for him because," she added softly, "he was a priest, thinking about leaving the church. I couldn't feel responsible for that."

Many women Sandra has counseled have online friendships and never want to go farther. Many have developed long-term friendships with one-time cyber lovers. Eventually, they evolve into online pals who can tell each other everything, and that facet of their relationship is more important than physical gratification. One key element of sexual attraction is proximity, which you get mentally, but not physically, online. Since most of us work our way up to sex by getting to know and trust an individual whom we can see and touch, the immediacy of online sex may seem superficial. The near-encounter just isn't enough.

But some women do wish to go farther, to take a virtual experience and make it real.

RULES OF THE ROAD FOR WEB CHATTING

1. Select a screen name or names that can't be traced to your regular account. Your online identities should tell others something about your ideals and wishes.
2. Don't chat on sites that have no moderators unless you don't mind the occasional flaming.
3. Go to chat rooms that reflect your interests rather than a romance or sex room.
4. Learn the language by visiting www.netlingo.com.
5. Set up a profile so that others can get to know you. If you decide to use a photo, it should show something about you that you'd like others to see.
6. Get to know a person in a group before you go into a private chat, but remember, if it doesn't turn out the way you'd like it, you can always block their emails.

DATING

Moving from Chatting (VL) to Dating (RL)

There are women like Rachel who would never consider meeting an online partner. There are others, however, who specifically use chatting as a bridge to meeting. Most of Sandra's patients who grew tired of Parents Without Partners and the entire array of local singles' events, frequented the chat rooms only with the intention of finding a real partner, for sex, and perhaps for a more committed RL relationship.

"The way we've been meeting and courting for thousands of years hasn't gotten us very far, because the divorce rate is still around 50 percent," says Dr. Al Cooper, a sex therapist whose practice is being reengineered thanks to the Net.[3] "Part of the reason for that is that romantic passionate relationships aren't stable—they are usually based on two people finding each other devastatingly attractive. In life, maybe you meet one hundred people over the course of a year and choose twenty who are attractive, and out of those, if you're lucky, you've got three you really enjoy spending time with and want to date.

"But on the Net, you can easily choose one hundred people you felt some commonality with, and out of those, you could develop online relationships with twenty, and out of those you might find ten you were interested in exploring the romantic dimension with, and maybe after some time, you narrow the field to three who seem appealing. Understand that those wouldn't be the same three people as those you met in real life . . . because in real life you look and judge first and get to know later. The main cut on the Net is common interest and liking they way they speak to you. And of course, if you're lucky, they may also turn out to be attractive—or may become more attractive after you get to know them."

The facility of chatting and flirting doesn't change the fact that the majority of actual meetings generated by virtual attraction won't work out. Like everything else on the Net, they involve a gamble. But wasted time online is generally safer than wasted time in a bar and cheaper than taking an adult-ed class for the sole purpose of meeting someone. You're honing your social skills and maybe, with each experience, becoming a little more clearheaded about your choices and your desires.

Most people want to see the one they're going to rendezvous with first. No matter how many private chats and phone conversations you've had, you still may hold out hope that the guy is not only wonderful, kind, and funny, but also looks like George Clooney. And the way to do this online is to include a pic or gif with your profile. Of course, this goes counter to the philosophy of the Web, that the mind is mightier than the body. By attaching your photo, you are saying to your potential partner that looks really do count, and acknowledging that the other person probably cares as much as you do about your physical attributes. Then, too, if you choose to download photos, you may very likely be leaving yourself open to contract a virus—which could be almost as bad as getting an STD from real-time contact if it wipes out everything in your computer! In addition, when you've posted your own photo, it, too, can be passed from computer to computer, and who wants to be the visual equivalent of sloppy seconds?

Many of my patients who've decided to meet a person they've had a close relationship with online are often astounded to see that the photo of their would-be lover bears little resemblance to the real person. The man in the picture may be young, thin, and sporting a full head of hair. Not so in real life. The deception you may encounter online can either be intriguing and sexy, or frustrating and annoying, depending on how seriously involved you've already become.

Marsha, a divorced mother of two from Kentucky, said that she found photos very useful. "I put up a picture of myself standing up in a canoe and it got a lot of responses. It was kind of funny, but brave, too. When I moved to Texas to take a better job, I didn't know anyone in the area. And I decided I wanted to take the dating game seriously and not waste time. A picture isn't worth a thousand words on the Net, but it is in real life.

"If you're in the market to meet someone, you have to get right down to business and write a personal ad. You'll know to stay away from the big meat-market sites, such as AOL, Yahoo, or Excite. You absolutely have to special-ize—if you're gay, there are many sites for GLBTs (gay, lesbian, bisexual, transgendered), if you're into kink or fetishes, find a site that caters to those interests. I personally have four dogs, so when I'm chatting, I go to a room for people who love pets to find a guy who likes dogs, breeds dogs, or some-thing like that. You can narrow the field more quickly by shopping in the right place.

"I go and look at the Personals and see how the guy presents himself," Marsha said. "I click on 'Texas/divorced male' and maybe get a list of a hun-dred people who fit that criteria. Then I wait to see who emails me from my profile. If they happen to be online, I'll send them an instant message and say hi to see if there's any chemistry in our conversation.

"The next step is we put each other on our buddy lists so we'll know when the other one is online. You hope he'll be there when you log on, but if not, then okay, no sweat. On the other hand, if he's there three nights in a row, you know he's probably interested and it's okay to move on to phone contact.

"You really don't know anything until you hear his voice and get to see how he is live-time—how the chemistry goes. I'd say I have to talk to a guy on the phone four or five times, plus exchange more email, before I'm ready to meet in real life. If there are no red flags at that point, I'll set up a meeting for a drink or coffee, usually in a public place like a Fridays or a Bennigans. I always arrange to be paged by a girlfriend about an hour into the date, just in case. If I'm desperate to get away, I answer and just say it was nice to meet him without giving him any hope that this event will be repeated. If I'm really turned off by him or I think he's a creep, I might drive my car in the oppo-site direction from home to make sure he's not following me. But if I like him and I want to stay, I ignore the page; when we're done with our drink, I sug-gest that we go home and think about it and talk later or the next day online about whether we think this is working out.

"There have been guys that I've gotten very sexy with online before we ever meet—there's like a pull right through the computer. That kind of sex appeal I find really disturbing but so enticing. If, when we meet, the thrill is still there, it can hasten the steps it would take to get me into bed."

The process sounds very cut-and-dried, and for some jaded singles, romance hardly enters the picture. Most experts recommend that if you do want to meet the person you've been flirting with, you wait no more than a month before taking the contact real-time.[4] The longer you wait, the more expectations you will surely have, and if the whole thing goes bust, the more painful it will be. But there's always that hope that in this huge wide world, you will stretch out a thin tentacle and reach the ultimate—true love and great sex. It's possible you will find some certified nuts—but you could do that in real life as well. If you keep your wits about you and follow the instructions on safely moving from cybersex to f2f (face-to-face) dating, you might just luck out and meet a gem.

SAFELY MOVING FROM CYBERSEX TO F2F DATING

1. Online, read between the lines. What kinds of information do you get from your would-be date? Is he or she behaving as you'd expect in a RL relationship? How long does it take between responses? Who initiates? If you're doing all the work online, you'll probably have to do the same when you really meet.
2. If you like what you hear in a private chat, make a phone date. If three phone conversations leave you just as interested, you can arrange to meet in real time.
3. Be sure you discuss on the phone what you both expect in your real-time meeting.
4. Select a public place, a coffee shop or restaurant, where there are plenty of people. Never agree to meet at your place or your partner's.
5. Ask a friend to call or page you during your date, and when you answer it, you can give a prearranged signal if things aren't going well and you want to escape.
6. Either arrange to be picked up by a friend, or park your car far away from the date and take a taxi to your car so that you can't be followed.
7. Agree to talk with your date by phone the next day, after you've both had time to reflect on how it went.

Cyber-Abuse

There are those individuals who are stuck in this intricate Web and can't seem to get *off*line. One study of 18,000 Internet users indicated that at least 5.5 percent of women and 5.6 percent of men report that they spend from eleven to twenty hours compulsively visiting sex sites and engaging in cyber-stimulation that they can't get in real life.[5] According to an MSNBC survey, 200,000 Americans spent eleven hours a week or more accessing sexual material online and admitted to being "addicted."[6]

At first you're just curious—you hang out in a few rooms, you meet a few people for private chats, and before you know it, you can't wait to return home to log on. A harmless pastime becomes an obsessive drive. It's so easy to get "involved" with someone quickly on the Net, and pseudo-intimacy is what many people crave. It's hidden, it's safe, and it's enormously satisfying. Pornography enhances the sexual high, and you can talk about anything that turns you on under cover of the computer—even illegal acts such as rape or child molestation.

Those who use the Net exclusively to provide excitement in their lives may start to spend less time with family and friends in f2f contact. This can erode a marriage, a family, or a career. The number of individuals who can make love to a cyber-partner but cannot bear the thought of that guy in the bedroom they swore to love, honor, and obey may be increasing.[7]

In some instances, the Web can be dangerous. Loners and paraphilics are just waiting for the right opportunity to meet the person whose fantasy matches theirs. Cyber-stalking raises its ugly head when the bond has become so intense that it becomes imperative to consummate a virtual relationship in the flesh. We've all heard horror stories about women slaughtered by an online lover who had sworn in email or a private chat that he was going to kill her. But the pull to come together is almost too compelling, and reason doesn't always enter into it. The sense of anonymity afforded by cyberspace leads to bigger risk-taking.

It is vital that, no matter how appealing and how safe you feel in the virtual embrace of a new lover, you follow the guidelines we recommend above in order to keep your anonymity and to stay safe. This may seem self-evident if you're the type of person who has to ask why anyone in her right mind would make a date to meet a person who has told her in graphic detail exactly what he wants to do to her. The answer is twofold—first, she doesn't consider him a stranger because she is sure from their correspondence and online chats that she knows him well enough. And second, all the things he suggests are undoubtedly the stuff of her own fantasies, which she would never have been able to realize without his support and encouragement.

If you are concerned that you are spending too much time online, or that you are close to taking a risk by meeting someone who has revealed a very dark side to his personality, it may be wise to schedule a consultation with a therapist. Although Sandra rarely sees women who feel they are addicted to online sexual pursuits, she does see many men, some brought by a worried spouse who feels that the lure of anonymous online sex has stolen her partner's attention from her. These are real issues and should be dealt with in counseling.[8]

Exploring vs. Cheating—How to Know the Difference

If you're in a committed relationship, is online sex with an unknown partner cheating? Is it adultery if all you do is go into a chat room and talk about sex? Or if you exchange steamy email with a friend who's become a cyber-lover? What if you have no plans to meet your paramour, but you give and receive sexual messages and instructions as you both masturbate in your separate bedrooms? You are at once apart and together in cyberspace, and in order to define "cheating," you must split hairs that are thinner than microfibers. It's hard to make clear distinctions.

There are, of course, different degrees of sexual exploration. Sandra has many women in her practice who have used their sexual forays as a way of remaining in a relationship that has become physically barren, either because of their partner's lack of interest or incapacity. "I knew my married sex life was over when my husband had prostate surgery and refused to get treatment for his erectile problems," said Janice, a professor in her early fifties. "He said he was giving up sex and had no interest in any kind of physical intimacy at all." She just couldn't live with his choice, because she was still a sexual person. "I forgave myself and got online to find a lover," she confessed.

Another patient said she felt entitled to enter chat rooms and talk sexually because she knew her husband did—he had been downloading pornography and surfing the Net for years after she went to bed. When he refused to discuss her feelings about his behavior, she decided to go online herself. When her husband discovered the extent of her online "romances," he became bitterly angry. But this was the impetus for the two of them to try to save their marriage by going into couples therapy.

For women with partners who are constantly rejecting or belittling, an online affair can supply a fantasy that they can use when they're in bed with their husbands. On the other hand, depending on the degree of guilt involved, the experience of Internet thrills with a person who really talks to you and seems to understand you can make married sex more deadly than it was before. It can propel some women to make the decision to end a marriage or long-term relationship. Would this have happened without the stimulus of that virtual partner? It's impossible to say.

If your online behavior feels secretive, shameful, and disloyal, then it's time to 'fess up and discuss it with your partner. Sometimes, this can lead to an increase in intimacy and a resolution to make sex more interesting at home; sometimes it leads to acrimony. In any event, it can be useful as a way of forcing couples to take stock of their sexual and emotional relationship. Are you and your partner spending enough time together? Do you feel valued, desired, and loved? Does online sexual exploration represent a failure or lack of intimacy in your present relationship? What are you prepared to do about it?

Any amount of secrecy, whether or not it involves infidelity, changes the nature of an intimate relationship because all the cards are not on the table. There are risks in becoming sexually active in cyberspace. Unlike men who surf, click, ogle the girls, and then click off, most women want some interactive participation along with their erotic stimulation. If you fit this profile, understand that cyber-flirting can make a bigger dent in your marriage because it allows you to avoid major issues. You have allowed your emotional and sexual needs to be fulfilled by another partner (even if you never meet) and you can therefore manage to avoid growth and change in your primary relationship.

Here's a revolutionary thought: Why not use the Net to fix your marriage? Just as the Internet causes problems by allowing people to be intimate yet separate, it can also serve as the necessary glue to mend the break in exactly the same way. Since cyberspace is an ideal medium for communication, why not communicate with the one you really desire to be intimate with?

Are you and your partner bored and sexually dissatisfied? Well, what are you waiting for? Run, do not walk, to the nearest computer terminal and start surfing—together. Make sure you're sitting close enough to make physical contact—let your thighs touch, or arms gently intertwine. This is a journey that will start to make you anticipate novelty in sex rather than bemoan the old vanilla standard you've been hanging on to for years.

How difficult is it for you to talk dirty to each other? If you are long-married parents of a few school-age kids, you have probably put a lot of energy into excising all four-letter words and double entendres from your vocabulary. That type of limitation may have crept into the bedroom when you weren't looking. But when you listen to other people going at it in chat rooms, or read erotica out loud to each other, you may find that you begin to loosen the reins a little. You may even be inspired by other couples' webcam erotic adventures to find new uses for your home video camera, which is not only useful for photographing the kids' ballet recitals and soccer games, but also adept at capturing the steamy sessions in your own bedroom or living room.

It's easy to make your own dirty movie, and no one has to know but you. Women who have never seen themselves lubricate or have an orgasm can truly blossom as they put away their inhibitions and watch themselves in the privacy and safety of their own inner sanctum. Couples can admire the way they look and what they've done together. Put the camera on a tripod and go at it, then watch yourselves on tape at another time for an additional turn-on. You don't have to put yourselves up on your own website to appreciate the thrill of voyeurism. Let the bolder couples inspire you.

What does it feel like to be completely abandoned with the partner you know so well? For those who are not as visually inclined, it may be easier to talk in cyberspace. You can at last open up to the person you share a life with and reveal what turns you on. There's undoubtedly something there for both of you—the porn sites, the lingerie, the chats, the steamy stories of seduction. Why not explore them all?

A chat room can become really interesting if you have two computers in different parts of the house. You'll know each other's identities, but no one else will understand that you're a couple. You can pretend you're just two strangers, meeting online for the first time, checking each other out, daring to be a little suggestive or even blatantly horny. You can use sites for role-playing together, for picking up another man or woman (if you've ever fantasized about a threesome), or you can exchange lascivious email that will indicate exactly what you'd like to do to each other when you're alone.

"My husband prides himself on never having learned to type," Melissa, a 33-year-old marketing consultant, said to me, "because he was always sure he was going to have a secretary do it for him. So when we went into a chat room, I had to be the scribe. He stood behind me, his hands on my shoulders, and whispered what he wanted me to write. Then people would answer him back and we'd both take note of his reaction. I felt like I was inside him—the reverse of intercourse—because he was sharing those intimate thoughts and feelings, and I got to express them in words. It occurred to me that I don't really pay attention to my fantasies while I'm in the middle of sex—I stop thinking and just act in this kind of animal way. But by having to put my excitement down on the screen, it made me conscious of asking for what I like in bed, something I hadn't done before because I was too caught up in the 'oohs' and 'aahs.' "

What is it about writing the words down or being shown images of bodies that saves us from speaking the words aloud or looking at ourselves in the mirror? The excitement of cyberspace has a great deal to do with the fact that you have to wait to get a response after you click—you've initiated something (a flirtation with another person or an image on the screen) and then it takes a few seconds to download the results. In that brief period of time, you are in suspense, hoping for the best, eager to get satisfaction. And as we know, in a long-term marriage, you don't always get what you want, but if you try, sometimes, meeting your partner in cyberspace, you can get what you need.

Sex Is More Than Virtual

The cyber-boom has clearly changed the way we look at relationships. A woman in her teens or twenties may have no recollection of a time when she didn't use a computer. For her, it doesn't seem at all unusual to meet a lover online and to have a closer relationship with him than anyone she knows in "real" life.[9]

But virtual reality is one remove away from human touch. The real reason that we delight in the instinctive drive to couple is that it heals the existential separation we all live with daily. The sights, sounds, smells, and tastes of real sex are more subtle and more complex than the jangle of cyber-stimulation. Go ahead and enjoy the Web as it grows larger and more inclusive, but never let it replace your gut desire to be one of two human beings, naked and vulnerable, having a wonderful time.

8

BETTER SEX
THROUGH CHEMISTRY

Sex is all about chemistry. Our hormones, our proteins, our enzymes, our neurotransmitters, and dozens of other bits and bytes of human effluvia all contribute to our sexuality. When you're sexually interested and turned on, your body can feel both light and substantial, relaxed and alert, thanks to chemicals that are naturally present. Who wouldn't like to enhance those wonderful sensations? Who doesn't sometimes wonder what potions you might *add* to the mix to make it even better?

You need three things at the very least to be receptive to sex: You have to be motivated to be intimate, even if you don't feel physical desire; you have to become aroused, maybe even to the point of orgasm; and you have to consider sex a satisfying and rewarding option as opposed to a frustrating chore. It also helps to have an interested and interesting partner. Through the magic of chemistry, you can fiddle with the first two elements—as for the third and fourth, well, those may be out of your control, but perhaps your better awareness of what turns you on will allow you to deal with those, too.

Unfortunately, chemistry not only works to enhance sex, it can also work against it. Usually, there isn't just one stumbling block to sexual fulfillment. You may desire sex, but be unable to be aroused; you may lubricate just fine, but have no interest in any sexual activity; you may feel acute pain in your clitoris and vagina, which will curtail both desire *and* arousal. There are categories and subcategories of these difficulties, one very often feeding into the other. And although some women don't judge their sex lives by their orgasms, if you never experience a climax, you may feel that you have somehow failed or been cheated of this supposedly "natural" activity. The last criterion necessary for sex is satisfaction. If you *don't get no satisfaction,* to paraphrase the immortal words of Mick Jagger, you may just give up. No more sex, thanks a lot.

Scientists are working fast and furiously to come up with a chemical panacea that will have an impact on a number of different systems—the hormonal, the central (the brain and nervous system), and the behavioral. In this chapter, we offer an overview of available drugs that inhibit sexual response and those that encourage it. We'll offer you guidelines to help you make the decision as to whether you should attempt a pharmacological approach to alter your sexual response. And finally, we'll discuss what you can do *without* drugs to make the chemistry just right.

ANTISEXUAL DRUGS

Medications That Inhibit Sexual Response

You may be surprised at the range and scope of stuff you can swallow that will tune your libido down to zilch or make it hard for you to become aroused or have an orgasm. In order to see how certain chemicals can wreak havoc with your sex life, you have to understand what must occur chemically in order to feel sexy. First, you need adequate *blood flow* to your genitals in order to become aroused and get that tingling, sexy feeling. Your nipples, clitoris, and vagina respond to stimulation only when your cardiovascular system is working properly. Then you need to *lubricate,* which happens when you become aroused. Sex when you're dry is uncomfortable, and may put a halt to all activity before it gets going. You also need an active libido. Feeling desire is partly related to chemicals in the brain known as *neurotransmitters,* and it's also *hormonal.* If you're taking a drug that prevents any one of these systems from doing its job, you may not care at all about sex.[1]

Let's take these one at a time.

Blood Flow (affects arousal):

Many **antihypertensive** medications are known culprits in contributing to sexual difficulties because these drugs either prevent the release of the neurotransmitter norepinephrine, deplete it, or block its receptors. Centrally active sympathetic blockers (Reserpine and Clonidine) meddle with desire, arousal, and orgasm. So do beta blockers Inderal and Blocadren, although the newer varieties Lopressor and Atenolol do not seem to cause as many problems with sexual function.

Diuretics such as Lasix and Aldactone may also prevent women from experiencing arousal and orgasm.

ALTERNATIVES: Ask your physician if you can try one of the newer drugs. Calcium channel blockers (Nifedipine or Verapamil) will leave most sexual function intact and also lack the sedative effect of some of the other drugs. Angiotensin-converting enzyme inhibitors (Captopril and Enalapril) may be the best antihypertensive drugs for sex, although they can cause a cough. The alpha-adrenergic blockers Prazosin and Terazosin may interfere with blood flow in the smooth muscles of the vaginal wall, but may not affect orgasm.

Lubrication (affects arousal):

Many drugs block the effects of acetylcholine, the neurotransmitter that helps to produce vaginal secretions and dilates blood vessels in your genitals (and elsewhere) when you're aroused. **Anticholinergic drugs** may dry you out and make you feel less sexy, including antihistamines, antipsychotics, some antidepressants, and some antinausea drugs.

 Antihistamines: Drugs like Benadryl, Atarax, and Periactin can also dry out your mucous membranes, including those of your mouth, vagina, and anus, and also tend to make you woozy, whether you select the regular or "nondrowsy" variety.

 ALTERNATIVE: Go without and take a herbal supplement such as Echinacea, zinc, or Vitamin C. You can also try saline nose drops to clear nasal passages. An over-the-counter water-based lubricant such as Astroglide, Slippery Stuff, or Acqua-lube may help with lubrication.

 Other common medications that may interfere with sex: Lomotil (for diarrhea), Urised (used to prevent urinary frequency), Scopolamine (for seasickness) and Ditropan (for overreactive bladders) may interfere with desire, but not with arousal and orgasm.

 ALTERNATIVE: None. Being sick to your stomach or having cramps will probably turn you off to sex anyway, so take your meds and wait it out.

 Antipsychotics: Haldol, Thorazine, and Mellaril may interfere with all phases of your sexual response, from desire to arousal to orgasm.

 ALTERNATIVES: If you must be on these meds, you should discuss timing of dosage with your physician. It's possible that you could plan a sexual encounter when the drug's effect is at its lowest in your system.

Neurotransmitter Production (affects desire):

Antidepressants: If you suffer from mild to moderate depression, one of the first things to go is usually your sex life. Unfortunately, many of the drugs that treat this condition also depress sexual interest and performance. Estrogen helps increase the production of norepinephrine, serotonin, and dopamine, the feel-good neurotransmitters. The balance among them is tricky—when serotonin is too high, or dopamine and norepinephrine are too low, it appears that desire wanes. They have to be in balance for you to feel that all's right with the world.

 The SSRIs (selective serotonin reuptake inhibitors) such as Prozac and Paxil often interfere with arousal or orgasm. They take their place alongside their earlier cousins, the MAO inhibitors (Parnate and Nardil) and tricyclics (Elavil, Norpramin, Tofranil, Asendin, Anafranil, Sinequan, and Pamelor) in wreaking havoc with desire, arousal, and orgasm.

 Regulating neurotransmitter movement is a very imprecise art. So Prozac and other SSRIs, while helping the meek to express themselves, and the angry to calm down, may also dampen sexual ardor on a regular basis.[2] In order for us to feel aroused and sense desire, we need fluctuating serotonin levels that move through our nervous system on an as-needed basis. When the neurotransmitter is altered chemically, we don't experience those highs and lows, that buildup and release of tension. And in addition, the SSRIs can bring on a battery of other symptoms, including nausea, loss of appetite (or weight gain with long-term use), excessive sweating, allergic rashes, dizziness, and headaches, all of which can be major sexual turnoffs.

ALTERNATIVES: There are several promising antidepressants that may overcome the sexual side-effects of SSRIs. Celexa (citalopram), Wellbutrin (buproprion), Serzone (nefazodone), Remeron (mirtazapine), and Desyrel (trazodone) seem to have the least antisexual effects and reduce depression at the same time. Some doctors prescribe Viagra to balance out the libido-lowering qualities of Prozac, and some counter it with Wellbutrin, which increases the amount of norepinephrine in the central nervous system, thus improving nerve transmission and enhancing the effect of the serotonin in the synapse.

You can also talk to your physician about taking a "drug holiday," possibly on weekends, when you might be more likely to have sex.

Anti-anxiety medication: Anxiety and panic, too, will turn off sexual response, and tranquilizers are usually prescribed to treat these conditions. The cause of these conditions is thought to be some type of imbalance in neurotransmitter production and output, specifically of brain hormones norepinephrine and serotonin. In this category are Valium, Xanax, Ativan, Tranxene, and Librium, as well as BuSpar, Atarax, and Vistaril (which also have an anticholinergic drying effect).

ALTERNATIVES: If you need these drugs, you must take them. However, you can talk to your physician about taking a "drug holiday."

In the future, it is likely that the medications we give to alter a woman's mood will help rather than hinder sexual function. The drugs currently on the market that manipulate the relay of emotional information are "dirty," that is, they affect many neurotransmitters simultaneously. In the next ten years, however, we will undoubtedly have a few "clean" drugs, which will go right to the target and knock it out, leaving all the other neurological functions and responses untouched. Medical science may actually come up with something that combines the mood elevation of a Prozac with the sexual stimulation of a Viagra.

Hormonal (affects desire and arousal):

Oral contraceptives: Many women report that certain OCs, which suppress the production of testosterone, an androgen that influences libido, have a distinctly *an*aphrodisiac effect. So while they can have sex as much as they want, they may not want to. The reason for this ironic chemical twist is that OCs must be absorbed by the gastrointestinal tract and reach the liver in a "bolus," or one large dose. The "bolus effect" induces the liver to increase the production of a chemical that binds to circulating testosterone, which means that there's less free testosterone to work positively on your sex drive. The drugs that do double duty as antiacne medications (those whose predominant active ingredient is either Desogestrel or Norgestimate) are the worst for sex precisely because of their low androgen nature.

ALTERNATIVES: If you're taking Ortho Tri-Cyclen, Desogen, or Mircette for lovely skin, you might want to switch to a drug whose primary active ingredient is Norethindrone, Norgestrel, or LevoNorgestrel, such as Triphasil, Alesse, or Ortho-Novum. You could also switch to a progestin-only pill, such as Micronor or Ovrette, although you may experience more breakthrough bleeding on these pills. Or forget the pills and choose a progestin-releasing IUD (which acts locally instead of systemically). The newest model, already in use in Europe and soon to be approved in the U.S., releases levonorgestrel for up to seven years.

A few other alternatives, though, are the old tried and true diaphragm, the new Nuva-Ring, or a latex condom!

Other hormonal drugs to treat **endometriosis** (Danazol, taken daily) and **infertility** (GnRH agonists and antagonists, administered as depo-injectables) will often quell desire. Usually, these drugs are taken on a short-term basis (about three months). Hopefully, desire will return when you're no longer on the medication.

Other drugs that interfere with sex: Medications to control diabetes, thyroid disorders, and Lyme disease all tend to quash desire. There are no alternatives for these drugs; however, some women who take them might be appropriate candidates for testosterone replacement (see below). **Opiate analgesics** like Demerol or Codeine may affect orgasm. Typically, a course of treatment on painkillers is short-lived, and the patient can step down to Tylenol or aspirin after a few days. **Chemotherapy** drugs, which are both toxic and also have antihormonal effects, are the worst offenders. The antiandrogens that are used, such as Tamoxifen, usually result in loss of libido, as well as vaginal atrophy (dry vagina), hot flashes, and mood swings. Since many women have chemotherapy in the aftermath of an estrogen-related cancer, they are not candidates for hormone replacement and must use natural treatments (see chapters 9 and 11) to restore any libido at all. Research is currently under way to determine whether natural substances are safe for patients who have experienced breast cancer.

And let us briefly mention the chemical mood changers that are only available illegally. Women do, of course, use marijuana, cocaine, Quaaludes, and the flavor of the year, Ecstasy, in order to get in the mood for sex. Some of these street drugs will relax you; others will pep you up—but most will inhibit sexual performance even if they enhance arousal. They are all potentially dangerous and involve a great deal of personal, physiological, and legal risk. A glass of wine, a massage, and some deep breathing may do as much for your sexual inhibitions as a few tokes on a joint or a line of coke. And more important, these will not land you in jail or in the hospital.

But if you're interested in playing with the light and shadow of chemicals, you might want to look at prescription drugs. There is nothing yet that's a sure bet, but there are many busy minds at work on the elaborate details of enhancing female sexual function.

Drugs That May Reduce Libido	Alternatives
1. Antihistamines	Treat your cold naturally, use lubricant
2. Blood pressure meds	Ask your doctor to switch medications
3. Diuretics	Ask your doctor to switch medications
4. Chemotherapy/radiation	Add nonhormonal lubricants
5. Meds for diabetes, thyroid, Lymes	Add nonhormonal lubricants
6. Antipsychotics	Ask doctor about timing of dosage
7. Opiate analgesics (drugs for pain)	Ask doctor about timing of dosage
8. Antidepressants	Switch meds; ask doctor about a drug holiday
9. Tranquilizers	Switch meds; ask doctor about a drug holiday
10. Oral contraceptives	Switch meds; use diaphragm, IUD, or latex condom
11. Drugs for endometriosis and infertility treatment	Wait for cycle to end; switch meds
12. Street drugs	Try a glass of wine and a massage instead

DRUGS THAT MIGHT HELP YOUR SEX LIFE

On the Drawing Board: A Pill to Make Sex Better

Debates are currently raging in medical think tanks, laboratories, and institutes of pharmacological research as to whether it is possible, by tinkering with chemistry, to make sex wonderful for a woman or restore sexual feeling to what it once was. Clearly this is a much more difficult task for a woman than a man. For most men, the erection that results from blood flowing into the penis is a visual stimulant for engaging in some sort of sexual activity. Thanks to men's predominant gonadal hormone, testosterone, desire is easy to muster, especially when a firm erection is obvious and palpable.

For women, it's not nearly this simple. First, they can't see anything happening when they get sexually excited. Nipples may become erect, but they are usually smothered in the confines of a brassiere. The clitoris certainly stands up, but very few women are in a position or of a mind to look at that. Many women don't actually feel that they are wet, even when a partner verifies that they are. Some women do become aware that their breath is shorter and raspier, but they may interpret that as being due to physical exertion rather than their increased arousal. As for feeling "horny," well, it's been described as a heavy, warm, tingling sensation in the genitals, and yet some women read this as only slightly different from what it's like when they have to urinate. Unfortunately, because of a lack of awareness and a cultural reluctance to discuss female sexuality directly, most of us grow up completely ignorant of what's going on in our bodies during an erotic interlude.

Hormones of Desire and Arousal

The two major gonadal hormones, estrogen and testosterone, are present in both males and females. Though both genders produce both hormones, it's the amount and balance of these chemical messengers that influences our sexual and reproductive well-being. The major sex hormones are the family of estrogens (the three principal ones are estriol, estradiol, and estrone), the progestins (the major one is progesterone), and the androgens (the major one is testosterone).

The libido, or sex drive, is in great part dependent on how much of which hormones are available and "free," that is, not bound to receptors, and their amount varies during any part of our menstrual cycle or our life cycle. So our interest in scratching that itch has an almost wavelike pattern—the rise and fall in our secretions has a big influence on whether or not we approach our partner with open arms, or turn over and go to sleep.

Testosterone for Zest, Strength, and Desire

Desire is regulated by a combination of what's going on inside us and what's going on outside us. Testosterone fuels sexual desire, but does not determine whether we'll turn to our partner or to ourselves for relief. Then too, we don't have to act on those urges. We may simply be aware of the increase in genital sensations and smile inwardly without satisfying them. (Men don't have as easy a time with this option as we do!) Some women equate desire with sexual fantasies, tingling sensations, and masturbatory urges. Other women feel a surge of desire only when they feel especially loved or close to a partner. Still others never experience spontaneous sexual desire but are quite receptive to sensual touch, which may ignite passion. And finally, still other women mirror the desire and arousal of their partners. In other words, each of us burns at different temperatures, ignited by different fuels, and this may change at different times of our lives.

In order to feel physical desire, a woman must have sufficient amounts of both estrogen *and* testosterone. Although it's more common for women to lack sufficient testosterone after the removal of their uterus and ovaries (hysterectomy and oophorectomy), androgen deficiency is not unknown in younger women. And *no* woman produces anywhere near the amount of this gonadal hormone as men do.

At puberty, boys start producing 300 to 1,000 picograms of testosterone per milliliter daily, and this gives them their muscles, pubic and underarm hair, deep voices, and preoccupation with sex. A female, who makes only a ninth of this amount in her adrenals and ovaries, relies on estrogen as her major gonadal hormone, but she has to have a little testosterone or her interest in sex will die on the vine. A woman who lacks sufficient testosterone will no longer fantasize about sex (if she ever did), or masturbate, or feel "in the mood," even when stimulated by an erotic film or a sexy look. Typically, she may also lack sensation in her nipples and clitoris and feel a general lack of vitality and energy.[3]

As we get older, we don't have the same number of testosterone receptors, nor do we produce the same number of enzymes that allow us to use this hormone on a cellular level. Just like men, most of our testosterone travels in the blood bound to the protein known as SHBG (sex-hormone binding globulin). And estrogen stimulates the production of more SHBG, which binds up more testosterone. We need more free testosterone to feel that urge to merge.

But there's no general rule for how much is enough, either bound or free. Two women with identical testosterone levels may have totally different sensitivities—one may experience her level as deprivation and the other may find it just the tonic she needs to get aroused.

What is a normal level of testosterone for a woman in her reproductive years? Ah, there's the question that no one seems to be able to answer. A variety of reliable laboratories come up with a pretty wide range for free testosterone, which is 1.3 to 6.8 pg/ml (picograms per milliliter) for women from 18 to 46. And the general consensus is that total testosterone decreases as much as 50 percent as women age from 20 to 50.[4] If a patient comes to therapy and says she has no interest in sex whatsoever, and that she once enjoyed it, Sandra recommends that she consult her gynecologist or an endocrinologist and ask to have her levels of DHEA and testosterone checked. If her levels fall into the lowest quarter of whatever is considered normal for a woman of her age, then adding testosterone to her hormonal brew may help. However, different laboratories use different assays and often, results from one lab don't jive with those from another. Also, because women's levels of testosterone are so much smaller than men's, it is difficult to get an accurate reading. It can be helpful to test once and then repeat the test at the same lab a year later, to see if there's been a significant decline in levels.

There are plenty of women who have higher than average levels who have problems with desire, and women who have lower than average levels who have no trouble at all feeling frisky. Which tells us, once again, that female sexuality is not about one thing but about many. But since replacement testosterone can make a difference in some women, Sandra recommends that if levels are low, you try to raise them. It's a start, because it may motivate you to think more about your sex life. Many women are concerned that taking testosterone will make them "masculine," that is, it will give them facial hair, deep voices, and huge muscles, as well as doing damage to their liver. But with the low dosages that are prescribed for women taking testosterone preparations, you should not have negative side effects if you take only the prescribed dose, and you might just reap additional benefits, such as more vitality, less fatigue, and stronger bones. Women respond differently to dosing—some will have a big increase in testosterone from a very small dose, and others, particularly those with immune system diseases who are very deficient in testosterone, seem to need a great deal more. Also, testosterone supplementation may depend on other drugs you are taking; for example, women on birth control pills (high in estrogen and progesterone) will see little or no effect.

Sandra's patient Adrienne had been on estrogen replacement after a hysterectomy, and she came to therapy a year after her surgery saying that she felt "completely neutered. I just don't ever want it," she said, "even though my husband is attentive and loving and lots of fun in bed. He's always been like that, but now it does nothing for me."

Sandra suggested that she might consider getting a prescription for a testosterone cream or ask about switching to Estratest, a product that combines estrogen and testosterone. When Sandra saw her six months later, she looked like she'd spent her time at a European spa. What was different? "When I first took it, I was dubious, but within a couple of weeks, I was unable to think of anything *but* sex. It was so distracting. Also, I found myself flying into rages at the least little thing. So my gynecologist lowered the dose a little, and now, sex is not just good, it's better than ever because I made an effort to get it back. I also feel that zing that testosterone is supposed to give— a feeling of self-confidence and personal strength."

Currently, there are a few ways you can take testosterone:

❀ **Topical cream:** Your physician can prescribe a topical cream or gel of natural micronized testosterone, which can be mixed for you by a custom-compounding pharmacy. When it is micronized—a powdered formulation of the hormone—it can be prescribed by your physician in any dosage to be made up as a cream or gel. (Most women prefer the topical preparations to the oral ones, since testosterone, applied directly to the clitoris or labia, can increase sensitivity in those areas. It can also be rubbed into the arm, thigh, or stomach.) The dosages can range from less than 1 mg to as much as 25 or 30 mg per day, depending on the results of your hormone test.

🌸 **Natural micronized capsules, lozenges, or sublingual drops:** Micronized testosterone can be prepared as an oral formulation suspended in olive or coconut oil.

🌸 **Topical gel:** Solvay Pharmaceutical is working on a testosterone gel, Androgel, that will dry into a patch and release an adequate amount of hormone into the bloodstream over a 24-hour period. There has been virtually no research done in women on the importance of testosterone cycling, so that it is highest in the morning and lower at other times of day, as is the case when it is naturally produced by the body. This appears to be very important in men. So it will be interesting to see whether the patch's continuous delivery of the hormone flattens the effect on desire.

🌸 **Combination pill (Estratest):** This pill contains estrogen and testosterone in combination. A woman with an intact uterus must also take a progestin or natural progesterone to prevent the uterine lining from overgrowing and developing precancerous cells, which might develop under the influence of unopposed estrogen. The derivative of testosterone in this medication is never actually converted by the body into natural testosterone, and in addition, it may compromise liver function and lower HDL levels. Many women feel that the medication is just enough to improve libido; others feel it is too low to be effective.

🌸 **Other formulations with additional hormones:** Many physicians are concerned about the natural conversion of testosterone to estrogen, particularly in patients who may be at risk for estrogen-dependent cancers. Progesterone can be mixed with the testosterone to diminish the conversion, and in addition, patients can also be advised to take herbs and supplements to further diminish the effect. Oral zinc, chrysin, and saw palmetto are recommended for this; ask your doctor about appropriate dosages. In Europe, pharmacists are using dihydrotestosterone, a different formulation that does not convert as easily, but it is not yet available in the United States.

In addition to the above possibilities, there is a new product on the drawing board, a *patch,* worn on the hip or buttock, that delivers testosterone using the skin as a semipermeable membrane. In 1995, the FDA approved the transdermal Androderm patch for men with low testosterone, and subsequently, researchers went on to consider the desire problem in women. They decided to study women who had had their ovaries removed, where the reduction in testosterone was immediate and the decline in their sexual function was most dramatic.

"The role of testosterone in female biology has never been appreciated," says Norm Mazer, vice president of clinical research at Watson Laboratories, the company that collaborated with Procter & Gamble on the female patch, which contains a low dose (only 0.15 mg to 0.3 mg) of testosterone, which is typically what the human ovary makes daily during the reproductive years.[5] It releases medication over a four-day period and uses the same testosterone molecule that the body produces naturally, as opposed to the derivatives used in tablets.

A recent multi-center study looked at 75 hysterectomized and oophorectomized women who were taking estrogen replacement therapy but complained of low sexual desire and arousal. A testosterone patch was used to determine whether additional testosterone would stimulate greater sexual interest. All the women in the study were married or in long-term partnered relationships, and each woman was given either placebo, a 150 mcg daily testosterone patch or a 300 mcg daily testosterone patch in a randomized order for twelve weeks. At the end of the three-month study, all the women said that their sexual lives were more satisfying, although the women at the highest dosage levels of testosterone reported the most significant increase in sexual frequency, pleasure, and well-being. They also said they were less depressed and more positive about life at the end of this time.[6]

But why did all the women do better, even those taking the placebo? And what does this say about replacement testosterone? Despite the fact that we know how important the effects of testosterone can be in terms of boosting desire, what may be more important is how *motivated* women are to get their sex lives back on track.

Clearly, sex means more than just the urge to have it. And there are many more steps involved, even after a woman feels desire. She still must feel physically aroused to be ready-set-go for sex, and this requires a pretty fair amount of estrogen.

Estrogen/Progesterone for Well-Being and Arousal

Estrogen counts. It may protect the bones and heart, keep the skin glowing, and the brain remembering where you parked the car. But it also is really important when we're talking about sex. The family of estrogens is responsible for the menstrual cycle, the development of breasts and hips suitable for childbearing, and a higher ratio of fat to muscle throughout the female body. It keeps the vagina elastic, and allows women to lubricate readily when aroused. It maintains the urethral lining and makes sure that the bladder is sufficiently elastic to contain urine. Because it helps to plump up the tissues, estrogen allows stimulation and friction of sensitive areas, like the clitoris, labia, and nipples.

Unopposed estrogen (that is, without the progestin) increases the risk of uterine cancer and may increase the risk of breast cancer. It also increases the density of the breasts, making the job of reading mammograms more difficult. There may be more false positives in women who are taking estrogen only.

While we're talking about estrogen and sexuality, we would be remiss not to mention progesterone, the counterbalance to estrogen. Although it's generally known as the hormone of pregnancy, because it prepares the lining of the uterus, the endometrium, for the implantation of a fertilized egg, it's got plenty of other functions. Although it can produce PMS-like symptoms, it also has its good side; it helps to lower the risk of uterine cancer.

So let us consider how this estrogen/progesterone mix figures in the cycle of sexuality. During our reproductive years, when our bodies give us specific monthly signals and we know when we're likely to bleed or when we're likely to feel moody, it's easier to understand how we might relate to a partner sexually. We can lubricate because estrogen keeps the vaginal tissues pumping out fluids; we can experience a warm flush throughout the body, specifically in the genitals, when our partner whispers sweet nothings and touches us.

In the mid-to-late forties, the mix of hormones begins to change. When a woman has been without a period for twelve consecutive months, her cycle is considered to be over and she is then called "postmenopausal." Her estrogen levels will have dropped to about a fifth of their peak level during the reproductive years, and her progesterone levels will have plummeted to zero.

Certainly, the effect of this hormonal landslide is felt in the sexual realm. The vagina shrinks and becomes less elastic. The endometrium becomes dry and friable without the lubrication afforded by estrogen production, and this thinner skin is more susceptible to irritation and infection. The pubic hair gets thinner and starts falling out; the clitoris and nipples no longer stand up readily when aroused. In addition, the ease and frequency of orgasm is somewhat reduced in midlife. This may be due to the altered feeling of the orgasm itself. A woman who used to be easily orgasmic and had many exciting peaks may be disappointed to find that she has fewer contractions. Some women may leak a little urine during orgasm due to a less firm closing of the urethral sphincter, and this, too, can be very unsettling. The most difficult change noted by some women in midlife is when orgasm itself is painful—whereas this experience was always an out-of-control, but wonderful, sensation, now it may be truly difficult to manage. There are other women, however, who have none of these problems, and in fact, only come into their sexual prime after 45. Reports of multiple and serial orgasm are more frequent in older women than in younger ones.

If you are perimenopausal or menopausal and find that your sexual interest is waning, it's a good idea to talk to your gynecologist about having your estrogen levels tested, especially if you are not really sure about taking HRT or ERT (estrogen replacement therapy, for those women who have no uterus). For decades, these two drug regimens have been the gold standard of postmenopausal treatment, whether natural or surgical. Estrogen has a positive effect on over three hundred tissues in the body, including the bones, heart, brain, bladder, and of course, the sexual organs.

Still, there are risks as well as benefits. Certain studies indicate that women may be at higher risk for breast and endometrial cancer after more than five years on ERT. Women who take HRT may also be more at risk for gallbladder disease, blood-clotting problems, and liver or kidney disease. There are newer, nonhormonal drugs for osteoporosis, and with all the hoopla about estrogen lowering the risk of heart disease and deaths from heart attacks in women, recent reports suggest that the hormone may not be effective in this area. However, if your major reason for considering this drug is to alleviate hot flashes or enhance your sex life, you can take it in a form that is extremely safe.

"I didn't like the idea of HRT, but I took it because my mother had advanced osteoporosis," Lena, a divorced fashion designer of 55 told me. "After two months, I'd gained seven pounds, and I really hated bleeding again after all those years. But I have to say I liked not having hot flashes, and sex was a lot more comfortable. So I switched to Fosamax for my bones, and started using an estrogen vaginal tablet, much neater than the cream, and it doesn't get absorbed into my bloodstream as readily. I'm really happy to see my new boyfriend these days, let me tell you!"

To have a sex life that gives you satisfaction, you need both *motivation* and *physical resources.* Estrogen does not affect libido as testosterone does, but it certainly influences mood, and you might be more likely to want sex if you feel positive about yourself and your life. As for the physical resources, estrogen is the linchpin to arousal, since it preserves the genital tissues and allows for lubrication. It keeps the tissues of the vagina and bladder elastic so that sex is comfortable. And it alleviates hot flashes that might interfere with a hot and heavy encounter.

"I wasn't sleeping because of night sweats, and sex felt like dry friction," a 53-year-old patient, Sonia, told Sandra. "So when I was thoroughly miserable, I took oral HRT on the advice of my gynecologist, although I'm a kind of natural, Birkenstock-and-granola type. I'd tried plenty of over-the-counter healthfood store supplements, like wild yam creams, and I ate enough soy products to choke a horse, but none of that really improved the symptoms. So I took estrogen. I've been on it for about a year, and I'm a total convert. I think it ought to be free to every woman past menopause—at least for five years."

Like Sonia, many postmenopausal patients do well on estrogen replacement. We do recommend it for serious consideration, since most women who take it are very pleased with the improvement in their sexual comfort, their skin, and even their mood. But this very personal decision must be made in consultation with your doctor, and the mode of treatment must be customized for each woman.

There are several ways to take estrogen:

⊛ **ERT:** If you have no uterus, and therefore no uterine lining that might become precancerous, you can take an oral estrogen alone. Oral estrogen alleviates menopausal symptoms and helps to improve sexual arousal. This is a systemic drug, affecting the entire body.

⊛ **HRT:** If you have a uterus, you must take a combination of estrogen and progesterone. Oral estrogen and progesterone alleviates menopausal symptoms and helps to improve sexual arousal. This is a systemic drug, affecting the entire body.

⊛ **Patch:** This transdermal patch emits estrogen in a timed-release fashion. You must take an oral progestin if you have a uterus. This is a systemic drug, affecting the entire body.

⊛ **Estring:** The recently FDA-approved estradiol vaginal ring (a 2 mg impregnated silicone ring inserted above the cervix) emits estrogen for three months, but acts locally, not systemically, so there is low systemic absorption of the drug. The ring alleviates sexual and urogenital symptoms, such as dryness, burning, or painful sex.[7]

⊛ **Estrogen cream:** The cream acts locally, not systemically. The amount of estrogen is not significant enough to thicken the endometrial lining if used daily but then tapered down to one to three times weekly. The **vaginal tablet** (Vagifem) has the same effect, and once again, there is low systemic absorption of the drug when taken as directed—one tablet daily for two weeks and then one tablet twice weekly.

Taking hormones is clearly not a one-size-fits-all decision. You need to assess your reasons for replacement estrogen, your personal and family medical history, and your expectations for the drug. As a patient, and as a sexual woman, you should ask a lot of questions and be as informed as you can about your options.

Suppose It's Natural? DHEA and L-Arginine

We know a good deal about replacement testosterone and estrogen because scientists have been involved in thorough, double-blind placebo studies on these hormones for years. But the newer candidates on the sexual horizon are not as well tested. If you're interested in trying supplements that might improve sex, remember that the evidence is mostly anecdotal. But the substances are legal, and in small amounts, they are probably pretty benign. The question is, will they make you feel sexier?

Some experts are very excited about the prospects of **DHEA** (dehydroepiandrosterone) for enhancing female sexuality. This steroid hormone is produced by the sex glands (the ovaries and testes) or the adrenal cortex and has the unusual property of being able to convert first to testosterone and then to estrogen, as the body requires. It seems to buffer the other hormones in the body against sudden changes in acidity or alkalinity, and in so doing, it protects against the stress response.

The claims for this hormone are many; the testing (mostly on laboratory animals) inconclusive in humans, but it has been suggested that supplemental doses of this hormone will double your sexual pleasure. Dr. Julia Heiman, a clinical psychologist at the University of Washington and author of a well-received popular book on orgasm, found that postmenopausal women in a study she conducted had a heightened subjective response to erotic stimuli on DHEA over placebo, although there were no substantial vaginal changes. This one small study suggests that DHEA may work on the central nervous system first, before having any peripheral or genital sexual response.[8]

Dr. Audré Guay, director of the Center for Sexual Function at the Lahey Clinic North Shore and clinical professor of medicine at Harvard Medical School, is even more enthusiastic about the hormone.[9] In his studies using Viagra on women, he found that the drug was not successful in women with low testosterone levels. And because there is currently no standardized dosage or administration for testosterone in women, he decided to try DHEA. If his patients complained of lack of energy and lack of libido, he started them on 50 mg of DHEA daily for two months and then would test their levels again. If they hadn't increased slightly, he'd increase the dosage to 75 mg for another two months, and then, if necessary, to 100 mg.

Dr. Guay feels that all the pharmaceutical efforts to help women to become more aroused are misguided, because they have to feel desire first. "If free testosterone is lower than 1.0 pc/ml, giving DHEA can make the difference," said Dr. Guay. "Within about three months, you can see more energy, more libido, more lubrication—although since DHEA converts to estrogen, the lubrication may be from the estrogenic effect. Of course, any woman who's had breast cancer can't take this hormone because of the increased estrogen. Young women have to be on birth control pills to take it, because if they should get pregnant and be taking DHEA during their first trimester, the fetus might be virilized [develop masculine characteristics] and end up with ambiguous genitalia. But for older women, if carefully monitored by a physician, DHEA could be a real boon because it puts T [testosterone] on board, and that's what they need first to improve their sex lives."

Another nonprescription combination that's been tested out is a marriage of L–arginine, an essential amino acid, the primary source of nitrogen molecules required to produce nitric oxide, and yohimbine *(Pausinystalia johimbe),* an alkaloid compound from the bark of a West African tree that has been shown to dilate blood vessels and which has been used successfully for male erectile dysfunction for years. Nitric oxide is part of the big chain reaction that causes erections to occur and can also assist in female arousal.

Dr. Cindy Meston, an associate professor at the University of Texas at Austin, conducted a small double-blind study on postmenopausal women with arousal disorder and found that the combination of L-arginine and yohimbine gave good results within one hour as compared with placebo. In this case, as opposed to the DHEA study, the women became more aroused and lubricated, but they didn't report feeling more sexually turned on.[10]

Both of these supplements are available at your local healthfood store, so you can try them if you choose to—but don't expect to see results for about three to six months. Unfortunately, the brands have many different dosages and varying degrees of purity—and few experts can say how much anyone should take, and whether they are worthwhile in women with adequate testosterone levels (which is a good reason to have your levels tested before you proceed). The few human studies that give any indication of success have used 50 mg daily of DHEA-S (sulfate), a cheaper form of the hormone with a longer half-life. We strongly recommend you work with your doctor if you want to try these supplements. We simply don't know enough about their downsides and side effects, so let your doctor monitor you carefully.

Several herbs are reputed aphrodisiacs. Damiana, kava kava, ginseng, muira puama—which either relax or stimulate the body and mind—are the best known, and these, too, are available over the counter in healthfood stores. (These should *not* be used by pregnant women, since reactions with the unborn fetus are unknown.) Since the FDA does not test these substances, it's impossible to say how much of which one will tweak your own body chemistry in just the right way to make you more receptive or interested in sex. On the other hand, trying something means that you are taking an active role in your sexual journey. Why not? What have you got to lose? Check with your doctor, then follow the package directions to the letter, and monitor yourself for any changes, sexual or otherwise.

But wait a minute. What about that little blue pill? If it did so much for men, couldn't it help women, too?

Viagra for Women?

Viagra (sildenafil) changed the sexual landscape for men. First, it brought a major lifestyle issue out into the open. With half of all men between 40 and 70 experiencing some degree of erectile dysfunction, wasn't it strange that the condition had stayed in the closet for so long?

There were desperate types who went to the doctor, but how many of them would use the admittedly unappealing available methods to take care of their problem? Few men would enthusiastically inject their penis with a drug cocktail of phentolamine and papaverine—or take happily to the idea of having silicone rods or pumps inserted in their testicles. There were drugs that relaxed smooth-muscle tissue, but none were widely effective and easily administrated (the Muse suppository had to be inserted into the urinary meatus!). It was difficult for most men to equate having a wonderful time in bed with all this unpleasant drug foreplay.

Then, by a fluky coincidence, as Pfizer chemists formulated a pill to regulate vasodilation in men with angina, they stumbled on the solution for that other disaster that had troubled them for so long.[11] And when that little blue pill was approved by the FDA in March 1998, an extraordinary turnabout occurred. Men, in many cases goaded by the deprived women in their lives, picked up the phone and made an appointment with their primary care physician or urologist. Men dug deep into their pockets and paid the $10 for the chance, once again, to see four inches become six, and to feel the delight and accomplishment of pleasing a partner as they pleased themselves.

Viagra works in the following way: Sexual stimulation causes penile nerves to produce a chemical called nitric oxide. The nitric oxide activates enzymes to produce cyclic GMP, which relaxes the blood vessels in the penis and lets them expand, causing an erection to occur. The medication inhibits the enzyme, PDE-5, which allows for cyclic GMP accumulation. With no PDE-5 appearing on the scene for about an hour, a man can happily enjoy sex play and intercourse.

Well, women need some type of physical response, too. Whether or not they are aware of it, genital tissues swell, the walls of the vagina lubricate, facial flushing occurs, breathing and respiration increase, and the nipples and clitoris engorge. Many partners of sexually renovated lovers found it frustrating to have a partner who was sexually enthusiastic when they themselves were not aroused. Moreover, too frequent intercourse sometimes brought on bladder and vaginal infections, particularly in older women who had been sexually abstinent or had had only occasional sex for the past few years.

It wasn't just that they were trying to keep up. Women wanted *their* pleasure, too. Thanks to the Pill, women have been happily able to control their reproductive lives now for the past four decades—why shouldn't they have the same freedom to control their sexual response? Without asking permission, lots of women pilfered their husbands' pills.

"I wanted to see what it would do for *me*," explained Linda, a 62-year-old gynecologist from Baltimore. "My husband asked me to write a prescription for him, and I told him he didn't need it, but I have to admit, we were both curious. After he took it about three times, he was sold. He was convinced that his erections were harder and he had a more dramatic orgasm and ejaculation.

"Like many women in a long-term relationship, I don't have the same level of desire I used to, and that made arousal more difficult. I was on estrogen and had tried Estratest, but when my husband's level of interest went down, so did mine. I've always been a woman who was motivated by my partner's excitement, even if my own level of intrinsic desire was low. Another change I didn't like was that I had stopped being coitally orgasmic. So we decided to try Viagra together to see what would happen."

She took 25 mg and he took 50, and they were delighted. For the first time in a very long time, she came when he was inside her. They used the medication seven or eight times with the same result and no problems other than some facial flushing. (They continued using a lubricant because Viagra didn't completely reverse her dryness, and the moist feeling of the topical application helped her to become aroused.) She took Advil to alleviate the slight fullness in her head. Once she tried the higher dosage, but was concerned about adverse effects. The FDA findings on deaths suggested that Viagra is not dangerous except for individuals with heart disease who are on medications containing nitrates. The twelve million men currently using Viagra are testimony to the fact that the drug works safely and effectively for most men.

Linda wonders, and many sex researchers echo her question, whether much of this renewed sexual buoyancy has to do with expectations. You think it's going to make things better, and it does. (Pfizer found a large placebo effect in the studies they conducted on men before the product was approved by the FDA.) Yes, it's important to get blood flow to the genitals and lubrication makes things feel better, but there's also that ineffable connection between partners who are engaged in doing something exciting together. "I think the best benefit of Viagra," said Linda, "is that it can create more enthusiastic lovers." Viagra takes about an hour to kick in, but that gives a couple time to take a shower, give each other a massage, sit and just touch gently, if they choose to.

Sandra has many women in her practice who have snitched their husbands' drugs. There seems to be no harm in trying it a few times if you are not on nitrates. (Again, check with your doctor.) Side effects include flushing, indigestion, blue vision, nasal congestion, urinary tract infections, abnormal vision, diarrhea, dizziness, dry mouth, and clitoral hypersensitivity, but these are quite uncommon. The most common complaint is headache, so many physicians recommend that their patients take aspirin with the Viagra.

The New Contenders—Other Drugs to Alleviate
Female Sexual Dysfunction

Dozens of drug companies are scurrying to find new products that circumvent the drawbacks of Viagra. They're eager to come up with a faster, more user-friendly method of getting blood flowing to the genitals, without unpleasant side effects. One candidate vying for attention is a phosphodiesterase inhibitor, a compound that blocks certain forms of the enzyme PDE-5. This drug, currently the hot topic in Bristol-Myers Squibb laboratories, appears to be as potent as Viagra in achieving relaxation of the smooth-muscle tissues, but has greater specificity for different types of the enzyme that triggers visual disturbances and facial flushing. Bayer Corporation's investigation of the drug Vardenafil is a promising candidate to rival Viagra. It takes only half an hour to begin working and seems to have a slightly better side-effect profile.

Vasomax (phentolamine metholate) was considered a real contender, and as of this writing has not obtained FDA approval. But rats who were taking the drug developed benign tumors, and Zonagen, the manufacturer, went back to testing. Now this vasoactive drug, which works on different enzymes than Viagra and circumvents the problems of blue vision, heartburn, and the other side effects, may not obtain FDA approval, at least in the near future. The company is also working on a vaginal gel, a preparation of phentolamine called Vasofem.[12]

There are a slew of new preparations that are made from the same stuff used in the injectables for male sexual dysfunction—papaverine, phentolamine, and alprostadil—but in a cream or gel formulation that can be used as part of foreplay, which is, of course, a big part of what women want.[13] A New Jersey company called NexMed is currently working on Femprox, an alprostadil-based cream currently in Phase II clinical trials. Topiglan is in the works from MacroChem Corporation. This topical formulation is intended to treat erectile dysfunction, but the manufacturers are hoping that it will work as nicely on the clitoris as it does on its homologue, the penis. In New York City, Dr. Jed Kaminetsky, a urologist, has developed two versions of his "Dream Cream," one made of L-arginine and an asthma medication that contains a phosphodiesterase inhibitor, and the other, an over-the-counter version that is mainly L-arginine. Patients report that the cream, at about $7 per dose, is worth every penny—the topical formulation is also considered a plus by most patients, although a few complain that the warmth generated by the cream can be irritating rather than erotic.[14]

At Harvard Scientific, a Florida-based pharmaceutical company, a gel and a spray for the vaginal area are in development. Another similar spray, created by the Japanese genius who brought us the floppy disk, is awaiting a U.S. patent. These products would last about an hour per dose and could be reapplied immediately.

But are these the answer for *women*? Most of Sandra's patients suffer from a lack of sexual desire, and getting back blood flow and lubrication are simply the tip of the iceberg.

It is apparent that if you have no desire for sex—for whatever reason— these vasodilating drugs won't help. And yet over half the women in the multisite study on Viagra, even those who weren't taking the active drug, said that sex was better, as do the women using various topical preparations that increase blood flow. What this means is that if you care enough to do *any-thing*—whether it's enter a study, talk to your partner about your wishes and desires, make more time to be sensual or sexual, or take a placebo and believe in it wholeheartedly—your sex life may improve. The key, then, is in the mind and the central nervous system.

Getting Your Groove Back: Wanting It Again

Testosterone for women with androgen insuffiency is one method of recapturing desire, but another way to achieve it is to fiddle with the neurotransmitters in the brain—you need serotonin to make you feel comfortable and in the mood for pleasure; and you need dopamine to have that wild intense joy you used to get as a kid racing downstairs on Christmas morning.

TAP Pharmaceuticals, a division of Takeda Chemical Industries, who later were subsumed under a company called Pentech, thought they had the problem solved when they went into their large Phase III trial on men with erectile dysfunction. Their drug, Uprima, is a dopamine agonist administered as a sublingual (under the tongue) tablet. The active ingredient of this medication, apomorphine, is fast-acting (twenty minutes as opposed to an hour for Viagra) and works on the central nervous system to initiate the genital relaxation. Unfortunately, in the trials, although men did get erections with Uprima, a few of them also experienced vomiting and fainting. The worrisome side effects of apomorphine, hardly conducive to sexual interest or activity, are major hurdles for the drug, which has not been approved in the United States, although it is doing a brisk business in Europe.

Finally, there is one FDA-approved method of treating sexual dysfunction that is not chemical, but mechanical. The EROS-CTD (clitoral therapy device), developed by UroMetrics in Minnesota, is a petite vacuum pump that looks like a computer mouse with a small funnel on the end. The funnel goes directly over the clitoris and produces a firm sucking or vacuum-like sensation when the device is turned on. The EROS device is noninvasive and has no side-effects—except for its $359 price tag, which may be covered by insurance. Opinions have been mixed—women with arousal dysfunction and those with low touch sensitivity think it's wonderful; women with normal function tend to feel it exerts too much pressure on a very delicate area, and they prefer a vibrator. But some sex therapists are trying it out with patients, particularly those who have gone through chemotherapy and have become anorgasmic.[15]

Although this is good news for some women, we know perfectly well that the genitals are not the only organs that respond sexually when you are turned on. The amazing mix of details—physical, psychological, emotional, situational—that come into play before, during, and after an erotic event means that it will probably be some time before science can piece together a panacea for female sexual dysfunction. And in this race for a solution, it would be foolish to bet everything on just one horse.[16]

Marian Dunn, Ph.D., director of the Center for Human Sexuality at the State University of New York Health Science Center, Brooklyn, who recommends Viagra for many of her male patients, points out that it's vital that doctors spend the time to educate couples in the use of this drug and others like it and encourage them to have realistic expectations for success.[17] "They can't simply be handed a prescription and given a wink and a pat on the back," said Dunn. "Physicians have a responsibility to explain to the couple that Viagra won't fix a troubled relationship—in some cases, a lack of sex has probably maintained the status quo, and shaking everything up with this little blue pill may cause additional problems between the two."[18]

Nevertheless, as of this writing, there are few cheerleaders for Viagra use in women. One multisite study of 577 women worldwide indicates that Viagra by itself is not the answer to a better sex life. Slightly over 50 percent on the active drug found it helpful and slightly over 50 percent on placebo found it helpful, which once again shows us how incredibly complex female sexual response can be.

"Nearly half of the women in the study suffered from low desire, about 30 percent had arousal problems, 20 percent had orgasmic disorder, and under 10 percent complained of lack of lubrication," reported Rosemary Basson, MD, physician and sex therapist, who was responsible for testing 15 women at the Vancouver site.[19] "The first group were either premenopausal or were taking estrogen; the second group were postmenopausal and not taking estrogen. So we had women from 18 to 55 who were recorded at baseline for a month, then on placebo or Viagra (at either 10, 50, or 100 mg doses) for another three months.

"But the important thing to remember about female sexual dysfunction is that there are so many subgroups—you can be excited in your mind but not feel pleasant sensations in your body and vice versa, or you can lack pleasure in mind and body." As Basson points out, what the women didn't get was satisfaction. And this is the major point. Men need an erection to be sexual, and Viagra can do that; women need to have their minds as well as their bodies altered, and vasodilation is not enough.[20]

In the clinical trials that are being done on these drugs with tiny groups of usually postmenopausal or hysterectomized women, the researchers are desperately longing to hear the words "increased lubrication," "warmth," "tingling," and most important, "satisfaction." Because what good are lubrication and blood flow if subjectively they don't make sex any more desirable?

When are you satisfied? Maybe it's having enough sleep, going for a three-mile run, then coming home to take a long hot shower and putting on a silk camisole under your Polartec sweater. But you can also feel satisfied after finishing a great novel, or listening to one of Beethoven's late quartets. Satisfaction, in sexual terms, means all of that—you want to feel physically fulfilled, not drained; you want to feel emotionally gratified, not regretful; and you want to feel mentally content and at peace. But it's not reasonable to expect a pill, or salve, or squirt to provide all three kinds of satisfaction.

PRESCRIPTION DRUGS AND SUPPLEMENTS THAT MAY ENHANCE SEX

Hormonal	*Neurotransmitter production*
Estrogen	Apomorphine (Uprima)
Testosterone	
DHEA-S (non-p.)	
	Mechanical
	Eros-CTD
Vasodilation	Vibrators
Viagra	
Vibrators	
Vardenafil	*Herbal*
Vasomax-Vasofem	Damiana
Phosphodiesterase inhibitor	Ginseng
Femprox (topical)	Kava kava
Topiglan	Muira puama
"Dream Cream"	
L-arginine (non-p.)	

Sexuality Is More Than Just Chemicals

We used to think of sexuality as a straight line. Masters and Johnson saw the model of excitement as fitting both partners: a path that progressed from desire to arousal to plateau to orgasm to resolution. But a newer model, designed by Rosemary Basson, MD, clinical professor and sexual medicine expert, suggests that it is the desire for intimacy that starts the cycle going for women, rather than the wish for physical release. We crave closeness with our partner, and this leads us to seek or be receptive to sexual stimulation. That stimulation causes arousal, which whets desire, which leads to even more arousal, culminating in orgasm. The cycle gets repeated because of our positive memories of the good feelings associated with our last sexual encounter.

A balance of estrogen and testosterone will modify the response of the limbic system; DHEA may increase energy and libido; a brand-new type of SSRI may enhance the good memories and temper the bad ones; a vasodilator will get the blood vessels ready for sex; a centrally acting drug will change neurotransmitter output; but science still hasn't figured out the whole equation. Some women may respond well to one drug or a combination of drugs;

others may not respond at all. It will undoubtedly take more, in the long run, to make that circle run smoothly.

Satisfaction is really not primarily physical—it has to do with expectations, with positive memories, with knowing what worked the last time and what might be good the next—or be even better in the future. If you're easily pleased, it won't take much (maybe just a smear of gel or a patch on your ass) to increase your satisfaction. If you imagine yourself as the doyen of a Turkish seraglio, with hot partners draped around you and in you, then a little spray on your vagina won't improve things much. You may be satisfied with one orgasm on Sunday, but on Thursday find that no less than ten will do.

The perfect aphrodisiac for women cannot be bottled, of course, because there would be too many ingredients that had to go into the mix of that little pill—physical, mental, emotional, and contextual. A drug or several drugs in combination will make eroticism possible, but probably won't ever be a panacea.

But it will be nice to know that it's there, waiting on the sidelines if it's needed.

COMING BACK TOGETHER:
RESTORATIVE SURGERY

The body is our home; the place where the furniture is familiar and comfortable and a lamp is always lit in the window. But when something happens to us—such as a serious illness or a surgery that changes the configuration of our internal or external organs—the house doesn't feel like home anymore. If you've been ill or survived a disfiguring surgery, more has been cut out of you than just a piece of tissue—it feels like a part of yourself has been excised. Sex may become a thing of the past.

If you have suffered from a disease that has had an impact on your sexuality, desire and arousal may feel like old memories to you. If you've had a breast or a cancerous lump removed; if you've had an ileostomy or colostomy that required a stoma; if you've undergone a prolapse that necessitated a pelvic-floor repair, you may think wistfully of a time when sex was familiar and easy and shake your head. Now you have other priorities; now what you rejoice in is being alive and simply functioning normally again.

But let us assure you that women who have lived with a mastectomy, ostomy, or pelvic-floor repair for some years report that life does get better. Sexuality not only can return, but sometimes, it can be better than ever, because the surgery has taken care of the disease or discomfort.

What does it mean—physically and emotionally—to be taken apart and put back together? At first, all you can think about is that you've survived. After that, you may think about your pain and how incredibly tired you feel. But once the recuperation period is past, you can reexperience joy in your life and the wonder of being alive. Sexuality can be one big part of that. Of course, a woman who is determined to return to "normal" or create a new idea of what normal is has a better chance of enjoying her sexuality than one who doesn't.

Will you ever feel good about taking off your clothes in front of a partner? Can you ever feel comfortable with your changed body? Fortunately, these days, there are a variety of surgeries that can repair nearly every bit of damage done by disease. And by restoring the body to normal function after illness, self-image can improve.

In this chapter, we will introduce you to women who have come out on the other side of breast, bladder, and bowel surgery. All of them have an active sex life; and for some it's better than it was before. The key, as we've found in so many women, is wanting to feel the pleasure and closeness that comes with satisfying connection and going after it deliberately. As one ostomy patient put it, "It's a gift to go back to life without pain. And it doesn't matter to me that I've been rearranged down there. It takes a little more time to do it right, and that's all to the good."

If you are currently dealing with major illness that has altered your body, you'll find here some information and inspiration to send you on your journey back to sexual pleasure.

Breast Surgery: Recalled to Life

As the lifetime breast cancer rates hover at one in eight women, we all live with the awareness that we are susceptible. Breast cancer has become a political cause—and although it's a sad comment on the times that women have to have a major medical crisis in order to show solidarity, it *is* one significant way that we band together. The role models of the movement—Jane Brody, Betty Ford, Marcia Wallace (of *The Simpsons*), Peggy Fleming, Jill Eikenberry, Linda Ellerbee—are all strong, savvy women who have gone public with this new female rite of passage. Those of us who have had friends making their way through the minefields of diagnosis and treatment—and who among us has not?—are heartened by being close to women who show that it's not just possible, but certain, that there is life and hope on the other side of the disease.

The breasts are known as "secondary" sex characteristics, but that's a cultural bias (organs only rank in first place if they help to make a baby!). Breasts are vital for feeding our infants, for body image, clothing selection, and of course, for sexual attraction and sensation. There are women who can orgasm just from having their breasts and nipples touched or kissed. Is there a way to compensate for their loss? Does being a woman—a *sexual* woman—rely more on your personality and your spirit? Or does your figure determine your comfort and pleasure in your sexuality? Undoubtedly, both affect your feelings about yourself as a sexual being.

There's a bigger issue here, and that is whether the prospect of death due to cancer can ever be wiped out when the lights are dim and someone is nibbling at your ear. "Having cancer obliterates a woman's sexual expectations for quite a while," says Kathleen Segraves, Ph.D., a breast cancer survivor and associate professor in the department of psychiatry at Case Western Reserve. "When you're newly diagnosed, you don't think about the aftermath of the surgery—all you want to do is live, and how you look is secondary."

Surveys from breast cancer survivors are filled with contradiction and ambivalence, because it really isn't just the loss of one or both breasts that alters self-image, sexual function, and sexual pleasure. There is evidence that there are changes in sexual sensations and arousal after breast cancer, and that, for some women, problems can persist even after treatment is over.[1] Many studies that extend beyond the first few years indicate that for some women, sexual appetite continues to diminish as they get farther from the active treatment aftermath of cancer. The women who have the greatest problems with sexual adjustment are those who've had changes in hormonal status (due to chemotherapy or removal of the ovaries), or who have relationship problems with their partners.

But there are other studies that give a much more positive view of the situation. These findings indicate that most breast cancer survivors, after the acute phase of treatment is over, are not much different from their healthy sisters in terms of quality of life and emotional and social well-being, and that their adjustment back to good health is, in fact, *superior* to those of women with other chronic diseases.[2] Their overall quality of life is similar to and, in some instances, better than women who've never had breast cancer.[3]

What does that mean? "Better" is surely as subjective a word as we've got in the lexicon, but we'd say that it means that this brush with mortality brings a heightened sense of personal awareness and a consideration of everything that must be done to improve our reason for being here. If you didn't talk to your partner before, you had better do it now; if you didn't look at yourself in the mirror and find something admirable, you had better do it now. The pain and suffering are transformative for many women.

One 48-year-old hospital worker confided to Judith, "Bill used to love to fondle my breasts, even when we were watching TV or lying around cuddled up together reading. I would feel, as we got closer, the two mounds of me pressing against his chest—I'm pretty well-endowed, so they would touch him first. And then I got cancer. I refused to believe it until I woke up from the double mastectomy. You know, when I opened my eyes, Bill was holding my hands, and he said, 'Hiya, Gorgeous,' even though that was not how I would have described me. I think he knew I needed to be reassured that I looked okay. That really helped when I was ready to show him the scars. He took it a lot better than I did. He touched my body, kissed the scars, and the look in his eye was just as turned on as it had ever been. But I don't enjoy breast caressing at all anymore—I'd rather concentrate on something else."

Breast cancer is like going ten rounds with Mike Tyson. There is so much trauma to the body and the psyche, you don't know how you'll come out of it. There's the biopsy, then the lumpectomy or mastectomy, and if there's a suspicion that the cancer has spread to the lymph nodes, an axillary node dissection. Then comes reconstruction. There's a flap created for expanders so that increasingly larger-sized saline pouches can be fitted inside, and then building of the breast mound, followed months later by the construction of the areola and nipple, and the pigmentation or tattooing of the areola. After all this surgery, it's nearly impossible to remember that you are a woman first, a patient second. Most women take the toughest blows in three very significant areas—their sexual self-concept, sexual functioning, or sexual relationship.

In this day of patient-centered managed care, you are forced to make quick decisions and hard choices. Of course, you must have several professional opinions, but in the end, you're the one who must decide which option to select—because it's your life and your body. You will be told either that the cancer is aggressive or in an advanced stage and you should have a mastectomy (this may also depend on your family history), or that you're in an early stage of a less rapidly growing cancer and it may be possible to conserve the breast and remove only a portion of it.

However, even a lumpectomy can deform the breast and nipple, and a mastectomy that involves the lymph nodes impairs use of the arm. If you've had one mastectomy, the fear of having the cancer return is palpable, at least for the first few years after the initial diagnosis. These days, many women are voluntarily electing to have the healthy breast removed as well, to allay their anxiety about recurrence.

Not only do you have to decide on what type of surgery you're having, you also have to decide what you're going to do about reconstruction and when to do it. If you opt for reconstruction, do you want to start immediately, when you have the mastectomy? Or do you want to recover from chemo first? If you don't do it now, isn't it likely that you never will—because who would want to go back for more surgery if it isn't absolutely necessary?

Maybe a prosthesis would be a better idea. These silicone shapes that fit into brassieres are usually fine for small-breasted women, but those who require a large insert say that they're bulky and heavy. Some women abandon them after a while and proudly flaunt their new, changed chests. And by the way, studies show it doesn't make much difference in terms of body image or psychosocial adjustment whether you have breast reconstruction or don't.[4] The way you feel about yourself is what counts when you're deciding what to do to restore your body.

The most popular current practice is a two-stage reconstruction procedure—one to build the breast mound, the second to construct the nipple/areola complex. Reconstruction is denied reimbursement by many insurers. They may allow the first procedure, but may not allow the second. Or they'll pay for reconstruction of the diseased breast but won't pay to alter the non-tumorous breast for symmetry. Although surgeons have greatly improved surgical procedures, it is impossible to predict what the final outcome will be, or how it will change down the road. As the body ages, the implanted breast remains perky whereas the natural breast starts drifting south.

Ironically, it's the woman with a family history of breast cancer or the one who's had a recurrence after her first mastectomy who ends up with the more idealized version of a chest. "I have a lot of friends who were really disappointed with their surgery," said Mary Anne, a 43-year-old patient whose mother had died of breast cancer and whose older sister had been recently diagnosed. "My second reconstruction made me look completely symmetrical, and that's great. But I don't know," she said soberly, "that these two even mounds on my chest compensate for the fact that my prognosis could be a lot worse than some woman with only one tumorous breast and no cancer in the family. But you know, I'm starting to feel good again, and that's what I concentrate on. One day at a time, as they say."

Surgery is not the end of the road—it only takes you to the next destination. Most women must follow surgery with radiation or chemotherapy or both, which burn the body's tissues and rob them of needed lubrication. Over a third of women complain of a dry, tight vagina and heavy sweats after chemotherapy, as well as diminished orgasm or loss of orgasm. The skin is hypersensitive, which means that touching all over—no matter how gently—can feel painful. Breast cancer is more than physical disfigurement; in many instances, it means loss of reproductive function. A young woman who goes into premature ovarian failure or has her ovaries removed prophylactically may have a great deal more trouble than an older one accommodating to sexual changes. Physiologically, she will be catapulted into early menopause; psychologically, the diagnosis may challenge her past image of herself as sexy.[5]

If you've had an estrogen-dependent cancer, you can't take hormone replacement therapy or use a testosterone cream (testosterone converts to estrogen in the body), and the more uncomfortable sex becomes, the more you may avoid it. Desire wanes as erotic fantasies lapse. Then, too, cancer and its treatments are enormously draining—it's hard to muster the energy to get through a normal day, let alone frolic in bed.[6]

"After my bout with breast cancer," said Danielle, a personal trainer in her late thirties, "I couldn't believe how bad I felt. I had always been a person who would jump out of bed every day and do my stretches in front of the wall-to-wall mirrors in my studio, and here I was so sick to my stomach, I could barely make it to the bathroom," she said.

Danielle had a lot of issues about the way she looked after surgery. A die-hard exerciser who was proud of her fine-tuned body, it was especially difficult to deal with her altered physical image. "I'd had the reconstruction at the same time as the mastectomy, and I kept telling myself it was impossible to tell the difference between my breasts, and then I'd feel so depressed because that was a total lie, and there was this huge difference. Of course I'd heard stories about the bad old days, when you lost muscle mass and tissue because they cut everything from your armpit down to your chest and your range of motion was a daily reminder that you were no longer whole.

"My surgery was great—it was just the cosmetic part that made me feel unsexy. My boyfriend said he didn't notice, and he was just as attentive in bed, but I couldn't bear him touching that side of me. It wasn't all psychological—my underarm and the side next to the breast were so incredibly sensitive that the least touch was unpleasant. I felt like a bionic person, made up of parts that weren't really me."

And her reaction is pretty common among women who go through this difficult procedure. Hair loss magnifies the effect of the illness—hair falls out in clumps when you brush it, and the eyelashes, eyebrows, and pubic hair may go as well. It takes at least a year for regrowth, and hair rarely returns the way it used to be. Curly may straighten out; soft may become wiry. More important than external cosmetics or camouflage, you need time. Time to accept that the image in the mirror, which may not look anything like your old self, is the new edition. Time to make peace with the inevitable changes we all go through, whether or not we've had cancer.

The effect on libido from chemotherapy can be disastrous—after treatment, it is common for sexual interest to plummet. Women who'd been interviewed four years after mastectomy with chemotherapy had more sexual dysfunction, poorer body image, and more psychological distress than the women who'd had surgery but no chemotherapy.[7] In addition, hormone therapy in the form of tamoxifen, an estrogen agonist, is often recommended to prevent a recurrence. But this drug, unfortunately, dries out the mucous membranes and can create a burning sensation in the vagina. When you're convinced sex won't feel good, it's hard to muster any enthusiasm for it.

What should you do? Don't force anything. If cuddling and gentle holding offer you some relief, ask for what you want from your partner. "I think we just lay there in bed together for weeks," said Elaine, who had a mastectomy at 43. "We didn't really talk about it; we'd just get into bed and read and listen to music and let our legs entwine. It felt warm and companionable more than sexy. I didn't feel any interest in sex at all until months later."

Accepting Yourself After Surgery

How do you make the transition back to health? After all this, how can you recapture your passion—your love of life and love of sex? More than anything else, you need to feel that you can take charge of your own recovery, be desired, and feel desire. It requires a strong will and good sexual self-esteem to make the leap from "cancer patient" to "sexy woman."

Ellen, who had her first mastectomy thirteen years ago, is currently struggling with cancer that has metastasized to her bone. But she claims that her sex life is much better now than it used to be. "When I had my first surgery, they weren't doing immediate reconstructions, and even after the ordeal of chemo was over, I couldn't really think about sex. I didn't like my body—it was scarred, and hairless, and I didn't want to be touched. I had absolutely no libido—I don't know if it was a reduction in testosterone or if it was psycho-logical, but sex was about the last thing on my mind.

"Then, after about two and a half years, I had a flap done and they put in an implant. Of course it didn't feel like a breast, and it had a poor excuse for a nipple, done with my own tissue, but I felt wonderful, even though I had no sensation in my breast when we made love. I used to get so excited when my husband touched my breasts—it was hard to give that up, even though Dr. Ruth says you never know how many parts of your body can make up for one breast. Then, two years ago, the cancer came back in the first breast and the sternum. I had bone pain, and the lesions in my skull made it hard to feel a kiss. When my husband pressed on me, it was painful. And then, when you're really battling the cancer, you can't catch your breath, you're nauseated, you're exhausted from the disease.

"But I got through that, too, and lately, I've been a lot better. My hair has come back, I'm not as fatigued, and I have a real desire to live fully—everything is more important—reading, my hobbies, my home, visits from my children. I'm in the world of the well, and I want to dance and be sexy and make love."

Joanne, who had a mastectomy at 40, didn't need to have chemotherapy or radiation afterward. "I felt great waking up from the anesthesia," she said, "since they'd done the reconstruction while I was out. Six months later they did the nipple and the tattooing for the areola. I actually have feeling in the upper part of the breast—the doctor says I'm lucky—it's just how my nerves connect. I was grateful to get such an early diagnosis. But my biggest shock was when my husband was diagnosed with cancer of the lymph nodes about a year later. He was the one who was self-conscious in bed. He'd say, 'Look at me with my caved-in neck,' and I'd say, 'Hey, I love you for what you are, just the way you do me with one fake breast.' My sexy image of myself never depended on my breasts."

Each of us has an inner vision of what our "self" consists of. If we like it a lot, we go out into the world bravely, hopefully, and we are more likely to embrace our sexuality. If we don't like it, if it embarrasses or shames us, we might turn away from sexual expression. So if our physical body is surgically altered, our perception of how it looks will determine how we react in sex-ual situations—either wholeheartedly or cautiously, or with avoidance.[8]

Sometimes the way back to self-acceptance is through the help of other women who've been there and come out on the other side. Nancy Kaplan Healey, associate director of the Breast Cancer Resource Center/Princeton YWCA in New Jersey, spoke about how she began to accept her new body after two bouts with cancer: "In the old days, women lost everything after breast surgery—muscle mass, tissue, range of motion. No one talked about it—you certainly wouldn't show your chest to a friend—even a good friend. But the surgeries are so much better these days, you can't tell even in a bathing suit or a low-cut gown. I had a lumpectomy first, then a mastectomy five years later, when the cancer returned. I woke up from the anesthesia with a new breast, and it was wonderful! Once I got the nipple it really felt like a breast—and it was so easy, an outpatient procedure—I would have driven bare-chested back to the office, it looked so good!"

Alyson, who was in her early thirties when she was diagnosed, said that she felt closer to her husband after her cancer experience, but it wasn't until after she'd talked with a therapist and with other women who'd been through the same thing that sex seemed at all appealing to her. "I'm the type who puts a big Band-Aid on everything. So I covered up all my fears and feelings about myself. I made jokes about how nice it was that the doctors had fixed my 'ski slopes,' you know, the kind of post-nursing breasts that are all flat on top. I took care of the kids and the house and my in-laws and my boss. And then, at night, when it was time for bed, I was just exhausted and I couldn't even remember a time when I liked sex. My husband said, 'Hey, didn't this experience teach you to slow down and smell the roses?' but that was really hard for me to do.

"I went into therapy and I finally learned to be proud of myself for having done all this. I joined a support group full of other amazing women who had also survived breast cancer. My self-esteem is much higher now. I realize I don't have to be liked by everyone—just by me. I'm learning how to say no. I'm starting to feel feminine and desirable again, and I'm hoping that before long, I'm going to feel that I want to share things physically with my husband. It's been a long haul."

Breast cancer support groups, springing up in hospitals, community centers, on the Internet (see chapter 7) and in YWCAs all over the country offer lifelines to women going throughout the process, from diagnosis through treatment and beyond. We cannot make a more fervent recommendation to join a group—it has been found that most women recovering from this traumatic illness actually live longer and fuller lives when they are able to normalize their experience by sharing their grief and hope with others going through the same ordeal.[9]

If you simply don't feel comfortable in a group, look for one individual you can talk to. Just one other woman mentor can ease the initial pain, according to Kathleen Segraves, Ph.D. "One patient of mine told me a story of going into a wig shop to get fitted before starting chemotherapy. She overheard another woman at the end of the counter who had just had a mastectomy and was also wig-shopping. 'I'll show you mine if you'll show me yours,' she joked, after a brief conversation. The two retired to a back room where they pulled up their T-shirts to compare scars, and were quite happily surprised. 'Hey, that doesn't look bad at all! Your doc did a really good job,' the other woman told her, and she gave her new friend the same type of affirmation. They suddenly felt bonded and have remained friendly—both are now eight years beyond their diagnoses." By sharing this experience with a buddy, and by looking—really looking—in the mirror on your own, it is possible to integrate a new self-image.

Most studies have found a strong correlation between a good marriage and a satisfying sexual relationship.[10] "I didn't do this for my husband, I did it for me," said April, now 62, who had a complete mastectomy with all thirty-two lymph nodes removed eight years earlier. "I had to sleep with a pillow under my arm to keep my right shoulder from caving in, which was very painful, and I'm a big-breasted woman, so the prosthesis I had to wear was terribly heavy. I thought about it for four years, and then, after the kids were through with college, I said to my husband, 'I want reconstruction.' He said, 'You're fine like you are, but if you want the surgery, go ahead.' I tell you, it was the best $20,000 I ever spent!" (The fee was for the two stages of reconstruction and the reduction of the opposite breast. Insurance paid for all but $7,000 or $8,000.)

"My husband never really told me how scared he was about my cancer, although I could tell. In bed, he was so careful with me, like he thought he was going to hurt me, and we're still careful with my arms and chest, but I can see I'm going to be a lot more comfortable about sex. He sees I like the way I look, and I think that gives him a boost, too. Because I can get aroused again, even if it's not quite as intense as it used to be. The surgery was recent, though, so I expect it will get better with time."

April is a woman who always enjoyed sex, even when her body wasn't pleasing to her. And having two breasts again has been a revelation. If you are a breast cancer survivor and are concerned that you still don't look quite right after surgery, you might want to try a few of the following tactics to ease the transition: Adjust the bedroom lighting with candles (romantic but not revealing), splurge on lacy lingerie to cover what you can't yet own up to. And be sure to experiment with activities other than intercourse, and other positions—spooning is good because you can keep your back to your partner. You may find that you enjoy cuddling, touching, and massage more than penetrative sex, and that being sexually "satisfied" means something different—something more profound—than it used to.

Beyond the physical alterations in your body and the changes in sexual desire and response is another huge factor—the relationship. How will your partner respond? Will things change between you? Is it easier if your partner is a woman? Interestingly enough, partnered lesbian women do not necessarily have less of a problem than straight women. Although their partner can sympathize, it may make no difference in the success or failure of the relationship. Another woman may identify *too* strongly—*there but for the grace of God go I*—and find it threatening to be close to a partner who is or has been ill.

Men's reactions, too, span the spectrum of possibilities. One man actually told his wife, who was going through chemotherapy and couldn't respond to his caresses, that she was "no fun anymore." But another, a big burly truck driver who came in for counseling with his wife, said that when they were intimate now, he liked to put his head where her breast used to be. That way, he could hear her heart beating and know she was very much alive. The length of the relationship also matters. A couple who have been together for decades may find it too painful or feel too angry at the turn of events to make love with the threat of recurrence hanging over them, whereas others may find it a positive way to affirm their love. For a single woman who is just beginning to explore new relationships, the question of when to tell is always on her mind. But this would be true if she'd been raped or in an abusive marriage—she would still have to trust someone enough to disclose such private and painful material.

You will undoubtedly go through many stages of recovery—as with any loss, it is necessary to deal with denial, anger, grief, resignation, and acceptance—and all the many steps in between. Some days may feel exhilarating, brimming over with possibility, and others feel gray or depressing. Just when you think you're past the worst, something else happens—the death of a parent, the loss of a job, the rejection of a lover—and you feel like you have to start all over. Sexual expression becomes possible again when you find that the gap between body and spirit is narrowing and that there are new reasons to celebrate being alive.

Bladder and Bowel Readjustments and Alterations

Although we associate loss of bladder function with extreme old age, the truth is that stress incontinence hits many women in midlife. "I play competitive tennis," a 55-year-old told me, "and I couldn't believe that every other time I hit the ball, I leaked. At first I thought it was like arousal—as though I was just excited—but then it started happening when I coughed or sneezed or had an orgasm. I was so embarrassed I started avoiding the things I used to love. And I never explained why when people asked. I just couldn't."

Enormous advances have been made in the treatment of stress incontinence, yet sadly, only 25 percent of women who suffer from urinary leakage actually admit to it. Incontinence remains a dirty little secret that women won't confess to their doctors or their lovers because it's so humiliating to lose control of a function that's been a breeze since they were three. But if you are suffering in silence, it's time to speak up, before it has a real impact on your ability to be intimate. It must be obvious that sex is very tricky if you have an unreliable bladder. When the penis enters the vagina, just in front of the uterus, which lies against the bladder, it can easily trigger an accident.

Incontinence also relates to a loss of estrogen, which helps the urethral sphincter to close properly. Kegel exercises—those invaluable squeezes of the pubococcygeal muscles we all should have been taught after we gave birth—

can make a big difference. Here's how to do a Kegel: Imagine that you are sitting on the toilet, about to release the flow of urine. Then squeeze the muscles that will stop the flow. That's one Kegel. You should do three sets of ten Kegels, alternating quickly and slowly, three times a day as a preventive measure. And, as an added bonus, strengthening those pubococcygeal muscles will increase sexual satisfaction for you and your partner, as well as protect against incontinence. Studies show that many women do Kegels incorrectly. Ask your doctor to check your technique. Then practice—while you're at your desk, stopped at a traffic light, watching TV.

There are also many new treatments and drugs available, if you make an appointment with your doctor to consider the medical options. But you must speak up! Family practitioners and gynecologists may not be aware of the latest treatments for this problem, but can refer you to a urologist if necessary. Weighted vaginal cones (see Resources for ordering information) are often recommended—you hold these tamponlike devices by squeezing your pubococcygeal muscles together, and you increase the weight you are able to hold as you would in a strength-training program for any other part of your body.

Several new anticholinergic drugs, such as Detrol and oxybutynin, work well for urge incontinence (having to urinate urgently even when you've just voided), and decongestants such as phenylpropanolamine and ephedrine will relax the bladder and increase capacity and urethral resistance. There are also collagen implants that are injected directly into the urethra to help it to close properly. And surgery is sometimes recommended when mechanical or pharmacological solutions have failed.

Pelvic-floor-suspension surgery requires extreme skill and delicacy on the part of the surgeon—think of the tiny tubing that snakes up the urethra to the bladder. The usual approach for stress incontinence is repositioning the bladder neck, suspending it with sutures or creating a sling from muscle tissue or some synthetic material. The gold-standard operation is known as a Burch retropubic colpo-suspension, and its newer variation, a laparoscopic Burch, is also popular because it is minimally invasive and requires only an overnight stay in the hospital. There's also a procedure that's being tested in Europe that is done with TVT (tension-free vaginal tape), where a mesh shield is placed under the urethra that self-fastens to the internal structures.

Another urogynecological condition that requires surgery is prolapse, where the uterus begins to slip downward into the vaginal area, and sometimes actually protrudes right through the vaginal introitus. This may be caused by difficult labor and childbirth, which injures the support structures of the pelvis, or by congenitally weak connective tissue. There seems to be a predisposition to prolapse in many families, where weak uterosacral ligaments are a legacy from one generation to the next. Prolapse can also affect women who are chronically constipated and strain in order to have a bowel movement.[11]

The perineal body is so vital to a woman's sexuality—nerves from the sacrum go to the rectum, perineum, the introitus of the vagina, and the clitoris. Multiple births can tear this nerve connection, allowing the uterus to sag. Disastrous as this may sound, some stages of prolapse are less problematic than others, and the sooner treatment begins, the more chance there is for success. If the uterus hangs down only to the level of the hymen, it's still possible to have intercourse and enjoy it. A ring pessary (kind of a rubber doughnut) is placed around the cervix to hold up the uterus and bladder; Kegel exercises and electronic stimulation (a gentle probe that zaps the muscles in order to contract the bladder) can strengthen the debilitated pelvis.

But if the condition worsens, you will probably need surgery. In some instances, the bladder protrudes into the vaginal canal (cystocele), causing pressure on the vaginal wall and the urethra. If you have this problem, you will have to hold back your vagina manually in order to urinate. Alternately, the rectum may sag into the back wall of the vagina (rectocele), and you must realign your organs and place a finger in your rectum in order to defecate. There are also complete prolapses, where the cervix protrudes all the way through the vaginal opening. How is sex possible when it feels like your insides are falling out?

"After my hysterectomy," said Roberta, a 56-year-old from upstate New York, "I began to notice a feeling like things were shifting down, almost like when your tampon is slipping. The doctor said my bladder had fallen because the muscles were gone, like an old stretched-out rubber band. Sex was, well, aggravating more than anything else. I still felt desire, but it was so difficult. So I had the suspension, and it was fine for about two years. And then it fell again. This is a tough kind of surgery—not everyone has success with it—and sometimes you have to have several surgeries until you get one that works. I guess that part of the body is like a real floor of a building—if the support system under it is no good, you can reconstruct the floor itself, but it won't hold. So the second time I had serious surgery—I went to a specialist who said the only option was to hook the vagina onto the muscles around the backbone. They just barely reached.

"Of course, what this did was to stretch out the vagina so it seems longer and tighter than it used to be. My husband is crazy about the change, and so am I. I have so much more feeling, it's a lot more intense. When I was recuperating the second time, I was a little apprehensive, but after eight weeks, I really started wanting sex again. We went slowly, but I was so much more relaxed and at ease—I don't know why.

"A lot of women I know—my two daughters who are in their twenties, and women at the office—they all said, Oh, you can't do this! But it was really no big deal. It was broke, and I got it fixed. And the sex is really terrific."

Repairing the pelvic floor is a big job—it may require rebuilding the delicate architecture of any one or several of seven different support systems made of ligaments, tendons, muscles, and nerves. The surgery usually alleviates the fear of incontinence and helps women relax and desire intimacy once again. Of course, there are cases where organs that have been patched and stitched just don't feel the way they used to. Genital sex involves such a complex mix of physiological and psychological elements that it may not be possible to retain feelings that used to connote arousal. But this does not mean that pleasure goes away. Even with women whose entire sexual apparatus has been decimated, excitement and fulfillment are still possible.

There are no guarantees with this type of surgery, which often has to be repeated after fifteen or twenty years. Loretta, who had both a prolapse and stress incontinence after a bad episiotomy with her second pregnancy, was told that her nerves might have been damaged and her condition could get worse. "I was just fed up with leaking every time I exercised or had sex. I really had hope that this thing would make a difference, so I decided on the surgery, although the outcome wasn't guaranteed to be positive.

"The doctor did a complete hysterectomy, an anterior and posterior repair, and put in a bladder sling. I have to say that it's wonderful to feel like everything's back in place—and sex is fine, but not totally wonderful. I really miss having a cervix—the doctor told me that some women really feel the penis hitting up against it during sex and that's very pleasurable. Well, now it's like an empty space, so I don't feel as much. But my husband is willing to try new things, and we use different positions more than we ever did. I think my desire is greater than it used to be, and I think about sex a lot, because now I'm not worried about leaking. I feel really good in bed."

If you liked sex before, no matter what illness or disability you suffer from, you will be motivated to try sex again once you have been treated. If you didn't enjoy sex, the disease or surgery can provide an excuse to retire from the bedroom.

This is also true if you have had an ostomy. From earliest childhood, we have been taught that bowels and urine are dirty and disgusting, and should never be handled. When we no longer have normal outlets for our waste, but still want to remain sexual, there has to be an accommodation that breaks the old taboo.

Women who've had ulcerative colitis, Crohn's disease, or cancer may require an ileostomy, where the large intestine and often the rectum are removed. If the colon is diseased, from cancer or diverticulitis, then a colostomy will be necessary. Cancer of the bladder or certain congenital conditions may necessitate a urostomy. All three procedures require a stoma (from the Greek word for "mouth") to be created—an opening by which waste can exit the body. Discharge is pretty much continuous in a urostomy and an ileostomy, and empties into a bag worn on the lower half of the abdomen that has to remain in place even during lovemaking. A colostomy is often just a temporary measure—the intestines are allowed to "rest" for six months and a stoma is put in place only for as long as it's needed; then the procedure is reversed after healing has taken place. (The colostomy may be slightly easier to deal with whether it's for good or just for a while—some women can simply wear a patch over the stoma if they time their eating appropriately.)[12]

For most women, there's a lot of grief and anger associated with this type of loss. And there is usually a change in vaginal sensation due to the displacement of the other organs. "I got Crohn's when I was 18," said Barb, who at 40, has been an ostomate for the last ten years. "I would scream every morning in the bathroom until I'd been able to get everything out. The bloody diarrhea left me with abscesses that would have to be lanced periodically. There I was with my butt up in the air, and I knew the doc was going to give me a local, and I'd get so tense. And then for days afterward, I'd leak while the abscesses were draining, and I'd have to wear Depends. I thought I had the ugliest butt in the world.

"My husband used to turn me on just by kissing and touching in the car. He was my only sexual partner, and I wish I could have liked sex more, at least then. I've never, to this day, had an orgasm, I don't think. But in our first year of marriage, I had the surgery, and it took three months of no work and no driving, and of course, no sex, for me to recuperate. The *idea* of sex made me tense.

"At the beginning, I named my stoma. I called her 'Lily,' so I'd be able to relate to her better. I'd change the bag and check it and the seal before we were going to have sex to be sure it didn't leak. I got these lacy covers to put over the pouch. But after a while, my husband would just push it away so he could get to me, and I figured it didn't matter whether I tried to make it look attractive or not.

"Sex is so animalistic—he's fast and not tender, although he always asks if he's hurting me. I tell you, I'd rather be gardening. My sense of my body is just bad—the summer is worst, because I have to find bathing suits with skirts so it doesn't look like I have a third leg. The rest of my life is fine, but I wish there were some way to tell my husband that I don't like sex. We never talk about it."

If Barb did muster the courage to discuss it, she might discover new ways to get pleasure from her body. When she came down with the disease, she was only 18, and she had had no sexual experience at all. The Crohn's disease, the subsequent surgery, and the stoma only reinforced her original feelings—she never liked sex to begin with. And her acceptance of her body is seriously wanting. Her first task must be to find a way of liking herself better. Once she feels good about herself, she may allow her body to be loved.

If you really love sex and want it to be an enjoyable part of your life, it doesn't matter how your body is cut up and pieced together. This is just how Fran felt, a very sexy woman who became an ostomate at 32, after her second child. "I think that there's a core of your mind and body that just wants it," she said. "I have had Crohn's since I was 16 and a half, but I had a sex drive then, too. I think I was a little self-conscious, after the surgery, because I have a very active ostomy and I always have to empty the pouch, sometimes right when we're in the middle of passion, but my husband doesn't mind that at all."

Fran loves sex. Having to go to the bathroom to change the pouch is just something that prolongs the time that she and her husband spend together. "If I feel something going on in there, I'll say, 'Hold that thought, I'll be right back,' and he just says, 'Don't worry, I'll think of something to get you back in the mood. Take your time.' Maybe it is all about time, and that time together is a gift, and now I know what it's like not to have constant diarrhea and pain."

I asked if she had ever had anal sex before the ostomy. "We did it that way once—my husband is the only person I've ever had sex with, and when we were young we wanted to experiment with everything. But let me tell you, it was so uncomfortable we never did it again. Now I have nothing back there— no nerves—and the opening is closed up. So it's not a part of our sex play. That's okay. We have plenty of other places that we touch and kiss that feel good. Sex is a state of mind. If your mind stays focused, your body can follow."

We urge you to seek out professionals who can help you, people who are knowledgeable and familiar with these illnesses. With time and guidance, you can learn to think about yourself positively, with a new way of approaching sexuality. You're going to have many concerns—how you look, whether the scarring around your incision will hurt when jostled by sexual maneuvers, and whether diminished blood circulation in the area makes lubrication more difficult. Next come all those practical issues—*will I smell, will I leak, what kind of noises will I make when gas escapes?* Fortunately, there are compassionate, humorous, and highly trained ostomy nurses and ETs (enterostomal therapists) who have seen it all and can make sense of it for you. There are also companies that manufacture lacy appliance covers and cummerbunds that hide the stoma—see Resources for information about where to order these. Most women who are longtime ostomates find that they don't need the camouflage once they've reclaimed themselves as sexual beings.

Female Genital Cutting

There is only one more surgical alteration that must be mentioned, but it lies off our continuum of appropriate remodeling and reconstruction. This is the heinous crime of female genital cutting (FGC), practiced in far too many cultures around the world on girls as young as three and sometimes right before puberty. According to a 1997 report by the World Health Organization (WHO), there were two million of these procedures performed in Africa, and in areas of the Middle East, Asia, and South America.

Although accurate numbers are nearly impossible to track down, it is estimated that at least 7,000 women and girls each year come to America from countries where the majority of their sisters have been cut. Some come seeking asylum since the procedures are banned in America. But others come with the intention of preserving their traditions, regardless of the law. How ironic it is that thousands of female circumcisions a year take place in California, New York, and Washington, D.C., in communities where refugees have settled in tight-knit groups, determined to hold on to at least part of their cultural heritage.

If you are a woman who underwent genital cutting at a tender age, you were brought up to believe that it was necessary. Without it, you may have been told, you would go wild and get into terrible trouble, no man would ever marry you, and you would suffer with menstruation and childbirth. Of course, your religious law demands it. And so, despite the pain and suffering you might have gone through yourself, you would risk anything to see that the same is done to your own daughters. Women who refuse the procedure may be social outcasts for the rest of their lives. If they accept, they are traitors to themselves.

There are those who contend that if we tolerate male circumcision, we have to adopt the same attitude about female circumcision. But the surgical procedure in a man in no way alters sexual function or decreases sexual appetite. In order for a male to undergo anything similar to even the least serious female procedure, the head of the penis would have to be cut off—not just the foreskin. Female circumcision, on the other hand, involves a continuum of surgeries that radically alter the genitalia. The three "feminine sorrows," as described by andrologist Dr. Jean Fourcroy,[13] include Type I clitoridectomy, in which the clitoral hood is excised; Type II clitoridectomy, which takes the entire clitoris and part of the labia minora; and Type III, infibulation, which removes all the external genitalia and involves stitching the vagina, so that it must then be torn open by a husband on the woman's wedding night to permit penetration. The gynecological complications are legion—infection, menstrual disorders, incontinence, fistulas, hemorrhage, and sterility are common. And the psychological complications are often worse.

Is there any treatment for this condition? Most clinicians who see circumcised women explain to them that they must be de-infibulated (or unstitched) prior to delivering their children if they don't want to have a cesarean. And this is one way for the circumcised woman to take back her sex life. Since it is illegal in the United States to re-infibulate or re-sew a woman, despite her request or that of her husband, she has no choice but to allow the introitus to remain open. But will this have a greater impact on her mental health—knowing that she has disobeyed a custom that has kept her "virginal" and subservient all these years?

Hanny Lightfoot-Klein, an anthropologist who lived in the Sudan for five years,[14] reported that 99 percent of the women interviewed who'd been cut *approved* of the procedure. In addition, most loved their husbands and said that they enjoyed sexual intimacy.

How can we believe this? It is nearly impossible to imagine these women having good sex, or actually, having any type of sex at all. Yet, it is true that sexuality is bigger than a bundle of nerves between the legs. Gina Ogden, a sex therapist who has made a study of nonphysical sexual pleasure, makes it clear in her book that extragenital sensation—even orgasm without touch or "thinking off,"[15] may offer women a greater outlet for excitement than they ever knew was possible. If they truly believe that their circumcision makes them desirable, maybe they really are able to overcome their physical pain and *think* their way to satisfaction.

FGC is despicable and should be outlawed worldwide. Yet the women who have been subjected to it, just like those who have learned to love sex again after breast or bladder or bowel reconstruction, seem to incorporate it into their self-image. Surgery can be either devastating or rehabilitative. What it does do in nearly every case is to peel away the layers of disease or self-criticism to reveal the person beneath. If the mind can get around the new body, anything is possible.

10

REBLOOMING THE ROSE: WILL COSMETIC SURGERY MAKE YOU SEXIER?

The mirror can be our greatest friend or our most dreaded foe. When we're young, it reflects the flaws that accidents of nature or genes are bound to cause. As we get older, we can see the changes that time and gravity inscribe on us. The face grows lined, the breasts sink or sag. Some of us— God forbid—start to look like our mothers. And the image of "mother" sure isn't sexy.

The question is, do you fix it if you can? Most women who have had cosmetic surgery say that they just wanted a little "refresher," similar to getting a new hair color or a brow reshaping. They didn't think of it as a big deal. Studies show that most reasonable people who choose to go under the knife are not doing it out of obsession with their looks or from extreme self-loathing, but rather from a considered awareness of aesthetics and self-perception. Most cosmetic surgery patients don't actually dislike their looks any more than the rest of the population, but are significantly more dissatisfied than a control group with the one or two offending parts that they feel need work.[1]

If you've decided to have some part of your body tucked, cut, and sewn, it's likely that you are doing it to satisfy some craving deep down in your soul. *You can be better than you are* is the credo of cosmetic surgery.

It is conceivable that your life could change after the procedure, allowing you to have a shot at a better job, a better mate, more money, more prestige. But will it really make you sexier?

What most women report post-surgery is that they definitely feel better about their looks, but the sexual benefit—if any—is indirect. It all depends on their priorities—whether they wanted an external effect, where their face and body became more appealing to them, or an internal effect, where they increased their self-confidence and self-esteem and therefore felt more desirable. Some women can get both from cosmetic surgery; others gain neither one, particularly those who end up with numbness, pain, and the headache of a big surgical bill. So if you're counting on the alteration to alter your attitude toward sexuality, to change you into a lusty babe with a libido as big as the universe, think again.

Appearance, of course, does not dictate sexuality. There are conventionally beautiful women who have lousy sex lives, and women who would never be judged attractive according to a *Cosmo* or *Vogue* survey who have enviable sex lives. And usually, once past the stage of flirting and fantasizing, most of their partners agree that it makes little difference what they look like—especially since so many people make love in the dark with their eyes closed!

Of course, this rational and reasonable piece of knowledge doesn't help every woman. There are those who have trouble feeling lovely, particularly as they age and see other women who have better skin, bouncier breasts, and cellulite-free butts. Some worry that their flattened appearance may cause their husbands to stray; others, that it may leave them vulnerable to getting passed over at the office for promotion. The mirror we have been taught to worship says that youth and beauty trump power and experience. And unfortunately, many of us buy the message sent by the media that there is something wrong with a woman's aging process.

The implication is that if we don't measure up to some impossible standard, no one will have us. If, on the other hand, we "fix" the bulges and smooth out the lines, we'll be admired, and then we'll admire ourselves, and then we'll want to be loved, and finally, sex will be fabulous.

Is it true? Can you make yourself sexier and feel more erotically inclined if you look twenty years younger? Will desire spark if you have your stomach lipoed or your breasts enlarged or reduced? What does changing your external image do to your internal vision, and what kind of impact does that have on your sex life?

If you're self-conscious about sagging breasts or wrinkles, you may feel too vulnerable to bare everything, and consequently may avoid sex. But if you're proud of the smile that has caused those deep laugh lines, and you love the children you nursed at those less-than-perky breasts, perhaps you can begin to see your new body as even more sexual than it was before. How can we feel sexy—at 30, 40, 80, or 100—when the face and body don't conform to a particular vision? In this chapter, we will examine the choices that women are making to alter their faces and bodies, and see whether cosmetic "improvements" actually help or hinder sexuality.

Remodeling the Face and Body

Any alteration, be it as simple as Botox in the wrinkles or as complex as a reshaping of the hips, thighs, and buttocks, is a temporary solution on one plane of our existence. Yes, the physical body echoes the psychological body, but if we are healthy, our self-concept is not derived solely from our body.

And what body are we talking about? The teen's supple limbs and pimply face? The young mother with her glowing skin and rounded hips? The menopausal woman with stand-out veins and breasts that sit a little closer to her waist than they used to? The same person morphs over and over again into someone slightly different because the human body is in constant flux. Every seven to ten years, we have a whole new set of bones; every few days, we slough off a layer of skin. What you've got at twenty is nothing like what you'll have at sixty—and each age has its own charms and drawbacks. Upstanding breasts courtesy of saline implants might make you feel hot at 28, but suppose they made it impossible for you to nurse a child in the future? Liposuction on your rear so that you can look beguiling in a thong might seem important at 50, but will you really want to wear that horrible undergarment at 80? The range of options to enhance our physical state is incredible, but if we can't go back, do we want to race forward? Being young and beautiful doesn't necessarily make you sexy; being old and gray doesn't mean you aren't.

Yet cosmetic surgery is a popular course of action for a lot of people searching for a new sense of themselves, despite the fact that these procedures are not without risk. There's cutting and blood and possible infection and all kinds of problems resulting from anesthesia, and then there's human error, which is more and more common in hospitals these days. Suppose they pull your eyes too tight? Suppose they lipo too much fluid along with your fat? Would you risk so much for such an uncertain outcome? The danger of serious complications from cosmetic surgery runs as high as 2 percent (according to *U.S. News & World Report*), and in addition, there is always the possibility of developing scar tissue in any area that is cut and stitched.

Yet more and more women seem to believe that changing the outside will resolve the conflicts and discontent going on within. In 1998, there were 946,784 cosmetic surgeries performed on American women (men had a measly 99,000).[2] One in ten women between the ages of 55 and 64 has had some type of cosmetic surgery—more than two times the number in any other age group.[3] In order to feel beautiful (and for some, in order to feel sexy), they must match an image or fantasy that probably began in childhood and developed with each passing year.

Which brings us to the four distinct reasons that women choose cosmetic surgery. The first two can offer benefit to women who want to feel sexier; the second two will probably work against a woman's feeling of desirability. Women might choose cosmetic surgery to fit better in their own skin; to be more visible in a society that ignores older women; to increase the likelihood of tangible benefits, like a new man or a new job; or to look—and be—absolutely perfect. For women who scrutinize their every flaw, looking good is a desperate goal rather than a hoped-for change.

REASONS FOR COSMETIC SURGERY: FROM THE REASONABLE TO THE RIDICULOUS

1. To Feel More Comfortable
   breast reduction for ease of movement and better personal image
   to fix a perceived flaw, such as a receding chin or a big nose
   to be a "normal" or comfortable size

2. To Feel More Visible
   to thwart the aging process
   to look more the way you feel—active and vital rather than tired
      and depressed
   to reenter society after a divorce or the death of spouse

3. To Achieve an Advantage
   to change the perception of yourself as undesirable, physically
      or otherwise
   to enhance a feature (breasts, lips, buttocks) associated with sex
   to convince the world you're young and ready for career advancement

4. To Look Perfect
   to conform to an unrealistic media image
   to fulfill an impossible standard for yourself
   to make everything "right" for a partner

When a woman selects a procedure that she feels will revitalize her sense of herself, she may gain sexual confidence as she peels away the physical flaws; if, however, she depends on that procedure to remake her in an image of something unattainable, there's little hope that her sex life will improve.

Enhancing the Original Face or Figure

Our feelings about what's aesthetically pleasing, of course, are based on ethnic, racial, and religious biases, as well as on the heavy hand of the media. In addition, if we happen to live with a younger man or younger woman, we may be more self-conscious about the hanging flesh under our necks or the crinkly lines around the eyes. If our partner looks young, we want to match. Through the art and science of plastic surgery, anything is possible.

The problem is that by remodeling the external body, we can't always change our internal vision. If we were told in childhood that we shouldn't stick our "big nose" in other people's business or were dubbed "Elsie" in adolescence because of larger-than-standard-size breasts, it's hard to lose the ugly-duckling mentality as we age.

"When I was a teenager, my sister got the surgery I wanted," said Kathy, who at 57 had a long-awaited nose job in addition to a face-lift. "I had always hated my nose, but it just wasn't the sort of thing that kids got in my small Midwestern town, especially because my parents thought of me as the brainy one and my sister as the pretty one. I used to leave my folks notes that read *Don't be nasty—give me a rhinoplasty,* and they'd completely ignore me. But my sister, who had a deviated septum, *she* got the nose job, which was terrible, by the way, and made her look like a pig. Meanwhile, my mother was dissolving into middle age, and looked so matronly—she let her hair go gray, she gained a lot of weight, she totally embraced matronhood. I was determined never to be like that, and to be a sexy woman. So I opted for surgery."

Most of us do just a little something to change our appearance, from makeup and nail polish to two-process hair-color jobs and weekly attention to our acrylics. A woman longing for a little change—nothing too drastic or expensive—can have body contouring with a personal trainer, have her teeth whitened, her eyebrows waxed, and her pubic hair cut in the shape of a heart or a lightning bolt. There's electrolysis and laser hair-removal, and fat-tissue massage to break down your cellulite.

But as we move up to more elaborate body-enhancement, we find dermabrasion; permanent lip and eye-liner tattoos; and cow collagen, human fat, or longer-lasting sugar gel (hyaluronic acid) to puff up the lips and fill in the laugh lines. The American Society of Plastic and Reconstructive Surgeons reports that after liposuction, the most popular surgeries are breast augmentation, eyelid tightening (blepharoplasty), face-lift (rhytidectomy), nose reshaping (rhinoplasty), chemical peels, collagen injections, and breast-implant removal (undoing the surgical work that was previously done). Good surgical candidates are repeat customers—21 percent of them come back for more—and there's no dearth of procedures, so you can easily become addicted.

Let us draw an important distinction between those who see their physical being as primary and those who give it high priority, yet can acknowledge that there's more to sex than a young face and a hot bod. So no matter how many points you give yourself for intelligence and personality, if you hate the way you look, it may be difficult for you to see yourself as desirable and sexual. The big question is whether feeling desirable actually makes us feel desire.

To be sexy and sexual requires a certain sense of abandon, of looseness, of confidence, flexibility, and fun. Cosmetic surgery can help to give us these attributes, or it can inhibit them—it all depends on the woman.

Making the Decision for Cosmetic Surgery

Let us start by assuming that you have thought long and hard about this revision to your face or body, and that you have an extra few thousand dollars earmarked for a procedure. It is vital that you approach this venture seriously, and learn exactly what is entailed in the surgery.

Examine your motives. Have you always hated one feature or one part of your body? Since body image is made up mostly of our ideas, attitudes, and beliefs, it's worthwhile to consider whether you evaluate yourself realistically or have a distorted idea of the way you should look. If you basically like what you see and simply want to alter one thing, then surgery may be an option. If you can't stand anything about yourself, it might be a good idea to have some talk therapy instead of going to see a cosmetic surgeon.[4]

Do your homework before selecting a surgeon. See several doctors who have been recommended either by friends who look fantastic, or by another physician who has had patients who are very happy with their results. Check out the doctors' credentials, and look at health regulatory agencies' listings to see if there are any complaints against these physicians.

Set up consultations with several surgeons. Most of the women interviewed for this book said that they saw at least three and sometimes more surgeons before making their choice. Many traveled across the country to visit the surgeon who had the best plan for their renovation. One of the great quandaries of cosmetic surgery is that each doctor you see has a different idea about what should be done. Some are motivated only by money—the more work, the higher the fees—but others are honest, ethical, and working from an experienced aesthetic perspective. Some women we spoke to made their decisions based on the doctor's bedside manner. A person who told them they looked tired and old didn't win as many points as the one who said they needed "just a little work."

If possible, have a friend or spouse accompany you to these visits. Changing your face or body is an extremely emotional venture, and you may not be completely rational about what you feel has to be done.

Some doctors insist that you begin a course of lifestyle change months before your operation. If you're having a face-lift, they may caution you not to drink alcohol or use recreational drugs or smoke or eat a rich diet. If you're having liposuction or body contouring, they may suggest that you lose some weight before surgery. If you are really making a commitment to this process, follow the instructions to the letter. It could make the difference between a physical change that lasts a year or two and one that looks great ten years out.

Before beginning the process, ask your surgeon:

⚜ What does this surgery consist of?
⚜ How much does it cost? When must I make payments?

- ❀ What must I do to prepare for surgery?
- ❀ How long is the operation? What kind of anesthesia will I have?
- ❀ How long will my recuperation be?
- ❀ Are there any things I should avoid or anything I should be doing while I'm recuperating?
- ❀ Are there any risks associated with this surgery?
- ❀ How long will it be before I look really good?
- ❀ How long will the results last?

If you are realistic about the possibilities of this surgery, you will likely be happy with the results. If, however, you have some expectations that could never be met (you want to look 25 when you're 50, for example), you'll be coming back for more before your scars are healed. And you'll never be satisfied with your results.

Getting Comfortable—Surgery as Reaffirmation

Most candidates for cosmetic surgery are very stable people who choose cosmetic surgery not out of disgust and self-loathing, but out of hopefulness. They may be more narcissistic than is good for them, but on the whole, they don't lack self-esteem or suffer from major social anxiety.[5] They know, inside, that the face and body they see in the mirror is okay, but they believe that it can be better. (The changes that are wrought through good surgery are very often so minor that no outsider can tell the difference, yet the patient is so delighted with her new image that she smiles more, she looks people in the eye, and generally appears more attractive because she feels better about herself.)

Louisa, a 39-year-old from Delaware, said that she had always liked her big body, but liposuction helped her to feel even better. Surgery provided a way for her to manipulate the raw goods and whittle them down to a manageable size.

"I'd always been heavy, since I was 10," Louisa said. "My wedding dress was a size 20. I was 5′3″ and 250 pounds. I used to ask my husband if he minded and he'd say, 'Are you kidding? I want as much of you as I can get.' We went to Hedonism in Jamaica for our honeymoon and spent most of our time on the nude beach. You know, there were all kinds of bodies there—nobody stares at a fat person, because there are so many of us.

"Anyhow, I got uterine cancer about six years ago and had a partial hysterectomy, and I had an incision that ran from an inch above my belly button to the top of my pubic hair. As I started recuperating, the weight dropped off, and I could exercise more and I did everything—hiking, Tae Bo, rock climbing. I got down to 160. But people kept asking me when I was due, because everything was hanging on me, like drapes. So I had a tummy tuck with liposuction, and for a while, I thought I was gorgeous. But then a surgical hernia formed after the hysterectomy, so my next surgery was to repair that incision. And at the same time, the plastic surgeon removed all the scar tissue; he also did a flank reduction for my football points—it was like I had a half a football on each hip, which he took off, bless him!

"Now I'm about 190 and I love the way I look. I feel sexually voracious—I think I'm harder to please now than I was. I have no hang-ups about my body; as a matter of fact, my husband and I had sex on the beach on a blanket next to my girlfriend—she didn't care, she was reading a book. Things I would never have done before. I told my husband, next I want a boob job, and he says, 'Hey, whatever you want. But right now, you're really hot.' "

According to life-insurance tables, Louisa would be considered greatly overweight. But the pounds on the scale have no bearing on her sexuality. Because she is so well adjusted and self-accepting, she feels sexy at a weight that most women would consider disastrous. For her, surgery was simply a matter of becoming more comfortable in her skin.

Extremely well-endowed women may also get a terrific effect from cosmetic surgery. Reducing the size of the breasts can expand the world that a woman lives in. "People used to stare," Joellen, a 32-year-old nurse, said. "I'd walk into a room, and every man in there, his head would swivel around so he could get a good look. Then there was the catcalling on the street—*Hey, baby, can I have a drink of milk?*—that kind of thing. I had to shop in special stores for bras and clothes. The doctor took me from a double E to a D cup, and it's wonderful. I can lie on my stomach, go jogging, do everything I want. And now when a man looks at me, I think he finds me attractive, not freakish."

There is good reason for excising breast tissue that causes physical problems. A very large woman may decide on surgery because she is plagued with backaches and fatigue just from trying to hold up all that flesh. Being overendowed becomes more difficult with age, when the muscles no longer hold up the fat tissue effectively, and the breasts may sag to the waist. Pendulous breasts, reminiscent of big old grandmothers or nannies, or women who have nursed too many babies, do not convey a particularly erotic image.

But after surgery, a woman with proportional breasts can take great pleasure in how she looks, feels, and moves, and this can motivate her to become more open and more sexual. If her shape and form aren't holding her back, she can really enjoy herself. After years of covering up and wearing loose-fitting clothes, the woman who is comfortable in her body can really flaunt it.

Coming Out of the Shadows—Looking as Good as You Feel

A second reason for cosmetic surgery is to reclaim a sense of self by becoming more visible. "I looked older than other women my age, and I felt older, too," said Nancy, who decided, at 50, to have some "work" done on her face. "I had grown totally disinterested in sex—it just didn't matter to me anymore—because no one looked at me as though I were a sexual being. I remember one day I bought this big rack for the back of my closet door, and it wouldn't fit in a cab, so I had to walk the ten blocks back to my apartment carrying it. And as I trudged along, I was aware of how ten years ago, when I was adorable and fetching, some man would have stopped and offered to help me out. This is a totally sexist way of looking at it, but I have to own up to my feelings. I honestly believed that only the pretty girls with the great hair and long legs *wanted* sex, because men found them desirable and that interest in them was what sparked their own desire. I thought if I fixed myself up a bit, I wouldn't be invisible, and then I'd feel sexy."

It's lousy to feel invisible. The idea of being taken for granted or passed over is an issue that many women deal with from childhood, when they find that it's necessary to turn handstands or act "fetching" to get their father's attention. And as we get older, and think that we're fading into the background, we lose the sense of being desired. So this is one way in which cosmetic surgery can help a woman to feel more sexual.

"I got to the point where I wasn't the heroine of my fantasies anymore," said Lucy, 57. "With my current husband and myself, it had been love at first sight, and I don't think he minded my too-narrow nose or my corrugated upper lip, which was just like my mother's. After we'd been married ten years, I started to think about looking exciting so I could feel more excited inside. I'd always wanted to get my nose done, and I thought, Hey, let's do the whole thing. After consultations with three different doctors, I decided on the nose job, my eyelids, a classic face-lift, a chin implant, and laser surgery on my upper lip followed by injections of fat taken from my hips.

"Right after surgery, I looked like I'd been in a terrible car accident. My husband took ten days off of work to take care of me, and he never let on that it was really hard to look at me. He was so nurturing and supportive, and it was okay that we couldn't kiss because I couldn't pucker up my lips, which really hurt.

"It's now a month from surgery, and my eyes are still dry, my face is still kind of numb. But I'm very happy with the results, and in about ten years, if I think I need it, I'll get refreshed again. I don't look younger—I still have wrinkles—but that's not the point. I suppose somewhere I hoped I'd look 30 again, but I'm delighted to look like a very attractive 50-something instead. The surgery didn't turn me into a different person, but I think if I hadn't done it, in time I would have eventually changed and become a woman who didn't feel desirable and therefore didn't feel desire."

Lucy was an ideal customer for cosmetic surgery because she knew what she wanted and she got exactly that. Reclaiming desire has a lot to do with being noticed and appreciating the other person appreciating you. When you are visible, you show yourself off to the world. And that's very sexy.

Practical Matters—Surgery That Will Get You Ahead

The third reason that women have cosmetic surgery is purely practical: They believe that it will help them get ahead or get a mate. For them, the physical body is a tool with which to conquer new territory, to start a new business, train for a marathon, or take a new lover. "In your twenties," says Denise Thomas, a cosmetic surgery consultant in New York City,[6] "your sex life takes off. And it can improve in your thirties. But you want to be better than you are, especially if you're in competition with other women for men and for good jobs. Especially as women age, they want to feel that they have an edge, or if they've lost it, they want it back. Many want younger men. And this is why a tighter face and renovated body can mean more than just being beautiful and sexy."

There are many who agree with Thomas's theory, or have been convinced that surgery makes good business sense and may open doors to new prospects both personally and professionally. Janice, a mother of three and a jewelry designer, decided to have a tummy tuck after her last child turned three and she was itching to move her business to a higher level. "I still looked pregnant—my belly was huge, even though I was back to my prepregnancy weight. I was in a lot of competition with really young, hip jewelry designers. The fashion industry—even accessories, which is my thing—is cruel; if you look like a suburban housewife, you're not going to get anywhere.

"The first doctor I saw wanted to do the surgery as an in-office procedure, same-day surgery. So I showed up, and the nurses looked around for my file and said, 'Whoops, we didn't do the preoperative tests, so you can't have the tuck.' The doctor showed up and said, 'Well, no problem, you're here so let's do it.' So the anesthesiologist put me under but the next thing I know, he's waking me up, saying I had an irregular heartbeat, so they weren't going to do the surgery without clearance from a cardiologist.

"It's scary to think about it—if anything had gone wrong!—but I guess I was so desperate, I really didn't think about my health. Anyhow, I found another surgeon, and he did all the necessary testing and I had the procedure done in the hospital for about $6,000.

"I was really happy with my nice flat stomach for a year . . . but then it started puffing out a little and I called the surgeon back and complained. He said I had really loose stomach muscles and this was to be expected unless I was doing my sit-ups every day (I wasn't), but that he'd do some liposuction and it would look great again. So I went for it. He lipoed my torso, trunk, and armpits, and it cost $3,000, but he wrote down on my insurance form that I had an umbilical hernia, so some of that got paid for. I have to say, though, the extra surgery wasn't worth it. I don't see a difference.

"Why did I go through the whole thing? I wanted to look better in clothes; I wanted to feel better about myself, and now I do. I wanted to look hip enough to really sell the cutting-edge product I was making. No, I don't parade around the house naked—I'm not that kind of person. My husband has always been really caustic about 'fat people,' and he criticizes my body now just like he did before the surgeries. I have to ignore it. There's no magic in this—it certainly didn't make sex better for me. But I'm selling more and that's what's important right now. I like the improvement. I never expected it to change my sex life."

If Janice's business didn't demand that she appear a certain way, if her husband didn't have disdain for anyone who looks overweight, would she have gone through all this? Liposuction is the most commonly performed cosmetic surgery in the lexicon, even though several people have died from the procedure.[7] Love handles, cellulite, flabby tummies, and the lot are all part of the human package, and as we age, they become more pronounced. Of course, it's not just those in the public eye or in typically youth-oriented businesses who feel their fat must be excised in order for them to feel beautiful and sexy. As we have become a video culture, a nation of visual consumers, we fear that all eyes are upon us. But it is really the inner eye that is so critical and demanding.

Breasts and Sex

We have not evolved a great deal when it comes to breast size. The ideal female form has changed drastically over the centuries, but Barbie—and Marilyn Monroe—still cast a long shadow over some women. They feel that in order to be sexy, they need generous breasts.

In America today, the perky breast is in. What's even more in is a skinny body that looks great in clothes, with pop-up breasts spilling out of deep cleavage.[8]

If you don't have it, but you want to flaunt it, you can stop in at your nearest cosmetic surgeon's office and come out a bigger woman. Although most sexual partners, male and female, say that "more than a mouthful is wasted," there's a sense that being voluptuous, spilling out of your cleavage—or just having some cleavage to begin with—is a desirable thing.

It is not just the size of the breast that confers sexual status, but the size of the nipple. Nipples are sexy—when you can see them, erect, through a shirt, it is evident that a woman is either very chilly or she is sexually aroused. These days, even though all manner of sexual footage appears on cable TV, most stations will put a genteel mosaic of fuzz around nipples, because they are simply too hot to handle. Although, as yet, women have not demanded nipple and areola augmentation, the concept cannot be too far from some ingenious plastic surgeon's mind. Imagine the day when you can stop into a beauty salon for a haircut or a manicure and then go next door to get your nipples plumped up!

"My husband I had gone through some rocky times," said Toni, a 37-year-old insurance adjuster. "Our sex life was in the dumper. So I thought, what can I do to make him sit up and pay attention? I thought maybe he was losing interest, but the implants really saved my marriage. He couldn't keep his hands off me. I really love to watch him watch me. I feel like a real woman now."

Toni's decision for surgery seems very practical, but it's hard to imagine that her new breasts will buoy up a marriage that's in trouble. Toni was worried that before her surgery, she wasn't a "real woman," which says a great deal about her lack of confidence in her own femininity. What's more to the point is that her marriage may have been built on some unreal ideals. Expecting new breasts or a new face to cement a relationship is completely unrealistic. And yet, there are women who cling to this hope like a life raft.

Great Expectations—How Realistic Are They?

It is very often not the outcome of the procedure but rather the inability to alter expectations that makes women unhappy with their cosmetic surgery. To an outsider, the recovered patient looks great, but to the woman who has looked in the mirror a thousand times and still can't embrace what she sees, the improvement isn't enough.

The benefits of any surgery last approximately ten years, which keeps you ten years ahead of yourself in chronological years, but doesn't, of course, stop the march of time. One day, like it or not, you will be old. Ten years here or there is just a few ounces of epithelial tissue in the bucket. Unless, of course, you keep having surgery.

"I decided to have a face-lift at 53, when my daughter told me she was going to get married the following year," Milagro said. She was a slender woman of indeterminate age, originally from Brazil, who was now living in California. "My husband said, 'Why do you want to do this? You look great, younger than anyone else your age.' But I was thinking about the future, and what I could be like down the road. I'd spent my whole life in the sun, and I was just starting to pay for it.

"After interviewing four surgeons, I decided on a wonderful doctor whose price was somewhere in the middle of everyone else. I'd gotten quotes that ranged from $15,000 to $56,000, depending on what surgeries they were suggesting.

"The surgery wasn't the bad part—it was afterward. You can't sleep at all—you have to be propped up and there are these staples where the drains are right at the temples, in front of the ears, behind the ears, and the killer one in back of the skull.

"After two weeks, my husband was begging me to come home. I was still all red and had to wear this greasy sunscreen, but I'd had my hair done, and I wore something he really liked for the plane trip. When he met me at the airport, he pretended not to know me. 'Excuse me, little girl, have you seen my wife?' he asked me, grinning.

"Within six months, I was mostly pleased with the results. I wasn't as drawn as I used to be, and my skin had a real glow. I suppose I do feel more attractive, in a way. But after another six months, I was starting to see some new wrinkles. My doctor said to me, when I complained, 'You do not have a plastic face. It's human, it's flesh and blood, so it changes. Time doesn't stop.'

"But I grinned and said, 'No, but we can slow it down. Doc, I'm going to put you on retainer.' "

The question is, when will Milagro come back for more? It's very clear that this woman has a picture in her head of a newer, rejuvenated, refreshed self, who conforms to her own personal ideal of womanhood—at least on the outside. But, already, only a year after surgery, she is getting perilously close to dissatisfaction. New lines will inevitably crop up, and repeated surgery can only do so much. How will she know when enough is enough? And if she doesn't figure that out, will her experience with the surgery ultimately leave her feeling worse about herself rather than better?

When Surgery Doesn't Solve the Problem

Not everyone is happy when they open their eyes and look at their bandaged or bruised face or stapled stomach. And even after the healing process has a chance to work, women may discover that the Fountain of Youth has a few rocks, and occasionally, some foul-tasting water. Who says that Venus was a young woman without lines or wrinkles? After all, she was a goddess—she'd been around for centuries. It's likely that her smile was wreathed in deep ridges and crow's feet surrounded her exquisite eyes. But we can only guess.

"Some years ago," 47-year-old Olivia told me, "I decided to have the deep bags removed from under my eyes. I look a lot like my mother, who had the same problem, but she waited till she was 69 for the surgery, so it didn't help much. Well, I figured, as long as I'm having anesthesia, why not do something else? I asked the doctor if he could do something about my chin and the jowls that were developing underneath, which made me look older. So he said he'd do a chin implant and liposuction the fat underneath, and he promised me I'd be really happy with the results. Recovery time wouldn't be any longer—I wouldn't be away from work very long. So I said yes.

"I woke up from surgery and my only complaint was the numbness in my lower lip. So I got home, and the next day I called the doctor to ask when the novocaine was supposed to wear off. He said the numb feeling was normal, that it would go away gradually. But it didn't and it hasn't, and now, it's been *nine* years since the surgery. I went back a few times and the doctor finally admitted that I had permanent nerve damage. I am always aware of it—when I eat, when I talk, obviously when I kiss. It's worse when it's humid out.

Sometimes I want to scream, it's so intense—the feeling isn't numbness, it's an abnormal sensation. Other times, it's milder, but it's always there.

"I don't regret doing it. Look, I have to say I got the cosmetic result I wanted. I know you'll think I'm crazy, but I'm actually thinking about a full face-lift when I hit 50. Obviously I won't go back to the same doctor. And I hope that there won't be complications like the last time. Okay, so I won't look 40 when I'm 70, but I *will* look 60. And to me, that's enough."

Olivia paid a heavy price for her chin. Is it logical to care more about an image than to value the face and body we were given at birth? At some point, we have to come to terms with who and what we are, and that includes the way we look. You can create something nearly new out of the whole cloth of surgery, cosmetics, creams, and potions, but what you end up with, basically, is that person underneath who day by day is getting older. If our self-concept doesn't change to keep step with our image, we will never be able to see ourselves as sexy when we hit 70, 80, and 90.

The Goal of Perfection

Joanne runs a modeling agency in Santa Barbara, and, at 54, is proud of the fact that she has made the leap from being a model herself to managing other beautiful women's careers. To look at her photos, one would say that she is barely into her forties. Her hair is dark and lustrous; her skin bears no signs of sun damage or late nights with too many martinis. She's gorgeous and she knows it.

"My boyfriend is twenty-three years younger than me and he loves my looks. And I make sure he'll continue to love them. I keep a mirror on my nightstand so I can see whether my mascara has run; I have a big mirror on the armoire across from the bed so I can check myself when we make love. If I get in a position where my tummy is hanging down or I look really gross, I can quickly change. I love to be looked at, but I don't like being messed up. I'm not the kind of girl who tears off her clothes on her way to bed and starts making love wearing only her glasses and socks. That would look so awful! I haven't had any cosmetic surgery yet, but believe me, the minute I see those folds start in my neck or some puffiness around my eyes, I'll do it. I certainly think it would make me look sexier to get things fixed when they started falling apart, but I don't have hope that it will make me *feel* sexier. Since menopause, I don't have much desire at all. I fake it and pretend for my boyfriend, but it's all so cool now. It's kind of sad—it feels like I've lost a good friend."

Joanne has been marbleized into her beautiful face and body, and her attitude is literally poison to good sex. In order to feel feminine and luscious, we have to throw a lot of structure to the winds—this is what is meant by "get down and get dirty." The woman who needs to be beautiful all the time is stuck in the form and can't get into the function. Her ideal look is frozen into a perfect face and body, but she can't breathe and let her belly out, let alone have an orgasm.

If we concentrate on the external—which is, of course, the ostensible reason for cosmetic surgery—we lose the most vital part of ourselves. This house that we inhabit shifts and changes from moment to moment, and we can either accept that or fight it. But change is natural and normal, and it's happening on the inside as well as the outside. A woman who thinks she can lock herself into an immutable physical form is deceiving herself. What's more, she has abandoned the real stuff of sexuality, which allows for all comers—rich and poor, beautiful and not so, young and quite old.

For Lucy and Nancy, who feel sexier because they can see themselves more clearly, and for Louisa, who although still a heavy woman likes the feeling of her body again, cosmetic surgery has been an enormous boon. For Olivia, who ended up with more pain and frustration than satisfaction, for Milagro, who has unreasonable demands for her image, and for Joanne, to whom the body is everything, tampering with the goods would be a mistake. We can only hope that they'll discover that before it's too late.

Coming to Terms with Face and Body

For most women, whose sexual lives are only one portion of a committed, loving relationship, the realization eventually dawns that looks don't matter *that* much. The longer you gaze with the eyes of love, the fewer flaws you see. And when that affection is reflected in the mirror, it may relieve any apprehension you might have had that you aren't a desirable, hot juicy babe.

If someone else sees you as desirable, why can't you? It's time for you to fall in love with yourself, with all your flaws and faults, and lines and sags. Why can't you be turned on by your own face—one that has seen sorrow and silliness and boredom and anger? What does a flat stomach or perfect-size breasts have to do with your sexuality? Nancy Etcoff, Ph.D., a psychologist at Harvard Medical School, was quoted in *Modern Maturity* magazine on the issue of coming to terms with the face and body we grow into over the decades. "When the skin is pulled tight [in a face-lift], you get that wide-eyed blank look. The little crinkles around the eyes and mouth that come from smiling, when we try to remove them, we remove a lot of that history. I think that's a real cost of surgery."[9]

Our personal history is what makes us sexy. Our awareness, our intelligence, our laughter, our pride, and of course, the way we fit in our skin. That will change as we get older. Perhaps we can grow more comfortable in older bodies by really looking at them—by letting the mirror be a daily reminder of how cherished and desired we are. And then, hopefully, we will be able to erase the nostalgia for the girl who's gone and develop a passion for the fabulous woman who's right there, staring us in the face.

Weighing the Exterior Vision: How Much Does It Really Matter?

What will we look like when we're old? Can we still feel desirable with flesh that is lined and flaccid? Is it possible to defy the equation youth+beauty=sexy? The body of a 70- or 80-year-old is constantly desexualized in our society—and indeed, how often do we get to see one?

If the face droops and the body sags, can we still attract a partner? Of course we can! Think of the women who embrace their wrinkles and gray hair and puffy eyes and say, Look at me, this is what 50 or 60 or 80 looks like. No makeup, no hair color, no artificial enhancement whatsoever. The striking images of Katharine Hepburn with her extraordinary bones, Renata Adler with her long white braid, and Germaine Greer with marked circles under her eyes are advertisements for faces you would never forget—faces with plenty of character. These women don't care what society says about conforming to any image—they are happy with who they are at their current stage of life.

In an interview published in *The New York Times Magazine,* Liv Ullmann, the great Swedish star whose face and figure inhabit the films of Ingmar Bergman, her longtime lover, talked about being 62. She has not had plastic surgery, despite the deep wrinkles, sagging skin, and incipient jowls that caused a woman in an airport to ask her, "Didn't you used to be Liv Ullmann?" Her reason for allowing time to do its job was that she had always loved her grandmother's face. "I thought if I could grow into that kind of face . . . I wanted to see what God wanted from mine, more out of curiosity."[10] This is a woman who sees her face and body, like her life, as a work in progress.

It is wonderful to think you look great, because when you're pleased with yourself, others catch on and find you irresistible. If removing the bump on your nose or tightening your upper arms really makes you feel like a sexy babe—then by all means, do it. But have no illusions. Sexuality is 90 percent mind and spirit. The physical part of it is significant only if you make it so, if your awareness of your exterior self overshadows your perception of the interior self. If you didn't feel desire and didn't get aroused before your surgery, it's highly unlikely that you will afterward. Your sexual feelings are too complex to be fixed by a scalpel and a few sutures.

There are ways, however, to dig deep down and do something about your sex life that will count at any age and with any face and body. In the next chapter, you'll learn exactly how to enhance your sexual pleasure. (P.S. It has almost nothing to do with the way you look.)

HOW TO SPARK DESIRE:
SEXUAL SOLUTIONS FOR BODY,
MIND, AND SPIRIT

Turn on any TV talk show or wander into any appropriate chat room and you will find vast numbers of women who are having a lousy time in bed. Not only don't they feel a burning desire for sex; they don't even feel a mild interest. So if you're not having a ball either, you're supposed to be comforted by the fact that you fit the pattern, and you're "normal."

But suppose you don't *feel* normal. You feel like you're missing something, like you're falling behind, like you've lost a limb or part of your sense of touch. You can surf the Net and take a pill and get your face lifted and your stomach liposuctioned, and desire may still elude you.

Don't be hard on yourself if you don't feel extremely sexual right now. People go through lulls, get bored, get busy, get into ruts, and the desire for sex may fade or disappear altogether. And then, either because they finally feel peaceful or tender toward their lover, or happen to see a sexy image, or perhaps do nothing at all except respond to a partner's kiss, desire sparks again, like an engine that was idling and is now ready to race.

Women living alone may find that their sexual desire goes underground without external stimulation. They may want to masturbate, or they may find that it really doesn't interest them. They may sometimes worry that the thrill is completely gone, but then a new person comes on the scene who finds them attractive or sexy or fascinating, and suddenly, their juices are flowing again.

We can wait out these periods of abstinence and sexual lassitude, or we can take action. And to that end, there are a huge number of activities, skills, and items that can make sex anticipated and delicious once again. In this chapter, we offer three pathways toward sparking your dormant desire. You can do it *externally, internally,* or *therapeutically,* or you can pick and choose from all three areas.

The external interventions include all sorts of sex toys (vibrators, dildos, and more exotic choices), flavored and textured condoms, dress-up (split-crotch panties, leather, costumes, stiletto heels), and equipment that can be a part of sex play (blindfolds, whips, harnesses, and restraints). You can decide to have sex in different places at different times, using sensory apparatus (food, wine, music, body paints, scarves, and other fabrics), reading pornography, listening to erotic audio, watching erotic films, and participating in fantasy games or role-playing. Any and all of these can be the fodder for some new excitement.

Then we have the internal interventions. By quieting the mind and focusing only on feeling, passion may unexpectedly return. The field of psychoneuroimmunology has allowed us to see the parallels between desire and personal awareness. The relationships among behavior, the brain, and the endocrine and immune systems are intertwined—just having a sexual thought can trigger the production of hormones and neurotransmitters that enhance physical experience. We'll offer guidelines for beginning a practice of sexuality that unites all the many facets of your being.

But it is also conceivable that there is something seriously askew that is preventing you from enjoying sex—something that may stem from early childhood relationships, trauma or abuse, or a dysfunctional pattern that has taken hold and refuses to let go. And so the therapeutic pathway may be the one for you. Sex therapy can offer a safe way to learn to be vulnerable and comfortable at the same time. The right therapist can serve as a mentor and can help women and couples eliminate or quell old fears and negative reactions. We'll explain exactly what therapy should and can't do, and you'll find appropriate therapeutic options listed in Resources.

If desire has disappeared temporarily, if sex just doesn't feel good, you may shrug and think it more prudent to leave it alone and move on in your life. But let us enthusiastically express our encouragement to keep the spark alive. Once you have stimulated that little flame, it may illuminate your entire life.

EXTERNAL SOLUTIONS FOR SEXUAL DOLDRUMS

Expanding Your Repertoire with Sex Toys, Equipment, and Games

What makes you horny? What gets you wet? Women are typically sensual creatures, and sensory stimulation may tweak sexual interest. Just lying in the sun can be stimulating to some women—the warmth, the light, the heat flowing into the body. What do *you* like to look at, listen to, taste, touch, and smell when you are completely at ease? The old saw about wining and dining a woman by candlelight with roses on the table isn't far off the mark, but may be unrealistic on most evenings when you have to feed the family or run to a committee meeting. Clearly, there are other ways to add eroticism.

Music helps—for some, an auditory enhancement can be soothing, for others, stimulating. The insistent beat of a great drum solo or the riff of a wailing saxophone can echo the buildup of sexual excitement. Select something that can set a mood or that matches your mood—Indian ragas, old jazz, New Age Windham Hill. Now, as for scent, you may love the unadorned smell of musk or fresh clean skin, but if you're into something more exotic, you can try **aromatherapy** candles and oils. They come in an array of delicious smells that coincide with your moods: If you're looking for an aphrodisiac, try jasmine, musk, patchouli, saffron, sandalwood, or ylang-ylang. If you're too hyped up for sex and need to calm down, try chamomile, jasmine, lavender, or neroli. And if what you need is a wake-up call to sex, try bergamot, lemon, nutmeg, or peppermint.

Taste can match an erotic appetite for sexual titillation. Using food in the bedroom is an adult version of finger painting, where you smear your own body or your lover's with something sweet or creamy, then lick it off, gratifying several urges at one time. Old favorites are chocolate sauce, whipped cream, wine, and cognac, but you can also use guacamole, creamy peanut butter, cream cheese, or hummus. Don't put food inside the vagina—you can get a nasty bacterial infection this way. But a bedroom picnic is a great way to overcome reluctance to perform oral sex if one of you happens to be squeamish about tasting bodily fluids or nervous about the scent or taste of their own.

Once your senses are heightened, and your body relaxed, you can spend some time getting to know what pleases you. **Masturbation** is a terrific way to reawaken the sexual spirit inside you. No matter what you were taught as a child, self-love is a way to enjoy sex without love, orgasm without commitment or recrimination. Many women don't even know where their sexual organs are, and by touching themselves, they are able to identify and feel pleasure in their clitoris, inner and outer labia, vaginal introitus, and anus. Many of Sandra's patients have come alive to sexuality without any partner, just by treating themselves well in the bedroom.

THE BENEFITS OF MASTURBATION

1. It feels good.
2. It is the only absolutely safe form of sex.
3. It teaches you how your body works.
4. It shows that you are independent, in charge of your pleasure.
5. It keeps the tissues lubricated, especially important in older women.
6. It's a way to expand your fantasies and learn a lot about yourself and your sexual interests, fears, and hopes in the process.
7. For women without partners, it offers physical release and all the benefits of pleasure and orgasm.
8. For women with partners, it offers a different sexual experience, one that you control and where you get exactly what you want each time.

9. For couples, it is a way to observe and learn about your partner's
    sexual wishes.
10. It can be a form of meditation, a way to bring mind and body
    into harmony. _____

Masturbating with a hand or a washcloth is fine, but it gets boring after a
while. And this is where **sex toys** come in. Have you ever considered putting something inside yourself to see whether you felt different sensations?
What about something that stimulated your vulva more intensely (and longer)
than a hand could?

Many of Sandra's patients are initially reluctant to use toys. They feel
they're just mechanical—cold and unromantic. The idea of buying a piece of
rubber or plastic for self-stimulation or even partner use seems unappetizing.
Many women find that their reluctance to use toys stems from unfamiliarity
rather than aversion, or from feeling that dildos and vibrators are too kinky for
"nice" girls to use. Other patients have reported feeling they're anxious about
growing dependent on a vibrator. What if orgasms by the dozen, courtesy of
their mechanical friend, become so desirable they can't have it any other way?

"I'm not that type," one 30-year-old patient told Sandra. She was in therapy because she had never had an orgasm. "I have never masturbated." She
described her partner as "kind of clumsy" in bed, and incapable of sensual
touch. He was either too gentle and tentative or else too rough.

Sandra suggested that she purchase a vibrator and try it out alone to discover whether she might become more aroused than she typically did during
sex with her partner. If she didn't like it after a few tries, she could throw it
out and they would find other ways of helping her achieve her first orgasm.

Two weeks later, she was back in Sandra's office with a big grin on her
face. "Bingo!" she said. "It was great. I had one orgasm, and then, before I
knew it, another and another. I couldn't believe I could feel so much so
quickly. It was almost too intense."

If you feel that sex toys are just too strange and unfamiliar, go online and
look at them for a while, or order one of the catalogues in Resources just to
go window-shopping. It may be easier to stimulate your imagination and
pique feelings of arousal to read about them and see pictures of them on the
Internet or in catalogues. Imagine how they might feel on your body. Fantasize a bit, and see what happens.

Even if you wouldn't buy a sexual device yourself, you may be introduced to the wide world of toys by a partner or another woman who's
recently discovered how great they are. Group parties for show-and-tell of
toys, tasty lubricants, exotic condoms, leatherwear, and provocative lingerie
are becoming more prevalent than Tupperware events. It really helps to have
a friendly group of women joking and ribbing each other about the possible
uses of these items. Often the enthusiasm and camaraderie help to squelch

inhibition. Part of the spice that gets lost in many established relationships is the lack of planning and preparation for something a little different. "When my boyfriend and I moved to New York City," a 40-year-old from Nebraska told Judith, "we wandered around the Village and found this sex shop with incredible lingerie in the window. We went inside just for a few laughs, but we ended up buying a vibrator and some edible body-paints and a cock ring. We couldn't wait to get home to use them! I think we were probably even more turned on by the shopping trip than by the equipment. It was just wonderful to fantasize and touch all this stuff. And I have to say that my interest in sex was really heightened."

If you don't live in an urban area, you can have the same experience buying online together, except that—at least until technology provides us with those virtual reality "feeler" gloves—you can't touch your purchase until it arrives several days later. Still, however you get them, sexual aids and devices offer an outlet for experimentation and the opportunity to experience different sensations.

Dildos (from the Latin *dilatare,* which means "to open wide") were the very first sex toys. During sexual arousal, the vagina balloons open, and many women feel that having something in that space while they are masturbating or engaged in sex play with a partner is extremely stimulating.

They come in many skin colors, smooth and ridged, for the vagina and anus, and there are dual dildos, so that two lovers can use them at the same time. Some are hollow so that they can contain a smaller-sized penis (these are worn on a harness that fits around the man's hips). And any dildo can be placed in a **strap-on** if no penis is available. Lesbians can select several sizes and trade back and forth wearing them—or one partner can always be the "top" and the other the "bottom." Dildos can be inserted all the way inside, or can just graze the entrance to the vagina, moving in and out between the labia to provide a maddeningly exciting tease. There are thick ones that will fill you entirely, and thin ones, which may be preferable if your partner is manipulating it inside you. If you've had any gynecological surgery, or if you've never had intercourse, or it's been years since your last sexual encounter, you'll want to start with a smaller model and work your way up.

Vibrators have come a very long way from their origins in the late 1800s as hand-held steam massagers, prescribed by physicians to treat "frigidity" in women. The next model, an electric "vibratory dilator" that delivered a shock to the vaginal walls, came on the scene in 1911. These were followed by battery-operated ones in the 1930s and 1940s. Today, there are models for vagina and anus; penis-shaped ones that fit right inside you; huge wands with one or two big soft heads that can be used directly on the exterior of the genitals and nipples. Some have crooked appendages that will hit your G-spot (the Gräfenberg spot, located on the anterior wall of the vagina, which feels something like a bean and which swells when stimulated). Some have a small extra finger (the "twig") to work on the clitoris while the main portion fills the vagina. In addition, there is the Swedish massager model. It resembles a flat iron with various attachments that can be added to change your sensations. These are still sold in drugstores ostensibly as back massagers, but if you look at the little knobs and rubber spiky things you can hook on, it's clear what they're intended for.[1]

Betty Dodson, the grande doyenne of masturbation (see chapter 6) recommends the Hitachi wand for self-stimulation—if you find the sensation too intense, you can use it on top of your underwear. Go slowly if you aren't used to a vibrator—if you get hooked on the enormous pleasure you're receiving and keep going indefinitely, you may numb the area, and it's possible to damage these delicate tissues, particularly the urethra—this can set up a urinary tract infection. Most of Sandra's patients become expert pretty quickly.

"I have MS and it's getting worse," Adrienne, a 40-year-old computer programmer told her. "Vibrators are particularly beneficial for women with disabilities because we have reduced sensitivity to touch and a vibrator can be turned on high to compensate for that. Also, my fingers really don't work well enough for masturbation, so they're a great boon to anyone like me with impaired muscular control—you don't need to hold them in your hands, but can simply put them inside the elastic band of your underwear and lie on top of them to achieve enormous pleasure."

You can use vibrators and dildos alone when you're masturbating (there are also models that can be used under water in the tub), you can use them with your partner as part of sex play, and they can increase stimulation during oral or anal sex or intercourse by keeping contact with the clitoris while another orifice is being penetrated.

Anal toys are an entire category unto themselves. The anus, despite its unsavory reputation, is an erogenous zone, just like the clitoris, labia, vagina, and nipples. Of course, hygiene is exceptionally important if you decide you'd like to try anal play or anal intercourse.

There are, first, butt plugs of various sizes, and anal vibrators. Wearing a plug when you're not having sex is a kind of sexual secret—and many women are into the idea of keeping something in there under their clothes, just to remind them of what might happen later and to loosen the anal sphincter muscle for anal intercourse. There are also anal beads—five plastic or rubber rounds strung on a nylon cord. You insert the whole string and then pop them out one by one, which provides a real thrill as the anus opens and closes over each bead.

Sex toys come in every conceivable shape. The best-known ones are phallic, but there are egg-shaped ones that can be inserted and then turned on with a battery-operated remote control, and something called a "Venus butterfly" that sits across your labia and is worn with straps that fit across the hips and buttocks. Ben-wa balls, which date back to ancient China, are small metal balls that may be inserted loose into the vagina or sometimes are connected with a string for easy removal. They are weighted so that, as you move— either walking around or gyrating your hips during sexual activity—they hit against the walls of the vagina. There's a sex toy called the Octopus with eight attachments for all your different needs, and even an "auto" arouser that plugs into the cigarette lighter of your car (park first, please). And there are remote-control stimulators, so that your partner can turn you on at a distance.

Don't substitute a banana or a cucumber for a sex toy. Plants break down under pressure, and you can end up with a walloping infection from a bit of zucchini that breaks off inside you. Dildos and vibrators are made of non-reactive material; veggies are filled with chemicals that will react with your own moist internal environment. Emergency room doctors love to regale friends about the many times they've had to remove mustard bottles, light-bulbs, flashlights, and worse from a patient's vagina or anus. So spend a little— most sex toys cost between $20 and $40 (although they can get much pricier)—and get your thrills safely. (See Resources for a guide to buying toys.)

And one more safety issue. Toys should be kept scrupulously clean, even if you are in a mutually monogamous relationship. Scrub them with hot water and mild nonallergenic soap after each use. If you're sharing a toy—particu-larly one that goes inside the anus—it's a good idea to place a condom over it and change it before the toy finds a new home. Always use lubrication—there are plenty of water-based lubricants available in drugstores, sex shops, and online, such as Astroglide, Slippery Stuff, Acqua-Lube, Fem-Glide, and even a new K–Y jelly that has a silky feel. (Massage oils are lovely, and can be ter-rific for massage, but should not be used with condoms, because oil or petro-leum jelly can break down latex and render it useless.)

As for the once mandatory spermicide nonoxynol-9, which was handed out routinely along with condoms in the 1980s in order to protect against the transmission of STDs, it is now considered *more* dangerous to use it than not. Women who used it long term complained of vaginal and cervical ulcers, yeast infections, and burning that was certainly not erotic. Nonoxynol-9 acts as an irritant to the delicate membranes, and these open sores may make the body more vulnerable to infection.

But ongoing research showed that by adding a buffer, avena sativa (the herbal extract of oats), you would neutralize the caustic effect of the chemi-cal. A newer nonoxynol, known as 15, has been in the works for some time and is being test-marketed as Erogel (see Resources) in seven American cities as well as two international sites. This may turn out to be the toothpaste of the twenty-first century, keeping a smile on your face as well as disease from your reproductive organs.

Sandra has had more than one patient tell her that she enjoys masturbat-ing with a vibrator, but that she's worried that it may "spoil" her for her hus-band. And others who say that their husband is so crazy about seeing them with their vibrator that he always insists on having it in bed. So does it become a fetish if you have to use it every time?

The same may be asked of any **sexual equipment** that adds a different dimension to the acts you perform. Suppose you and your partner get off on high heels, or crotchless pants, or rubber, and then you start playing games where you always use this stuff to get turned on? "My husband really had a thing for leather," said Merillee, a 32-year-old landscape gardener. "We visited some friends in the country and when we got ready for bed, he came out of the bathroom with his collar and thong on. I just laughed. It was so inappropriate to take that stuff to someone else's house! But he was really hurt and humiliated, and then he told me he couldn't get it up if he wasn't wearing it. The way I read it, it was like armor, protecting him from his sexual feelings. Me, I feel sexy sometimes in leather and sometimes just completely naked, like I was then. It was sort of becoming an issue in our relationship, but we're working on it."

Fantasy play is fun—dressing up, dressing down, role-playing add spice for many. It becomes a problem only when one partner finds it necessary and the other finds it objectionable, particularly when it turns into an invariant part of the sexual script. Say you rented an erotic video, and it was great because you could learn from watching the couple onscreen and mimic what they were doing—which would expand your repertoire. But then you started getting into the films and you became aroused only when you did what the characters did. It might rob you of your own imagination and improvisational skills, which is what makes sex so delightful. Or suppose you decided to try out a little light bondage, maybe with scarves or leather. You began to enjoy that so much that it escalated, and you went on to chains, rope, and cat-o'-nine-tails. And you have to do it every time in order to get turned on. Is this a dangerous thing? Does the sex become more about the equipment and objects than about what you can give to each other? Yes, it can become a problem, in which case one of you may have to suggest scaling back, or perhaps create a new sexual scenario together.

But instead of constricting sexual interest, you can build on fantasy in order to make sex even better. Imagination sends us to places that would be frightening, dangerous, or ridiculous in real life. For a woman with a fragile ego, it may be hard to get into fantasies that challenge her ideas about herself. For example, it may be too difficult for a woman who is ambivalent about her sexuality to fantasize about making love with a woman, or for someone who once had an incestuous experience with her brother to think back to those stolen moments together.

On the other hand, if our vision of ourselves is strong enough, we can have some pretty wild dreams and find them enthralling. "My husband ordered a paddle online and wanted to use it on me," one corporate executive of 50 told Sandra. "I couldn't believe that I got aroused when I pictured myself being held down and spanked. I mean, that's so politically incorrect, and yet I found it very exciting. But you know, it was an enormous relief not to have to be the one making the decisions and corrections! I really got into it!" This was a woman who had been the oldest of four girls, and everyone always depended on her. So to give herself up to pleasure, to abandon all control, was extremely erotic for her.

For most, experimentation with toys or costumes or games is a sometime thing. In fact, it's much more common that we need prodding to stick a toe in the water, not that we're going to jump in the deep end. Most of us struggle under years of repression or, at the very least, inhibition that make us feel inept or embarrassed about even wanting to do something that breaks our regular bedtime patterns. The biggest hurdle is making the commitment to try something new.

You can start to overcome your automatic tendency to say no by following these questions and then creating your own wish list:

Q: Do you value your relationship? IF YES, THEN CONTINUE
Q: Is the relationship stagnant? Is this partly due to your reluctance to be physical? IF YES, THEN CONTINUE
Q: What risks will you take in order to make changes? CREATE WISH LIST

WISH LIST FOR MORE ADVENTUROUS SEX
- I'd like to give my husband of twenty years a hand-job, just like I did in college.
- I'd like to sit on his face and have him tongue me.
- I'd like to make a date for sex, planning all the trimmings.
- I'd like to make love outside.
- I'd like to try an ice cube melting inside me while he goes down on me.
- I'd like to make love in front of a full-length mirror and see how we fit together.
- I'd like to try a soft manual toothbrush or a new, thin paintbrush on all my delicate tissues.
- I'd like to have phone sex while we're both at the office.
- I'd like to play strip poker or even sex Monopoly, with a separate act designated for each property I land on.
- I want to share fantasies with my partner—as long as they're not hurtful.
- I'd like to set up a camera on a tripod and videotape us making love.
- I'd like to go out to dinner sans underwear and talk dirty throughout the meal.

Write down all your secret wishes on separate pieces of paper and toss them into a hat. By writing them down, you get a chance to think about them, solo, and then present them to your partner for consideration rather than blurting them out and risking embarrassment.

Q: What are your goals? CREATE LIST in order of importance; for example,

❀ to be comfortable in my body
❀ to be comfortable with more physical contact
❀ to feel something more
❀ to learn how to play sexually
❀ to improve my relationship before time runs out.

Finally, when you have selected goals, set a date by which you will make the effort to try a few new things.

Start by talking about the kinds of things you like—things you've done and things you've only heard or read about. (Erotic books and films are excellent sources of ideas.) You can give each other a lot of thrills with a sex game, where you take turns acting out wishes from your wish list. You should not agree to anything that you find objectionable—that will only make you resentful. On the other hand, don't reject unusual requests out of hand. You may find that you're pleasantly surprised by them. And don't end every sex session with intercourse . . . that may have been what got you bored and uninterested in the first place.

Sex lives that have become routine and predictable lose appeal. As one of our colleagues says, in order to want sex, it has to be sex worth wanting. Evaluate your sex life and consider whether it needs updating or modification—a new coat of paint, as it were. You may just discover that adding just a little color will be an effective solution to sexual doldrums.

SEXPERT HINTS FOR PLENTY OF PLEASURE

1. Go to bed naked (you're more likely to have sex if you have skin rubbing skin under the covers).
2. Go braless around the house for a whole weekend to feel fabric against your nipples.
3. Wear silk underwear.
4. Use body lotion, and spend time putting it on your most sensitive areas, on the inner thighs and around the breasts.
5. Buy crotchless panties.
6. Wear a clitoral vibrator under your clothes in a public place.
7. Get a tattoo where only you and your lover will see it.
8. Go to a male strip show with a group of women friends.

9. Get a tape of a book of women's top fantasies by Lonnie Barbach or Nancy Friday and go for a walk outside wearing headphones.
10. If you have a partner, take a shower or bath together every week.
11. Keep a wish-basket in the bedroom of things you'd like to try and swap turns with your partner so that you each get a chance to experience some new sex treat.

Pornography and Antipornography

"I love reading really good porn," said Pam, a single elementary-school teacher who grew up in New Hampshire. "It's probably the thing my mother warned me most about, and the thing I enjoy most about sex. When I get into one of those books that Anne Rice wrote under her 'dirty' pseudonym, you can't disturb me. I get hot and I masturbate, and I read some more, and I stay hot. I can spend a whole Sunday just feeling like a sexpot, even though in real life, I'm teased for dressing so conservatively."

The word "pornography" comes from the Greek, meaning "writing of prostitutes." It has classically been the province of men—a slimy, degrading, obscene look at sex. The old hard-core porn films are a meaningless collection of crotch shots, huge penises entering tiny vulvas, breasts bigger than melons with nipples to match. No people, no plots—just disjointed sexual acts.

The advent of the Web has made porn much more accessible—no longer do you have to hide out at the back of the video store or local magazine stand. You don't have to write away for dirty pictures, but if you surrender your credit card number, you can get them with the click of a mouse.

Feminists decry porn because it dehumanizes both women and men and turns women into objects—a long leg ending in a spike heel, an open mouth dripping with cum, a pair of buttocks being spread apart. Traditional pornography is not only not sexually stimulating to a lot of women, it can be repellent, since it implies that the female body is simply a collection of orifices to be used and abused. (The classic male fantasy was supposed to be a gorgeous woman who fucked all night long and then, at the end of the evening, turned into a pizza that the man could gobble up.)

But today's career porn-stars are doing very well with live masturbation scenes and X-rated Web chats—one e-entrepreneur is said to have made $50,000 from her website. They design their own sites and their own online dramas, and they collect the paycheck.

Some of the best new porn is addressed directly to women. Candida Royalle is a savvy producer and director of women's erotic films who has found a way to turn on women visually. A former porn star who got sick of the relentless focus on body parts, not passion, she started making films that spoke to the excitement inside her and other women she knew. "I wanted to show that the entire body is an erogenous zone, to see touching and kissing and couples looking at each other. I decided to present lovers in a way that's holistic . . . more encompassing. The way the couple touch and what they're feeling is the turn-on.

"In my own life, I was finding that really good sex takes effort. It takes a lot more of the relationship than the physical part of it. I recently began a sexual relationship with someone I'd been seeing for several months. And we didn't have intercourse. We just touched and caressed . . . he made me feel beautiful by touching me. It was also incredibly exciting. I try to show this in the films—to present lovers making love in a way that's holistic. It's goal-less, it goes way beyond the old lick, suck, fuck, and fall asleep in half an hour.

"The physical expression of love, especially when it's deeply sensual and non-coital, wakes up the body and the mind. It's a continuum of all the other things that go on in a relationship," Candida says sincerely. "It's a deep connection that opens people up to each other and invites a level of intimacy that otherwise won't be there. Within this type of special union is the potential for elevation, for ecstasy. So few people understand the depth of where lovemaking can take them."[2]

The depth, of course, is not easy to investigate through external means. In order to understand what sexual passion is about and where it lives inside us, we have to turn within.

INTERNAL SOLUTIONS FOR SEXUAL DOLDRUMS

Mind Meets Body and Spirit in the Bedroom

More stimulation—whether it's through vibration or titillation—is just that. It's a momentary high, and it expands the playing field, but for most women, it's not the key to rekindling desire. Because, of course, the biggest sexual organ is between the ears, so if you want a real awakening, you must turn on the mind.

Every second, 100 million messages are sent from the nervous system to the brain.[3] We are assaulted with stimulation of every kind, from sensory input to cognitive thought. It seems impossible that anyone could actually tune out long enough to achieve orgasm. And in fact, this is the problem many women have. The busy paraphernalia of their days keep recycling, even at a time when the mind craves active consciousness but *not* active thinking.

The old belief that the left brain is the "accountant," keeping tabs on all our busywork, and the right brain is the "artist," creatively and intuitively exploring the world, has been debunked by recent research on brain damage. As it happens, either hemisphere can take over any function if necessary. Research in psychoneuroimmunology (the science that combines psychology, neurology, and immunology) indicates that the corpus callosum, the band of fibers connecting the hemispheres, is larger in women than in men. It is easier for a female's right and left brain to communicate, especially during moments when the frontal lobes (the "thinking" brain) take a backseat to the limbic system (the "emotional" brain). This happens most frequently during meditation, trance states, and orgasm.

One reason that many women claim that sex doesn't do it for them is that they can't get into the mood, or looking at it from a neurological perspective, that they can't switch gears and stop the mental chatter, the monkey-mind. They can't turn from the thinking to the feeling brain, mostly because they're tired and preoccupied and feel overwhelmed with their second full-time job as wife, mother, chief cook-and-bottle-washer, etc. And if they have a partner who's less than helpful around the house, they may resent his easy suggestion that they drop everything and come to bed.

Let's imagine it's 11 PM, right after the news. You are lying beside your sweetheart, and he begins to kiss you. Your mind is processing the inventory of what happened during the day and what you have to do tomorrow. Let's listen in:

Kiss. Shirt ruined at cleaners—will they pay? Hand on thigh. Billy needs to pack a lunch for the soccer tournament Sunday. Didn't do that last load of wash. Hate it that Dad is sick. He was nauseated when I spoke to him—he's losing so much weight! Mouth on breast—don't think I can fly out to see Dad right now. Guilt.

There is too much going on here! How can you possibly let yourself experience the infinite possibilities of sexual feeling when you're reviewing a list of activities and doubts in your head? Women who find sex an annoyance may simply be reacting to the fact that they have not switched over from cognitive thought (those beta waves hurtling through the brain as we categorize and organize things) to the sexual state of mind (conscious and alert, relaxed but energized, brought on by the slower alpha waves). They may simply need to learn to quiet down and get centered on themselves.

Mindfulness, a very user-friendly meditative practice adopted from Buddhism, can change the nature of your thinking and allow you to open yourself to those precious moments of connection that you're now missing. As described by Jon Kabat-Zinn, founder and director of the Stress Reduction Clinic at the University of Massachusetts Medical Center, mindfulness is "the regular, disciplined practice of moment-to-moment awareness, the complete 'owning' of each moment of your experience, good, bad, or ugly."[4] When you are mindful of what you are doing, whether it's signing your name or stroking your lover's arm, you are participating fully in life, rather than letting moments slip away unnoticed. What this means for your sex life is crucial: Instead of getting distracted by the hundred things you might be doing if you weren't making love, you can let go of all this extraneous stuff and throw yourself into sex with abandon.

Mindfulness takes practice. As you move through your activity, you must be aware of what you're thinking and feeling and continually bring yourself back to what's really happening rather than your perception of what's happening. As a method of learning, let's take one thing that you do on a regular basis and break it down into its various components. How about something sensual, like washing your face.

- Begin by looking at yourself in the mirror. Examine your face; don't judge it.
- Turn on the water and run your hand under it. Feel what it's like to have one dry and one wet hand. Feel the temperature and adjust it.
- Pick up the soap, feel how slippery it is. Wet the soap and feel the difference in the texture.
- Wet your face, and look up at yourself. Notice the difference— moistened eyelashes and eyebrows, water on your cheeks.
- Soap your face and enjoy the sensation, the slickness on your skin. Explore each plane and cavity—the forehead, temples, cheeks, eyes, nose. Taste soap on lips.
- Wash off the soap, and with each splash of water, feel your face lose the suds.
- Dry your face, and enjoy the softness, the fluffiness, of the towel.

Now let's try it with sex. Pay close attention to every move, every sound and scent, and what you and your partner are sharing. Listen to the messages you give yourself and keep bringing your focus back to the present moment. Now, as you give and take with your partner in an intimate way, the running monologue in your mind hopefully will be more like the following:

Kiss. Lips very soft, taste of chocolate and saliva. Teeth click, then move away. Licking his lower lip, then face. A little stubble. His hands on my ass, pulling cheeks apart, massaging closer toward my opening. Breath comes faster. Eager. Melting.

You can also carry mindfulness into movement. Take off your clothes (you may want to leave your underwear on), and give each other sensual massages—but stay in the moment. Use massage oil or a body lotion so that your hands will slide with no friction from one body part to the next. Focus now both on the breath and on your partner's body. If you're touching an arm, *really touch it*—feel the texture of the skin and hair and the warmth or coolness of the fingers. Smell your partner's scent and see the body under your hands as a gift. Handle it carefully, with mindfulness.

During the next week or two, refrain from sexual activity. Allow the deep connection between you to grow. You may want to investigate **acupressure points that stimulate sexual energy.** Pressing the points—which according to Chinese medicine lie along fourteen meridians, or energy pathways, in the body—can trigger the production of beta endorphins, those neurotransmitters that alleviate pain and also provide a unity between the yin and yang, the excess and deficiency throughout the body. The points that may help to turn you on are the center of the nipple, the center of the sternum, the center of the perineum (the strip of skin between the genitals and the anus), the center of the crease where the leg joins the torso, the lower abdomen between the navel and the pubic bone, and the lower back on the spine directly opposite the belly button.[5]

After this, you might wish to experiment with a technique known as **pelvic rocking.** Sitting naked opposite your partner on your knees—place a cushion or two between your legs to take the pressure off—begin to rock your pelvis back and forth by first arching the small of your back and then contracting it. The two of you should make eye contact, although you may find, as your pleasure builds, that your eyes close involuntarily. The movement of the hips can be very slight, but as you get into a rhythm, you'll want to feel an expansion and contraction in your genitals and anus. You can inhale and exhale as you grip with the muscles around the perineum (the pubococcygeal, or PC, muscles) and then let go. Understand that you and your partner are experiencing the same physical sensation, but may appreciate it in very different ways—just as you do sex. It's really important to acknowledge this. As close as you may be, you cannot crawl inside each other's skin to be sexually in sync. On the other hand, you can share enjoyment as you are now.

Reach out and hold hands as you continue the pelvic rocking. This is the time to establish deep eye contact so that you can transmit nonverbal messages about being together. See if you can match your breath and your rocking. Continue this for ten or fifteen minutes, and at the end, be silent together, allowing your breathing to come back to normal. You may feel a tingling in your genitals—or you may not. The experience itself may be enough to share right now.[6]

Of course, delving into desire can't be done merely by adding new skills to your repertoire. It's mainly in your attitude. In learning these skills, you have to see your sexual time as primary, inviolable. You have to be in the moment and let nothing come between you and your pleasure. Over time, you will see that you stop judging yourself and your partner—you stop criticizing your bodies or your techniques and stop feeling that you should or shouldn't do one thing or another. You begin to ask for what you need without feeling needy or neglected. And finally, you *let go*. What happens, happens. Lovemaking or masturbation becomes pure sensation, a way to get out of your head, into your body, and into unquestioning delight.

After doing your meditation and relaxation exercises, work your way back to lovemaking slowly. You may want to refrain from intercourse for a while, but do everything else. You are looking for a state of consciousness that allows you to be in the moment, experience sensation, and be aware of your partner, if you have one.

Mindfulness is only one form of meditation. You might be interested in trying the more conventional type of **seated meditation,** similar to what you might do in a yoga or tai chi class, which involves going within and quieting the mind. Meditation is a way to approach sexuality because it cultivates "being" rather than "doing." You don't have to think about whether or not you're pleasing your partner, or whether you're going to have an orgasm. All you have to do is be there—really *be* there. It has been likened to peeling an onion—you remove one layer of thought and feeling after another until you reach the deeper core inside. You can detach from all the petty concerns that hold you back. More important, you can gain patience with yourself and your partner. In the 1960s, Herbert Benson of the Harvard Medical School began a series of clinical studies on experienced meditators and found that they were actually able to control what had previously been thought of as involuntary physical responses.[7] The "relaxation response," as he called it, shuts down the habitual thinking process so that the practitioner can achieve clarity. The mind functions as a backdrop to the various faculties that make you human—your emotions, your will, your spirit.

If you're interested in trying out a mind/body connection to enhance your sexuality, it's best to start by yourself. Give yourself twenty minutes or more each day to sit in a quiet place, close your eyes, and begin to focus on your breath. Pay attention to the inhale and exhale, understanding that other thoughts will enter your mind. Let them appear and then disappear, as though you were sitting in the passenger seat of a car, watching the scenery pass by. Keep bringing your focus back to the breath. This will be very difficult at first, as your brain chatters away and scattered thoughts intrude. Don't give up when this happens. Just return your focus to your breath and keep trying.

The discipline of doing this offers enormous benefits, not the least in the sexual realm. After you've experimented on your own with clearing the mind, ask your partner to join you. Sit cross-legged facing each other, and begin the breathing. Listen to each other's rhythm and try to synchronize. Feel the warmth of your partner's body close enough to touch but not touching. Sense everything around you—the feeling of your hands on your knees, the sounds of the street or the night, the smell of the meal you just cooked or the flowers in the vase on the table, see the sunlight through the backs of your closed lids. Take in the sensations but don't label them with thoughts.

There are many other mind/body techniques that may prove effective for you. You might try **visualization,** where you make up a fantasy and imagine a partner and a sexy scenario that turns you on. You might attempt a relaxation technique known as **autogenics** (which comes from a word meaning "self-generation"), where you do a body scan, encouraging each limb and organ to become heavy, warm, and relaxed. You can suggest the same to your genitals and tell yourself that you are calm and open to touch. Another method is to use **recall**—you can conjure up one place and time in your life when you felt completely, utterly relaxed and at peace. And in re-creating that feeling in your body, you can teach yourself to assume that attitude of ease and acceptance at any time you'd like.[8]

To be sensually aware, you have to explore areas that you have previously not even considered in a sexual context. One very interesting realm of current investigation is **pheromones,** chemical messengers that pass from our skin into the air and have the power to attract others to us. The pheromones are picked up by a sensory organ at the base of the nasal septum, the VNO (vomeronasal organ) and delivered via a neural pathway right to the hypothalamus in the brain. This, of course, is the master gland that is responsible for our most basic emotions, such as anger, fear, and sexual passion.

In one study, men who were allowed to choose from a selection of ties in a department store homed in on the display that lies on top of pads that had been tucked into women's armpits for a few hours. Pheromones (from the Greek "I carry excitement") influence our behavior a great deal more than we suspect.

There are plenty of companies manufacturing pheromone sprays (to catch the lover of your dreams or keep the one you've got interested), but you might forgo the expensive colognes and start using your nose as an active participant in your sex life. Sleep closer together, don't bathe before bed (you'll wash off the good stuff), and don't shy away from your lover's essential juices. Pheromones can serve as a reminder that sex smells and tastes wonderful and that we may be a lot more exciting than we give ourselves credit for.

Women who have begun to blend their new awareness into their sex life talk about sex in a different way. They speak of concepts like "flow," "timelessness," and "being lost or immersed" in the experience. They are occasionally able to reach what they speak of as "euphoria," a high that is unequaled in the world of recreational drugs and which affords true peacefulness as opposed to spacey-ness. One 40-year-old patient of Sandra's described it this way: "Last night when my lover and I were making love, I had the picture in my mind of this huge vat of yellow paint being swirled around—you know, like you're stirring the sediment up from the bottom to mix it in. And the sediment comes up orange, so there are warm tones in the bright yellow. And that's me! I'm the paint and I'm the vat containing the paint and I'm the implement stirring it up. I love getting stirred up in sex. When I come, I can see this breaking of the pattern of paint—a kind of incredible Jackson Pollock deep inside me."

The concept of mind, body, and spirit combining is as old as written history and probably predates it. In the most ancient cultures, sexuality was considered a merging with the godhead, and mortals had to be in an appropriate altered state in order to achieve this temporary uplifting that we might call divinity.

In the Indian Tantric tradition, which dates back to 5000 BC, sexual union is seen as a state of enlightenment, and in Chinese Taoism, the yin and yang of two individuals becomes a complete circle when they are joined. These are two similar philosophies that incorporate a vision of wholeness, which extends not only to sexuality of course, but to all of life. Both traditions encourage the discovery of the divine through the celebration of the total human. They use all of the senses, the mind and the spirit, to reach mystical peaks. A partner, then, is not simply a manipulator of your limbs and flesh, someone who can scratch an itch better than you can yourself; rather, your partner is the complementary side of your own life force. Together you are not two halves but one whole, moving, breathing, changing together, both mass and energy at once. You can transcend personality, body, and space, and reach a type of spiritual union that is undreamt of in *Playboy* philosophy.[9]

Does this sound too esoteric? According to those who derive incredible results from Tantra, you just have to do it. The belief comes later. You start with deep relaxation, lying in a pool of sunlight, or in a completely quiet room, listening to your breath, becoming aware of your body. You might hold the hand of your partner beside you and feel the pulse of life exchanged through your fingertips. You might use massage to stimulate the physical body, but you could train yourself to be more sensitive by almost touching your partner—keeping your hand about a half inch away so that you can feel each other's heat, yet not have the satisfaction of complete connection. In Tantra, heightened excitement and orgasm are not the goal. The first and more important thing is sensation—the warmth of light on your bodies, the smell of the bedsheets or of your partner's hair, the salty taste of skin.

Some of the most convincing literature on this practice comes from those who cannot have sex in a traditional way—paraplegics, quadriplegics, and those who either from accident, disease, or congenital malformation have no sensation in their genitalia and can't have an orgasm in the "traditional" way. Gary Karp, a paraplegic, realized after studying Tantra all that he'd missed by racing toward old-fashioned orgasm and ejaculation.[10] An orgasm gives you a thrill, and then it's over. A state of ecstasy, on the other hand, allows an exchange of vital energy between two partners that can go on indefinitely. He discusses, as many other converts to Tantric sex do, the fact that excitement is just the beginning, rather than the means to an end. As soon as the body responds to sexual signals, instead of climaxing, a Tantric practitioner stays in the moment, slows her breathing and her activities, and relaxes into . . . who knows what? For some, an extraordinary energy seems to blossom in their heads or bodies. For others, who describe out-of-body experiences, the practice can be transcendent. By accepting whatever happens, by not attaching to any goal or vision of what we think sex should be, we may enter uncharted territory that gives new meaning to the words "pleasure" and "joy."

Like Tantra, the Tao (which means "the Path" or "the Way") teaches that we must let go of all our expectations of sex and simply enjoy the journey. All of life is based on the interweaving of the yin and the yang—a white teardrop head-to-toe with a black teardrop, which each contain a dot of the complementary color. The two sides are absolutely equal, in complete balance, one side about to change into the other. Whatever happens when we are with our other half—our partner—is perfect.[11]

There is no goal to Taoist sex. An orgasm might detract from the experience of taking this leisurely and often unexpected trip that may lead its travelers away from their sexual demands, away from achieving anything at all. A sensual kiss can be prolonged indefinitely; a mere placement of the tongue on the perineum can be so erotic that it completely overshadows the function of oral sex.

Sex becomes spiritual when excitement turns to heightened consciousness. The arousal becomes richer, more relaxing, and it nourishes itself the longer it goes on. When you have no expectations about getting off, or performing, or making your partner happy, you are no longer just a bean counter in bed, figuring who did what to whom. You can't be jealous or frustrated, or feel shame, guilt, or anxiety. When you take the time to prepare the ritual of kissing, touching, breathing together, it's all part of the experience, and it may bring you closer to yourself, your partner, and a feeling that transcends physical sex. For some, this mind/body connection will open a new pathway to desire. At the very least, it will give sexual exchange a new focus, an opportunity for self-exploration and self-awareness in addition to pleasure.

There's another way to approach sexuality internally, and that's to make it an integral part of your life, with the same priority as you give household chores and the kids' homework. This means that you have to carve out time in your schedule for play and pleasure. If you're exhausted, there's no way you're going to be in the mood. You need to be motivated to get more rest. Here are just a few ways to take the pressure off so you can start to enjoy your sex life:

SEXPERT HINTS FOR MAKING TIME FOR YOURSELF

✺ Make restful sleep a priority. Cut back on watching TV or other activities that keep you from turning in early.

✺ Get a sitter once a week *without fail* who will take your kids to her house. If you're all alone, fine, take a nap. If both you and your partner are bushed, take a nap together—naked. You never know where it might lead.

✺ Make a deal with your husband or partner to share all chores. (Hint: Let him know the purpose of this deal, which is to bring more sex into your life, and it might work.)

✺ If you have kids over the age of eight, let them make a simple, cold dinner once a week and serve it to you and your partner. (They should probably be in high school to use the stove alone.) You'll have to organize this and get the ingredients for them, but afterward, don't meddle. Your job here is to enjoy being waited on.

⚛ If you wear glasses or contacts, spend at least one waking hour without wearing them. Seeing the world in soft focus allows you to concentrate inwardly rather than outside yourself.

⚛ Take a twenty-minute vacation once a day. (Yes! You have twenty minutes just for you.) Sit in the sun with your cat, play music and dance, take a bubble bath, go to the local playground and get on the swing-set. Anything fun!

⚛ Hone down your life to what's really important and don't take on new commitments just because people say they need you. Say no when asked if you can do just one more chore, one more job, or take one more volunteer position.

THERAPEUTIC SOLUTIONS FOR SEXUAL PROBLEMS

Is Sex Therapy for Me?

If you feel as if you've tried everything—sexy underwear or no underwear, self-help books and videos, visits to the gynecologist or urologist, but are still at an impasse, it's time to seek consultation with a trained sex therapist.

We pointed out at the beginning of this chapter that external treatments are very useful for some individuals in a sexual slump, but will do absolutely nothing for people who are having serious problems. Sex therapy can be the answer—or at least the beginning of a long-term solution. There are many possible situations that might make you decide it's time to get professional help.

Maybe you find yourself having flashbacks to a horrendous experience in childhood every time you have oral sex; maybe you climb the mountain of arousal but never reach the peak of orgasm; or maybe you cannot tolerate anything inside your vagina. Maybe, if you're single, you are dismayed at the fact that you never enjoy sex with the men you feel attracted to. Maybe, if you have a partner, you've reached a point where you just avoid "doing it." The magic that was once there has been replaced by daily snipes and subtle sabotage. You go to bed at different times and avoid physical contact. Or maybe you're in the midst of an ongoing battle about how often you have sex, and you're fed up with those unpleasant fights about whether three times a week is too much or too little. If you feel stuck, and problems in the bedroom are beginning to make the rest of your relationship toxic, it's time to consult an expert.

Therapy helps women reclaim permission to be sexual and to find a way to make sexuality a part of themselves, not split off from the whole. We are all entitled to a sexual life and to pleasure—it is not okay to tolerate bad behavior from a partner or to accept any type of emotional blackmail. Women who've been abused in any way come to expect the same thing to happen again, and this makes them helpless. Sex therapy gives them a map out of the dark forest, into the light.

Sex therapy is talk therapy, but it invites a particular kind of talking—the discussion centers on all the contributions, past and present, that complicate or thwart sexual life. It may involve a trip back to the past and the sexual messages, myths, and injunctions you learned—usually without conscious awareness—as you grew up. Certainly, you'll talk about the present blocks that interfere with sexual freedom. And since sex is typically a two-person activity, you not only talk but also listen to what the other person who is intimately involved with you has to say.

Sex therapy costs the same as psychotherapy and is covered by insurance, HMOs, and third-party payers. While prices vary across the country, tending to be more expensive on both coasts than in the heartland, treatment is generally short-term and well worth the expense. For those with limited budgets or no insurance, graduate and medical schools often have training clinics where services are rendered by interns or residents and fees are more modest. In addition to a therapeutic session, Sandra also recommends and runs women's sexual enhancement groups. When women get together to talk about their problems, they are at once surprised and relieved to find that they are not alone. By talking in this time-limited group, they can feel supported.

Getting yourself into therapy takes some courage. It's embarrassing to admit you're going to a doctor for therapy—especially *that* kind. Imagine telling the insurance person at work, if anything should go wrong with your claim, exactly what that mental health service you're getting is all about. And if you have a partner, you may find that he or she is more resistant to the idea of seeing a therapist than actually going. *We don't need it; we'll work it out; let's give it another month or so,* are all typical responses. Steel yourself and don't allow the moment to slip away. You know if you're miserable; you are well aware of how many techniques and treatments you've already tried. A good answer to the "no way, not me" is "Well, I'm going to go and check it out, and just see what happens. You may be a lot happier with me in bed after this." And then, don't hesitate, just *go.*

Or maybe you feel you could use therapy but would rather see a marital therapist, or perhaps a pastor, counselor, or social worker. But if you really are having trouble in the bedroom, it's best to go to the person who's the most knowledgeable about those problems. Other professionals may be compassionate and sympathetic and offer excellent insights, but they are not specifically trained to recognize both the medical and psychological contributions to sexual problems. Today, more than ever, it is necessary to be aware of new pharmacological options as well as both the physical and interpersonal factors that can impede sex. And sex therapists have this type of training.

How do you find a good sex therapist? Start by asking your own doctor. (You don't have to discuss the specifics of your situation if you don't feel comfortable doing so with the family doc.) You may be referred by a gynecologist or urologist or your primary care physician. You can also consult your state's psychological association or the department of psychiatry at a local medical school, if you live near one. You can also get referrals from one of the excellent organizations that deal with sexual issues, either AASECT (American Association for Sex Educators, Counselors, and Therapists) or SSTAR (Society for Sex Therapy and Research). See Resources for addresses and phone numbers.

Once you've got several names, you'll talk with the therapists briefly over the phone and make an appointment for a consultation with one of them. The first meeting should probably tell you whether this is a person you could bare your soul to—obviously, you're looking for a good listener, someone who's open, not defensive or judgmental, someone who doesn't place blame but sees all sides to each situation—and can put things in perspective. It's also a great idea to find someone with a sense of humor, because sex (and lack of sex) can be really funny at times. A good therapist will tell you about his or her credentials, answer all your questions, and treat you with respect. If you encounter someone who does not fill those criteria—or if you feel uncomfortable talking to this person—*get out and find someone else.* Remember, you are paying for a service, and you deserve to get what you want from your sessions.

Initially, the sex therapist will undertake a comprehensive assessment of your difficulties and will spend time taking a sexual history from both you and your partner if you have one. Usually, you will each have your own time to share your perceptions and theories about why sex is just not working. Like a detective, you and the therapist want to track down every lead, physical and psychological. And although only one of you will receive an official "diagnosis" (which will justify reimbursement from third-party payers), typically it takes two to have an ongoing sexual problem.

The most common sexual complaint of women is that of low or absent sexual interest or desire. And desire, as we've seen, is a complicated thing. Androgen insufficiency is sometimes the culprit—so your therapist might suggest that you have an evaluation of your testosterone levels. Lack of androgen is associated not only with lack of desire, but also with reduced feelings of well-being and energy (see chapter 8). Testosterone levels decline slowly and steadily after the age of 35, but in a woman who has had a hysterectomy or has had both ovaries removed, or both, the levels plummet rapidly. If you had a sexual appetite before menopause or before the surgeries just mentioned, and now have none, then it's worth considering androgen replacement.

On the other hand, your lack of interest may be due to an underlying depression, low self-esteem, situational stresses, or a partner who is unloving and uninterested in you. Even distractions and disruptions such as a child's illness, loss of a job, divorce, elderly parents who need care, a rotten boss, or money problems can pose a distraction from sex. And most often, lack of desire—as well as other sexual problems—are due to a combination of factors.

So all of this and anything else that might be pertinent must be discussed in therapy. You'll talk about your family history, critical experiences that might have shaped your beliefs, emotional reactions to sex, whether you take recreational or prescription drugs, and recent experiences in bed and out of it that are relevant to your problem.

Sex therapy is not very dissimilar to other types of psychotherapy. The focus here, of course, is on sexual and relationship problems, and your therapist may suggest videos, books, or films, as well as at-home "exercises" for the two of you that are intended to enhance sexual satisfaction. And despite the jokes about sexual surrogates, almost no one uses them.

There are many different reasons for seeking the services of a sex therapist.[12] Pain on penetration is certainly one. Vulvar pain, or vulvodynia, may be excruciating to some women, who may find any type of genital touching impossible. Consider a recent patient of Sandra's, Alison, a 33-year-old computer programmer. She met her husband, Ted, an engineer, when they were in college. "We've been married for eight years," she told Sandra, "and we've always had a great relationship." Sandra asked her, then, why had she come to see her. "Because we've never had intercourse. We can't. There's no way. We do everything else, like manual and oral sex, and really enjoy it. But the minute Ted tries to enter me, I freeze."

They had tried every trick they could think of in order to get Alison to relax, but nothing worked. So they gave up trying and just enjoyed the sexual relationship that they did have. But as Alison began to think about wanting a child, she realized she needed professional help. She wanted to overcome the problem—but she really didn't know what the problem was.

And then one day, she was looking through a sex manual in the bookstore and saw the word "vaginismus."

"The minute I read the description, I had this great sense of relief. It's me. There's a word for it—other people have it! So I got online and typed in the diagnosis and I found this huge chat room filled with 260 women who all had or used to have my problem. It was like finding my family. I hung back and just listened to them talk, and read these incredible stories that were much worse than mine—most of the women hated sex, and I loved it—and I told Ted and he was thrilled. For a while, I went to the chat room all the time, but it got a little tired, and someone suggested to me that I find a therapist. So I called my regular doctor and got a referral and I can't tell you how amazing it was. Dr. Leiblum was enormously sympathetic and comforting. She gave us the whole story about vaginismus and I learned it was physical, yes, but there was a big emotional component.

"I realized that I'd been shutting out the possibility of pregnancy from a very young age. Both my parents died when I was about 14, and I was on my own completely by the time I was 17. I just knew I couldn't afford to mess up my life with a baby. I had to keep on track, finish college and lifeguard when I wasn't studying—it was exhausting. So I closed myself off to having kids—literally."

There are several steps in the treatment of vaginismus. First, the woman has to learn to relax the pubococcygeal muscles (the muscles that allow you to "grip" and stop the flow of urine). She must practice relaxation exercises and slowly get comfortable about using a set of dilators of increasing size. They begin at about the width of a finger or junior tampon and increase up to that of an erect penis. The therapist guides the woman's treatment, suggesting at-home exercises. She also challenges any misconceptions the woman may have about the size of her vagina and old myths she may have heard about the pain involved in vaginal penetration.

The woman inserts the dilators into her vagina by herself, using a lubricant, and then when she's ready, she allows her partner to insert them. The therapist explains in each session what the couple is to do, and then gives them "homework." These sessions together, of course, are not just physical. Both individuals are encouraged to talk about all their feelings while doing this activity—the fear, the excitement, the reluctance, the relief.

"When Ted and I got up to the largest dilator, and I wasn't having any trouble, Dr. Leiblum said it was time to try intercourse, but that we shouldn't be upset if we couldn't manage it at first. Actually, it was nowhere near as difficult as we thought it would be. We were so exhilarated—it was like discovering each other's bodies all over again. I think because we know each other so well and love making love, this was just a new and terrific thing to add to our repertoire. And did it ever work! I'd say I have orgasms eight out of ten times without any clitoral stimulation. I wish we'd gone to therapy sooner, but now it's like being 18 all over again. We just can't wait to get each other into bed."

Not all sex therapy is as direct or simple. A lot of sex therapy revolves around the ways that a couple deal with each other and how they express both positive and negative feelings. Since good sex comes from the heart and mind as well as the body, attention must be paid to all aspects of the couple's relationship and lifestyle. Often, they spend too little intimate time together to get comfortable enough for good sex. But it's also possible that more complicated factors contribute to their problems. People really believe that old hooey about "love conquers all," and are sure that if they're passionate about each other, that they should be able to read each other's minds. This deeply rooted belief, reinforced by generations of Harlequin romances and Hollywood films, can be torn out by the roots only when both members of the couple start to say exactly what they're thinking.

In sex therapy, you are encouraged to state your preferences and be out-spoken about your likes, dislikes, irritations, fantasies, disappointments, and anxiety and reluctance about trying new things. You are also helped to under-stand that many of your fears and misgivings are outdated. They belong to the "old" you, not to the new circumstances in your life. And you and your part-ner are encouraged to reconsider how and what you say and do to each other. As your relationship improves, so does the sex, and vice versa. If you were sexually abused in the past, and if memories and feelings continue to intrude on your present, you will be helped to come to peace with it and to feel not only safe, but deserving of pleasure.

At times, the therapist may suggest homework—exercises that increase sensual and sexual feelings. Sensate focus, a step-by-step program of increas-ingly intimate caressing exercises, is sometimes recommended. Most women love the long, leisurely, and loving massage sessions with their partner. And even if it causes them some anxiety, the exercises become a means for explor-ing feelings about being passive, about giving up control, about asking for what you want and instructing a partner in your likes and dislikes.

The benefits of this are enormous. First, neither member of the couple gets bogged down in performance anxiety. This is just a time to be intimate and to respond to each other. In therapy sessions, when we get to discuss the response to sensate focus, it serves as a bridge to talking about the psycholog-ical reactions one has to only giving or only receiving pleasure. What thoughts does it bring up? Is the giver grudging or jealous or bored? Is the receiver threatened or directive or not turned on by anything the partner attempts? Any and every feeling is possible and permissible. This was one of the ways in which Sandra helped a 37-year-old patient named Vivien, who had been married for nineteen years. Despite her outwardly sexy appearance and comfortable way of relating, Vivien had never had an orgasm.

Vivien reported, "I never really felt very physically attracted to my hus-band, but when Max and I got pregnant, I felt we had to get married. What did I know? I was 18. Max was always a great person—good, caring, but his attitude toward me was very condescending. He never makes me feel val-ued—he hardly listens when I talk. I'd say I really liked a movie we had seen and he'd say in a patronizing way that I missed the symbolism. Finally I just withdrew—I didn't even bother to defend or express myself anymore."

As time went on, Vivien's lack of sexual interest became more apparent, but her husband wouldn't give up, plying her with self-help books and ques-tioning her about her orgasm at each encounter. "It was like that old 'Was it good for you, sweetheart?' every single time. The more he pumped me for information, the less interest I had.

"I have to say that I wasn't completely sexually turned off. Max's best friend was a real flirt, and he really seemed to appreciate me. I imagined sleeping with him, but I just couldn't follow through. It would have been such a betrayal, and I couldn't have lived with myself. So instead, I got a vibrator and fantasized about how James might touch me. And within a few days, I had my first orgasm."

In individual sessions, Vivien came to realize that although she was attracted to James, there were many things she valued about her husband. He was a good father, a good provider, and genuinely protective of her. These were things she had always wanted in a partner. With encouragement, she was able to tell Max more directly how she felt devalued and disrespected by him, and how these feelings made her resent him and withdraw from him emotionally. With help, Max was able to "hear" Vivien for the first time. He still has his lapses, but he certainly is more careful about the way he talks to her. While intercourse with her husband is still not her favorite activity, Vivien is capable of having an orgasm when and if she decides to. She is in charge.

There are women who have undergone horrendous physical, sexual, and emotional abuse who have sexual or relationship problems, although not all do. It seems impossible that anyone could go through years of incest or a violent rape and come out sexually unscathed, but there are those with such strong self-concepts that they are able to put these experiences behind them. For those who still suffer, however, therapy can be an enormous boon. There are no quick fixes here, certainly, and for some women, the insights alleviate only a small amount of the pain, but even that can be beneficial. And it doesn't matter how long ago the events occurred or how old you are when you start therapy. There is always something to be gained by sharing the past with a professional who can guide you, like Charon of the Greek myths, who rowed people on the river Styx back and forth from the underworld, allowing them, every once in a while, a glimpse of the sun.

Some people are simply better at sex than others—they like it more, they are more responsive, they get aroused more quickly and with more intensity. Who knows why a woman ends up adoring sex more than her friends? Is it because of the amount of dopamine her brain produces or the amount of free testosterone she has available? Is it the freedom and pleasure in her body she had growing up? Is it that she had tolerant and pleasure-loving parents who never clamped down on her sexual experimentation? Is it that her first lover was so caring and skilled, her first taste of ecstasy set her up for life? For those who aren't sexually adept or really very interested, it doesn't mean you're cold and unfeeling; it doesn't mean you don't excel in other areas—being a funny, loving, nurturing partner is obviously just as important as being a hot ticket in bed. But most women who are motivated can find sexual help in some form—if they are willing to take the journey and pursue it.

In the ancient tale of Amor and Psyche, the family of a beautiful, brilliant maiden is ordered by an oracle of Apollo to abandon her on a craggy hilltop.

She is subsequently carried by the wind to her new home, a mysterious castle where her lover comes to her only under cover of darkness, telling her she must never ask to see his face. He is devoted to her; he adores her; he makes passionate love to her that curls her toes; but he tells her she cannot look at him or she will lose him.

Clever and curious Psyche figures that she can get away with just lighting a lamp for a moment after her husband has fallen asleep. She intends to blow it out immediately. But as she strikes her tinder and lights the lamp, she is mesmerized by his extraordinary beauty. It is Amor, the son of Venus, the god of Love. He is perfection in manhood, lying there naked except for his huge white wings. She accidentally pricks herself with one of the arrows from his quiver and the shock of its effect—love at first prick, as it were—causes her to drop burning oil from the lamp on his shoulder, waking him. He chastises her for disobeying, for investigating desire instead of simply accepting it, and he casts her from his home, vowing that she will never find him again.

As in any hero myth, of course, Psyche fulfills a lot of impossible tasks, including going to the underworld to search him out, nearly resulting in her own death. But she eventually earns the prize—in this case, her husband, immortality, and the baby already growing inside her, a girl named Pleasure.

Luckily for us, it's never as tough as that to achieve pleasure. Whether your sex life would benefit by a trip to Victoria's Secret or an online toy store or it needs major renovation, let us counsel you to act on your inclination to do something. By speaking the forbidden words, by coming out of the dark that's allowed you to hide from yourself, you are overturning the status quo in your bedroom. When you buy a vibrator, meditate together, enjoy sensual massage, or see a therapist, you are intentionally turning on the pilot light. When you think about something sexual, you increase sexual awareness and stimulate hormonal activity that may lead, in time, to delight—and even to desire.

CODA:
THE FACE OF JOY

There is no "normal" when it comes to sex. There is only experience and the knowledge that the longer we live, the more opportunity we have to make constructive changes. Sex, and the qualities that surround it, play a vital role in our lives from cradle to death. When we look at our desire and our behavior with forethought and clarity, when we make conscious choices about the role we would like sex to play rather than passively accepting an unsatisfactory situation, then we are on the road to uncovering the best of ourselves.

Sex has so many faces, and many are not recognizable. We can be celibate and intimate, we can love and yet not want physical touch, we can come from sitting on a warm rock or from a fleeting thought that travels on a spring breeze. We can shrink inside and turn away from all stimuli, or feel swollen with anticipation and desire. The comfort of domestic pleasures and gentle cuddling seesaws with the wild passion of a new affair that kicks and bucks and yells out loud. We can feel wild and then contained; we can be attracted to men, then to women, then both; we can love ourselves and hate what our body is becoming; we can know sex deeply and fully, and then in an instant, feel it subsiding and slipping away. It can lie dormant, nestled in those corners of our consciousness until another time when it roars forth, ready to make the earth tremble anew.

It has been said that we crave orgasm because it is in these lightning flashes that we are shown, for just an instant, the hidden face of God. But we have been looking in the wrong places for the wrong rewards. "God," or what we think of as the Supreme, is what we're made of. All we have to do is find a way to search out the inclinations and intentions that are deep inside us. Sex is a vehicle, a means to explore what we really need in order to feel like whole women. And at each stage of life, at each juncture in our emotional and spiritual development, we need something new.

Women have been told for decades that female sexuality is complex, many-faceted, and hard to pin down. The truth, as we have seen, is that sex is so flexible, so changeable, that for each woman it may be a continually shifting pattern, a series of kaleidoscopic images based on where we are, who we're with, how much we trust ourselves and others, and what our goals are.

So let us celebrate and curse the fact that we were born women. It's wonderful to have so many options; terrible to realize that some of them drive us nuts and others leave us cold. It is our birthright to delve into that mysterious place that turns us on and makes us go, even if at times it seems overwhelming and hard to handle. One day, maybe, we'll know exactly how it works—but for now, it's much more interesting to ride the power of those underground forces and wait to see what the next phase holds in store.

There will always be a next phase. Whether you are a young single, a married mother, a lesbian loner, a midlife explorer, or a highlife crone, whether you search off-line or on, with pills or without, whether your body is just as it's always been or slightly altered, you have a chance to change again. When you peel away the years of frustration and anxiety you've had over sex and reveal the naked woman beneath the skin, you may find her not only beautiful, but more accessible than you imagined.

Sex may be the first thing you think of when you wake each morning or the last thing on your mind, but if you open yourself to its possibilities, it can teach you the value of your self-worth, your sense of humor, and your creativity. What's more, it will help you get on your feet again if you're down. It will add privacy, secrecy, a sense of the unknown, and just a little risk to your life. And if you despair of ever finding the erotic impulse, or you think you had it and lost it, understand that you are not done. Turn around again and sex will be there, staring you in the face. What you do with it, and how you choose to make it part of your life, is entirely up to you.

NOTES

1. Childhood and Adolescence

[1] Many cultures have special rituals for the onset of menses—Jewish women slap their daughters across the face to welcome them into the tribe. (At best, it means "May you never have any pain greater than this"; at worst, it means "Life is tough—get used to it." A kinder version of the ritual includes a hug after the slap—to welcome the woman after driving away the child.) The Arapesh, a South Pacific tribe described by Margaret Mead, made a big deal of a girl's first menses: Her brothers built her a menstrual hut where she would be isolated far from the village in order to keep it safe from the supernatural strength she would now have as a menstruating woman. She was then required to throw away her old child's grass skirt and armlets and the older women inserted stinging nettle leaves in her vulva to make her breasts develop. She then fasted in her hut for five or six days, after which (the bleeding ostensibly having ended), she came out to be painted and decorated. It was considered a very happy time for everyone. In many African cultures today, horrific female genital mutilation—which may be carried out on children as young as 3 or as old as 13—shows to what extent society can be perverted by the fear of the power of female sexuality.

[2] Alice Schlegel, "Status, property, and the value on virginity" (1991) *American Ethnologist* 18(4): 719–734. Virginity just doesn't mean what it used to now that women tend to wait decades between the onset of puberty (when they might become sexually active and become pregnant) and the establishment of a family. In most cultures, when a teenage girl was ripe for marriage, she had to be intact. Schlegel, a cultural anthropologist at the University of Arizona, writes, " 'Nature' designs us to begin our sexual lives at biological adolescence, but 'culture' intervenes with a social adolescence that does not include unconstrained sexuality." She explains that virginity is most likely to be valued when the families of daughters give property at their marriages in the form of dowry, indirect dowry, or extensive gift exchange, since they are, in effect, buying a son-in-law. In those societies, a girl who is not a virgin is not just damaged goods, but any progeny that come of her will be in doubt. Why would a man want to bring up someone else's child?

[3] It would be nice if we could get right in there at the age when all this physical and emotional turmoil is going on and help children to cope. The schools, now mandated to explain more than "the facts of life," must educate children about puberty, reproduction, contraception, STDs, and all the nuts and bolts of human sexuality. (Unfortunately, all they get is a few nuts—the crucial stuff about communication, pleasure, and experimentation with sexual activities safer than intercourse is generally missing.) In New Jersey, family-life educators lobbied to take the material about menstruation and move it into the fourth grade, where it now belongs. But the Whitman administration deemed it more "appropriate" not to tamper with the Core Curriculum Standards, which require that this advanced stuff be taught later—there

are some kids who don't get the information until eighth grade, when it is clearly ancient history. (Personal communication, Susan Wilson, executive coordinator of the Network for Family Life Education, Rutgers University.)

⁴Edward O. Laumann, et al., *The Social Organization of Sexuality* (Chicago: University of Chicago Press, 1994).

⁵Sharon Thompson, *Going All the Way: Teenage Girls' Tales of Sex, Romance, and Pregnancy* (New York: Hill and Wang, 1995).

⁶Although most lesbian girls don't come out until college, many reports indicate that about 17 percent knew of their gender preference in elementary school and 6 percent more were convinced by the time they got to junior high. Many women feel desire for other women but don't consider themselves gay, nor do they act on their desires. The University of Chicago survey (Laumann, et al.) found that a full 59 percent of their female sample said that they had at one time felt desire for another woman, although only 13 percent identified themselves as lesbians and felt desire, and another 13 percent acted on their desire although they didn't identify themselves as lesbians. This is quite different for homosexual men, who are much more likely to identify themselves as gay, whether or not they desire or engage in sexual acts with other men.

⁷J. Brooks-Gunn and Frank F. Furstenberg, Jr., "Adolescent Sexual Behavior," *American Psychologist* 44, (1989) 249–257.

⁸Alan Guttmacher Institute, reporting figures from the National Center for Health Statistics.

⁹Doreen A. Rosenthal, et al., "Personal and Social Factors Influencing Age at First Intercourse," *Arch Sex Behav* 28:4 (1999): 319–333.

¹⁰Abstinence is not only encouraged, in certain states private counseling centers are handsomely endorsed by the federal government's Department of Health and Human Services for advocating this type of sex education *and no other.* The Baptist Church has instituted an abstinence contract, which can actually confer "secondary virginity" upon the girl or boy who's already foolishly indulged.

¹¹Sharon Thompson, "Putting a Big Thing Into a Little Hole: Teenage Girls' Accounts of Sexual Initiation," *Journal of Sex Research* 27:3 (August 1990): 341–361.

¹²Leonore Tiefer, *Sex Is Not a Natural Act and Other Essays* (Westview Press, 1995).

¹³Thomas R. Eng and William T. Butler, eds., *The Hidden Epidemic: Confronting Sexually Transmitted Diseases* (Washington, DC: National Academy Press, 1997): 28.

¹⁴Alan Guttmacher Institute, reporting figures from the Centers for Disease Control and Prevention and the National Center for Health Statistics.

¹⁵National Crime Victimization Survey, Bureau of Justice Statistics, U.S. Department of Justice, 1996.

¹⁶Of the 905,000 teen pregnancies in 1996, more than half resulted in births. Approximately 31 percent of teen pregnancies end in abortion; 14 percent end in miscarriage; 43 percent end in unintended birth; 7 percent end in an intended birth; and less than 3 percent had the baby but placed it for adoption, according to the 1995 National Survey of Family Growth. Adolescents account for less than one-third of abortions performed each year, and a full 61 percent of these are to middle- or upper-income girls. African-American teens are the most likely to keep their babies and raise them by themselves or within the bosom of their fam-

ily—this often continues a tradition of their mother and grandmother, who also raised children as single parents after unintentional pregnancies.

[17]Although American sex educators pride themselves on school-based programs that explain the risks of early pregnancy and stress condom use for the prevention of both pregnancy and STDs, we are way behind our French colleagues in the dissemination of the 72-hour pill. Marketed under the name of Norvelo, this anti-implantation drug is available free to all French schoolchildren through the school nurse—without parental consent. It is also available over the counter without a prescription (*The New York Times,* "France Provides Morning-After Pill to Schoolgirls," by Suzanne Daley, Feb. 8, 2000).

[18]Parental involvement laws require approval for a minor child to obtain an abortion, and these are on the books in AL, AR, DE, GA, IA, IN, KS, KY, LA, MD, MA, MI, MN, MS, MO, NE, NC, ND, OH, PA, RI, SC, SD, UT, VA, WI, WV, and WY.

2. The Young Single Woman

[1]J. Townsend, "Sex without emotional involvement: An evolutionary interpretation of sex differences," *Arch. Sex. Behav.* 24:2 (1995): 173–203.

[2]Luis Garcia, Ph.D., "Self-Ideal Discrepancy and Sexual Esteem," presented at the annual national conference for the Society for the Scientific Study of Sex (SSSS), Los Angeles, CA, November 1998.

[3]Susan Brownmiller, *Against Our Will* (New York: Bantam Books, 1976).

[4]Brownmiller, *op. cit.* The author discusses "victim precipitation," a concept from the criminology texts that puts a huge burden on the victim. Anything the victim does, says, or is can be fodder for the attacker's action. In effect, the victim isn't responsible for the rape, but she may have contributed to the circumstances that led up to it. And it can be very flukey as to what contributes—one woman crying may inflame a rapist, but soften another. One woman interviewed for this book described how she looked her attacker in the eye and asked, "What would your mother think of you right now?" He let her go immediately and slunk off into the night.

[5]Christine Gorman, "Who Needs a Period?" *Time* magazine, Sept. 18, (2000): 56.

[6]S. L. Thomas and C. Ellertson, "Nuisance or natural and healthy—should monthly menstruation be optional for women?" *Lancet* 2000 Mar 11; 355 (9207): 922–924. By fine-tuning the dosage and keeping estrogen as low as possible, a woman will produce very little endometrial tissue, and it is not necessary for the body to get rid of it on a monthly basis. In primitive societies, where repeated pregnancy and breast-feeding suppress ovulation naturally, women average about 100 periods per lifetime as opposed to 350 or 400 in the West. It was always apparent that the Pill could eliminate menstruation entirely, but when Enovid first came on the market, the 21-day method of administration served to retain a period. The reason for this is religious rather than medical. Dr. John Rock, the physician who is largely responsible for the development of the Pill, was a devout Catholic, and hoped to convince the Church that the Pill was a "natural" method of birth control, similar to the rhythm method, because it used the very hormones produced by the body. Rock was delighted when Pope Pius VII approved use of the Pill as long as it was only intended to correct irregular menses—Rock knew that to get this medication into the hands of Catholic women, they had to bleed.

[7]See Laura S. Brown, "Lesbian Identities: Concepts and Issues," in Anthony R. D'Augelli and Charlotte J. Patterson, eds., *Lesbian, Gay, and Bisexual Identities Over the Lifespan* (New York: Oxford University Press, 1995).

[8]Beverly Whipple, "Beyond the G-Spot: Sexuality in the New Millennium." Talk presented at the Society for Sex Therapy and Research, March 4, 2000. Whipple says that in some women, G-spot stimulation, orgasm, and female ejaculation are related and in other women they aren't. Some women have reported experiencing ejaculation with orgasm from clitoral stimulation and some have reported experiencing ejaculation without orgasm.

[9]Women who suffer from this physical condition, known as vaginismus, are plagued by involuntary tightening of the vaginal muscles, which clamp shut so as to prohibit entrance of a finger, a tampon, or a penis. The treatment, which can be very successful, involves desensitization by using a series of dilators that increase in size, as well as partner-assisted exercises. And of course, the biggest balm is good communication between the partners.

3. Coupling

[1]Philip Blumstein and Pepper Schwartz, *The American Couple* (New York: William Morrow & Co., 1983).

[2]Edward O. Laumann, et al., *The Social Organization of Sexuality* (Chicago: University of Chicago Press, 1994).

[3]Laumann, *op. cit.,* 229.

[4]Helen Fisher, "Lust, Attraction and Attachment in Mammalian Reproduction," *Human Nature* Vol. 9, No. 1 (1998): 23–52.

[5]U.S. Bureau of the Census, Monthly Vital Statistics Report, Vol. 43, No. 12 (issue date tk).

[6]Laumann, *op. cit.,* 92.

[7]Blumstein and Schwartz, *ibid.*

[8]U.S. Bureau of the Census, Monthly Vital Statistics Report, Vol. 43, No. 12 (issue date tk).

[9]Laumann, *op. cit.,* 89.

[10]Pepper Schwartz and Virginia Rutter, *The Gender of Sexuality* (city tk: Pine Forge Press, 1998).

[11]Schwartz and Rutter, *op. cit.,* 125–126.

[12]Manijeh Daneshpour, "Muslim Families and Family Therapy," *Journal of Marital and Family Therapy*, Vol. 24, no. 3 (1998): 355–390.

[13]Suzanne Iasenza, "The Big Lie: Debunking Lesbian Bed Death," *In the Family* (1999). The author quotes Marilyn Frye, who questions the Schwartz/Blumstein data on lesbians. She contends that what lesbians do together when they are making love typically takes about half an hour, as contrasted with the typical heterosexual couple, who spend about eight minutes, tops, having intercourse.

[14]Pepper Schwartz, *Peer Marriage: How Love Between Equals Really Works* (New York: The Free Press, 1994).

[15]Pepper Schwartz coined this phrase to express the equality of the two individuals in a marriage.

[16]Dalma Heyn, *Marriage Shock: The Transformation of Women Into Wives* (New York: Villard Books, 1997).

4. Mothering

[1]E. O. Laumann, et al., *The Social Organization of Sexuality* (Chicago: University of Chicago Press, 1994). The findings from this major survey of sexuality in America indicate that 97 percent of sexually active adult heterosexuals have had vaginal intercourse, an activity that could result in birth. However, other factors intervene, such as fertility, contraception, abortion, and miscarriage. Then, too, some individuals practice other forms of sexual behavior (oral, anal, and manual sex) that would not result in conception.

[2]Jane Riblett Wilkie, "The Trend Toward Delayed Parenthood," *Journal of Marriage and the Family* (August 1981).

[3]Nancy Chodorow, *The Reproduction of Mothering: Psychoanalysis and the Sociology of Gender* (Berkeley, CA: University of California Press, 1978).

[4]Sandra Risa Leiblum, "Love, Sex, and Infertility: The Impact of Infertility on the Couple," *In Session: Psychotherapy in Practice,* Vol. 2, No. 2 (1996): 29–39.

[5]Robert May, *Sex and Fantasy* (New York: W. W. Norton & Co., 1980).

[6]Sarah Blaffer Hrdy, *Mother Nature: A History of Mothers, Infants, and Natural Selection* (New York: Pantheon, 1999).

[7]Charlotte Patterson, "Children of Lesbian and Gay Parents," *Child Development* 63 (1993): 1025–1042.

[8]Charlotte Patterson, "Lesbians choosing motherhood: A comparative study of lesbian and heterosexual parents and their children," *Developmental Psychology,* Vol. 31, No. 1 (1995): 105–114.

[9]E. O. Laumann, et al., *ibid.,* p. 83. Laumann points out that masturbation is associated with "sexual failure" because it implies you have no partner temporarily or over a long period of time. However, among women (who masturbate less than men), there is no difference in the frequency or incidence of this activity in younger women who are living with a partner, older women living with a partner, and women who have never married.

5. The Woman in Midlife

[1]E. O. Laumann, et al., *The Social Organization of Sexuality* (Chicago: University of Chicago Press, 1994).

[2]Judith Daniluk, *Women's Sexuality Across the Lifespan* (New York: The Guilford Press, 1998).

[3]Premenopause, which for most American women begins around 35 and continues to the early forties, refers to the years when ovulation is less certain, and therefore it is increasingly difficult to conceive, although monthly cycles continue to be regular. Perimenopause refers to the period just after this, typically from the mid to late forties, when the cycle becomes irregular and many women experience signs or symptoms such as hot flashes and vaginal dryness. Menopause, which commonly occurs at around 51 or 52, although for some it may be as early as 30 or as late as 58, is marked by one continuous year without menstrual cycles.

[4]Irwin Goldstein and Jennifer Berman, "Vasculogenic female sexual dysfunction: Vaginal engorgement and clitoral erectile insufficiency syndrome," *International Journal of Impotence Research* 10, Supplement 2 (1998): S84–S90.

[5]S. R. Leiblum and R. T. Segraves, "Sex therapy with Aging Adults," in S. R. Leiblum and R. C. Rosen, eds., *Principles and Practice of Sex Therapy: Update for the 1990s* (New York: Guilford Press, 1989).

[6]For this reason, many in the medical community are becoming increasingly interested in SERMs (selective estrogen receptor modulators) like raloxifene and tamoxifen. These drugs bind to estrogen receptors, producing estrogen-like (agonistic) effects on some tissues and estrogen-blocking (antagonistic) effects on others. In this way, the breast and uterus can be protected, and so can the heart and bones. The SERMs do not seem to have any sexual benefits, however, and in addition, may cause vaginal bleeding and hot flashes, neither of which make women feel sexy.

[7]Susan Rako, *The Hormone of Desire* (New York: Harmony Books, 1996).

[8]B. Sherwin and M. M. Gelfand, MD, "The Role of Androgen in the Maintenance of Sexual Functioning in Oophorectomized Women," *Psychosomatic Medicine* 49 (1987): 397–409.

[9]Lonnie Barbach, *For Each Other* (New York: Signet/Penguin, 1984).

[10]Warren Hoge, "The Stately 'Calendar Girls' Dressed So Simply in Pearls," *The New York Times* (January 23, 2000).

[11]G. Khastgir and J. Studd, "Hysterectomy, ovarian failure, and depression," *Menopause* 2 (1998): 113–122.

[12]Winnifred Cutler, Ph.D., *Hysterectomy: Before & After* (New York: Harper & Row Publishers, 1988).

[13]Julia C. Rhodes, et al., "Hysterectomy and Sexual Functioning," *Journal of the American Medical Association* 282:20 (1999): 1934–1941.

[14]Anastasia Toufexis, "Preserving Fertility While Treating Cervical Cancer," *The New York Times,* July 31, 2001.

[15]Rosemary Basson, MRCP, Sexual Medicine, Vancouver, BC, "The female sexual response: A different model," *Journal of Sex and Marital Therapy* 26 (2000): 51–65.

[16]Lonnie Barbach, Ph.D., "Loss of Sexual Desire," *Menopause Management* (January/February, 1998).

[17]Stephen B. Levine, MD, *Sexuality in Mid-Life* (New York: Plenum Press, 1998).

[18]Ellen Cole, "Lesbian Sex at Menopause: As Good As or Better Than Ever," in B. Sang, J. Warshow, and A. Smith, eds., *Lesbians at Midlife: The Creative Transition* (San Francisco: Spinsters Book Company), 184–193.

6. The Woman in Highlife

[1]Bernice L. Neugarten, ed., *Middle Age and Aging* (Chicago: University of Chicago Press, 1968). Excerpt from William H. Masters and Virginia Johnson, *Human Sexual Response,* "The Aging Female and Aging Male," 272.

[2]W. H. Masters, "Sex and aging—expectations and reality," *Hospital Practice* (August 15, 1986): 175–198.

[3]"Aging by the Numbers—Longer, Healthier, Better," *The New York Times Magazine* (March 9, 1997).

[4]Widows typically do better than widowers after the death of a spouse, even on more limited funds and resources. The rates of depression and suicide in widowers are markedly higher than that of widows, despite the fact that older men tend not to have as many chronic, long-term disease patterns (e.g., heart disease, kidney disease, diabetes) as older women. According to a January 1996 report from the Centers for Disease Control entitled "Suicide Among Older Persons," covering a survey that ran from 1980 to 1992, men account for 81 percent of all suicides over the age of 65. The rate for divorced men and widowers was markedly higher than for married men. One of the biggest reasons for this skewed statistic is that men are used to having women take care of their health, nourishment, and scheduling, and without a woman present to do this, they may feel lost and helpless.

[5]L. Speroff, et al., *Clinical Endocrinology and Infertility,* sixth edition (Lippincott, Williams & Wilkins, 1999).

[6]D. Bernard Starr and Marcella Bakur Weiner, Ed.D., *The Starr-Weiner Report on Sex and Sexuality in the Mature Years* (New York: Stein & Day Publishers, 1981).

[7]Judy Bretschneider and Norma McCoy, MD, "Sexual Interest and Behavior in Healthy 80- to 102-Year-Olds," *Archives of Sexual Behavior* 17 (1988): 109–129.

[8]AARP/Modern Maturity Sexuality Survey by mail of 1,384 adults age 45 or older. This survey was designed by the *Modern Maturity* editorial staff and the AARP Research Group with the assistance of Dr. John McKinlay of the New England Research Institutes.

[9]J. Alexander, et al., eds. *Women and Aging: An Anthology by Women* (Corvallis, OR: Calyx Books, 1986). Essay by Baba Cooper, "Voices: On Becoming Old Women."

[10]Vicki Goldberg, "The Effects of Aging: Viewed Unblinkingly," *The New York Times* (January 2, 2000).

[11]Robert Butler, personal communication, November 10, 1999. See also Robert N. Butler, MD, et al., *Aging and Mental Health: Positive Psychosocial and Biomedical Approaches* (Boston: Allyn & Bacon, 1998).

[12]Sandra L. Welner, MD, "Gynecologic Care and Sexuality Issues for Women with Disabilities," *Sexuality and Disability* 15:1 (1997). Supplemental information from the author's presentation at the North American Menopause Society 1999 conference, and personal communication.

[13]Erik Erikson, *Childhood and Society* (New York: W. W. Norton, 1963).

7. Cybersex

[1]Stanford Institute for the Quantitative Study of Society, from a survey based on a nationwide random sampling of 4,113 individuals over the age of 18. As reported in *The New York Times,* February 16, 2000.

[2]For a complete tour of the possibilities you may encounter online and in a variety of relevant websites, see Deb Levine, *The Joy of Cybersex* (New York: Ballantine Books, 1998), and

Anne Semans and Cathy Winks, *The Woman's Guide to Sex on the Web* (San Francisco: HarperSanFrancisco, 1999).

[3]Personal communication, February 27, 2000. See also Al Cooper, "Sexuality and the Internet: Surfing Into the New Millennium," *CyberPsychology & Behavior* 1 (1998): 181–187.

[4]Deb Levine, MA, "Virtual Attraction: What Rocks Your Boat," in *Journal of CyberPsychology and Behavior* (August 2000).

[5]Dana E. Putnam, *Journal of CyberPsychology and Behavior* (September 1999). A study of 300,000 adult sites examined the number of hours logged on and various indications of addictive behavior.

[6]"Technotes," *Newsweek,* March 13, 2000.

[7]J. Shaw, "Treatment rationale for Internet infidelity," *Journal of Sex Education and Therapy* 22:1 (1997).

[8]Sandra R. Leiblum, "Sex and the Net: Clinical Implications," *Journal of Sex Education and Therapy,* 22:1 (1997).

[9]A recent marriage reported in the March 30, 2000 edition of *The New York Times* recounts the tale of two players of an online role-playing game set in the Middle Ages. Ultima Online, which boasts 160,000 players internationally, is a complete social and ethical world (most players log in more than twenty-two hours a week, on average) where your created character is designed to be quite similar to your own personality. After the two players' characters had married online, they met and repeated their vows in Minnesota.

8. Better Sex Through Chemistry

[1]For more information on drugs that affect sexual function, see Cynthia Mervis Watson, MD, *Love Potions: A Guide to Aphrodisiacs and Sexual Pleasures* (Los Angeles: Jeremy P. Tarcher/Perigee Books, 1993).

[2]Vladlen Kurnov, "Sex and drugs: A review of the literature on effects of medications as well as other chemicals on sexual/reproductive function," *RWJMS*—II (January, 1999).

[3]Susan Rako, author of *The Hormone of Desire* (New York: Harmony Books, 1996), points out that a lack of testosterone may be responsible for the draining fatigue and exhaustion that deplete a woman of her zest for life as well as for sex.

[4]Jan Shifren, et al., *NEJM*-343 (2000): 682–688. See also Zumoff, et al., JCEM 80 (1995): 1429–1430.

[5]Personal communication, Dr. Norman Mazer, August 22, 2000.

[6]Shifren, et al., "Transdermal testosterone treatment in women with impaired sexual function after oophorectomy," *NEJM,* Sept 7, 343:10 (2000) 682–688.

[7]E. Weisberg, et al., "Efficacy, bleeding patterns, and side effects of a 1-Year Contraceptive Vaginal Ring," *Contraception* 59 (1999): 311–318.

[8]Personal communication, Dr. Julia Heiman, October 6, 2000.

[9]Personal communication, Dr. André Guay, January 15, 2001.

[10]Personal communication, Dr. Cindy Meston, October 4, 2000.

[11]Daniel McGinn, "Viagra's Hothouse," *Newsweek,* December 21, 1998.

[12]Personal communication with Dr. Paul Lammers, senior vice president of Clinical and Regulatory Affairs, Zonagen.

[13]Personal communication with Dr. David Ferguson, consultant to several pharmaceutical companies on sexual dysfunction and incontinence, August 29, 2000.

[14]Personal communication, Ted Kaminetsky, M.D., January 7, 2001.

[15]Sarah Janosik, MSW, sees a considerable number of breast cancer survivors in her Austin, Texas, practice and reported that some of her anorgasmic patients who had tried vibrators came to her and asked for a prescription for the EROS. They were using it repeatedly both alone and with their partners and had no trouble achieving orgasm.

[16]L. A. Berman, J. R. Berman, S. Chhabra, and I. Goldstein, "Novel approaches to female sexual dysfunction," *Expert Opin Investig Drug,* 10:1 Jan 2001: 85–95.

[17]Personal communication, Marian Dunn, Ph.D., November 19, 1998.

[18]Medical News and Perspectives, "New Drug for Erectile Dysfunction Boon for Many; 'Viagravation' for Some," *JAMA,* Vol. 280, No 10 (September 9, 1998).

[19]Personal communication, Rosemary Basson, M.D., October 4, 2000.

[20]S. A. Kaplan et al., "Safety and efficacy of sildenafil in postmenopausal women with sexual dysfunction," *Urology* (1999) March; 53 (3): 481–486. This study at Columbia University on postmenopausal women indicated that Viagra improved blood flow to the clitoris but it didn't translate into sexual satisfaction.

9. Coming Back Together

[1]P. A. Ganz, et al., "Breast cancer survivors: Psychosocial concerns and quality of life," *Breast Cancer Res Treat,* 38 (1996): 183–199.

[2]P. A. Ganz, et al., "Life after breast cancer: Understanding women's health-related quality of life and sexual functioning, *Journal of Clinical Oncology* 16:2 (1998): 501–514.

[3]B. E. Meyrowitz, et al., "Sexuality following breast cancer," *Journal of Sex & Marital Therapy,* 25 (1999): 237–250.

[4]L. R. Schover, "Sexuality and body image in younger women with breast cancer," *J Natl Cancer Inst Monogr* 16 (1994): 177–182.

[5]Schover, *ibid.*

[6]Lisa Anjou, Ph.D., a cancer survivor and sex therapist, director of mental health services at the Mt. Sinai Center for Breast Health in Beechwood, Ohio, is conducting a study using Viagra with women post–breast-cancer. Since it's a nonhormonal sexual enhancer, it might at least restore some feeling and lubrication to a woman who's lost the ability to be aroused.

[7]L. R. Schover, et al., "Partial mastectomy and breast reconstruction. A comparison of their effects on psychosocial adjustment, body image, and sexual function," *Cancer* 1995 Jan 1; 75(1): 54–64.

[8]B. Anderson and J. van der Does, "Surviving gynecologic cancer and coping with sexual

morbidity: An international problem," *International Journal of Gynecologic Cancer* 4 (1994): 225–240.

[9]D. Spiegel, et al., "Effect of psychosocial treatment on survival of patients with metastatic breast cancer," *Lancet* 1989 Oct 14; 2 (8668):888–91. David Spiegel's landmark study at Stanford University School of Medicine in 1989 showed that women recovering from breast cancer lived longer when they were in a therapeutic support group with others like themselves.

[10]A. Ghizzani, et al., "The Evaluation of Some Factors Influencing the Sexual Life of Women Affected by Breast Cancer," *Journal of Sex & Marital Therapy,* Vol. 21, No. 1 (1995).

[11]David S. Chapin, MD, Director of Gynecology, Beth Israel Deaconess Medical Center, Boston. Personal communication, January 2001.

[12]"Dating, Sex, and the Single Ostomate," Sally Chapralis, *Ostomy Quarterly,* Vol. 30, No. 1, Winter 1992.

[13]J. L. Fourcroy, "The three feminine sorrows," *Hosp Prac* (Off Ed) July 15; 33(7) (1998): 15–16, 21.

[14]Hanny Lightfoot-Klein, MA, "The sexual experience and marital adjustment of genitally circumcised and infibulated females in the Sudan," *Journal of Sex Research*, Vol. 26, No. 3 (1989):375–392. Klein's books, *Prisoners of Ritual* and *An Odyssey into Female Genital Circumcision in Africa* (New York: Haworth Press, 1989) brought this problem to public attention in the West for the first time.

[15]Gina Ogden, *Women Who Love Sex* (New York: Pocket Books, 1994), p. 142.

10. Reblooming the Rose

[1]D. B. Sarwer, et al., "Body image dissatisfaction and body dysmorphic disorder in 132 cosmetic surgery patients," *Plast Reconstr Surg* May; 101(6) (1998): 1644–1649.

[2]*Newsweek,* Issue 2000, Special Edition, December 1999, p. 65.

[3]Priscilla Grant, "Face Time," *Modern Maturity,* March/April 2001.

[4]M. Rankin and G. L. Borah, "Anxiety disorders in plastic surgery," *Plast Reconstr Surg* 1997 Aug; 100(2):535–542.

[5]M. Dunofsky, "Psychological characteristics of women who undergo single and multiple cosmetic surgeries," *Ann Plast Surg* Sep; 39(3) (1997): 223–228.

[6]Personal communication with Denise Thomas, January 2001.

[7]R. B. Rao and S. F. Ely, "Deaths related to liposuction," *New England Journal of Medicine* 340 (19) (1999): 1471–1475. The various reasons for these deaths entailed clotting problems, possible drug interactions, bacterial infections, fluid overload, and the volume of fat removed. A newer version of this procedure, tumescent liposuction, performed with the assistance of ultrasound, makes fat cells easier to suction out and reduces the extraction of nonfat tissue. The cannula or sucking tube is also smaller, so it barely leaves a scar. Doctors must be highly skilled and experienced with this procedure and the new equipment, but ultimately, there should be less trauma, faster recovery time, and less risk of complications and infection.

[8]From Ernst Brücke, *Schönheit und Fehler der menschlichen Gestalt* (Vienna: Braumüller, 1891). As quoted and illustrated in Sander L. Gilman, *Making the Body Beautiful,* Princeton, NJ: (Princeton University Press, 2001), p. 220.

[9]Priscilla Grant, *Modern Maturity, ibid.,* p. 7.

[10]Daphne Merkin, "An Independent Woman," *The New York Times Magazine,* January 21, 2001.

11. How to Spark Desire

[1]Cathy Winks and Anne Semans, *The New Good Vibrations Guide to Sex,* 2nd ed. (San Francisco: Cleis Press, Inc., 1997).

[2]Personal communication, Candida Royale, May 2000.

[3]Jack Maguire, *Care and Feeding of the Brain* (New York: Doubleday, 1990).

[4]Jon Kabat-Zinn, *Full Catastrophe Living: Using the Wisdom of Your Body and Mind to Face Stress, Pain, and Illness* (New York: Delta Books, 1990).

[5]Michael Reed Gach, Ph.D., *Acupressure for Lovers* (New York: Bantam Books, 1997).

[6]Margo Anand, *The Art of Sexual Ecstasy* (New York: Jeremy P. Tarcher/Perigee Books, 1989).

[7]Herbert Benson, *The Relaxation Response* (New York: William Morrow, 1975). See also his later popular work, *Your Maximum Mind* (New York: Random House, 1987).

[8]Daniel A. Girdano, et al., *Controlling Stress and Tension: A Holistic Approach,* 4th ed. (Englewood Cliffs, NJ: Prentice Hall, 1993).

[9]Richard Craze, *The Spiritual Traditions of Sex* (New York: Harmony Books, 1996).

[10]Gary Karp, *Life on Wheels: For the Active Wheelchair User* (Sebastopol, CA: O'Reilly & Assoc., 1999).

[11]Mantak Chia and Douglas Abrams Arava, *The Multi-Orgasmic Man* (HarperSanFrancisco, 1996).

[12]Sandra Leiblum and Ray Rosen, *Principles and Practice of Sex Therapy: An Update for the 1990's* (New York: Guilford Press, 1989).

RESOURCES

Organizations Dedicated to Sex Education

Sex Education and Information Council of the US (SIECUS)
130 West 42 St., Ste. 350
New York, NY 10036
(212) 819–9770
(siecus@siecus.org)

American Association of Sex Educators, Counselors, and Therapists
    (AASECT)
PO Box 5488
Richmond, VA 23220–0488
www.aasect.org/AASECT@mediaone.net

Society for Sex Therapy and Research (SSTAR)
409 12th St., SW
PO Box 96920
Washington, DC 20024
(202) 863–1646

Society for the Scientific Study of Sexuality (SSSS)
c/o David Fleming
PO Box 416
Allentown, PA 18105–0416
(610) 530–2483

The Kinsey Institute for Research in Sex, Gender, and Reproduction
University of Indiana
Morrison Hall 313
Bloomington, IN 47405–2501

Institute for Advanced Study of Human Sexuality
1523 Franklin St.
San Francisco, CA 94109
(415) 928–1133
(Information on nonoxynol-15 (Erogel))

Websites for sexuality information
www.askisadora.com (The Sexuality Forum, offering advice and
    information)
www.bianca.com (sex information and erotica at Bianca's Smut Shack)
www.libida.com (sex information, chats, boards, erotica)
www.nerve.com (sex information, chats, boards, erotica)
www.xandria.com (sex information and education as well as online
    sex shopping)
www.sexuality.org (sex information at the official website of AASECT)
www.safersex.org (the latest on safer sex, both hetero- and homosexual)
www.positive.org (website of the Coalition for Positive Sexuality)
www.bettydodson.com (information on sexuality and masturbation)

Websites for teen support and sexuality education
www.cybergrrl.com
www.webgrrls.com
www.goaskalice.columbia.edu
www.femina.com
www.gURL.com
www.chickclick.com
www.theglobe.com

Organizations Dedicated to Women's Health

American College of Obstetricians and Gynecologists (ACOG)
409 12th St., SW
Washington, DC 20024
(202) 638–5577
www.acog.org

American College of Nurse-Midwives
818 Connecticut Avenue, NW, Ste. 900
Washington, DC 20006
(202) 728–9860 or 1–888–MIDWIFE
www.acnm.org

American Urogynecologic Society
2025 M St., NW, Ste. 800
Washington, DC 20036
(202) 367–1167
www.augs.org

Association of Reproductive Health Professionals
2401 Pennsylvania Avenue, NW, Ste. 350
Washington, DC 20037–1718
(202) 466–3825
Perimenopausal information: (202) 723–7374
www.arhp.org

American Society for Reproductive Medicine (ASRM)
1209 Montgomery Hwy.
Birmingham, AL 35216–2809
(205) 978–5000
www.asrm.org

North American Menopause Society
11000 Euclid Ave.
Cleveland, OH 44106
www.menopause.org

HERS (Hysterectomy Educational Resources & Services)
422 Bryn Mawr Ave.
Bala Cynwyd, PA 19004
(610) 667–7757
www.ccon.com/hers

The National Women's Health Information Center
Office on Women's Health, Dept. of Health and Human Services
1325 G St., NW
Washington, DC 20005
(202) 347–1140
www.4women.gov

The Pelvic Floor Institute at Graduate Hospital (Pelvic-floor reconstruction)
1800 Lombard St., Ste. 900
Philadelphia, PA 19146
(215) 893–2643

The Center for Sexual and Marital Health (Sex therapy)
Robert Wood Johnson Medical School
675 Hoes Ln.
Piscataway, NJ 08854–5635
(732) 235–4273

Websites for women's health
womenshealth.medscape.com
www.my.webmd.com
www.intelihealth.com
www.womenssexualhealth.com
www.womens-health.com

Vulvar Pain (Vulvodynia)
Vulvar Pain Foundation
PO Drawer 177
Graham, NC 27253
(336) 226–0704
www.vulvarpainfoundation.org

National Vulvodynia Association
PO Box 4491
Silver Spring, MD 20914–4491
(410) 299–0775
www.nva.org

This group publishes newsletters from which you can order attractive stoma covers, etc.

Ostomy

United Ostomy Association, Inc.
19772 McArthur Blvd., Ste. 200
Irvine, CA 92612–2405
(949) 660–8624 or 1–800–826–0826
www.uoa.org

Incontinence
National Association for Continence (NAFC)
PO Box 8310
Spartanburg, SC 29305–8310
(864) 579–7900 or 1–800–BLADDER (252–3337)
www.nafc.org

Simon Foundation for Continence
PO Box 835-F
Wilmette, IL 60091
1–800–23 SIMON (237–4666)
www.simonfoundation.org

Sex and Disability
Sexuality and Disability Training Center
Boston University Medical Center
88 East Newton St.
Boston, MA 02118
(617) 726–2748
A group of health professionals exploring physical disability and sexuality. They publish *The Journal of Sexuality and Disability.*

It's Okay! a magazine on sexuality and disability
Sureen Publishing
PO Box 23102
124 Welland Ave.
St. Catharines, Ontario
Canada L2R 7P6

Restorative and Cosmetic Surgery
The American Society of Plastic Surgeons (ASPS) and the Plastic Surgery
    Educational Foundation
444 E. Algonquin Rd.
Arlington Heights, IL 60005
1–888–4–PLASTIC
www.plasticsurgery.org

The American Board of Facial Plastic and Reconstructive Surgery
115C South Saint Asaph St.
Alexandria, VA 22314
(703) 549–3223
www.abfprs.org

Transgender and Cross-Dressing Resources
Transgender Resource Guide
www.cdspub.com

Sexual Toys and Aids for Women
Eve's Garden
119 West 57 St., Ste. 420
New York, NY 10019
www.evesgarden.com
(Catalogue for $3.)

Vaginal Weights for Kegel Practice
Kegel Exercise Kones
Milex Products, Inc.
(312) 631–6484

FemTone
ConvatTec
(908) 281–2200

Femina Vaginal Weights
Urohealth Systems, Inc.
1–800–879–3111

Sexual Toys and Aids for Men and Women
Adam and Eve
PO Box 800
Carrboro, NC 27510
(1–800–765–ADAM)
www.adameve.com
(Free catalogue arrives in brown paper wrapper.)

Good Vibrations
938 Howard St.
San Francisco, CA 94103
(1–800–289–8423)
www.goodvibes.com
(Catalogue of toys, books, and videos arrive in plain packaging.)

SomethingSexyPlanet
4242 N. Federal Hwy.
Ft. Lauderdale, FL 33308
(877) 423–7399
www.somethingsexyplanet.com

Xandria Collection
Lawrence Research Group
165 Valley Dr.
Brisbane, CA 94005
1–800–242–2823
(415) 468–3812 customer service
www.xandria.com
(Collector's Gold Catalogue of toys, books, and videos $4, with coupon for that amount good toward a purchase; leather catalogue $5; lingerie catalogue $2, with coupons good toward purchase. Special edition catalogue free of charge for disabled people.)

Materials and purchases arrive in plain packaging. This company does not rent, sell, or trade customers' names.

Other sex toy sites
www.sexshop2000.dk
www.blowfish.com

Condoms
Condomania
351 Bleecker St.
New York, NY 10014
and other locations
(212) 691–9442
www.condomania.com

Safe Sense
888–70 CONDOM (702–6636)
www.condoms.net

Only Condoms
1–877–B4U–DOIT
www.onlycondoms.com

Prescriptions for Natural Hormones
Following are sources for custom-compounding pharmacies that supply natural estrogen, progesterone, and testosterone products. You will need a prescription from your physician. To get a list of pharmacies by states:
www.dmoz.org/Health/Pharmacy/Pharmacies/Compounding

Transitions for Health
621 SW Alder, Ste. 900
Portland, OR 97205–3267
1–800–888–6814
www.transitionsforhealth.com

Women's International Pharmacy
5708 Monona Dr.
Madison, WI 53716
1–800–279–5708
www.womensinternational.com

Natural Woman Institute
8539 Sunset Blvd., Ste. 135
Los Angeles, CA 90069
www.naturalwoman.org

Rape, Violence, and Sexual Abuse
RAINN (Rape, Abuse, and Incest National Network)
635 B Pennsylvania Ave., SE
Washington, DC 20002
(202) 544–1034
HOTLINE: 1–800–656–HOPE (4673)
www.rainn.org

National Sexual Violence Resource Center
125 Enola Dr.
Enola, PA 17025
(717) 909–0710

National Center for Victims of Crime
2111 Wilson Blvd., Ste. 300
Arlington, VA 22201
(703) 276–2880
www.ncvc.org

National Women's Law Center
11 Dupont Circle NW, Ste. 800
Washington, DC 20036
(202) 588–5180
www.nwlc.org

Emergency and Alternative Contraception
1–888–not–2–late or ec.princeton.edu
www.plannedparenthood.org

Lifestyle Choices: Polyfidelity
IntiNet Resource Center (IRC)
PO Box 150474-L
San Rafael, CA 94915–0474
National organization for resources and support to those exploring non-monogamy. Membership $30 a year, including a subscription to quarterly newsletter, online consultation, and referrals.

RECOMMENDED BOOKS, TAPES, AND VIDEOS

Books

Anand, Margo. *The Art of Sexual Ecstasy.* New York: Jeremy P. Tarcher/Perigee Books, 1989.
Angier, Natalie. *Woman: An Intimate Geography.* New York: Houghton Mifflin Company, 1999.
Barbach, Lonnie. *For Yourself.* New York: Signet Books, 2000.
———. *Turn Ons: Pleasing Yourself While Pleasing Your Lover.* New York: Plume, 1998.
———. *For Each Other.* New York: New American Library, 1984.
Bright, Susie. *Susie Bright's Sexual State of the Union.* New York: Touchstone/Simon & Schuster, 1997.
Corn, Laura. *101 Nights of Grrreat Sex.* New York: Park Avenue Publishers, 1995.
Dodson, Betty. *Sex For One: The Joy of Selfloving.* New York: Crown Publishers, 1996.
Dworkin, Andrea. *Pornography: Men Possessing Women.* New York: E. P. Dutton, 1979, 1989.
Friday, Nancy. *My Secret Garden: Women's Sexual Fantasies.* New York: Pocket Books, 1998.
———. *Forbidden Flowers: More Women's Sexual Fantasies.* New York: Pocket Books, 1993.
Heiman, Julia and Joseph LoPiccolo. *Becoming Orgasmic.* New York: Simon & Schuster, 1988.
Heyn, Dalma. *The Erotic Silence of the American Wife.* Turtle Bay Press, 1994.

————. *Marriage Shock: The Transformation of Women Into Wives.* New York: Villard Books, 1997.

Joannides, Paul. *The Guide to Getting It On.* Goofy Foot Press, 2000.

Leiblum, Sandra and Ray Rosen. *Principles and Practice of Sex Therapy,* 3rd ed. New York: Guilford Press, 2000.

Morin, Jack. *Anal Pleasure & Health.* San Francisco: Down There Press, 1986.

Ogden, Gina. *Women Who Love Sex.* New York: Simon & Schuster, 1994.

Sachs, Judith. *The Healing Power of Sex.* Englewood Cliffs, NJ: Prentice Hall Press, 1994.

Siegal, Diana Laskin. *The New Ourselves, Growing Older.* Boston: Boston Women's Health Collective, 1996.

Thompson, Sharon. *Going All the Way: Teenage Girls' Tales of Sex, Romance, and Pregnancy.* New York: Hill and Wang, 1995.

Walsleben, Joyce and Rita Baron-Faust. *A Woman's Guide to Sleep.* New York: Crown, 2000.

Winks, Cathy and Anne Semans. *The New Good Vibrations Guide to Sex,* 2nd ed. San Francisco: Cleis Press, Inc., 1997.

Wolf, Naomi. *The Beauty Myth.* New York: Anchor Books, Doubleday, 1991.

Hot Graphic Novels

All erotica, tapes, and videos are available through the Good Vibrations Sexuality Library, www.goodvibes.com

Adventures of a Lesbian College School Girl, 1997

Manara's Kama Sutra, Milo Manara, 1998

Quiver: A Book of Erotic Tales, Tobsha Learner, 1998

Hot & Bothered 2, Karen X. Tulchinsky, ed. (lesbian), 1999

Herotica, Volume 6, Marcy Sheiner, ed., 1999

Audio

"Exit to Eden," Anne Rice, 1992. Read by Gillian Anderson. Cassette only

"Of Dreams and Bedtime Stories," 1996. Cassette or CD

"Ear Candy," 1997 (collection of erotic tales). Cassette or CD

"Herotica, Vol. 1–3," Susie Bright, ed., 1995–1997

"Encounters Erotica" (including sounds of sexual encounters), 1996. CD only

"Cyborgasm, Vol. 1 & 2," 1993–1994 (erotic stories and fantasies). Cassette or CD

Videos

How-To
"Nina Hartley's Guide to Seduction," 1997
"Nina Hartley's Guide to Fellatio," 1994
"Nina Hartley's Guide to Cunnilingus," 1994
"The Incredible G-Spot," Laura Corn 1995
"Fire in the Valley," Annie Sprinkle and Joseph Kramer, 1999
Erotic Educational Series, "Behind the Bedroom Door," and
    "Sex—A Lifelong Pleasure," Dutch-produced

Classic Erotica
"Autobiography of a Flea," 1976
"Alice in Wonderland," 1976
"Insatiable," 1980
"Behind the Green Door," 1972
"3 A.M.," 1976
"Devil in Miss Jones," 1972

Women-Centered Erotica
Films of Candida Royalle:
"Eyes of Desire," 1998
"One Size Fits All," 1998
"The Gift," 1997
"The Bridal Shower," 1997
"My Surrender," 1996

Films of Betty Dodson: Masturbation Techniques for Women
"Viva la Vulva," 1998
"Celebrating Orgasm," 1996
"Selfloving," 1991

Other Recommended Films
"Annie Sprinkle's Herstory of Porn," Annie Sprinkle, 1999
"Every Woman Has a Fantasy," Edwin Durell, 1995
"Dirty Little Mind," Jean-Pierre Errand, 1995
"Sluts and Goddesses," Maria Beatty, 1992
"The Swap," Paul Thomas, 1994
"Contract for Service," Ernest Greene, 1994 (lesbian S/M)
"Prison World," Ernest Greene, 1994 (lesbian S/M)
"Possessions," Andrew Blake, 1998 (lesbian)
"The Hills Have Bi's," Josh Elliot, 1996 (bisexual)

BIBLIOGRAPHY

Alexander, Jo, Debi Berrow, et al., eds. *Women and Aging.* Corvallis, OR: Calyx Books, 1986.

Alexander, Shoshana. *In Praise of Single Parents: Mothers and Fathers Embracing the Challenge.* New York: Houghton Mifflin Co., 1994.

Allgeier, Elizabeth Rice and Naomi B. McCormick, eds. *Changing Boundaries: Gender Roles and Sexual Behavior.* Palo Alto, CA: Mayfield Publishing Co., 1983.

American Cancer Society. "A Significant Journey: Breast Cancer Survivors and the Men Who Love Them." Minnesota Chapter (Video).

Anand, Margo. *The Art of Sexual Ecstasy.* New York: Jeremy P. Tarcher/Perigee Books, 1989.

Anapol, Deborah M. *Love Without Limits: The Quest for Sustainable Intimate Relationships.* San Rafael, CA: IntiNet Resource Center, 1992.

Angier, Natalie. *Woman: An Intimate Geography.* New York: Houghton Mifflin Company, 1999.

Bakos, Susan Crain. *Kink: The Shocking Hidden Sex Lives of Americans.* New York: St. Martin's Paperbacks, 1995.

Benkov, Laura, Ph.D. *Reinventing the Family: The Emerging Story of Lesbian and Gay Parents.* New York: Crown Publishers, Inc., 1994.

Blum, Deborah. *Sex on the Brain.* New York: Penguin Books, 1997.

Bright, Susie. *The Sexual State of the Union.* New York: Touchstone/Simon & Schuster, 1997.

Bromberg, Joan Jacobs. *The Body Project: An Intimate History of American Girls.* New York: Random House/Vintage, 1997.

Brooks-Gunn, J. and Frank F. Furstenberg, Jr. "Adolescent Sexual Behavior." *American Psychologist* 44, 1989, 249–257.

Brownmiller, Susan. *Against Our Will: Men, Women and Rape.* New York: Simon & Schuster, 1975.

Buckley, Thomas and Alma Gottlieb, eds. *Blood Magic: The Anthropology of Menstruation.* Berkeley and Los Angeles: University of California Press, 1988.

Chia, Mantak and Douglas Abrams Arava. *The Multi-Orgasmic Man.* San Francisco: HarperSanFrancisco, 1996.

Chodorow, Nancy. *The Reproduction of Mothering.* Berkeley and Los Angeles: University of California Press, 1978.

Clunis, D. Merilee and G. Dorsey Green. *The Lesbian Parenting Book: A Guide to Creating Families and Raising Children.* Seattle, WA: Seal Press, 1995.

Craze, Richard. *The Spiritual Traditions of Sex.* New York: Harmony Books, 1996.

Dackman, Linda. *Up Front: Sex and the Post-Mastectomy Woman.* New York: Viking/Penguin, 1990.

D'Augelli, Anthony R. and Charlotte Patterson, eds. *Lesbian, Gay, and Bisexual Identities Over the Lifespan.* New York: Oxford University Press, 1995.

Delaney, Janice, Mary Jane Lupton, and Emily Toth. *The Curse: A Cultural History of Menstruation.* New York: E. P. Dutton, Inc., 1976.

Dodson, Betty. *Sex for One: The Joy of Selfloving.* New York: Crown Publishers, 1996.

Dworkin, Andrea. *Pornography: Men Possessing Women.* New York: E. P. Dutton, 1979, 1989.

Ehrenreich, Barbara and Deirdre English. *For Her Own Good: 150 Years of the Experts' Advice to Women.* Garden City, NY: Anchor Press/Doubleday, 1978.

Ericksen, Julia A. with Sally A. Steffen. *Kiss and Tell: Surveying Sex in the Twentieth Century.* Cambridge, MA: Harvard University Press, 1999.

Estes, Clarissa Pinkola. *Women Who Run with the Wolves.* New York: Ballantine Books, 1992, 1995.

Fein, Ellen and Sherrie Schneider. *The Rules.* New York: Warner Books, 1995.

Fisher, Helen. *Anatomy of Love.* New York: Fawcett, 1994.

———. *The First Sex: The Natural Talents of Women and How They Are Changing the World.* New York: Ballantine, 2000.

Gilman, Sander L. *Making the Body Beautiful: A Cultural History of Aesthetic Surgery.* Princeton, NJ: Princeton University Press, 1999.

Heyn, Dalma. *The Erotic Silence of the American Wife.* Turtle Bay Press, 1994.

———. *Marriage Shock: The Transformation of Women Into Wives.* New York: Villard Books, 1997.

Husain, Shakrukh. *The Goddess: An Illustrated Guide to the Divine Feminine.* New York: Little, Brown & Co., 1997.

Kennedy, Eugene. *Sexual Counseling: A Practical Guide for Those Who Help Others.* New York: The Continuum Publishing Company, 1989.

Klein, Marty. *Ask Me Anything: A Sex Therapist Answers the Most Important Questions for the '90s.* New York: Fireside Press, 1992.

Kraig, Donald Michael. *Modern Sex Magick: Secrets of Erotic Spirituality.* St. Paul, MN: Llewellyn Publications, 1999.

Kramer, Jonathon, Ph.D. and Diane Dunaway. *Why Men Don't Get Enough Sex and Women Don't Get Enough Love.* New York: Pocket Books, 1990.

Ladas, Alice Kahn, Beverly Whipple, and John D. Perry, *The G-Spot: And Other Discoveries About Human Sexuality.* New York: Dell Publishing Company, 1982.

Laumann, Edward O., John H. Gagnon, Robert T. Michael, and Stuart Michaels. *The Social Organization of Sexuality: Sexual Practices in the United States.* Chicago: University of Chicago Press, 1994.

Lieblum, Sandra and Ray Rosen. *Sexual Desire Disorders.* New York: Guilford Press, 1988.

Lieblum, Sandra. *Infertility: Psychological Issues and Counseling Strategies.* Boston: John Wiley & Co. 1997.

Lieblum, Sandra and Ray Rosen. *Principles and Practices of Sex Therapy,* 3rd edition. New York: Guilford Press, 2000.

Lerner, Gerda. *The Creation of Patriarchy.* New York: Oxford University Press, 1986.

Levine, Stephen B. *Sexuality in Mid-Life.* New York: Plenum Press, 1998.

Mattes, Jane, CSW. *Single Mothers by Choice: A Guidebook for Single Women Who Are Considering or Have Chosen Motherhood.* New York: Times Books, 1994.

Michael, Robert T., et al. *Sex in America: A Definitive Survey.* Boston: Little, Brown and Co., 1994.

Moore, Thomas. *The Soul of Sex: Cultivating Life as an Act of Love.* New York: HarperCollins, 1998.

Neugarten, Bernice L., ed. *Middle Age and Aging.* Chicago: University of Chicago Press, 1968.

Neuman, Leslea. *Heather Has Two Mommies.* Boston: Alyson Publications, 1989.

Nevid, Jeffrey S. *Choices: Sex in the Age of STDs,* 2nd edition. Needham Heights, MA: Allyn & Bacon, 1997.

Ogden, Gina. *Women Who Love Sex.* New York: Simon & Schuster, 1994.

Panati, Charles. *Sexy Origins and Intimate Things: The Rites and Rituals of Straights, Gays, Bi's, Drags, Trans, Virgins, and Others.* New York: Penguin Books, 1998.

Plaskow, Judith and Carol P. Christ. *Weaving the Visions: New Patterns in Feminist Spirituality.* San Francisco: HarperSanFrancisco, 1989.

Rako, Susan, MD. *The Hormone of Desire: The Truth About Testosterone, Sexuality and Menopause.* New York: Three Rivers Press, 1999.

Rubin, Lillian B. *Women of a Certain Age: The Midlife Search for Self.* New York: Harper & Row Publishers, Inc., 1979.

Sachs, Judith. *The Healing Power of Sex.* Englewood Cliffs, NJ: Prentice Hall, 1994.

———. *Sensual Rejuvenation: Maintaining Sexual Vigor Through Midlife and Beyond.* New York: Dell Publishing, 1999.

Scantling, Sandra and Sue Browder. *Ordinary Women, Extraordinary Sex: Every Woman's Guide to Pleasure and Beyond.* New York: Dutton, 1993.

Schachter-Shalomi, Zalman and Ronald S. Miller. *From Age-ing to Sage-ing: A Profound New Vision of Growing Older.* New York: Warner Books, Inc., 1995.

Schwartz, Pepper. *Peer Marriage.* New York: The Free Press, 1994.

Schwartz, Pepper and Philip Blumstein. *American Couples: Money, Work, Sex.* New York: William Morrow & Co., Inc., 1983.

Schwartz, Pepper and Virginia Rutter. *The Gender of Sexuality.* Pine Forge Press, 1998.

Shalit, Wendy. *A Return to Modesty: Discovering the Lost Virtue.* New York: The Free Press, 1999.

Solomon, Robert C. *About Love: Reinventing Romance for Our Times.* New York: Simon & Schuster, 1988.

Sternberg, Esther M., MD. *The Balance Within: The Science Connecting Health and Emotions.* New York: W. H. Freeman and Co., 2000.

Stone, Merlin. *When God Was a Woman.* San Diego, CA: Harcourt, Brace and Company, 1976.

Thompson, Sharon. *Going All the Way: Teenage Girls' Tales of Sex, Romance, and Pregnancy.* New York: Hill and Wang, 1995.

Vance, Carole S., ed. *Pleasure and Danger: Exploring Female Sexuality.* Boston: Routledge & Kegan Paul, 1984.

Wallerstein, Judith S. and Sandra Blakeslee. *The Good Marriage: How & Why Love Lasts.* Boston: Houghton Mifflin Co., 1995.

Winks, Cathy and Anne Semans. *The New Good Vibrations Guide to Sex,* 2nd ed. San Francisco: Cleis Press, Inc., 1997.

Wiseman, Jay. *SM 101: A Realistic Introduction.* San Francisco: Greenery Press, 1996.

Wolf, Naomi. *The Beauty Myth.* New York: Anchor Books, Doubleday, 1991.

Woyshner, Christine A. and Holly S. Gelfond, eds. *Minding Women: Reshaping the Educational Realm.* Cambridge, MA: Harvard Educational Review, Reprint Series #30, 1998.

INDEX

abortion, 34–35
abstinence, 36–38, 44–46
acupressure, 243–44
adolescence, 16–38
  abortion in, 34–35
  academic achievers in, 24
  danger in, 16–17, 19, 22, 25
  doctor's visits in, 30–31
  eating disorders in, 20, 21
  emotion in, 19
  exercise in, 20–21
  falling in love in, 29
  father/daughter relationships,
    15–16
  gays and lesbians in, 24–25
  getting it (sex) over with in,
    26, 27
  girls in groups, 22–25
  loss of virginity in, 27–30
  masturbation in, 21–22, 26
  menstruation, 16–18
  motherhood in, 35–36
  popularity in, 23–24, 27
  pregnancy and, 33–36
  puberty and, 16–17, 181
  rape and, 31–33
  self–esteem in, 18, 19–21
  sex information in, 19–20
  sexual experimentation in, 25–27
affairs, extra–marital, 122–25
aging process, 129–30, 132–33
  extreme old age, 144–45

and health problems, 136–38,
  141–43
and independence, 144
and intimacy, 136
and memory, 133–36
and testosterone, 181
see also highlife
alternate lifestyles, 137
analgesics, 179
anal stimulation, 61
anal toys, 235
anti–anxiety medication, 177
anticholinergic drugs, 176, 207
antidepressants, 176–77, 179
antihistamines, 176, 179
antihypertensive drugs, 175
antinausea drugs, 176
antipsychotics, 176, 179
aromatherapy, 232
arousal, 129, 175, 180
attachment, 72
attraction, 72
autogenics, 245

baby boomers, 63
"Baby Think It Over" doll, 33
Bartholin glands, 111
Ben–wa balls, 235–36
blood flow, drugs affecting, 175
blood pressure medications, 179
blow job, 26–27
body fat, prejudice against, 18

ABOUT THE AUTHORS

DR. SANDRA LEIBLUM is known nationally for her leadership in the field of human sexuality. As a sex therapist, she has treated thousands of individuals and couples over the last thirty years. The Society for Sex Therapy and Research awarded her the Masters and Johnson Lifetime Achievement Award, and the American Society of Sex Educators, Counselors, and Therapists recognized her expertise with the Career Accomplishments Award. She is the first elected president of the Female Sexual Function Forum, past president of the Society for Sex Therapy and Research, and a Fellow of the Society for the Scientific Study of Sex.

The author or coeditor of nine books on the treatment of sexual dysfunction and infertility, Dr. Leiblum is Professor of Psychiatry and Obstetrics/Gynecology and Director of the Center for Sexual and Marital Health at UMDNJ–Robert Wood Johnson Medical School in Piscataway, New Jersey. In addition to her clinical work, she is also a consultant to many major pharmaceutical companies in their investigations into chemical enhancement of female sexual response.

In her spare time, she enjoys hiking, biking, shopping, and . . . sex.

JUDITH SACHS, daughter and granddaughter of physicians, was probably destined to write and speak about preventive healthcare. She has been publishing books and lecturing for the past twenty years. An advocate for the expression of healthy sexuality, she conducts workshops and seminars that encourage women to take charge of their own sexual health.

She is the author or coauthor of more than twenty books on preventive healthcare, including *The Healing Power of Sex, Rewinding Your Biological Clock: Motherhood Late in Life,* and *Break the Stress Cycle: 10 Steps to Reducing Stress for Women.* She has taught stress management at the College of New Jersey and the Human Resource Development Institute of New Jersey, and is trained as an HIV/AIDS educator for the American Red Cross. A longtime practitioner of the Chinese art of tai chi chuan, she feels that martial-arts sparring with the right partner is the next best thing to sex.